P9-DIF-982

GOVERNING MORALS
A Social History of Moral Regulation

This evocative and broad-ranging book traces the history of moral regulation in Britain and the US from the late seventeenth century to the present day. Specific coverage is given to movements such as the Society for the Reformation of Manners and the Vice Society, the sexual abuse and anti-pornography movements, and contemporary self-help movements. Hunt argues that the main impetus for moral regulations often stems from the middle classes, rather than those with institutional power, but most significantly they provide classic instances of the intimate link between the 'governance of others' and the 'governance of the self'. Using the work of Foucault, this book analyses how projects of self-regulation can manifest themselves into the regulation of others. Concurrent with this is the rise of health discourses, which play a central role in contemporary discussions of moral governance.

Having previously taught in England, Alan Hunt is now Professor of Sociology and Law at Carleton University. His previous books include *Governance of the Consuming Passions* (1996), *Foucault and Law* with Gary Wickham (1994), and *Explorations in Law and Society* (1993).

CAMBRIDGE STUDIES IN LAW AND SOCIETY

Series editors:
Chris Arup, Martin Chanock, Pat O'Malley
School of Law and Legal Studies, La Trobe University
Sally Engle Merry, Susan Silbey
Departments of Anthropology and Sociology, Wellesley College

Editorial board:
Richard Abel, Harry Arthurs, Sandra Burman, Peter Fitzpatrick, Marc Galanter, Yash Ghai, Nicola Lacey, Bonaventura da Sousa Santos, Sol Picciotto, Jonathan Simon, Frank Snyder

The broad area of law and society has become a remarkably rich and dynamic field of study. At the same time, the social sciences have increasingly engaged with questions of law. In this process, the borders between legal scholarship and the social, political and cultural sciences have been transcended, and the result is a time of fundamental re-thinking both within and about law. In this vital period, Cambridge Studies in Law and Society provides a significant new book series with an international focus and a concern with the global transformation of the legal arena. The series aims to publish the best scholarly work on legal discourse and practice in social context, combining theoretical insights and empirical research.

Already published:
Anthony Woodiwiss *Globalization, Human Rights and Labour Law in Pacific Asia*
0 521 62144 5 hardback 0 521 62883 0 paperback
Mariana Valverde *Diseases of the Will: Alcoholism and the Dilemmas of Freedom*
0 521 62300 6 hardback 0 521 64469 0 paperback

Forthcoming titles:
John Torpey *The Invention of the Passport: Surveillance, Citizenship and the State*
0 521 63249 8 hardback 0 521 63493 8 paperback
Ronen Shamir *The Colonies of Law: Colonialism, Zionism and Law in Early Mandate Palestine* 0 521 63183 1 hardback

GOVERNING MORALS

A Social History of Moral Regulation

Alan Hunt
Carleton University

CAMBRIDGE UNIVERSITY PRESS

PUBLISHED BY THE PRESS SYNDICATE OF THE UNIVERSITY OF CAMBRIDGE
The Pitt Building, Trumpington Street, Cambridge, United Kingdom

CAMBRIDGE UNIVERSITY PRESS
The Edinburgh Building, Cambridge CB2 2RU, UK http://www.cup.cam.ac.uk
40 West 20th Street, New York, NY 10011–4211, USA http://www.cup.org
10 Stamford Road, Oakleigh, Melbourne 3166, Australia
Ruiz de Alarcón 13, 28014, Madrid, Spain

© Cambridge University Press 1999

This book is in copyright. Subject to statutory exception
and to the provisions of relevant collective licensing agreements,
no reproduction of any part may take place without
the written permission of Cambridge University Press.

First published 1999

Printed in Singapore by Craft Print Pte Ltd

Typeface New Baskerville 10/12 pt (Adobe). System QuarkXPress® [PH]

A catalogue record for this book is available from the British Library

National Library of Australia Cataloguing in Publication data

Hunt, Alan, 1942– .
Governing morals: a social history of moral regulation.

Bibliography.
Includes index.
ISBN 0 521 64071 7.

ISBN 0 521 64689 8 (pbk).

1. Conduct of life – History. 2. Ethics – History. I.
Title. (Series: Cambridge studies in law and society).

ISBN 0 521 640717 hardback
ISBN 0 521 64689 8 paperback

CONTENTS

PREFACE

This venture took shape slowly and, as is often the case, it came about through the conjunction of rather different lines of inquiry. In my first venture into historical sociology I was concerned to try to make sense of why it was that great social and political energy had been expended during the rise of urban societies in attempts to regulate conspicuous consumption through the enactment of sumptuary laws (Hunt 1996). It became clear that such projects were exemplars of projects of 'moral regulation', which involve practices whereby some social agents problematise some aspect of the conduct, values or culture of others on moral grounds and seek to impose regulation upon them. While moral politics is often complexly linked to the pursuit of economic or other interests, such politics is never reducible to a smokescreen or cover for more mundane class or sectional interests. There is an irreducible core in which people are mobilised and drawn into action by the passionate conviction that there is something inherently wrong or immoral about the conduct of others.

Once moral regulation had been identified as a distinctive form of discursive and political practice, it became clear that a great deal of what I had previously thought of under the generic label of politics could better be understood as moral politics. Thus the long-running battles that have transected societies over poverty involved the moralisation of the poor; whether in the name of charity, philanthropy or welfare the poor did not escape the moralising brush that castigated their morals, their idleness or their degeneracy. It was apparent that the great energies invested in attempts to regulate some aspect of sexuality cannot be engaged with without taking account of the moral imperatives and preoccupations that stimulate and sustain them. In addition my interest was engaged by the fact that many of these projects were not initiated by state agencies or institutions, but bubbled upwards from what have aptly, but somewhat imprecisely, been termed the respectable classes.

As I began to explore some early moral regulation movements, I became increasingly conscious that moral regulation was playing an increasingly active part in contemporary life. Moral politics was everywhere, and not just in traditional fields such as prostitution, alcohol and obscenity (now renamed pornography). Most startling was the realisation that, tempting though it was, it was inadequate to view the clamour of moral indignation as just part of a conservative backlash that had sought to sweep aside the presumed 'permissiveness' of the 1960s and 1970s. Moral politics was being generated from all across the political spectrum. Alongside the moral traditionalism of religious fundamentalism, with its appeal to family values and sexual austerity, moral campaigns were promoted by social forces with self-consciously transformative agendas. Radical feminism attacked pornography, sexual abuse and harassment in the name of progressive goals of transformed gender relations. Race activists promoted projects to criminalise racial abuse and hate-speech. In addition, it was apparent that while state agencies were prominent in a series of decreasingly successful 'wars' on drug use, most projects of moral reform came from below and not just from the respectable classes.

It was at this stage that my project took shape. I was struck by the intractability of many of the controversies engendered by contemporary moral politics exemplified by the degeneration of the abortion debate into fire-bombings, assassinations and vigilantism. There seemed little point in adding another contentious voice to the babble of current controversy over any of these moral conflicts. Instead I decided that it might be possible to throw some light on contemporary conflicts by undertaking a study of earlier moral reform campaigns. Not only would this provide potentially useful comparisons, but it would be much easier to sustain some critical distance. While I am intuitively unsympathetic to eighteenth-century campaigns to impose Sunday observance on a recalcitrant population, I do not feel the same strong commitments as I do over abortion, pornography and the other fields of today's moral politics.

While there have over the last three decades been a number of studies of individual moral regulation movements, little attempt has been made to compare and contrast these projects. It is my hope that the comparative dimension of my study will open up fresh approaches to making sense of the moral politics of our own time. In addition, while earlier studies operate with a generic, all-purpose concept of moral regulation, my aim is to contribute to breathing fresh life into the general theoretical debate that has, more recently, been taking place over the utility of the concept of moral regulation.

In venturing into unfamiliar subject matter and periods my task was made easier and my route faster by the patient and unhurried assistance of library workers in Britain, the United States and Canada; to them all my thanks. I acknowledge with appreciation a research grant from the Social Sciences and Humanities Research Council (SSHRC) of Canada which enabled me to carry out this project.

INTRODUCTION: THE THEORY AND POLITICS OF MORAL REGULATION

SITUATING MORAL REGULATION

In the city of Berne in 1688 restrictions were placed on winter sleigh riding; women were prohibited from riding in sleighs except when accompanied by their fathers or husbands (Vincent 1935: 367–8). In 1911 the Chicago Vice Commission called for the regulation of the city's ice-cream parlours, which it judged to be locations in which scores of girls took their first steps towards immorality and prostitution (Chicago Vice Commission 1911/1970). In Britain in 1955 legislation, the *Children and Young Persons (Harmful Publications) Act*, was passed imposing restrictions on American-style comics (Barker 1984).[1] In 1983 the city of Minneapolis, at the prompting of prominent feminists, instituted an anti-pornography ordinance. Some of these episodes are familiar, while others are shrouded in unfamiliar historical contexts. All such regulatory activity speaks to us of the anxieties and concerns of its period. Prohibitions on sleigh riding sound bizarre, but we can intuit concern with the weakening of patriarchal rule and condemnation of frivolity and possible sexual opportunity. Calls to regulate ice-cream parlours suggest concern with sites of heterosocial contact and come more into focus when we note that the discourses of the period stressed that it was immigrants, particularly Italians, who owned them. Attempts to restrict comics speak of persistent concerns about juveniles mixed with cultural chauvinism.

Moral regulation projects are an interesting and significant form of politics in which some people act to problematise the conduct, values or culture of others and seek to impose regulation upon them. There are three major grounds for insisting on the importance of moral regulation. The first is that moral regulation projects are often initiated from below;

the primary initiators and agents are frequently not holders of institutional power. I will show that the social origin of such movements frequently comes from 'the middle', from the middle classes. Of especial significance is the important role women have played as agents of moral regulation over the last century. The importance of moral regulation stems from the scope it provides for a variety of different social forces to articulate projects outside the mainstream of official politics and state institutions – sometimes so successfully that these projects get forced upon mainstream political parties and the state. While there are many studies of specific projects of moral reform, there has been surprisingly little attention to the general form or impact of moral regulation movements. However, not all moral reform projects emanate from below. There are some which seem to be the exclusive property of state institutions: a classic instance is the near monopoly by state agencies of anti-drug projects. These dual forms, movements from above and below, invite inquiry into how we should understand the significance of this duality.

The second reason for pressing the significance of moral regulation movements is that they provide classic instances of an intimate link between the 'governance of others' and the 'governance of the self'. In one of his last interviews Foucault identified his major concerns as being "to show how the government of the self is integrated with the government of others" (1989: 296). I want, not only to substantiate this general connection, but to explore the different forms in which projects stimulating self-governance manifest themselves in attempts to regulate others. Projects are not 'strategies' – the latter imply some more or less coherent planned course of action; projects may be conscious, but this is not a necessary condition. In particular I will emphasise the way that these projects seem to spill over and become transformed into their opposite. Movements that originate in attempts to promote male sexual self-control find themselves pressing for extensions to the criminalisation of sexual conduct.

The third ground for insisting on the pertinence of studying moral regulation is that such forms of regulation have a continuing significance today. The politics of moral regulation has become increasingly visible over the last two decades. Not only is there a series of persisting traditional moral problems, often with new names, which continue to occupy political and legislative attention – the classic exemplars being abortion, surrogacy and euthanasia – but a wider and more diverse range of social issues is contested in strongly moralised terms. Most strikingly there is a distinctive return to issues that had been prominent at the end of the nineteenth century. Great care needs to be taken to avoid falling into an all too easy cyclical account that emphasises a fashionable *fin de siècle* preoccupation. Yet while the form and trappings of current campaigns are different, there is a striking return to some of the prominent themes of late nineteenth-century moral politics. Politics organised around the sexual victimisation of women and children echo the calls for sexual purity and action against 'white slavery'; anti-pornography campaigns reverberate with the extension of obscenity laws at the end of the nineteenth century. Even alcohol regulation, perhaps the central target of nineteenth-century moral regulation, has made a significant return to the political agenda. Alongside these persistent themes the current agenda features a set of issues that are at one and the same time old and new: probably the best example is provided by the moral regulation of consumption. Common items of daily consumption – tea, coffee and tobacco being prime examples – have long been moralised, but there have been profound transformations in the moral discourses within which they are located. The discourses of health now play a disproportionate role; this is significant because to locate the grounds for not drinking coffee as a response to the presence of caffeine at first glance appears to take the issue outside the sphere of moral regulation. But closer inspection reveals a strange persistence of the status dimensions of consumption patterns: located within a medical discourse abstention now signifies a responsible care for the self, evidence of mastery over the simple pleasures in the name of health and longevity. And as with other fields we encounter differential roles played by public institutions: while smoking was for centuries locked into the politics of status and distinction, today it has been substantially harnessed by a powerful constellation of class cultures and state and medical institutions.

The similarities and dissimilarities between the multiple intersecting instances of moral regulation across time suggest a pressing need to grapple with the field of moral politics. The general pattern has been for debate and inquiry to focus on individual projects of moral regulation. In this form the encounters are often unproductive, bringing to light radically different normative evaluations of the projects under discussion. This book pursues a different approach, seeking a greater sociological distance from the immediate controversies by employing two connected research tactics. First, in order to provide some distance from our current preferences and prejudices, it locates these current controversies within a longer historical perspective. And, second, it aims to contribute to that distancing by employing a comparative approach intentionally looking at similar moral reform movements but in different historical and cultural contexts.

In order to provide a context for these wider historical issues, I will consider whether there is evidence to support the suggestion that there has been a shift from moral regulation of conduct through legislative activity of social institutions to a contemporary situation in which there is a 'pluralism of authorities', which require individuals to take responsibility and make choices for their own "self-constitution" (Bauman 1992b: 201–4). This claim resonates closely with arguments that modern liberal modes of government have come increasingly to work through stimulating the active engagement of individuals in projects of self-governance. I will argue that, while there is much to commend this thesis, it is important to recognise that self-governance is not new, but rather that the forms of self-governance have shifted significantly. I will show that there has been a shift from a negative or coercive form of self-governance, epitomised by the quest for 'self-control', to a more positive concern with 'self-formation'.

This transition in the forms of self-governance is exemplified by the shift from the nineteenth century's preoccupation with the promotion and formation of 'character' conceived of as a set of external virtues (perseverance, honesty, etc.) to be mastered and incorporated into the self.[2] By the mid-twentieth century the quest for character had been replaced by the pursuit of 'personality' without the fixed content of character, but concerned with personal self-formation through self-discovery and thus with the 'work' of forming a distinctive individual identity. Another expression of this shift is the tendency present in a range of modern social movements, particularly in self-help movements, towards an increasing preoccupation with issues of 'identity' (Laraña et al. 1994: 10). These trends can also be seen as exemplifying the shift from the 'struggle for existence' to the 'struggle for recognition' explored by Axel Honneth (1995). This book is concerned to chart the pattern of these shifts in the belief that a better understanding of moral reform movements will promote a more perceptive understanding and engagement with the passions and commitments called into play by today's moral reform movements.

GOVERNING THROUGH MORAL REGULATION

This study addresses moral regulation as a practice of governing in order to focus attention on social action that attempts to influence the conduct of human agents. This involves an expanded conception of governing that

> designates the way in which the conduct of individuals or states might be directed: the government of children, of souls, of communities, of families, of the sick. It did not cover only the legitimately constituted forms of political or economic subjection, but also modes of action, more or less considered, which were designed to act upon the possibilities of action of other people. To govern, in this sense, is to structure the possible field of action of others (Foucault 1982: 221).

The powerful claim at the heart of the sociology of governance is that a wide range of social agents are involved in practices of governing directed at diverse targets. Governing is not restricted to institutions that intentionally set out to engage in governmental activities such as state governments or municipal authorities. Many other institutions and social agencies engage in governing: schools govern pupils, hospitals govern patients, stores govern customers and so on.

An important feature of my argument is that moral regulation can be generated from a variety of different social positions. For simplicity's sake these distinct positions can be designated as regulation from above, from 'the middle' and from below. Moral regulation from above can be illustrated by state-sponsored anti-drug projects relying heavily on official agencies and criminal law. Regulation from 'the middle' is exemplified by the current anti-abortion campaign emanating, for example, from non-dominant religious organisations such as the Catholic Church and fundamentalist Protestantism. Such campaigns are often left well alone by central political and economic forces. Moral regulation from below is exemplified by medieval practices of 'rough music' or 'charivari' through which local hostility to wife-beating or to an adulterous wife is expressed by, for example, disturbing a fractious household by banging pots and pans in the middle of the night or mounting the husband backwards on a horse (Ingram 1984a; Thompson 1991). Today action from below is witnessed by the 'posting' of the addresses of presumed 'child molesters'. This simple model of three variants can be made more complex when various combinations of regulatory agents act in concert, as when state action from above is linked with popular action from below: for example, when state action is against the poor when the reduction of welfare benefits articulates and fuels hostility from the respectable working class against 'welfare scroungers'. In general, importance will be attached to identifying the social location of the regulatory agents and the forms of alliance exhibited in projects of moral regulation. The diverse sources of moral regulation support the general contention of the sociology of governance that 'governing' cannot be adequately encompassed within a hierarchical conception focused on the state or on dominant social or economic classes.

Since governing is not always a top-down process by some formally authorised superior, it follows that all sorts of agents are involved in governing. Thus beggars attempt through an array of tactics to govern those from whom they solicit. Further, governing is not necessarily successful or completed action, but always involves attempts that are more or less successful, and more or less failures; thus pupils attempt to govern their teachers, patients to elicit the medication they desire from doctors, and they do so with varying degrees of success and failure. The controversial aspect of this conception of governing is that it disrupts the conventional notion of power as something differentially possessed by different kinds of social agents and that those that 'have' power govern those that do not. From such a perspective it is scandalous to speak of beggars or children as 'governing'. The merit of this approach is that it focuses attention on the relational aspect of governing. The relative positions and resources of participants influence the likelihood of success or failure of the various projects in play, even though that calculus is more complex than analysis couched in terms of more or less power.

Governing rarely involves exclusively instrumental or external action directed at the governance of the conduct of others. Even such apparently instrumental mechanisms as highway speed limits intended to influence the speed of motor vehicles also involve a more general concern to sensitise drivers to safety considerations. Thus while speed regulations specify rules under which motorists can be stopped by police, ticketed or prosecuted, the rules also act upon the self-governance of motorists by inducing them to take account of changing road conditions such as bends or junctions ahead. Many forms of governing involve some mix of 'governing others' and 'governing the self'. This study focuses attention on one important and pervasive form of this mix of 'governing others' and 'governing the self' that takes the form of 'moral regulation'.

All practices of governing involve some element of moral regulation. The fact that moral regulation varies in intensity has played a significant part in stimulating the present inquiry. On the verge of the millennium we are experiencing an intensification of projects of moral regulation. The contested issues of our times range across economic, social and cultural fields that are struggled over in distinctively moralising terms. For example, in the economic realm the ethically neutral 'unemployed', who were the subject matter of economic and social policy for most of the twentieth century, have been reconstructed as 'welfare scroungers' in a way that is reminiscent of the 'paupers' and 'undeserving poor' who inhabited earlier periods of the politics of poverty. New categories of the socially dangerous (youth gangs, drug dealers, sex offenders and persistent offenders) inhabit a space that in the nineteenth century was occupied by the 'dangerous classes'. And in the cultural field angry moralisation in the discourses of sexuality reveal both continuity and change with the discourses of the nineteenth century; today paedophiles and rapists stand in the places occupied by the seducers and white-slavers in the nineteenth century.

Moral regulation involves the deployment of distinctively moral discourses which construct a moralised subject and an object or target which is acted upon by means of moralising practices. Moral discourses seek to act on conduct that is deemed to be intrinsically bad or wrong.[3] For example, when parents are advised by experts on child-rearing, this is never simply a technical question, but always, to a greater or lesser extent, includes a moral component that invests parents with responsibility for the conduct, present and future, of their children. It is helpful to isolate the following elements of moral regulation and this can be made more concrete by reference to child-rearing:

- a moralised subject (the parents);
- a moralised object or target (the child);[4]
- knowledge (informal or expert);
- a discourse within which the knowledge is given a normative content (parents should monitor the television watching of their children);
- a set of practices (potty training, school attendance);
- a 'harm' to be avoided or overcome (poorly socialised children, undisciplined workers, etc.).

The implication of this conceptualisation of moral regulation is that 'the moral' dimension is not an intrinsic characteristic of the regulatory target, since there is no set of issues that are necessarily moral issues; rather the moral dimension is the result of the linkage posited between subject, object, knowledge, discourse, practices and their projected social consequences.

The 'moral' element in moral regulation involves any normative judgement that some conduct is intrinsically bad, wrong or immoral. It is an important supplement that moralising discourses frequently invoke some utilitarian consideration linking the immoral practice to some form of harm. Such utilitarian elements become increasingly significant as moral discourses become detached from some taken-for-granted religious framework. Thus, while in Christian and other moral codes adultery is inherently sinful, with the rise of secular currents and religious heterogeneity, moralising discourses increasingly linked immorality to utilitarian claims about the personal or social harm associated with the wrong.[5] However, the association between wrong and 'harm' is significant. Harm has two distinguishable dimensions: it invokes both some specific harm resulting from the wrong conduct and some enhanced or symbolic harm. Take, for example, the late nineteenth-century purity discourses about prostitution; here the specific harm identified was that men resorting to prostitutes infected 'innocent' wives and children with venereal diseases and the symbolic harm was that prostitution exemplified the 'double standard' of sexual morality.

By focusing attention on moral regulation, I seek to avoid atrophying the concept as if it were some fixed or self-sufficient entity. We conventionally make distinctions, such as those between social, economic and moral realms; such categories are useful, even necessary, so long as we

BRIDWELL LIBRARY
SOUTHERN METHODIST UNIVERSITY
DALLAS, TEXAS 75275

do not fall into the trap of imagining that these terms create real separations as if there is some field, realm or space that is exclusively social, moral or economic. It is important to stress that there is no 'moral field', no place where 'the moral' rules alone or even predominates. Morality is to be found everywhere: in the workplace, at home, in every activity. Our conceptual distinctions are elaborated for analytical purposes only; in the real world they are always found in complex connection with other elements.

Moral regulation is a process in which moral discourses, techniques and practices make up the primary field of contestation. As I have indicated, moral discourses frequently link moralised subjects and objects with some moralised practices in such a way as to impute some wider social harm that will be occasioned unless subjects, objects and practices are appropriately regulated. Moral regulation comprises 'moralisation' rather than 'morality,' and thus is relational, asserting some generalised sense of the wrongness of some conduct, habit or disposition. One important aspect of moralisation involves what Foucault has called 'dividing practices' (1982: 210). A classic instance is the construction of the division between the 'deserving' and the 'undeserving' poor. Such a distinction has two immediate consequences; first it moralises the categories, delineates between good and bad; second, it operates as a legitimation for the differential treatment of the divided categories – for example, the deserving poor are granted relief that is denied to the undeserving poor.

Dividing practices impact upon those who are caught up by them. They thus become components of the ways in which those who are the targets of moral regulation become 'subjects'. It is one of the ways in which people are constructed, both through the actions of others and their action upon themselves, as subjects. They may attempt to refuse the subjectification imposed on them and thus create the possibility of resistance and the formation of an alternate subjectivity. On the other hand they may accept membership within the constructed category; the deserving poor may accept that status, claim relief, and support the denial of relief to the 'undeserving'. Such processes not only include potential contestation and struggle, but will always involve some form of self-understanding or reflexivity; this reflexivity may be mediated through the participation of others, such as external 'experts' who construct, reinforce or interpret the dividing practice.[6] Another way of describing the role of external agents is provided by what Bauman calls "asymmetric surveillance", which draws attention to the separation of watchers and watched and the objectivising practices of counting, measuring and classifying behind which techniques moralisation, explicit or implicit, is ever present (1992a: 6).

BRIDWELL LIBRARY
SOUTHERN METHODIST UNIVERSITY
DALLAS, TEXAS 75275

This general perspective provides a conceptual framework within which to embark on the exploration of the selected moral regulation movements. Singling out specific movements from the many diverse projects and campaigns could tend to create an impression of discrete movements which are then only brought into connection by means of external comparison. This would be misleading. It would omit the strong sense of enduring linkages between moral regulation movements. Others have drawn attention to the close links that existed between the activists in contemporaneous movements. Harrison (1974) charts the cross-cutting participation in Victorian movements in England concerned with Sunday observance, sexual purity, women's suffrage, animal cruelty and temperance, and anti-vaccination movements.

My contention is a stronger one. It is that moral regulation movements form an interconnected web of discourses, symbols and practices exhibiting persistent continuities that stretch across time and place. The deep anxieties that are roused and stirred in moral politics involve the condensation of a number of different discourses, different fears, within a single image – perhaps the classic instance being the role played by the persistent thematic of 'abolition' that provides a linkage, at work on both sides of the Atlantic, that linked moral reform movements of both the nineteenth and twentieth centuries to the symbols of the anti-slavery movement. In a similar vein, Ian Hacking demonstrates the linkages that exist between the current 'child abuse' movements beyond the immediate consciousness of participants, not only to anti-slavery, but to child labour, temperance, anti-vivisection and cruelty to animals, and above all women's rights (1995: 56). In brief, I will seek to show that such movements are not to be understood in isolation but as part of a shifting complex of projects of governance in which the long-run changes are not so much the shift from one target to another, but rather in the location of moral regulation within the field of governing others and governing selves.

Another dimension of moral reform movements is that they frequently succeed in establishing an 'umbrella effect' whereby they secure support from an array of otherwise diverse political and ideological trends.[7] This idea helps make sense of one of the troubling features of moral reform movements. Some campaigns had a major and lasting impact, while others did little more than elicit a superior smile from a knowing world about the strange obsessions of others. E. S. Turner (1950) gives a delightful account of opposition to nineteenth-century law reform by those predicting disaster and the end of civilisation as we know it when confronted with such initiatives as the outlawry of man traps, the introduction of Saturday half-day working and the rescinding of the prohibition on marriage to a deceased wife's sister. Would we have been successful in predicting that the campaign against the *Contagious Diseases Acts* in Britain from the 1870s would forge an alliance that resulted in major changes in criminal law? Would we have been any more likely to spot the significance of the fervour with which women in Washington Court House and Hillsboro', Ohio, in December 1873 sparked a crusade against saloons? There are other movements whose issues are just as significant and persistent but which have never succeeded in becoming mass movements. It is hazardous to name such movements because they are likely to flare immediately into active life. One would have been forgiven for thinking that the movement against cruelty to animals was a long-running concern of an enthusiastic minority rarely able to capture any political initiative. However, the dramatic movements in Britain in the mid-1990s against the conditions under which livestock is exported provide a telling instance of the umbrella thesis. It was only when the issue of cruelty was articulated alongside an anxiety-ridden nationalism and an outbreak of xenophobia against Continental Europe that for the first time in nearly 200 years an anti-cruelty campaign achieved national significance; in so doing it reignited the campaign against fox-hunting which had long simmered as much as a class issue as one about cruelty to animals.

The capacity to bring disparate trends together into an umbrella is a condition of the success of moral reform movements. This occurs where some specific social problem serves to mobilise an array or umbrella of different social forces that otherwise would not only have had no contact, but might have lined up as part of opposed social blocs. This mode of analysis suggests its value in addressing such contemporary issues as sexual victimisation, substance abuse and the like by focusing attention on the way these issues bring together an umbrella of otherwise rather different activists and how such alliances are constituted through the discursive construction of the field. To use the more traditional terms promoted by C. Wright Mills, the challenge is to attend to the construction of 'public problems' by social currents emanating from different ideological and political positions.

Moral regulation movements are often thought of as if they were some archaic throwback and almost inevitably conservative in content. It is important rigorously to exclude any such assumption. Yet it should be recognised that it is all too easy to err in this direction; intuitively I find myself out of sympathy with many of the movements I have studied. Yet rather than the conventional view which sees moral regulation movements as anti-modern, I will explore the suggestion that the persistence of moral regulation movements is a manifestation of an ongoing anxiety that has beset modernity about the governability of urbanised masses living without any evident structure of rule under conditions where traditional authorities, such as the Church or a visible dominant class, are weakened or no longer present and where class and other forms of deference are fragile.[8] Today there is no 'natural' system of social order and no possibility of promoting a Durkheimian moral education which could inculcate the rules of morality "elaborated by society" (Durkheim 1973: 162). Any system of moral regulation requires the existence of mechanisms of self-restraint and self-discipline that are generalised and disseminated. The agency of first resort is often the family, as witnessed in the persistent invoking of 'family values'. However, the family is itself increasingly perceived as fallible, and is today often seen as the source of disorder and immorality. Under such conditions the quest emerges, prompted by concerns about various aspects of social order, for the promotion and enforcement of a 'moral order' conceived as the necessary condition for 'social order'.

Most projects of moral regulation, but not necessarily all, are articulated within a language of decline or degeneration; 'things' are represented as not being what they used to be and this change is articulated within a moral discourse. One common form invokes an imagined golden age of community or national greatness and moral rectitude that is confronted by a 'present danger' that threatens future social ills of decline, degeneration, and social disorder – often, but not always, a fear of the insubordination of the poor or of labouring classes, or – occasionally – of the dissoluteness of some dominant section. The proposed moral reform is presented as necessary to overcome the decline and generally has a dual thrust: a specific cure for the identified ill and an expanded or symbolic dimension. Again citing the example of the prostitution controversies at the end of the nineteenth century, it was argued that securing male sexual purity would not only end the scourge of venereal disease, but would also restore national strength and honour.

However, it is important not to treat the evident conservatism of the above description of moral regulation as a necessary corollary of all projects. Rather it is crucial to insist that moral regulation has no necessary political valence. There is, however, an elective affinity between a conservative social imaginary and moral regulation projects, but this can be transcended in order to promote transformative projects.

MORAL REGULATION AND THE DEPLOYMENT OF LAW

One aspect of grappling with the relationship between social movements and institutional structure and apparatuses is to explore the way in which law becomes involved, is created, invoked, deployed, avoided or just ignored in the process. There have been studies that explore the way in which legislation has resulted from specific moral regulation campaigns. Such studies have often been linked to the 'moral panic' tradition in which the promotion of a public campaign produces demands for greater action to combat the targeted evil which, in turn, results in a combination of institutional expansion and legislative action.[9] Classic examples are Howard Becker's study of the emergence of the *Marihuana Tax Act* 1937 (1963) and Joseph Gusfield's analysis of prohibition (1963).

Much less attention has been paid to the relation between reform movements and the way in which they make use of legal resources. It will emerge that there occur significant tensions around the practices of moral reform movements with regard to the deployment of law. The present study will pay particular attention to the part played by law, whether positively or negatively, in the strategies and practices of moral reform. There is a persistent strand in which moral regulation movements articulate their demands in the form of calls for symbolic legislation; there are a number of other legal tactics which have received less attention. Some movements have been organised around attempts to enforce existing law, even going so far as to organise systematic drives to inform against offenders and to initiate prosecutions. Others have manifested considerable reservations about the desirability and effectiveness of coercive or regulatory legislation. It will be important to highlight the tensions between regulationism and anti-regulationism as a central dilemma of moral regulation.

One manifestation of this friction has been that moral reform movements have become increasingly attentive to questions about how they position themselves not only over the question of the content of law, but also with issues of the administration and enforcement of law. I will explore the implications of a growing legalisation of the politics of moral regulation manifested in the way in which issues of law, legislation, administration and enforcement became central issues and lines of cleavage. I will, in particular, be concerned to probe the implications of an increasing reticence about legal strategies which is one of the cumulative legacies of the modern history of moral regulation. Nowhere is this friction more clear than in the long-running argument within feminism over the deployment of law with some arguing that it is an essential component of any transformative strategy and others who insist that the very foundations of law are inimical to women's interests.

THEORETICAL RESOURCES FOR A THEORY OF MORAL REGULATION

This study will draw upon a range of theoretical resources. The strands that will be drawn on can be briefly indicated. A few basic strands can be identified to alert the reader to debates that will subsequently be pursued in more detail. The importance of Foucault will already be apparent. It is the interrelated themes of a concern with the deployment of discourses and techniques in the practices of power, and the interconnection between the governance of others and the governance of the self that will resonate throughout this study. It is again Foucault who underpins the concern with questions of governmentality, that is the mentalities and rationalities embedded in practices of governing (Burchell et al. 1991; Dean 1991; Rose & Miller 1992; Rose 1993; Hunt & Wickham 1994).

From Norbert Elias comes the recognition that the acquisition of the set of learned constraints on the personality is the hallmark of the unplanned advance of what he calls civilisation. What is dazzling about Elias is the way he sustains the linkage between long-run historical processes taking centuries to unfold and their detailed impact on the personality structures of individuals whereby a mundane change, such as learning to eat with implements rather than with the fingers, acquires world-historical significance. Projects of moral regulation (a term he does not use) fit into his focus upon "the social constraint towards self-constraint" (1982: 230). What is lacking in Elias is attention to the contested nature of these processes; he is too willing to hypostatise 'society', to make it an active agent that requires and demands things of individuals, with the result that his account comes dangerously close to social control theory that I reject in the next section.

Some greater attention to the contested nature of these civilising processes is made available by Peter Burke's concept the 'reform of popular culture'. Burke first proposed an historically specific focus on the reform of popular culture and 'civilising offensives' to refer to systematic attempts by sections of dominant classes to change the attitudes, values and cultural practices of subordinate classes in England in the period between the fifteenth and eighteenth centuries (1978). The process is exemplified in attempts to suppress 'riotous games', 'carnivals' and other popular festivities. The contestation over the maypole as a primitive fertility ritual ends with May festivities today having become a sanitised public holiday with no substantive content. Other traditional festivities, such as Halloween and Valentine's Day, have been infantilised.

The reform of popular culture embraces systematic attempts by some social forces to change the attitudes, values and practices of other sections of the population. These projects revolve around the multi-layered meaning of 'reformation' as something far wider than the theological disputes involved in their capitalised form as 'the Reformation'. Reformation exhibits a preoccupation with decency, diligence, gravity, modesty, orderliness, prudence, reason, self-control, sobriety and thrift; it is organised around a set of values well captured by Weber's notion of 'this-worldly asceticism'.[10] Central to the reform of popular culture is the emergence of a widening gulf between an elite and a mass culture, or between two previously associated social positions that exhibit an increasing rift or social cleavage. In his study of early modern England, Burke detected a complex realignment of the 'middling sort', the classes of yeoman farmers and small landowners becoming increasingly separated from the mass of agricultural labourers (1978).[11] During this process a class cleavage opens up in which some aspect of popular culture, which had previously been shared within the community, becomes increasingly moralised and subjected to external pressures for reform as, for example, when the landowning classes become estranged from popular rituals that come to be viewed as 'pagan'.[12]

The concept 'reform of popular culture' can find a wider range of application in order to address other manifestations of contestations over the content of cultural practices. Typical of the conflicts that have been studied are contests between Church and alehouse in England as sites organising and promoting popular recreations. The struggle over drinking became a continuing social drama that has persisted down to the present and still provides a target for moral regulation. The idea of reform of popular culture has gradually acquired a wider historical reach, being applied to later periods and to an expanded geographical range. It is of particular importance to stress the persistence of issues around the reform of popular culture down to the present. There is rarely a period in which the recreations and pastimes of the poor, of the working population, or of some socially visible minority have not been the target for the moralisation and projects of governance by some other section of the population. Alcohol has been a persistent target of moral regulation while tobacco smoking has moved in and out of the moralising reach. It should be noted that moralising discourses are frequently linked with other discursive components such as concern with national decline and with individual and collective health. We are only at a very early stage in the writing of the collective histories of the moralising discourses. The present work seeks to transform the idea of the reform of popular culture into a general sociological concept.

My conception of moral regulation is close to Philip Corrigan's early sketch of 'moral regulation' (Corrigan 1981). His focus is on the part played by moral regulation in state-formation. My concerns differ somewhat in that I am keen to explore the way in which conflicts over competing discourses within popular culture construct arenas within which the targets of regulation are formed and acted upon by both state and non-state agencies. In brief, it is important to avoid any suggestion that the state, conceived as some institutional personalisation, is an autonomous agent that selects its targets as part of some wider strategic objective and then organises their moralisation in order to subject them to moral regulation. Yet it is important to avoid a polarisation between state projects of the reform of morals and non-state movements; as I have suggested, I will be very much concerned to explore this complex configuration of state and non-state projects.

The central concern that I share with Corrigan is the insistence that social formations necessarily involve, along with economic and political frameworks, modes of social discipline that involve moral projects reproducing a culture of manners, customs and rituals. These processes are socially constitutive in so far as they form the identities and subjectivities which render social relations natural or taken for granted. The sum of these processes sustains forms of social life. The essential point is that moral regulation has a dual character as both externally regulative and internally constitutive (Corrigan & Sayer 1985: 194). It needs to be stressed that this conception of the constitutive role of moral regulation differs from Durkheim's classical account of 'moral order' in that it refuses the hypostatisation of 'society' as the active agent that 'produces' moral order. Rather moral regulation should be understood as ongoing contestations that involve a continuous, and more or less coercive, suppression of some identities and forms of life and the encouragement and enhancement of preferred forms.

Mitchell Dean takes issue with this conception of moral regulation. He argues that the concentration by Corrigan and Sayer on the state leads to a lack of attention to the practices of the self (1994). It should be remembered that the Corrigan–Sayer account emerged from a project whose immediate object was precisely to provide an account of state-formation; it seems to be beside the point to criticise such a project for being state-centred. Dean contends that the concept of moral regulation cannot adequately address the processes of self-regulation and self-formation. Here he follows Foucault in insisting on a distinction between 'morals' and 'ethics', that is between external moral codes and ethics as the practices of self-formation.

Dean's preferred alternative is to identify the object of study as the exploration of the relation between ethical practices (the practices of self-formation) and governmental practices concerned with political subjectification and the regulation of citizens. He distinguishes between two forms of self-formation: 'governmental self-formation' in which authorities seek to shape the conduct, aspirations, needs, desires and capacities of individuals, and the 'ethical self-formation' by which individuals seek to know, decipher and act on themselves. While Foucault's distinction between morals and ethics is helpful in drawing a line between these two realms, it has another important implication that needs to be recognised. The danger of conflating morals and ethics arises only if the two processes are conceived as necessarily moving in parallel; that is, of assuming that the external imposition of a moral code is mirrored in internal processes of self-formation. This tendency is, as I have suggested above, found in Elias' account of the civilising process, in which societal imperatives march hand in hand with changes in human personalities. The Corrigan–Sayer account of moral regulation escapes this tendency precisely because they insist on the contested nature of projects of moral regulation by drawing attention to the dual processes of suppressing some practices while encouraging others.

The differences between Dean and Corrigan–Sayer about the implications of the concept of moral regulation lead me to the conclusion that there is, in fact, no fundamental conflict. Projects of moral regulation and ethical self-formation frequently come together in the complex and varied forms of interaction between governing others and governing the self. Indeed, as I have already suggested, a significant dimension of moral regulation projects is that they are projects directed at governing others while at the same time they result in self-governing effects. But this is not a one-way process; projects of self-formation can and do play an important role in the making of governmental systems. Nowhere is this more dramatically illustrated than in Weber's account of the Puritan 'calling':

> When asceticism was carried out of the monastic cells into everyday life, and began to dominate worldly morality, it did its part in building the cosmos of the modern economic order (Weber 1930: 181).

We need have no fear that the term moral regulation refers only to projects to impose external moral codes, even though history is replete with just such endeavours; moral regulation is often directed at inducing projects of self-formation, manifest in ubiquitous incitements to 'self-control'.[13] What the concept of moral regulation succeeds in capturing – and here it is significant that my project is different from Dean's – is that these projects are always 'social' because they exhort their targets and seek to render them governable. In this respect I am not primarily concerned with reflexive self-formation save in so far as self-governance is one of the tactics employed or advocated. For Dean ethics is the action of the self on the self; my concern is to emphasise the ways in which the self comes to be induced to act upon itself. I am, for example, less concerned about how we diet than with how to come to feel the need to diet. To use Dean's own terminology, I view moral regulation as being more concerned with 'governmental self-formation' than 'ethical self-formation', but with the important proviso that I do not restrict 'governmental' to the practices of official authorities. More prosaically,

I am less engaged by the last two volumes of Foucault's history of sexuality than I am with the first. In the final analysis, I see no necessary incompatibility between Dean's position and my own, but rather detect a somewhat different focus of attention. I find no difficulty in endorsing Dean's conclusion that:

> The citizen is formed not only as an active member of a political community and a dependent subject but also as one who works on her or himself and is, as a consequence, an ethical being (1994: 166).

There is, however, one difference of substance between myself and Dean which remains. He raises the objection against the concept of moral regulation that it "delineates no clear domain" that is distinguishable from the general field of political regulation (1994: 155). I suggest he is wrong because, while moral regulation may be pursued as a political project, it is important to take account of the fact that moral regulation can be distinguished from political regulation in two ways. First, moral regulation projects are undertaken by a wide range of different agents falling outside the general ambit of the political and state institutions. The central focus of this book will document the part played by a diversity of social movements. Second, moral regulation manifests itself in many different guises: it may present itself as a medical project, a sanitary undertaking, a religious imperative or as a political strategy.[14] Moral regulation frequently coexists with other forms of regulation. For example, moral discourses are found closely associated with medical discourses, key instances being the long-running regulatory struggles over alcohol and tobacco that illustrate the shifting combination of medical and moral discourses.

It is necessary to stress that moral regulation is not simply a disguise or mask for economic or political interests; it is not some ideology behind which, once penetrated, can be found 'real' objectives or motives. From this follows the strong contention that this book seeks to substantiate, namely, that moral regulation is a discrete mode of regulation existing alongside and interacting with political and economic modes of regulation. Moral regulation as a form of regulation is not itself static; it changes its forms, its language and also its associates. In the nineteenth century it appeared in evangelical tracts and Victorian serialised novels. Today it is more likely to be found in the guise of self-help texts or the discourses of 'addiction' and 'recovery'. Yet such projects remain attempts at moral regulation in that they are concerned to effect changes in the conduct and ethical subjectivity of individuals.

In order to give weight to the general concern with the place of agency in moral regulation, this study will pay attention to the social movements that give substance and specificity to projects of moral regulation. This concern to explore these projects as social movements has significant implications. First I will draw on a variant of social movement theory. A chasm has opened up between the two camps of 'resource mobilisation' theory and 'new social movement' theory. My own inclinations are closer to new social movement theory if only because it is more attentive to the role of discourse in constituting movements, but I will also draw on resource mobilisation studies in order to pay attention to the organisational characteristics of moral reform movements which I will argue are significant in constructing the often bewildering shifting alliances that characterise moral reform movements. As I have already indicated, I will not simply be concerned with the internal organisation of moral reform movements, but will be attentive to their links with other forms of social, cultural and political action. This concern with the social movement dimensions of moral regulation plays some part in the selection of movements for detailed study to be outlined below. This also largely accounts for the exclusion of what might otherwise have been a prime candidate, namely, the temperance movement, because the sheer size and diversity of its organisational manifestations make it difficult to condense into a comparative study.

It should perhaps be noted that the range of different theoretical positions canvassed contain tensions and these will be explored when necessary. Different theories are rarely, if ever, simple alternatives or negations. More often they involve differential expressions of attempts to come to grips with some intellectual problem through the mobilisation of distinctive conceptual resources. Rather than being in direct opposition to one another, they can usually be best understood as mobilising differential emphases. Thus I feel no need to make a choice, say, between Elias and Foucault; both have much to offer, but each leads inquiry in somewhat different directions and both have certain 'costs' measured in terms of the issues they emphasise and those they marginalise.

ON SOCIAL CONTROL, MORAL PANICS AND ANXIETY

I turn briefly to discuss some theoretical positions that I will not make use of, and one that I will use, but about which I wish to enter a caution. I address these issues in order further to clarify my own position.

The idea of 'social control' has a long and influential history, but it is one that has no place in this book. My primary objection is that it pushes aside what for me is a central issue of all processes of governing and regulating, namely, that of agency. Who it is that attempts to govern whom and how those targeted respond should be central questions. Active people simply get squeezed out of accounts written under the sign of social control because there it is 'society', society-in-general as some unitary entity, that acts.[15] It is necessary to reject the Durkheimian focus on 'social control' by insisting that it is never 'society' that acts, but always and only people who act.[16] It is because the results of that action rarely correspond directly with the intentions of the acting subjects that it appears as if people are controlled by disembodied and impersonal entities such as 'society' or 'the economy'. These entities – which it is often convenient to speak of – are nothing more than a rough and ready shorthand for the aggregate of active people, their relations, conflicts and interactions. Once we take a step further and disrupt the common sense which equates 'society' with the 'nation-state', then it becomes even more clear that 'society' is a convenient but provisional demarcation for some social aggregate about which we want to talk. It is necessary to expunge the Durkheimian myth that 'society' acts through 'social control'. Moral regulation involves some people acting on other people and in so doing acting upon themselves.

There is a second concept that I need to reject. Much discussion of moral reform movements takes place under the label of 'moral panics'. Important studies have been produced under the imprint of the concept of moral panic (Cohen 1972; Cohen & Young 1973; Goode & Ben-Yehuda 1994). However, I avoid the concept itself because of its tendency to import a negative normative judgement. The term 'panic' implies that the response to some social problem is an over-reaction or exaggerated. To this should be added a warning against any self-righteous ascription of irrationality to projects of moral regulation. To assume that such movements involve over-reaction and irrationality is but a short step from a conspiracy theory in which some agent – for example, the state or the mass media – actively sets out to fan the smoke of anxiety into the flames of panic. It is not that there are no conspiracies in which social anxieties are manipulated or that the media do not amplify social anxieties, but that not all campaigns of moral regulation are the result of such manipulation. It is thus wise to avoid starting out from concepts that tend to import such assumptions. Moral politics addresses 'real' issues, although not always in the form presented by the reformers. Furthermore, projects of moral regulation have no necessary political label stamped on them and assumptions about their political tendency should, as I have suggested, be avoided.

Some attention is needed to the relationship between moral regulation and social anxieties. Many sociological and historical attempts to explain various forms of social change invoke the idea that they are responses to some anxiety. For example, Stuart Hall's classic study of the mugging panic in Britain in the early 1970s analyses the crisis as a response to widely diffused anxieties about changes in intergenerational relations, a decline in community in inner-city areas and heightened tension in race relations (Hall et al. 1978). The general form of such accounts is that the occurrence and timing of some social phenomenon is to be explained by reference to the presence of some elevated state of anxiety which elicits social or political responses by an identifiable group of social agents. Anxiety accounts share a common general form: they explain socio-historical phenomena as responses to anxieties generated by social change. Such accounts offer the prospect of going beyond the experience of participants to some sense of what is 'really going on', of causal mechanisms that are at work behind the consciousness of participants. The explanatory mechanism at work in anxiety theory is a variant of structuralism. It offers a 'deep' cause that underlies the phenomenal form through which the anxieties impact on social conduct so as to reveal mechanisms and connections not necessarily accessible to consciousness. But this claim should alert us to a real difficulty: if what constitutes the evidence is not dependent on the consciousness of the participants, how are we to establish the causal link between cause and phenomenal manifestation?[17]

There is a risk associated with anxiety analysis in that it suggests too direct a connection between cause and effect. In the analyses that make up this book I strive to avoid the hasty conclusions which anxiety theory seems to induce. I do not outlaw such arguments, but merely try to ensure that they are buttressed by adequate supports.

THE SELECTION OF CASE STUDIES

Moral regulation projects have exhibited a diverse, but seemingly unquenchable, concern to regulate everyday life. These regulatory incursions exhibit a persistent moralisation of some target category, whether it be the poor, prostitutes or young men, in attempts to discipline unruly forms of popular autonomy. The disciplinary projects produced profound, and more or less violent, changes in social relations. The moralisation of facets of popular culture has gone hand in hand with a shifting combinatory articulation in which new targets and new anxieties emerge and replace earlier combinations. We encounter an extraordinary diversity of regulatory targets. Some of these targets seem to fade away, such as the concern to enforce the discipline of religion in general and Sunday observance in particular, and yet even here we find that such projects experience a reprise, as in recent debates over Sunday opening of stores.[18] Other projects, although they undergo radical changes in their form, exhibit remarkable durability. Similarly concern with alcohol and with gambling, whether in the name of economic rationality or of morality, exhibits a long and complex history.

It hardly needs to be said that sex, sexuality and sexual conduct have rarely been far from the centre of attention – to such an extent that for at least the last 200 years sex and morals have been virtually synonymous. This fusion of sex and morals has resulted in its being taken for granted that sex is paramountly a moral question – so much so that it seems to be important to ask the seemingly naive question: why is sex so important? This issue constitutes an important element in one of the significant developments in the recent past, namely, the discovery that sex and sexuality have a social history. Spearheaded by Foucault, this realisation has stimulated an outpouring of historical scholarship and a deepening of political debate. This study seeks to contribute by attending to the shifts and changes in the part played by the discourses of sex and sexuality in moral reform movements.

The discourses of morality condense a plethora of representations that jostle for attention and their configuration shifts over time. Morality is a synonym for culture and civilisation or their absence or fragility. Moral discourses attribute blame and responsibility for social ills. Perhaps most significantly they articulate a specific domain or field of sexuality that both constructs what sexuality is and how it is to be experienced by particular categories of people, and links sexuality and sexual conduct to other aspects of social life, in particular to issues of health, well-being and prosperity or their opposites.

The discourses of sexuality also actively shape and regulate the emergence of distinctive class and gender relations. Lines of fissure within the working class became particularly sharp with the growth of a respectable working class associated with ideas of sexual respectability alongside a class hostility to upper-class exploitation of working-class women and girls. I will need to explore the link between sex and class with respect to the formation of a virtuous middle class dedicated to 'self-denial' and 'self-control' and their specific gendered articulations. These emotionally reassuring techniques helped to forge a lifestyle that, on the one hand, disparaged a dissolute upper class and, on the other, kept a distance from the threatening disorder of the public and private lives of the working class.

It is important to stress that deep inconsistencies characterise the discourses of sexuality. We will encounter views that treat sex as both natural and unnatural, that view women and children as innocent and perverse. In particular, ambivalence about female sexuality has remained one of the central tensions in the modern history of sexuality. These issues raise a general theoretical question concerning the relation between structural social change and the everyday realm of family, sexual relations and sexual practices.

The criteria of selection for the moral regulation movements to be discussed in detail are as follows. First, the movements studied move from simple individual movements in the earlier phases of the study, single movements at the beginning of the eighteenth century (Societies for Reformation of Manners) and the beginning of the nineteenth century (the Vice Society) to more complex movements. At the end of the nineteenth century the 'sexual purity' movements were a complex and overlapping cluster of organisations with no institutional centre, and the 'sexual victim movements' of the late twentieth are an even more complex array manifesting both dispersion and a variety of attempts at co-ordination.

Second, the movements discussed are widely spaced over time. A gap of roughly a century divides the four main phases of this study. This serves to underline the comparative nature of the project, the movements being sufficiently separated in time to ensure that the differences are evident and pronounced. This mode of historical comparison is supplemented by a cross-cultural comparison: for the last two phases of the study, 'sexual purity' and 'sexual victim' movements are investigated in both Britain and North America.

It is an inevitable consequence of the selection of specific moral regulation movements for detailed attention that other movements will not receive detailed attention. I have already commented on the significance of the exclusion of movements concerned with the regulation of alcohol as specific objects of inquiry because of their size and complexity. But much will have to be said about temperance and prohibition movements because of their links with and impact upon other moral regulation movements. Nowhere will this be more evident than with respect to the Women's Christian Temperance Union because of its key role in the formation of the American feminism and sexual purity tradition. Other movements, while themselves not specific objects of study, will figure in so far as they form part of the complex interconnecting texture of the web of moral reform movements whose different patterns are so important in both the nineteenth- and twentieth-century configurations.

This emphasis on the complex structure of the moral regulation tradition underlines the self-understanding of this study as a work of historical sociology. While it is to be hoped that there is material that is historically useful, it does not set out to provide an exhaustive account of any particular movement. It is undertaken in order to participate in debate about the changing place of moral regulation movements. Any contribution that this study makes to the understanding of any particular movement is an added bonus. However, it should be noted that more detailed attention is given to the first movement studied, the Societies for Reformation of Manners in early eighteenth-century England, precisely because this movement has not been the subject of detailed attention.

This work is organised around a tentative periodisation of moral regulation movements. It starts with a study of an English movement, the Societies for Reformation of Manners (SRM), active from the early 1690s and fading in the 1730s. In an important sense this was the first moral reform movement. I say this while being mindful of the importance of earlier moral regulation projects. Martin Ingram has traced currents of 'reformation of manners' focused upon attempts to regulate sexual morality back into the late middle ages. Peter Burke has documented the active concern with the reform of popular culture manifested in a widening fracture between farmers and agricultural labourers which led to explicit projects to intervene with regard to the everyday conduct and leisure of the latter. What is different about the SRM is that they were a membership organisation, to a significant extent independent of the governing classes, formed by a still amorphous and indistinct urban middle class. Their unique characteristic as a moral reform movement was that their primary focus was upon the enforcement of existing criminal legislation. Chapter 1 provides an extended account and analysis of the SRM.

The second movement studied, the Vice Society, active in the early years of the nineteenth century, exhibits a continuity with the project of the reformation of manners, but also marks significant breaks which make it possible to map some of the trends and tendencies that impact on the subsequent history of moral regulation movements. The Vice Society was active at the beginning of the nineteenth century. Its social base was closer to the Establishment, both civil and ecclesiastical, and it had access to the state apparatus and to Parliament. Like the SRM it was initially mainly concerned with the enforcement of existing law, but its tactics differed markedly being much more selective in the prosecutions it sponsored or stimulated. It gradually became more concerned with what I argue is a distinctive characteristic of 'modern' reform movements, namely the promotion of moral reform through state legislation. This characteristic also exists alongside the other great manifestation of nineteenth-century reform movements – the increasing centrality of socio-economic reform. What becomes crucial as the century progresses is the way in which socio-economic reform is both profoundly a matter of moral regulation, but at the same time comes to distinguish itself from the discursive framework provided by theology, which had played a central role in the prevailing moral reform discourses.

It is, of course, significant that the heart of this study focuses on the late nineteenth century. In an important sense we may regard this as the classical phase of moral regulation movements. A whole complex of moral regulation movements came into existence in Britain and the United States from the mid-Victorian period onwards. By the last decade of the century it had become clear that the core of this complexity was a set of projects that came to understand themselves through the designation of 'social purity'.[19]

These movements cover a decisive historical transition from a period in which moral discourses could still be articulated in the assumption of a generalised Christian doctrinal framework, in particular that of evangelical Protestantism, to an emergent necessity to locate moral projects within secular discourses that drew not on theology, but on the social sciences. One primary discursive and political medium through which this transformation was effected was that of feminism, and in particular through maternal feminism that sought to press for expanded rights grounded in an acceptance of the ideology of separate spheres and the valorisation of domesticity and maternity. Not only was this significant in that sexual purity demands brought significant numbers of middle-class women into active participation in the public sphere, but its rhetoric partook of a fascinating transition between evangelism and social science. At the same time purity politics also experienced a particularly sharp strategic tension, embedded not just in feminism, but more generally in liberalism, between coercive reform projects and those focused on stimulating active participation in self-formation activities. This major shift and its associated tensions were brought forward into the twentieth century when purity movements experienced a sharp decline in their power and influence in the period just before and after the First World War, when more secularised and instrumental politics came not only to dominate, but also to marginalise traditional moral reform movements.

Foucault argues that the nineteenth century witnessed the rise of the 'bio-politics of population', which involved the governmentalisation of issues impinging on the size, health and productivity of the whole population. There was an intensification of the production of knowledge about the population, a concern with birth-rate and fertility, with illegitimacy and with contraception; medicine was similarly governmentalised as exemplified in programmes of immunisation, notification of diseases, classification of causes of mortality, etc. He argues that at the heart of this new preoccupation with the "economic and political problem of population was sex" (1978: 25). As a result, sex and sexuality became a political issue. I extend Foucault's thesis by suggesting that the governmentalisation of sex does not only take place within the state. The rise and diversification of moral regulation movements with an array of different target groups and populations was precisely a set of interventions in the politics of population.

We do not have to search too far to decide why it was that issues around sex, sexuality, masturbation, prostitution and homosexuality became such key concerns during the later part of the nineteenth century. Increasing economic and military rivalry between the European powers along with the growing influence of the USA made the health, fitness and productivity of the working population increasingly important. To these concerns, especially in the case of Britain, needs to be added what may be termed the stress of empire, which involves a mix of unstable elements: on the one hand is the celebration of 'the greatest empire the world has ever seen' that coexisted with an anxiety as to whether so small an island and its population could sustain the burden of ruling. This apprehension sharpened after the 1850s with the military disaster of the Crimean War and the mutinies in India. My contention is that late nineteenth-century moral politics should be understood as being located within the discursive complex of nationalism, population and sexuality.

Foucault's account of the birth of bio-politics focuses attention on the moralisation of the working class that occurred during the nineteenth century. "It was absolutely necessary to constitute the populace as a moral subject and to break its commerce with criminality, and hence to segregate the delinquents and to show them to be dangerous not only to the rich but to the poor as well" (1980: 41). I concur with the importance of this complex of dividing practices which acted to pull apart the respectable from the unrespectable working class. However, I want to add an insistence on the importance of the moralisation of the middle classes, that is, on the self-formation of those who shared the sentiments of national obligation and national burden.

Chapter 6 makes a calculated leap from the late nineteenth century to the twentieth century that requires some explanation. This chapter is different in important respects from those that precede it. In the first place this move underlines the insistence that this work does not pretend to provide a chronological history of moral regulation. Had this been the intention, it would have been necessary to dwell at length on the intervening periods that punctuated the gaps between the movements explored in earlier chapters. This should not be read as implying that moral regulation was either absent or dormant. A more particular set of reasons motivates the jump from the aftermath of the First World War to our recent past.

In truth there was much of interest in the inter-war period. However, to investigate that period would require detailed attention to the way in which moral regulation was imbricated with the projects of bio-politics that found expression in the complex apparatus of welfare that took shape during this period. Such an undertaking would require attention to the complex of state interventions and the wider history of welfare politics. While non-state moral regulation organisations were still present during this period, they were of less significance than those either of the late Victorian period or of the post-1960s.

Taking the decision to bridge between the long nineteenth century and the pre-millennial period has profound implications for the treatment offered of contemporary moral regulation projects. No attempt is made to offer the type of studies of individual moral reform projects that characterise the treatments offered in Chapters 1 to 5. This change in the style of inquiry is motivated in part by the fact that readers will have some general familiarity with these more recent developments. The striking proliferation of moral politics would make a lengthy undertaking and, as will be seen, some useful efforts have been made in this direction. More importantly, the purpose of the final chapter is to open up a comparative debate about the place of moral politics during the two turn-of-the-century periods.

A key feature of the linkages of contemporary movements with the nineteenth-century purity movements is provided by the central intellectual, ideological and activist role played by second-wave feminism. Thus attention will be focused on movements and projects that have had a substantial feminist engagement. I will argue that there has been a reworking of the tension between coercive and non-coercive strategies that beset the maternal feminists of the late nineteenth century. This engagement has taken place in the context of major public divergent tendencies within contemporary feminism. It is no easy task to characterise these differences; it is certainly essential to reject any simply binary distinction such as the widely employed one between 'radical' and 'liberal' feminism. Rather attention will be focused on one major axis of the cross-currents within contemporary feminism, namely, to draw attention to the persistent role of radicalised versions of the maternal feminism which the earlier argument establishes as the dominant tradition within Victorian feminism. It is important at this point to stress that the internal debates are marked by a variety of resistances to that continuity. If more attention is paid to the ongoing influence of maternal feminism this should not be read as a failure of recognition of oppositional currents. Indeed it will be clear that the analysis offered shares much of the inspiration of these attempts to supersede the reprise of Victorian feminism. As a result of these markedly different currents within feminism, it is necessary to insist that the political valence of moral reform in the late twentieth century is unstable.

The controversies around contemporary moral reform projects are not simply replays of earlier debates. It will not be possible to pay full attention to all these features. One feature is of particular importance. Moral reform movements will be located in the context of their coexistence with an extraordinary proliferation of self-help movements. The nineteenth century witnessed a burgeoning and highly commercialised advice literature focused, as will be seen in Chapter 5, not only on conduct, etiquette and domestic management, but also on highly moralised treatments of marriage, sexuality and child-rearing. Today's bookstores have an analogous array, but the key difference is the shift towards self-help movements and organisations that combine therapy and activism. For instance action over sexual abuse is not confined to protest movements, but expresses itself in a variety of self-help and victims' organisations.

The arguments offered in this final chapter use this comparative treatment of moral regulation movements to open up a framework for debate. It is hoped that discussion can transcend the entrenched oppositions that have, for example, characterised debates over pornography by locating contemporary controversies within a comparative historical context. Such an approach may also facilitate consideration of the likely place of moral politics in the politics of next century. Will the trend towards the displacement of the politics of economic or material interests by highly charged moralised politics continue? Will moralising projects experience a decline as the reality of social and cultural pluralism renders attempts to impose a unitary moral code increasingly anachronistic?

CHAPTER 1

COMPULSION TO VIRTUE: SOCIETIES FOR THE REFORMATION OF MANNERS AND THE PROSECUTION OF VICE

AN EARLY MORAL REGULATION MOVEMENT

This chapter focuses on the Societies for Reformation of Manners (hereafter referred to as SRM or as the Societies).[1] These functioned actively from around 1690 until 1738, during which time they were responsible for over 100,000 prosecutions for moral offences, mainly in and around London.[2] The SRM provide a major instance of a moral regulation movement and will be treated as an early instance of an organised social movement. The SRM have the advantage of being sufficiently distant from our current preoccupations that they can be approached with some dispassion.

The conceptual apparatus employed draws on a sociology of governance outlined in the Introduction. A 'project' is a process of governance, practices directed towards the control of some other social agents, institutions or other social entities. All projects involve five main elements. Projects are undertaken by (1) 'agents' – the agents in this study are the SRM and their activists. They act with respect to (2) a 'target' – usually human persons or associations, in this case offenders against the moral order and a wider target of urban populations. In this activity agents deploy (3) 'tactics' or 'techniques' – the tactics of SRM involve informing against and prosecuting the target offenders. In so acting the agents locate their action within (4) discourses, for example, those used in the SRM texts or sermons. Every project is located within (5) a political context, for example, the forms of resistance generated by SRM prosecutions. My order of presentation employs this schema.

This approach to moral regulation projects can, I suggest, be understood as more or less closely linked to social movement theory. To make my point sharply, but, hopefully, without exaggeration, I will treat the

SRM as a 'new social movement'. To do so has the significant advantage of immediately dispelling the view that the SRM project was archaic and anachronistic. I hope to show that these interventions share many similarities with contemporary social movements.

The major thesis I will put forward about the SRM requires some advance explanation. The thesis claims that the SRM were a project of moral regulation which acted upon 'the social' *before* the discovery of the social. Recent sociological work has argued that 'the social' is not a universal synonym for 'society'; rather it is a specific historical stage during which 'the social' became an object of governmental action. Thus Dean (1991) and Steinmetz (1993) both locate the invention of 'the social' during the nineteenth century as the period in which the working class becomes an object of governmental regulation. I push back this 'discovery' by around 150 years. For this reason I speak of the discovery of the social 'before' the social, because I suggest that SRM intervention was indeed action on 'the social'. The social on which the SRM acted, however, has the important characteristics that Dean and Steinmetz identify: namely, it was a distinctively urban target, the street and the places of public resort (fairs, theatres, etc.) were its spatial targets. Second, these sites were characterised by 'social unruliness', not just unruly people, but unruly categories of people – categories captured well by the phrase that Beier uses in another context, 'masterless men'; that is, those who live outside structures of authority (1985), and even more to the point, 'masterless women' (whom Beier does not mention). This 'social' target is manifest in the way in which immorality was constructed by the SRM such that they pursued, as we will see, the social immorality of lewdness, but not the private vice of fornication.

The significance of my claim that the SRM were engaged in the regulation of 'the social before the social' is that it radically pushes back 'the social' from the nineteenth to the seventeenth century. This move breaks the association between 'the social' and the advent of industrial capitalism and the formation of a modern working class. This sense of 'the social' is at its core a conception of a disorganised site of social uncertainty; this uncertainty manifests itself in social and moral anxieties which in turn stimulate a compulsion to intervene. I next offer a general description of the SRM project for the reform of manners and locate it in historical context. I then explore in successive sections its agents, targets, tactics and political context.

THE PROJECT OF THE REFORMATION OF MANNERS

The project of the reformation of manners was a double project involving both a continuation of 'the Reformation' and a distinct 'reformation' or project of moral regulation. The constitutional settlement of 1688 unleashed a series of reformations encompassing a range of overlapping projects in which it is significant that religion remained the central focus. There was a revitalisation of the powerful motif of 'Reformation', echoing the older Tudor project of a national Church radically separated from Rome.[3] In the English case, it should be noted that the Reformation had been much more than a religious realignment; it was also a process of state-formation through which an established Church was bound closely to the state.

After 1688 there were competing versions of this project within the Church of England and they alternated within its leadership. The High-Church wing wanted a national Church, relatively non-sectarian in its theology, which could bind together Church, state and gentry. The other wing, the Low Church, had a more radical commitment to the Protestant breach with Rome and was prepared to collaborate with other, non-established, Protestant sects. Both wings made use of a more or less radical discourse condemning the immorality of the Restoration period, in the sense in which Bahlman (1957) refers to the period as one of 'moral revolution'. In this context the slogan 'reformation of manners' had broad resonances and was invoked in many different social and religious contexts and, we may presume, reflected a widely diffused popular sentiment. In modern usage 'manners' has narrowed to refer to the rules of civility. In the early modern period it had a wider meaning: 'manners' designated not only the rules of moral conduct, but the dispositions, attitudes and practices that marked civilised conduct and theological conformity (Ingram 1996).

Restoration Anglicanism bequeathed to the reformation of manners movement the idea of providentialism.[4] Providence manifested itself in a belief in the coexistence of divine care and divine wrath. These sentiments linked the morality of the populace to the fate and well-being of the nation and provided persuasive grounds for the demand for obedience and good order. A potentially wrathful deity was prone to strike at nations in which immorality was rife, and the Great Fire of London in 1666 was viewed as the most recent confirmation of that truth. The doctrine of providence provided an important legitimation for the coercion of individual sinners; since divine providence was inflicted upon the entire nation, it was necessary to reform the sinner in order to protect the whole community.

Another characteristic of the Low-Church party that distinctively influenced the SRM was a theological trend that became increasingly important over the next two centuries. Its core idea was that of the responsibilisation of the laity.[5] To follow the leadership of the clergy was not a sufficient commitment either for the individual's spiritual life or for the Christian's obligations in the secular realm. The key feature was an enhanced emphasis on the participatory responsibilities of the devout Christian.[6] This view found a fuller expression in the mid-eighteenth century, when many of those holding this view split away from Anglicanism to found English Methodism, which was to have a profound impact on both Christian and social action thereafter. In the late seventeenth and early eighteenth centuries this view found its expression in the formation of a wide variety of specifically Christian lay associations concerned to create an expanded space, not only for evangelical commitment by believers, but for such autonomous institutions to act upon the secular world in the name, not so much of the Church, but of Christianity. The SRM were the first of these great lay associations on the margins of organised religion; other important contemporaneous associations were the Society for the Promotion of Christian Knowledge (SPCK), established in 1699, and the Society for Propagation of the Gospel in Foreign Parts (SPG), founded in 1701.[7]

The emphasis on lay participation in both religious and social action laid the SRM open to the objection, from the High-Church party, that this emphasis on the role of the laity undermined the role of the clergy (Sacheverell 1709a; Hole 1699). To rebut such charges, the SRM devoted much energy to denying that they were a factional or schismatic movement (Stanhope 1702). SRM tracts and sermons devoted much attention to rebutting the charge of factionalism.

The expanded conception of 'reformation' involved a project akin to what Peter Burke (1978) has described as a 'reform of popular culture'. This involves a process in which a fissure opens up between social strata whereby the stratum seeking to assert dominance first moralises some part of the culture of the lower strata and then – and this is the significant step – acts upon it as something that can be 'reformed'. In Burke's discussion the gap that opened and was then acted upon was that between yeoman farmers and agricultural labourers. The SRM were agents who reinforced the separation between a respectable urban merchant class and the unruly urban populace that spanned the social distance from small traders, artisans and apprentices, to the working poor and the underclass of street prostitutes, beggars and discharged soldiers. These strata were to be 'reformed'; in the first stage aspects of their conduct and the sites where it occurred (the streets, taverns, fairs, markets and brothels of rapidly urbanising London) were moralised under the broad heads of 'immorality' and 'vice', which was then acted upon through the prosecution of some, if not all, forms of popular immorality. Hayton articulates this essentially urban character of the crisis which the SRM understood themselves as confronting. They engaged with

> major social problems resulting from rapid urban growth and aggravated by the economic dislocation brought on by war – poverty, vagrancy, drunkenness, prostitution and crime. The two strands, religious revival and social regulation, were united by a common belief in the existence of a moral crisis facing post-Revolution England (Hayton 1990: 51).

The Societies' sense of the project for the reform of popular culture can be contrasted with its nineteenth-century variant, that of 'improvement', in which the underclasses were to be harnessed to their own transformation through projects of self-improvement, where the governance of others is supplemented by the governance of the self.

What was distinctive about the SRM was that they had a program of action to carry forward this reformation of manners.[8] They proposed and carried out the systematic legal arraignment of a number of forms of public vice; later in this chapter I consider the specific targets of this project. The significant point is that in an organised fashion they made use of the currently available legal processes of 'informing' by laying information against offenders before Justices of the Peace (JPs).

THE AGENTS OF REFORMATION

In order to situate the SRM, it is necessary to consider both their institutional location and the characteristics of their agents. In brief, both the SRM and the activists constituted the agents of moral regulation. The SRM were lay associations; while there were a number of clerics who gave enthusiastic support, they do not seem to have been members. However, it is important to stress that the Societies were not movements from below, for, while they drew into action sections of the emerging middle classes, they actively pursued the support of the upper classes. Aside from seeking clerical support, the SRM also sought to enlist the active assistance of the Church hierarchy. For example, they secured the active encouragement of John Tillotson, Archbishop of Canterbury, between 1691 and 1694, and his successor, Thomas Tenison, who was persuaded to issue a circular letter to his Bishops commending the SRM.

The SRM also sought royal patronage and, in particular, pressed, with some success, for the issuing of Royal Proclamations against vice and immorality. One of the very earliest was a Proclamation in the name of Queen Mary in 1691, requiring JPs to enforce laws against profaneness and immorality.[9] The Queen also sent a letter to Middlesex JPs urging them to prosecute vice and, as a significant endorsement of SRM strategy, urged "all good Christians" to lay information against offenders. On the accession of Queen Anne in 1702, a *Proclamation for the Encouragement of Piety and Virtue and for the Preventing and Punishing of Vice, Prophaneness and Immorality*[10] was issued, and further Proclamations followed at fairly regular intervals. The SRM also sought declarations of support from high places: many of their numerous publicity materials reprinted a declaration signed by twenty-nine Lords Temporal and nine Lords Spiritual endorsing the SRM strategy. This concern with securing support and assistance from above may explain why it was that the SRM presented themselves as acting in support of the secular authorities, and never challenged them. Similarly the SRM denied that they had distinctive religious goals, although as we will see, their latitudinarian willingness to accept Dissenters was a persistent source of tension as the Church increasingly became linked to political conservatism.

One of the intriguing facets of the SRM was their relations with Parliament. Hayton demonstrates that there were many MPs who shared the SRM's attitudes towards the reformation of manners (1990).[11] However, there was no legislative activity during the period of the greatest SRM activism. Nor does the SRM literature pay any attention to Parliament. This is entirely consistent with their formal policy position that the problem did not lie with the law, but with its widespread non-enforcement. Accepting, for the time being at least, that this represents the SRM position, it still seems likely that this issue of non-enforcement would have been aired in Parliament by SRM supporters or others with a similar agenda. But we get no sense of this from the SRM. It may be noted that, while Bills seeking to advance the reformation of manners came before Parliament from a variety of sources, none was successful.[12]

The SRM were thus located within civil society, but had significant links with both Church and state.[13] Attention may now be turned to the organisation itself. In London the organisation had four distinct tiers; these may reveal something of the social composition of the Societies. It was an exclusively male organisation; there was no role for women. The first layer was the 'Original Society of Gentlemen', a body of persons of eminence (lawyers, MPs, JPs) who, along with the founding members, "consult of the best methods" to carry out the reformation of manners; they also raised money to meet the expenses of prosecution (SRM 1699a).[14] The 'Second Society', which in 1699 had fifty members, was composed mainly of tradesmen, who applied themselves to the suppression of 'lewdness' and disorderly houses. It was this group that for many years published the annual 'blacklist' naming offenders. Although the link between tradesmen and the suppression of prostitution was often mentioned, no explanation was offered. Was prostitution bad for business? Was it regarded as more sinful than drunkenness or gambling?

The third tier consisted of constables, who met to consider the most effective way to discharge their oaths and to divide themselves so as to inspect disorderly houses and to "take up" drunkards, lewd persons, swearers and other miscreants. The Association of Constables met weekly on Tuesdays at 5.00 p.m. at Hamlin's Coffeehouse, where each had "to furnish an account of his week's efforts for the cause" (Portus 1912: 44). The 'fourth rank', the "corner stone" of the Societies, were the informers who laid information concerning breaches of the law before the Magistrates. Contemporary accounts suggest that these lay members were local tradesmen and artisans.[15] The activities of this 'rank and file' are largely the focus of this study. As the SRM spread outside London, local Societies seem to have had a higher proportion of members drawn from the higher ranks of society.[16]

The Societies seem to have been surprisingly tightly knit organisations, self-consciously designed to produce a centralised and disciplined movement. They held weekly meetings and members paid fines for non-attendance. New members were only admitted with much caution: they had to be proposed on at least two occasions, thereafter two members were deputed to inquire into their "lives and conversations". The discussion and business of the meetings were secret, probably explaining why few internal records have survived; there were no membership lists and no minutes of meetings. Decisions were taken by majority vote, a decidedly advanced idea for the period.

The organisational structure suggests that the SRM were a distinctively urban movement and, unless otherwise indicated, my discussion focuses on London. Despite the elements of democratic and participatory principles, they retained a patrician hierarchy. The broad picture seems to be that the SRM membership involved a small stratum of urban gentlemen and a wider base of the urban petty bourgeoisie. It would be of interest to know if the informers were socially distinct from one of their major targets, those who traded on Sundays, in particular butchers and bakers. We know very little about the membership.[17] It seems clear that few SRM activists were drawn from the ranks of either high social status or new wealth.

THE TARGETS OF REFORMATION: PUBLIC VICE AND IMMORALITY

I have suggested that the SRM project was directed at an urban populace and the sites and spaces which it occupied during a period of rapid urbanisation. I now consider the construction of this target, urban immorality or vice, in more detail. The Societies projected a generalised fear of a profound national crisis whose origin lay in the immorality of the people. There is little or no trace of the critique of the immorality of Crown and Court which had been so important in destabilising the Restoration monarchy and precipitating the constitutional revolution of 1688.

The sins identified were decidedly 'everyday sins'. Robert Drew's sermon for the SRM is representative. In his catalogue of the causes of the dissoluteness of popular manners he cites: parents and masters who fail to set a good example at home; the neglect of public worship and the "misspending of Sundays"; "the luxury and profuseness that abounds among us"; the idleness of the poor; the snares and temptations that beset the good; and adds, significantly, the "strange notion of liberty that is abroad" (1731: 16).

These rebukes are entirely conventional; most are enduring elements of social moralisation. They would not have been out of place in the sixteenth century and most, if not all, would not have been incongruous on a nineteenth-century purity platform. Drew's list is a *mélange* of everyday anxieties (domestic discipline), social analysis (the idle poor), political critique ("strange notion of liberty"). I will have cause to comment further on the forms of discursive construction used by the SRM below. Here I am concerned to identify the specific targets which were seen as exemplifying the moral crisis.

The targets selected exhibit a significant continuity. As Table 1 shows, not only did the offences attacked remain virtually unchanged between 1694 and 1738, but their proportions shifted very little. These offences included lewd and disorderly practices, Sabbath violations, profanity and swearing, keeping of bawdy and disorderly houses, keeping a common gaming house and drunkenness. The pattern of prosecutions that emerged must have resulted from some policy decisions since, by the 1730s, it had become standard practice for the Annual Reports to contain a firm instruction that prosecutions should be restricted to offences itemised in the Reports, and not others. Outside London this disciplined strategy was less evident; local groups seem to have attacked more dispersed targets.[18]

In every year for which records exist, 'lewd and disorderly practices' were the most numerous prosecutions and in many years outnumbered all others. Unfortunately, we know little about the social characteristics of the defendants. It seems likely that the 'lewd and disorderly' were female street prostitutes. We have more detail of those prosecuted for Sabbath breaking since the figures often itemised the number of butchers and, less often, bakers. This indicates that the concern was predominantly with Sunday trading offences rather than with Church attendance, although SRM rhetoric was directed at the social and moral dangers attendant on the decline in religious observation. The Societies also targeted employers who paid out wages at inns on Sunday mornings; not only did this encourage Sunday drinking, but necessitated wives shopping on Sunday. However, they strenuously denied that they had ever prosecuted people for cooking Sunday dinner (SRM 1737).

It is not possible to identify the gender or occupation of those prosecuted for profanity and swearing. The figures for drunkenness are

TABLE 1 The pattern of prosecution, 1694–1738

Year	Account No.	Lewd & Disorderly	Keeping Bawdy or Disorderly House	Sabbath Breaking	Profanity and Swearing	Drunkenness	Keeping Common Gaming House	Sodomy	Annual Total	Total Prosecuted (Since Inception)
1694	1	269 f 40 m							309	
1695–98					No Records Extant				–	
1699	5				No Records Extant				–	
1700	6	682 f 161 m	70						843	
1701	7	635 f 209 m	50						944	
1702	8	758 f 100 m	74						858	
1703	9				No Records Extant				[628]	
1704	10	1175	15						863	
1705 }	11				No Records Extant				1619	
1706 }	12				No Records Extant					
1707	13	602 f 104 m	57						706	
1708	14	1255	51	1187	625	150	30	–	3298	
1709	15	794	32	1523	547	42	10	–	2948	
1710–14					No Records Extant					
1715	21	1152	36	1066	263	46	8	–	2571	
1716	22	1066	9	621	102	14	8	–	1820	
1717	23	1927	33	524	400	25	0	–	2909	
1718	24	1253	31	492	204	17	8		2005	

1719	No Records Extant									
1720	26	1189	14	615	114	11	10	–	1953	75,270[1]
1721	27	1197	15	709	161	13	–	4	2099	77,469[2]
1722	28	1223	35	658	201	8	104		2229	84,720
1723	29	1622	36	648	96	4	42		2449	86,944
1724	30	1951	21	600	108	12	23		2715	89,393
1725	31	–	–	–	–	–	–		2506	91,899
1726	32	–	–	–	–	–	–	x[3]	1060	92,959
1727	33	–	–	–	–	–	–	x	1363	94,322
1728	33	"a considerable number of persons"							[778][4]	95,100
1729	35	"a considerable number of persons"						x	[895]	96,326
1730	36	251	30	424	22	0	15	x	754	97,076
1731	No Records Extant									
1732	38	230	9	275	14	0	0	x	528	98,453
1733	39	89	3	395	–	0	15	x	487[5]	98,970
1734[6]	40	170	–	240	–	–			410	99,380
1735	41	318	–	268	–	–	–	x	586	99,970
1736[7]	42	212	–	457	–	–	–	x	545	100,650
1737	43	95	–	393	–	–	–	x	488	101,138
1738	44	52		493				x	545	101,683

1 There is a wide discrepancy between this first cumulative total of 75,270 and that arrived at by totalling figures for 1694–1720, even allowing generous average figures for years for which figures were not published or are missing.
2 The SRM cumulative figures are often at variance with the results of the annual totals derived from the figures published for the offence categories.
3 Sodomy offences referred to, but no figures given.
4 By subtraction of cumulative total for 1727 from that for 1728.
5 The British Library version of the 39th Account has the same figures as those in the 40th Account for 1734; Isaacs' figures have been preferred.
6 Both the 39th and 40th Accounts give figures for period 1/12/1732 – 1/12/1733, but figures for prosecutions differ. The 40th Account treated as report for 1734.
7 The British Library version of the 42nd Report gives the same figures as the 31st Account, including the cumulative total. Isaacs' figures have been preferred.

remarkably low, given what is known from contemporary accounts of the drinking habits of all classes in eighteenth-century London. The highest annual figure for drunkenness was 150 cases in 1708, and the average was around fifteen cases per year; it may be that even the vigilant SRM activists were forced to compromise with the drinking habits of the time or that it was not regarded as a serious offence.

There was one offence that had a peculiar status in the SRM lexicon, namely that of sodomy. There was no separation here between public and private vice. The SRM secured the prosecution of Capt. Edward Rigby, Commander of *HMS Dragon*, for attempted sodomy of a servant and of a friend of the Revd Thomas Bray.[19] Rigby was acquitted by a Court Martial. He subsequently underwent a criminal trial at the Old Bailey in December 1698, after he had been discovered *in flagrante delicto* at 'The George', an inn on The Mall; he was charged with blasphemy and attempted sodomy and was sentenced, without trial, to stand three times in the pillories and to pay £1000 fine and to serve one year's imprisonment.[20] The SRM sustained their attack with the publication of *The Sodomite's Shame and Doom* (SRM 1699b). The 1703 version of the *Account of the Progress* reported that "since the trial and punishment of the sea captain [Rigby] . . . 3 persons, by the diligence of the Society for Reformation of Manners, were found guilty of sodomy before LCJ Holt . . . and were accordingly executed" (1703: 27). The Revd Thomas Bray constructs sodomy, as so many other vices in island Britain, as a foreign invasion. "Alas, we hear of a much more fearful . . . host approaching, . . . the Sodomites are Invading Our Land" (Bray 1709: 30). Little further is heard until the SRM's *A Representation* in 1715; in this text the SRM emerged with a clear statement of a 'public vice' approach to both female prostitution and homoerotic sex. It claims as one of the SRM's achievements that

> our streets have been very much cleared of those lewd women, who used to solicit openly there to debauchery, night-walkers have been suppressed, and gangs of detestable sodomites dispersed (1715: 11–12).

There was a further period of silence on the topic. Not until the 1720s and 1730s was reference again made to sodomy in the Annual Reports.[21] In only one year, 1721, was the number of prosecutions for sodomy (four) specifically mentioned. In ten subsequent reports sodomy is mentioned and it is clear that there had been a shift in the SRM's target away from individuals towards the prosecution of homosexual brothels, "sodomitical houses". The absence of homophobic rhetoric in early reports suggests that homosexual prostitution was not visible until the 1720s. This later anti-homosexual campaign in the mid-1720s, led by two clerics, Bishop Edmund Gibson and Archbishop William Wake, with long association with the Societies, seems to have been a coded component of a wider anti-Catholic campaign.

In addition to their standard targets, the SRM periodically engaged in specific single-issue campaigns. At the beginning of the eighteenth century they launched an attack upon the London stage. The SRM joined with others in a campaign against the theatres: for example, they even promoted a pamphlet by a Catholic author attacking the immorality of the London theatres. Prominent SRM propagandists published anti-theatre tracts (Woodward 1704; Bedford 1705). They pressed the Archbishop of Canterbury for action against the stage in an open letter (SRM nd3). Although the theatre was a significant site for resistance to the SRM project, these attacks did have significant impact; as Isaacs observes, "the reformation of manners gave birth to genteel (and dull) sentimental comedies" (1979: 32–3).

They also took up other campaigns that fit Peter Burke's concept of the reform of popular culture with onslaughts on the London fairs, singled out as sites of immorality and drunkenness (Bray 1709). Also targeted was the early eighteenth-century vogue for public masquerades, dances at which participants wore face masks, where anonymity facilitated sexual licence (Porter 1985). Edmund Gibson, Bishop of London, directed an SRM sermon against masquerades on the grounds that they deprive virtue and religion of their last resort, that of shame (1723). Later their attention was turned to gambling houses, particularly between 1715 and 1725. A number of gaming houses were closed, although the general increase in gambling during this period suggests that these prosecutions may have served only to deflect and harass organised gambling rather than having a significant impact upon it.

Perhaps just as interesting as the selected targets for attack by the SRM were those that were excluded. Most significant is the absence of any mention of adultery or fornication. Why did the SRM not pursue the full range of moral offences? There was no overt discussion of this matter. There existed adequate legal grounds for pursuing such offences, since fornication and adultery were, nominally, criminal offences.[22] The explanation for these omissions seems to be that the SRM were decidedly less interested in individual or personal immorality; their target was public vice, their goal community virtue and orderliness. In an exchange in the 'Observator', an accuser claimed that the SRM "invade the private Rights of Persons"; the editorial reply stated firmly that the SRM do not "meddle with the private conduct of persons and families, but only take up such . . . as are openly guilty" (Isaacs 1979: 43). Their preoccupation was with outward conformity to the moral code.

There is, however, a real tension here. Isaacs' claim that the SRM strategy had little real interest in men's souls (1979: 44) is, I suggest, incorrect in important respects. A central element in their justification for informing against offenders was in order to save their souls. In the very first sermon preached on behalf of the SRM, Josiah Woodward stakes out the concern for the souls of others as the justification for intervening in their lives (1698). One of the most frequently invoked biblical texts was the rhetorical question "Am I my brother's keeper?" To which inquiry the answer was always an unqualified "Yes". However, I suggest that more is at stake here. First, the reformers had a developed sense of deterrence theory; they held out little prospect for prosecuting all offenders, but they persisted with prosecutions in order to deter as many as possible from the path of immorality. This links to a second theme, which suggests that we should not look so much at the characteristics of the particular offences, but rather should focus attention on the social character of the offenders. The SRM activity shows all the hallmarks of a reform of popular culture in Peter Burke's sense, in that the individual offenders were beyond hope, but the target was made up of diverse social strata whose cultural practices were to be moralised, pursued and finally overcome. The real target was a broad stratum of London life, the people, from small artisans and street-traders downwards.

What then does this say about all the preoccupations with individual souls in the SRM sermons? I will return to this issue. For the present it is sufficient to note that sermons occupied a distinctive discursive position which had an individualist frame of reference. The soul and salvation of the individual were the explicit focus of the sermons, but not of their meaning. The question was what to do in order to save the nation from the inevitable wrath of the deity. Another way of expressing this argument is to note that the anxieties which underpinned the action of informing against offenders were not with the individuals who had fallen into sexual temptation – sexual failing was always-already present; rather it was social disorderliness and insubordination that were the target of SRM attention. John Disney, an important ideologue, expressed the issue in dramatic contemporary terms. He invoked anxiety about social order as a fear of 'Popery'; for since Catholicism is soft on sin, sinners will support Papist plots and endanger Protestant supremacy. A further benefit that will accrue from enforcing the law is that it will disarm the Dissenters, who are all too ready to accuse the state and the Church of being soft on sin (1708).

One significant dimension of the fear of the people, and of the streets, was an intergenerational anxiety about increasingly mobile and insubordinate youth, epitomised by male apprentices and female servants. Samuel Price captured this concern in a 1725 sermon:

> This is a day of great liberty, wherein the generality of younger persons are uneasy under the most reasonable restraints, and it is to be fear'd that licentiousness will increase, unless family worship and discipline revives (1725: 19).

What is revealed is not a contradiction in the ideology of the SRM, but a discursive formation which is not constituted along the same private/public dichotomy that forms the common sense of the twentieth century. The reformers were remarkably clear as to their strategic orientation; we merely need to be able to grasp the logic which coherently links the salvation of souls with the fate of the nation.

THE TACTICS OF REFORMATION: PROPAGANDA AND PROSECUTION

The practices of the SRM have a feel that is both familiar and unfamiliar to late twentieth-century observers. The highly organised production and dissemination of propaganda matches that of today's successful 'new social movements'. Their systematic prosecution of offenders has a certain similarity with 'law and order' campaign tactics or even with vigilantism, but their systematic administration of a prosecution machine against everyday offences and everyday offenders has few recent parallels.

The most distinctive traces of the activities of the SRM are provided by the enormous volume of promotional or propaganda material that they produced and in the systematic prosecutions that they undertook. One compelling reason for treating the Societies as a social movement is precisely that they engaged in these systematic activities. The most important source was a series of overlapping published 'Accounts' of their activities. These texts, some in the form of broadsheets and others in book form, usually running to a hundred pages or more, appeared under varying titles, such as *An Account of the Rise and Progress of Reformation of Manners, An Account of the Progress of Societies for Reformation of Manners, An Account of the Societies for Reformation of Manners* and other variants. The authorship of these texts remains obscure.[23] It seems clear from the variety of formats and styles that a number of pens were at work in what was a prodigious output. Thus *An Account of the Societies for Reformation of Manners* first appeared in 1699 and by 1704 was in its twentieth edition. The first edition of Woodward's *Account of the Rise and Progress* also appeared in 1699 and was in its fourteenth edition by 1704.

These 'Accounts' took two major forms. *The Account of the Progress of Societies for Reformation of Manners* started out in broadsheet format of one or two sheets which briefly summarised the aims and objectives of the SRM, gave details of their prosecutions and published a 'blacklist' of offenders. This format covered thirteen documents spanning the period 1694–1707. Thereafter they take the form of an annual report detailing the prosecutions for the previous year; it is from these that the pattern of prosecutions is drawn (Table 1). Most are also available as appendixes to the *Sermons Preach'd Before the Societies for Reformation of Manners*, but some reports are extant in self-standing format. The '14th Account' in the new format of a lengthy annual report appeared in 1707; then there was a gap between 1710 and 1715 (possibly suggesting a decline in SRM activity). They resume with the '21st Account' in 1716 and then run continuously down to the '44th Report' in 1739.[24]

Other versions of the *Accounts* take a more literary form. Most start conversationally – "You may have heard about the Societies for Reformation of Manners" – and proceed to provide a stylised account of their formation by "certain young gentlemen of the Church of England" or "five or six gentlemen of the Church of England".[25] This sets up a persistent theme which keeps the identity of the founders secret. The reasons for this secrecy are unclear. It may be that the volatility of the preceding decades generated a security consciousness, but thereafter their work was conducted in a more open fashion. On the other hand, the secrecy of the Societies may be explained as a manifestation of the self-induced elan of a 'secret society' (Simmel 1950: 345–76). Yet their public character is attested by the long lists of official support for their project in the form of Royal Proclamations and letters from the Archbishop of Canterbury and other bishops.[26]

Key sections of these texts provided justification for the necessity of the formation of the Societies. These asserted the immorality of the times, in a way that assumed that this was known to all, since little or no evidence was provided. Much more space was taken up by the justification of their strategy, whose content varied over time. For example, some defended the collaboration between Church of England members and Dissenters, which was attacked from High-Church circles. These accounts stressed the dangers and oppositions encountered. The most persistent form of self-justification was the defence of the tactic of informing; this goes to confirm that this issue was the key objection levelled against the SRM.

The practical organisational role of these texts is revealed by the fact that they all reproduce a series of practical documents. The following were frequently included: Queen Anne's Proclamation of 25 February 1702; a list of the obligations of JPs; the *Presentment of the Gentlemen of the Grand Jury of Middlesex, 2 June 1701.*[27] The very practical nature of the SRM project is made clear from the fact that the *Accounts* also included examples of blank warrants, and summaries of the existing penal law (SRM 1700a). One publication bears an uncanny resemblance to a modern social movement handbook; it contains all the key documents (laws, proclamations, etc.) and the relevant forms for the prosecution of offenders (SRM 1700b).

In addition to the larger tracts, the SRM produced a vast body of occasional works, all directly linked to the advancement of their project. There were polemics, "dissuasives", against specific moral wrongs intended to be handed to offenders as an act of warning that the next time prosecution would be initiated (SRM nd1). The dissuasive against drunkenness was designed to be given to offenders when they appeared before magistrates (SRM nd2). Closely related were what today would be called 'open letters' on some current campaign: for example, there was one addressed to the Archbishop of Canterbury calling for action against the immorality of the stage (SRM nd3). Other pamphlets and open letters, 'To a Friend' or 'To a Country Parson', were intended to provide the reader with intellectual ammunition to defend the reformation of manners project and to rebut criticism of the SRM (SRM 1710). Another propagandist publication was a shortened version of the *Account* printed in parallel columns in English and French (SRM 1715).[28]

This varied productivity was not only distributed by the SRM members and advertised in their own catalogue (SRM 1708), but was also handled by the SPCK, who ran a 'mail-order' distribution system, which was probably not surpassed in scale until the rise of the mail-order catalogue in the twentieth century. While the SPCK later distanced itself from the SRM it is clear that at the beginning of the eighteenth century they were closely connected. One SRM broadsheet urged sympathisers to join both the SRM and the SPCK. The SPCK catalogues were full of SRM texts and pamphlets.

The prosecution of moral offenders was the major form of action undertaken by the SRM. They developed a businesslike method of prosecuting those who breached the code of legal morality. The process was as follows. Agents were employed by the Societies; they were allocated to different parts of the City and supplied with blank warrants. The informers, usually SRM activists, merely had to go to an agent and by reporting names and offences get a warrant filled out. This warrant was taken to a JP and, after the informer had sworn his information, the warrant was dated, signed and issued. It is significant to note that the legal effect of the warrant was to find the named party guilty of the offence even though it was issued in their absence and without their knowledge. The general form of the warrant was as follows:

> Whereas [John Doe], being above 16, is convicted before me of profane swearing [x times], within the parish of [—], this being the [second] time of his conviction, I charge and command you to demand of the said [John Doe], [20 shillings] for the use of the poor of the parish. If he refuse or

> neglect, you are to levy the same by distress, and in default of this set him in the stocks for [two hours]. And this shall be your warrant.

The only possibility of a trial arose if the offender refused to pay the fine or resisted distress.

The warrant, now issued, was taken by the informer back to the agent. Another SRM employee would call on each agent, collect the warrants, and deliver them to the relevant constable for the parish in which the offender resided. The constable served the warrant, collected the fine, or imposed the penalty in default of the fine. A register of signed warrants was kept by each SRM agent. Armed with this register the agent attended Quarter Sessions where parish constables were required to 'present' or report arrests and fines before a grand jury.

A number of volumes of these warrants are extant.[29] There are register books in which SRM-initiated warrants were recorded for the period 1704–13, also seven volumes recording actions taken by JPs subsequent to conviction for offences between 1704 and 1715. They have been examined in some detail by Isaacs (1979), who reports the following interesting features: that for long periods the names of two informers, Wright and Beggarly, dominate; between thirty and fifty per cent of offenders were vintners, chandlers, butchers, bakers and barbers; and there was only one gentleman among over 1000 offenders. A dramatic eighty per cent of the warrants were for Sunday trading, and the majority of the remainder were for swearing, and a few for drunkenness.[30] In the magistrates' records only fifty-four out of 8400 records did not concern Sunday trading. However, it seems that conviction was not quite as inescapable as the above accounts suggest; between January 1711 and December 1713, eighty-five per cent were excused by the magistrate either on the grounds that it was a first offence, or the JP himself had not attended, or the complainant had failed to appear (Isaacs 1979: 244–7). Strangely those prosecuted seem to have been excused if they themselves failed to appear to answer the summons.

The process of informing and prosecuting was, in practice, less smooth than this procedural description suggests. It was often difficult to track down a JP, and when found there was no guarantee that he would be receptive; many regarded the SRM as intruding upon their jurisdiction. The constables, lay officials elected within each parish, were a constant source of difficulty and obstruction; many were apathetic and were often unwilling to serve warrants or to follow them up. Both JPs and constables seem to have viewed the SRM prosecutions as disrupting their relations with the communities in which they operated. Yet, despite these difficulties and the overt opposition (to be discussed below), the

SRM achieved a remarkable level of political intervention in the everyday life of the London streets.

THE DISCOURSES OF REFORMATION: READING SERMONS

Access to an important strand of the discourses of moral regulation can be found in the sermons that were regularly preached before the assembled members and supporters of the Societies. I have located 135 sermons delivered between 1696 and 1739.[31] These sermons can be readily divided into two main groups: those delivered by Anglicans and those by Dissenters.[32] In the late 1690s these sermons were delivered quarterly. From the early 1700s there was an annual sermon, delivered at the end of the year and thus fitting well with the publication of the 'Annual Reports' as appendixes. The first sermon appears to have been delivered in 1696, by Josiah Woodward, probably the most important SRM publicist. Between 1697 and 1702 there were between six and eleven sermons each year. Thereafter the numbers decreased to between one and four per annum, but it is significant to note that even in the years of lowest activity between 1710 and 1714, sermons were delivered. There is not a single year between 1696 and 1739 when an SRM sermon was not delivered.

Some of the most famous and distinguished divines of the period delivered sermons to the Societies: Gilbert Burnet, White Kennet, William Nicholson, Edmund Gibson, Edmund Calamy, among others. This is a good indication of the intellectual respectability of the SRM project. It must also be true that the person who arranged the sermon schedule must have been well connected with the religious intelligentsia. In addition to the regular SRM sermons, another significant source of sermons was those presented at Assizes and at Mayoral Inaugurations, suggesting a pattern of strong links with the civic and legal establishment.

Before considering the content of these sermons, it is necessary to consider their form. They all had a common structure. They started with a biblical text; some of these texts were used time and time again, for example, "Am I my brother's keeper?", and a generally sectarian inflection was given to "He that is not with me, is against me". There followed a formal explanation of the text, its context and its meaning. A major portion of the sermon was given over to proving the moral necessity of the text, often supported by copious supporting biblical citations. Next, the contemporary relevance of the text to the work of the Societies was expounded. The sermon ended with practical advice to the Societies or warnings about how they should proceed. The sermons frequently shared a common background structure. They were built around four major themes: the contention that immorality displeases God; that the nation is beset by immorality; that the means for saving society is through a general reformation of manners; and that the prosecution of immorality is the most efficacious means of securing such a reformation.

A number of persistent themes in the SRM sermons can be identified. The first recurrent theme is that of the 'duty of rebuking' rather than standing aside to leave a soul in peril. Not only can souls be saved, but there is a duty to save souls that justifies the prosecution of evil-doers. It is significant that 'saving' is widely equated with 'prosecuting'. Mayo's treatment of this theme is interesting in that he is aware that the text's concern is with 'saving' through the repentance of the sinner rather than coercion. Consequently he calls for the joining of 'instruction' with 'correction'. His doubt is vocalised in a "fear that the methods taken by these Societies will not convert sinners" (1717: 35). This doubt was rarely expressed so clearly, but its presence can often be sensed. It is the fundamental contradiction of all purity work, that coercion to virtue may secure compliance but cannot guarantee reformation. The pragmatic solution is present in the common formulation: be compassionate to sinners, but when advice and reproof do not reform them, then resolute action is necessary and justified.

Many of the sermons had an exhortatory style. Such noble work will inevitably meet with discouragements and opposition; the sermon thus serves to "strengthen your hands" (Emlyn 1698).[33] The virtuous must expect opposition from the evil, against whom they are urged to stand firm. They will undoubtedly have to pay a heavy price for their diligence in "running imminent dangers from lewd mobs" (Fowler 1699: 29).

Another theme explicitly commended 'joining together' in the work of reformation. This conveyed a double meaning: it justified the formation of Societies outside the Church which could act in consort to suppress vice and irreligion; and it also offered a coded approval of collaboration between Anglicans and Dissenters. The other side of this theme was the concern to deny the charge, emanating from High-Church quarters, that the Societies were factional or schismatic. Few were as explicit as Samuel Palmer, who argued:

> These Societies [SRM] are not a private, but a publick *UNION* for the Common Good, and therefore cannot be an illegal *COMBINATION*; nor can the common-Stock to support their Expense be what the *Law calls Maintenance* (1706: 29–30).[34]

Another common theme explored the relationship between the deity, the magistracy and the Societies. It is the duty of both government and magistrates to act as 'God's Ministers', and the SRM, in turn, is presented as 'helping' the magistrates. Conceived thus, the reformation project was simply a natural extension of God's endowment to the civil power.

The motif of the reformer as an agent of the deity was often a prelude to one of the most powerful and persistent themes in these sermons, namely, the defence of informing. Time and time again, they insist that the term 'informer' should be no reproach to the virtuous. They reject the charge that informers intend to injure those against whom they inform; the SRM intend no harm, only benefit to their victims. The simplest version of the argument for informing and prosecuting was that profanity and immorality are evil, and that the virtuous have a duty to struggle against evil; hence to inform against evil-doers is itself virtuous.

The various versions of *An Account* repeated the following justifications for the tactic of informing. First, it is a "kindness to the poor" since fines collected went directly to poor relief. Second, that it is universally acknowledged that all have a Christian duty to be concerned for the souls of others. Third, a more pragmatic reason was given, that moral offences would not be prosecuted unless someone laid information before the magistrates, and in any case, the Royal Proclamation enjoins magistrates to enforce these laws. These arguments were articulated within a military metaphor, a war against vice and immorality, "the Christian life is a warfare" (SRM 1699a: 74).

The Dissenter John Ryther asked: "Must we all turn informer against our Neighbours and Acquaintances?" His solution distinguished the reformation of manners from other more secular forms of informing. The first should be encouraged, the latter not. He somewhat blandly asserts that there is no injury done to the guilty since their prosecution aids their salvation; he does not concede that the accused might not see matters in this light (1699: 61). However, in endorsing the practice of informing, he urges: "Be sure when you do so, you do it uprightly, for God's Honour . . . and not to vent your ill-will against the party" (1699: 62). In similar vein, Richard Willis, Dean of Lincoln, argued that it is a kindness to restrain offenders from evil (1704: 31).

Sometimes a more secular and nationalistic theme is stated that must have appealed to the entrepreneurial ethic of many SRM members. "YOU are providing the surest way to revive our *Trade*, prolong our *Peace*, and recover *England's Glory*," since God favours virtuous nations (Howe 1698: 35). A more religious expression of the same theme is found in the popular text: "Righteousness exalteth a Nation, but sin is a Reproach to any People" (Proverbs 14: 34), in accord with which "good Government in all Ages, has to inflict *Temporal* and *Bodily* Punishments on the Transgressors of the *Moral Law*; who at the same Time they sin against *God*, are Enemies to the *State* they live under" (Hayley 1699: 26).

Now and again, an explicit debate can be detected. The charge that the Societies favoured the rich and targeted the poor must have caused some concern. We find Gilbert Burnet, Bishop of Salisbury and a significant contemporary historian, advising his SRM audience against reproving their social superiors (1700). On the other hand, Samuel Pomfret (1701) recommended that informers should more diligently prosecute the powerful. Whatever the balance of the discourses on the selection of targets, there was never any doubt that their practices were directed against their social subordinates, and not their superiors. There was, however, agreement from most of those who preached sermons, that prosecutions should be undertaken with caution and circumspection. Informers should avoid any suspicion that they acted on grounds of religious difference, nor should they vent personal ill-will against any party. Entrapment was to be avoided at all costs. Informing required attention to personal virtue; "no man should offer to reprove another, who is eminently and notoriously faulty himself" (Burnet 1700). They were warned to use kind and gentle methods: to persuade the lewd to be won to virtue by rational argument; but those evil ones who persisted must be met resolutely (Ward 1700).

This mix of leniency and severity was a persistent theme. Some confidence was placed in the possibility that the prosecution of offenders would result in the deterrence of others who

> will be restrained by the Example, and kept in Awe, by the Fear or Shame of their Punishment. Good Men will also be edified thereby, as the Severity used against notorious Sinners confirms them in their Duty, and makes some Reparation for the Scandal given by the Crimes of Other Men (Wynne 1725: 19).

I have avoided using the term Puritan in connection with the SRM since this would greatly distort the theological roots of the SRM and their religious mentors, and also because the term implies an over-simplified model of the religious discourses of the period. However, there is one feature present in some of the sermons that resonates with a providentialism shared with Puritanism. Occasionally a preacher invoked an imagery of a vengeful deity active in sending earthquakes and other disasters thereby revealing his wrath and also his power to perform miracles such as the providential defeat of the Spanish Armada. One SRM text (1694) attributes the 'Great Fire' of 1666 to God's wrath at the immoralities of the period.[35] In a similar vein the 1699 *Account* invokes a dramaturgy of the 'decline and fall' of empires as a result not only of vice, but also of luxury, and details "God's wrath" against immorality with a list of recent epidemics and disasters (SRM 1699a: 12).

THE POLITICS OF INFORMING: RESISTANCE AND OPPOSITION

The SRM campaigns employing existing legal apparatus to mount a reformation of manners by prosecuting moral offences achieved, as we have seen, considerable support from sections of the Establishment and from the urban petty bourgeoisie. However, they also encountered considerable opposition, both popular and from the Establishment. Identifying these different sources of resistance and opposition helps to locate the project of the reformation of manners in its political context. It is significant that the SRM failed to secure a stable consolidation of support. The Tories distrusted their toleration and collaboration with the forces of Dissent, while the Whigs, in principle more sympathetic, were disturbed by the hostility their informing practices unleashed. The High Church shared the suspicions about collaboration with Dissenters, and added to this an anxiety that the Societies were undermining the Church's own authority. In particular they disliked the SRM's use of secular, rather than the ecclesiastical courts.[36] The magistrates considered that the Societies interfered with the administration of justice, and in particular with their own local legitimacy. Finally, and most prominently, the common people of London regarded them as spies and informers, and were only too happy to set about them when the opportunity presented itself.

The unsavoury reputation of 'informing' had deep roots. 'Common informers', mercenary informers, had been active for much of the previous century.[37] They had been the chief agents of enforcement of economic regulation, being particularly active with regard to tariff and customs violations and other market offences such as weights and measures. The informing activities of the SRM were a reminder of the campaign of informing against Dissenters that had been launched in February 1673 and epitomised the royalist Restoration. The role of 'informer' carried widespread opprobrious and pejorative connotations. As one commentator expressed it, while the Societies were well-intentioned, this was not the case with those who carried out much of their work who did so for private gain (Ward 1709: 40). Common though this accusation of extortion and racketeering was, I have come across no direct evidence to support it. However, this and other widespread beliefs about the reformers and their activities provided a base for both popular hostility and strong reservation from important sections of urban merchants and artisans.

There was concerted hostility from the majority of the Middlesex JPs.[38] Their hostility drew on a number of different sources. In addition to a dislike of informing, many magistrates regarded the activities of the SRM as an interference with their own jurisdiction. They were very sensitive to the importance of their relationships with the local communities over which they exercised jurisdiction. In the absence of any substantial administrative or coercive resources, they depended heavily for the maintenance of their legitimacy on a carefully modulated play of severity and discretion, in which as much as possible of their role was carried out by a variety of informal mediation activities. Their role can be described in very much the same terms that Douglas Hay (1977) has used to describe the critical role of discretion in the administration of the criminal law later on in the eighteenth century. Both the SRM informers and the JPs who supported them were viewed as problematic interventions ever likely to disturb the fragile legitimacy of their own authority.

These issues became visible in the most dramatic scandal to affect the SRM. It occurred at their inception and left a legacy that persisted as long as the Societies survived. In October 1691 the Middlesex JPs received a complaint about the activities of one of their number, Ralph Hartley, who was a JP and senior SRM member. He collaborated with one Sir Richard Bulkeley, who set up an office in Lincoln's Inn where he printed blank warrants and orders. He received information from a large number of informers. Bulkeley filled out the warrants and Hartley, in his capacity as a magistrate, signed over 500 of these warrants. It is significant that many warrants related to offenders and offences outside Hartley's own jurisdiction.[39]

A complaint reached the Middlesex Justices about the conduct of Hartley and Bulkeley. The complaint revolved around erroneous warrants. It was alleged that they maintained the office in order to collect the reward due to the informers. It was further alleged that Bulkeley pressured constables into executing these warrants. It emerged that some of those named were deceased or incorrectly named, or innocent persons. In October 1691, the Justices appointed a committee. They established the truth of the allegations of illegal convictions against Hartley (e.g. two deceased persons were convicted, another was fined for the offence of 'tippling' [drinking] in his own house). Bulkeley was charged with the 'impersonation' of a JP in purporting to give orders to constables. The Middlesex Bench suspended the execution of all Hartley's warrants, labelling them "illegal, arbitrary, and oppressive, and a great wrong and hardship to their Majesties subjects". They petitioned the Commissioners of the Great Seal to relieve Hartley of his commission as a Justice of the Peace. He was removed from the Bench, but significantly he was back again by 1704. They also recommended changes in procedure, in particular, that offenders be told the name of their accusers and that Justices should not convict anyone in their absence.[40] Although many SRM tracts and sermons defended Hartley with vigour, there can be no doubt that the case provided ammunition which was used by their opponents for many years to come.[41] The SRM did not always come off so badly. In 1716 some SRM constables were taking offenders (presumably prostitutes) to the Bridewell house of correction. Ingram, the Chief Constable for Fleet Street, challenged their authority and arrested the constables, presumably because, like the Middlesex JPs, he viewed the SRM as infringing on his jurisdiction. In this case it was the SRM who went to court: they sued Ingram for false imprisonment. The case was tried by the Lord Chief Justice, who found for the SRM and awarded £20 damages against Ingram (Portus 1912: 254).

Orthodox Anglicans, particularly those with High-Church views, suspected that the SRM amounted to a secret faction within the Church promoting schisms, a fear compounded by their open collaboration with Dissenters. Henry Sacheverell epitomised the right wing of the High-Church–Tory position; he was suspicious of anything that potentially disrupted the close interdependence of Church and state. His sermons and writings were directed against all Low-Church manifestations, non-conformity, and Whiggery, all of which he believed, whilst posing as being against vice, actually increased vice and cloaked their own wickedness. The substance of his attack was that

> instead of this *Ancient, Primitive, Discipline* of the *Church* which for so many Ages has, like a Rampart, secur'd its Religion from *Vice* and *Immorality*, *Schism* and *Heresy*, we must have substituted in its Place, a Society for the *Reformation of Manners*, wherein every *Tradesman* and *Mechanik* is to take upon himself the Gift of the Spirit, and to expound the difficult Passages of Scripture, and every *Justice of Peace* is allow'd to settle Its Canon, and Infallibly Decide what is Orthodox or Heretical (1702: 11–12).

In a sermon Sacheverell uses the text "Lay hands suddenly on no man, neither be partaken of other men's sins" (I Tim. 5: 22). His key formulation, a surprisingly liberal, and probably opportunist, argument was that the

> injunctions of Utility, Religion and Justice oblige us . . . not to thrust ourselves Pragmatically into his [our Brother's] business, or meddle with those concerns that do not belong to us; or under the Sanctified Pretence of Reformation of Manners, to turn Informer, assume an odious and factious office, arrogantly intrench [*sic*] upon other's Christian Liberty and Innocence, and under the show of Zeal and Purity (the most infallible Token of a dexterous and refined Hypocrite and Knave) turn the World-upside-down, and set all mankind into quarrels and confusion (1709a: 14–15).

It should be noted that this critique resonated with popular criticisms of the SRM as interfering 'busybodies'. Sacheverell himself soon became the target of attack not only by the SRM, but also by the political establishment. Josiah Woodward leapt to the defence of the SRM by arguing the virtue of an active participation by all Christians in the struggle against evil (1711).[42]

A more modulated criticism of the Societies came from the pen of Daniel Defoe. While he was a strong Sabbatarian, for example opposing hackney carriages on Sundays, nevertheless he espoused a populist critique of the SRM in the name of the people. "But we of the Plebeii find ourselves justly aggrieved in all this work of Reformation" (1698: 6). This is because the just and necessary laws are enforced against 'us', but not against 'you' ("the vicious part of the Nobility and the Gentry").

> These are all Cobweb laws, in which small flies are catch'd, and the great ones break through . . .' Tis hard, Gentlemen, to be punished for a Crime by a man as guilty as ourselves (1698: 11).[43]

He castigates the upper classes for their "corrupt Appetites" and for having perfected the vices of drunkenness and whoring (1698: 15). The standard SRM response to this criticism was that they overlooked the transgressions of the rich and attacked only the delinquencies of the lower orders, because the rich conduct their vices in private, and as such these are less pernicious than those conducted publicly by the lower classes.

Jonathan Swift articulated another aspect of Tory populism. He identifies himself with the projects of the reformation of manners, but he jibes against its institutional manifestation:

> Religious Societies, though begun with excellent intention, [have] . . . become a trade to enrich little knavish informers of the meanest rank, such as common constables and broken shop-keepers (1709: 70).

It is significant that Swift's own ideas for reformation are naively inadequate ("appoint pious men"), but his criticism of informing undoubtedly struck a popular chord.

A more interesting criticism of the SRM came, surprisingly, in a sermon by Samuel Bradford, who was the Rector of the church used for so many SRM sermons, St Mary-le-Bow. He produces a scintillating defence of liberal tolerance. Although the SRM is not mentioned explicitly, he attacks those who seek to use the law for the "Preservation of Church". He defends moderation, tolerance and the need to be peaceful with each other (Bradford 1710).

Another influential publicist, Bernard de Mandeville, satirically dedicated his *Modest Defence of Publick Stews* (1730), which defended the inevitability of prostitution, to "the gentlemen of the Societies". Following the thesis advanced in his notorious *The Fable of the Bees* (1705/1957) of the necessity of rulers adjusting to that which they cannot prohibit, he argues a case for state brothels. His contention against the SRM was that since it is impossible to prohibit vice, their actions could never do more than make vice more illicit and better organised. We see here the strands of what were to be the long-running hostilities between the abolitionists and the regulationists, which were to resurface with the late nineteenth-century struggles over the regulation of prostitution.

Mandeville's pragmatism also found less flamboyant expression from James Vernon, principal Secretary of State. While much concerned with the reformation of manners, William III was apprehensive about the SRM; he commissioned an investigation into their activities in London in 1698. Vernon's report, the epitome of modernist pragmatism, concluded:

> I am inclined to be of the opinion that this [SRM's informing campaign] may be a way of setting up hypocrisy, but will not much advance real honesty or virtue. When men have run through the circle of severities that are almost inseparable from sudden reformation, they will return to a natural state of being as good or bad as they please (quoted in Bahlman 1957: 86).

A less modulated version of the same was articulated by Edward Ward exemplifying a widespread criticism:

> They [SRM constables] are only Encouragers of what they pretend to suppress, Protecting those People, for Bribes, which they should Punish; well knowing each Bawdy-House they break in is a weekly stipend out of their Pockets (1709: 40).

Aside from all these argumentative criticisms, there were also further attacks on the SRM in the form of doggerel verses, satires and offensive notices in the press.

The resistance to the reformation of manners campaign also took more active and dramatic forms. On 12 May 1702 John Cooper, a reforming constable with a long association with the Societies, was helping several Westminster constables to arrest some prostitutes during the annual May Fair when he was attacked by "a company of soldiers, who, to the number of above thirty . . . fell upon the civil officers and their assistants, with their swords in their hands . . . while the constables were endeavouring to prevent the abominable disorders that were there committed" (SRM 1704: 17–18). Cooper died from his injuries and achieved the status of a martyr. On 21 May a commemorative service was held, attended by many dignitaries including the Lord Mayor, at which Josiah Woodward delivered a sermon dedicated to his memory. Woodward used the occasion for a militant assertion that it was high time for the magistrates to draw their swords against vice and impiety. "Once lawless Persons get such an ascendant as to be able to resist and outrage our civil officers in the just execution of their offices, all civil government is but a ludicrous pageant." Cooper himself was praised as "that worthy person who lately lost his life in some of the hotter parts of the service" (1702: 55).[44]

In March 1709 another constable, John Dent, an early SRM member and frequent informer, was murdered by three "private soldiers" while trying to make an arrest, presumably of a prostitute, near a playhouse. Thomas Bray delivered a funeral oration at a grand funeral, attended by a "great train of gentlemen of quality" and over a thousand citizens (1709). From the sermon we learn that Dent had been involved in the reformation of manners for seventeen to eighteen years and had been involved in the apprehension of "several thousand lewd and profligate swearers and drunkards" (1709: 15). He had also been the first to come to the aid of the injured John Cooper, seven years earlier, at the May Fair riots.

Cooper and Dent seem to have been the only fatalities, but there were other violent encounters between activists and their opponents. For example, during the course of an action against one of the largest gaming houses, Vandernand's in Drury Lane, the serving of the warrants required the protection of a squadron of soldiers; one person opposing service of the warrants was shot by soldiers and two Constables were wounded (Portus 1912: 321).

That these encounters between the moral reformers and their opponents resulted in fatalities is significant. E. P. Thompson's thesis, that the English mob operated within a well-understood framework of restraints and limits, 'the moral economy' (1971), rightly commands much support. Were the fatalities of the SRM activists riots gone wrong? The fact that there was no immediate or widespread repressive response from the authorities suggests not. Rather it is likely that the combination of theatre and violence that lay at the heart of the eighteenth century resulted in encounters that were immediate and explosive. Especially on carnivalesque occasions, such as the May Fair, the Constables executing the SRM projects were probably viewed as fair game for crowds enjoying the emotional and physical release of these occasions. The volatility of the allegiances of the crowd was itself also governed by routines and rituals. Thus the prostitutes who were seen as needing defence on some occasions were on others the targets of riotous action. Each Shrove Tuesday the prostitutes and the brothels in which they worked became the targets for ritual attacks from gangs of London apprentices (Harris 1986). While it is important to retain the core of Thompson's idea, namely, that the moral economy involves more or less coherent action to secure objectives resonating in popular consciousness, this should not lead to an impression that the mob was pacifist or anything close to it. These were times in which the streets were sites of direct political action which the authorities rarely had the capacity to control, even though they had techniques at their disposal both to frighten and placate their occupants.

The street riots and mob actions, of which the SRM were but one target, were changing at the beginning of the eighteenth century. What was taking place was the emergence of 'politics', as persistent, if not stable, sets of partisan allegiances; the result was that mobs with selective loyalties could be mobilised. The local communities were becoming more differentiated with localities exhibiting contrasting commitments. As we have seen, it was often necessary, in the eyes of local magistrates, for them to take account of local sympathies. Many areas of London, for example around the Strand, became virtual 'no go' areas for SRM agents. By the end of the century it was no longer legitimate, if it ever was, to speak of 'the London mob' as if it were a unitary entity.

THE SIGNIFICANCE OF THE SOCIETIES FOR REFORMATION

Commentators have spoken of the 'failure' of the SRM project. I think this assessment is incorrect. Certainly their campaign, like all political interventions, had its peaks and troughs, and it declined steadily from the mid-1720s and disappeared after 1738. Yet the significant fact was that for over four decades they sustained an active intervention against many aspects of the economy of the streets, whether street prostitution, Sunday trading or public drunkenness. These interventions must have been resented and resisted by their targets and were generally unpopular with not only the lower orders, but many of the becoming-respectable classes. To sustain this campaign, to employ extensive and well co-ordinated techniques of public propaganda, and to activate the application of a far from coherent legal apparatus was a very significant achievement.

It is, however, important to recognise the limits, or more accurately self-restraints, within which the reformation campaign operated. Despite the cumbersome nature of the prosecution and enforcement procedures available for use against criminal misdemeanours, the Societies made no effort to change that procedure. They grumbled mightily when officials, whether magistrates or local constables, evaded implementation, but despite the fact that they had access to the legislative process, they made no effort to change the legal procedures. Indeed they do not seem to have attached high priority to any form of legal change. While they were linked to a number of parliamentarians who were involved, generally unsuccessfully, in promoting moral legislation, the SRM did not campaign for legal change. Or, if they did give it any priority, they certainly did not make this concern public. In their extensive propaganda they made no use of calls to change either the substance or the procedure of the law. In making this point it should be borne in mind that intentional projects of law-making, what Hayek calls 'legal constructivism', were unusual in the early eighteenth century. Law tended to be viewed as a declaratory mechanism, it declared a law that was presumed to exist rather than making law, although it was necessary now and again to repeat and reinforce the law, particularly when there was evidence of widespread breach or neglect. Since the SRM's strategy and practice were, as I have argued, in other respects so 'modern', it is significant that they did not add a law-making component to their armoury.

There was just one exception to this studied indifference to legal procedure, a proverbial exception to the rule. In a sermon by John Heylyn 1728, in an interesting and novel passage he implies that SRM had found some deficiencies in the existing law. "[H]as it not been found . . . that some of these laws want reformation? Have they not often proved ineffectual by reason of certain defects, intricacies and obscurities, through which they greatly evade . . ."; he expresses the hope that the legislature would put matters right (1729). This approach to law is entirely original and distinctively modern; since it seems to have had no other reverberations we can note it as an historical possibility that had to wait its time.

However, I suggest that Curtis and Speck's assessment that the SRM simply wanted the authorities to enforce the existing law with the consequences of a "determined dependence" on the gentry fails to recognise their innovatory significance (1976: 60). This I think misunderstands the SRM's relations with the upper classes. They certainly actively sought out the support of lords and bishops, but they did not depend on them any more than they did on the magistrates. If a particular group of JPs stood in their way or opposed them, they would seek to manoeuvre to avoid the obstruction or they would engage in blunt criticism of both individual JPs and the Bench collectively. They succeeded in mobilising an alliance of some depth and breadth. They had serious and powerful backers in both Church and state, and they put together a substantial membership of activists, drawn from among the urban petty bourgeoisie. In other words, it is precisely this combination of an active quest for alliances with a practical strategic autonomy that leads me to think of the SRM in terms of the categories of modern social movements and to go as far as to say that the Societies for Reformation of Manners had many, if not all, of the attributes of a 'new social movement'.

CHAPTER 2

MORAL REGULATION FROM ABOVE: THE VICE SOCIETY

MORALS IN AN AGE OF ANXIETY

This chapter explores the implications of the thesis that an intensification of projects of moral regulation in early nineteenth-century Britain resulted from the interacting social, economic and political anxieties of the propertied classes generated by the dual revolutions, the Industrial Revolution and the French Revolution. While much attention has been paid to these social and economic transformations, less attention has been devoted to the cultural politics of the period. One major expression was the concern with the moral conditions of the stirring mass of the working and non-working poor. The respectable classes experienced deep apprehensions about the currents they perceived as flowing through the society. To these they responded with a disparate array of projects of moral regulation, which this chapter investigates.

The forebodings of crisis were mercurial; their peaks and troughs were stimulated by the shifts and stirrings occurring within British society. There was an expanding body of commentary and detailed study avidly consumed by the literate classes. The external circumstances not only bore upon intensifying international rivalries, but at the same time had political and ideological dimensions. Thus the loss of the American colonies finally conceded in 1782 was a stunning blow to British military power. It also heralded a political danger that was represented by the publication in 1791 of Thomas Paine's *The Rights of Man*. Similarly the French Revolution led to the military confrontation of the Napoleonic Wars that were to last with brief intermissions from 1793 until 1815, but brought with it the portentous spectre of radical demands for democratic reform that went beyond the calls for equal representation sparked by the American Revolution.

At home a deep foreboding manifested itself in a preoccupation with social conditions that in a very real sense created 'the social' as a focus for debate. The social was to become the object of self-conscious inquiry exemplified in Arthur Young's massive statistical undertaking of the *Annals of Agriculture* (1784–1815). From these investigations he berated the "supineness of the gentry" and urged the political conclusion that farmers should not only make liberal donations for relief of the poor, but should enrol in the yeomanry since revolt from below was a decided possibility. The propertied classes needed to be armed and weapons should be issued to all those with substantial incomes (Young 1797). More familiar is the enormous effort expended on inquiries into the conditions of the rural poor, the workings of the Poor Laws and urban social conditions that were represented by Sir Frederick Eden (1797) and Patrick Colquhoun (1799).

These diverse concerns found common expression in a persistent sense of anxiety that erupted with varying intensity from the 1790s onwards and was heightened by a series of severe economic crises. The articulation of these concerns took many forms. Anxiety bred a deeply conservative reaction that refused all innovation and unleashed the dark forces of 'King and country' mobs. At the same time it stimulated urgent demands for reforms of many different hues of which agricultural improvement and Poor Law reform were major instances. It manifested itself in that complex of interventions in the social for which the term philanthropy, although barely adequate, will serve for the present. Such apprehension revived providential religious ideas that interpreted each symptom of crisis as evidence of God's wrath with a sinful nation brought low by admixtures of the immorality of the lower orders and the luxury, pride and folly of the upper classes – sentiments that were to play a key role in forming the ideas of religious revivalism and, specifically, of the moral reform movements that form my specific focus.

Yet at the same time as these religious ideas were potent they existed amidst a religious differentiation that saw the established Church lose its unquestioned dominance, and which heralded a distinctive secularisation. The emergence of deists and agnostics added new fears of a Godless radicalism, but perhaps more pervasively resulted in a generalised separation between religion and everyday life; religion increasingly became a matter of personal choice and conviction and a Sunday that was separable from workaday life. Currents of secularisation amidst surges of religious revivalism are complex; for the present purpose it is perhaps sufficient to point towards E. P. Thompson's discussion of the role of Methodism in which he demonstrates that the "psychological terrorism" of a creed obsessed by guilt and sin contributed to the emerging political self-confidence of the working classes (1968: 411–40).

It is always risky to lean too heavily on the idea of crisis, since crisis tends to become a permanent condition. It would not be until well into the nineteenth century that a new complex of relations of ruling became secured. A strong case can be made for the early 1830s as a turning point with the first tentative reform of Parliament and the new Poor Law. The late 1840s can lay claim to being decisive, with the repeal of the Corn Laws finally attesting to the predominance of urban over rural capital and the state surviving the challenge of Chartism. For my purposes the key process is one of longer duration that laid the conditions of possibility for new relations of ruling.

A process of critical importance was the formation of an extended and complex civil society. The parameters of the old order had been in place since the Tudor consolidation of a centralised state whose local mode of rule relied upon the dominance of landed property and a propertied clergy. Even the law, an important instrument of that rule, was little more than the state and gentry in judicial robes. The trinity of state, property and Church ruled without the aid of civil associations or a police apparatus.

This sketch is only adequate to characterise a complex reality in so far as it focuses attention on the decisive process of the emergence of a civil society founded on a dense web of civil associations. If dates are required I would hazard the period between 1760 and 1830. It will be recalled that one of the things that made the Societies for Reformation of Manners so distinctive was that they were one of the first associations that separated themselves from the Church and were not economic associations. From the middle of the eighteenth century there came into existence a great mass of associations which not only linked the propertied classes together in cross-cutting relations but also produced links to the expanding middle and artisan classes. The evangelical activists were typically members of associations such as the Bible Society, Church Missionary Society, London Society for the Promotion of Christianity Among the Jews, School Society, Sunday School Society, Climbing Boy Society, 'Bettering Society' (Brown 1961: 329). From these roots was born a system of political representation which came to acquire the characteristics of a system of political parties that was able to articulate something more than crude economic interests. Politics increasingly came to be struggled over by means of organised associations. The French Revolution induced the formation of associations that distinguished friend from enemy. The great political issues of the period, whether it was the reform of the Poor Laws, the Corn Laws or parliamentary reform, all spawned their associational articulations.

More important for my purposes is the emergence of societies and associations that strove to act upon others, to pursue projects that sought to govern what was still termed the manners, or, we might say, the morals, of the populace. The institutional expressions were legion and came into being at an increasing rate. There is no familiar term to describe what I will call the web of civil society. The significance of the elaboration and complexification of civil society is that it works in two directions. On the one hand, it is an essential aspect of state formation in that it provides an infrastructure which enables the expansion of a dense system of administration – for example, the production of state knowledge commonly emerged from initiatives within civil society with unofficial statistical societies providing the base on which grew systems of official statistics. On the other hand, as civil society became more dense, it was increasingly able to act more or less independently of the state. And, most significantly, it provided the capacity to resist state action such that the state had to take account of responses emanating from within civil society.

I will focus attention on the emergence of just two forms of civil associations that are important to the study of the moral regulation movements in the early nineteenth century. The first concerns policing and the second philanthropy. The very growth of civil society generated an increasing concern with social order and stability. In England the politics of the formation of apparatuses of policing was deeply affected by resistance to centralised coercive apparatuses; police forces and standing armies were viewed by both conservatives and radicals alike as epitomising a trend towards an absolutist state. This hostility to centralised policing ensured that the Metropolitan Police did not come into being until 1829. This does not undermine the contention that there was a growing concern with social order. Rather it explains the significance of the emergence of a complex of prosecution societies.

During the last quarter of the eighteenth century the propertied classes became increasingly concerned about problems of social order. Local societies, characteristically called 'Associations for the Prosecution of Felons', were formed as private organisations of property owners, combining to share the costs incurred in locating, arresting and prosecuting offenders (Shubert 1981; Philips 1989; King 1989). These associations were, like the Societies for Reformation of Manners, concerned exclusively with enforcing the existing laws; they expressed no inclination to propose new laws or procedures. They can be contrasted with their contemporaries in America, the vigilantes who took law enforcement into their own hands and bequeathed the lynch mob to posterity (Brown 1975; Culberson 1990).

The prosecution associations were located in the existing procedures of the criminal law which still depended on the private initiation of prosecution and on the private apprehension of offenders. In this respect there was a lineage with the earlier Societies for Reformation of Manners in that they relied on the techniques of informing and made use of payments to informers. While these associations did not address themselves explicitly to issues of moral regulation, one late attempt to revive the older reform societies reveals a fascinating linkage. The rules of the Society for Reformation of Manners in Pontefract formed in 1786 specified that the principal inhabitants shall unite together

> for the better purpose of detecting felons, cheats, vagrants, night-walkers, and night-poachers, pawn-brokers, . . . sellers by false weights and measures, persons adulterating, or improperly mixing meal, flour, etc. (Zouch 1786: Appendix).

Here we see the defence of property mingled with some of the persisting targets of the reformation of manners. Occasional concern is also revealed with offences concerning alehouses and drinking and Sabbath observation, providing reminders of the older Societies. However, the concerns of the associated gentlemen were largely instrumental: they focused their activities on crimes against property and, occasionally, offences against the person. The gentry subsidised these prosecutions, but it may be significant that they also harnessed small property owners to the general defence of property. Some local agreements required members to act as a posse in pursuit of offenders; other associations (particularly in London) mounted their own foot patrols. It is worth noting that the prosecution associations favoured the establishment of local police forces. In short, they were civil society protecting its own, albeit sectional, interests and coming to the aid of the state; in so doing they hastened the critical phase of state-formation involving a more or less systematic policing apparatus. They and the Loyalist Associations movement of the 1790s, spurred by the threat of radicalism and the French Revolution, accustomed religious and social conservatives to voluntary combination and political action.[1]

The second broad category of civil associations was those that may be loosely labelled philanthropic. I suggest that this needs to be understood broadly, because consequent upon my earlier remarks about the coexistence of an intensification of religiosity and emergent secularisation, the philanthropic associations embraced many that were overtly religious, such as the Religious Tract Society (founded 1799), that was a domestic missionary project active in the expanding industrial towns barely reached by the Anglican Church. Of particular significance in the early Victorian period was the Sunday School movement which, as Laqueur has demonstrated, was at one and the same time an agency of the middle class in subverting the nascent class consciousness of the working class and also "a uniquely working-class cultural constellation"

(1976: 239). The connection between such religious projects and moral regulation is very clear from the objects of the early Sunday School Society (founded 1785):

> To prevent vice – to encourage industry and virtue – to dispel the darkness of ignorance – to diffuse the light of knowledge – to bring men cheerfully to submit to their stations – to obey the laws of God and their country – to make that part of the community, the country poor, happy – to lead them in the pleasant paths of religion here, and to endeavour to prepare them for a glorious eternity (Laqueur 1976: 34).

Other overtly religious bodies were more directly coercive and carried forward the long-running struggle over the people's Sunday that we encountered as a key element of the activities of the Societies for Reformation of Manners. Bodies such as the Society for Promoting the Observance of the Sabbath (founded 1809) and the Society for Promoting the Due Observance of the Lord's Day (founded 1831), later simplified to Lord's Day Observance Society, were moral regulation movements in that they focused on the perceived dissolution of manners and the threat to civil order stemming from a decline in religious observance. We will encounter in later chapters how organisations such as the Young Men's Christian Association (YMCA) and the Young Women's Christian Association (YWCA) were to play important roles in moral regulation politics in both Britain and North America.

The evangelicalism of the established Church was an explicit attempt at the reform of popular culture. One of its most influential articulations came from the copious pen of Hannah More who defined the project as being

> to improve the habits and raise the principles of the mass of the people at a time when the dangers and temptations, moral and political, were multiplied beyond the example of any other period in our history (quoted in Bradley 1976: 112).

The most important condition for the subsequent extension of the range and scope of moral regulation movements in Britain was the rise of philanthropy. This is not the occasion to offer more than a brief characterisation of the complex lineages of these projects whose most important feature was that they were directed towards the moralisation of the poor. The most persistent theme was the intimate moral association of vice and idleness; it found a powerful discursive linkage in the valorisation of 'restraint' and 'self-control' whose great power lay in the capacity to move effortlessly between the economic and sexual realms. It should be recalled that at the turn of the century the central preoccupation was with the working poor in rural England. However, the rise of philanthropy marked the emergence of a distinctive engagement with an urban experience. The towns and cities of this new world were perceived to be full of moral danger, insecurity and an ever-present risk of disorder.

Philanthropy involved new forms of knowledge and interventions in the urban world that were a transition from the familiar themes that had structured the practices of charity. Charity involved no personal knowledge of individuals, but as the frequent bequests to 'our poor' attest, to a known and familiar social category, one that was captured by the dictum that the poor are always with us. The world of philanthropy necessitated the exploration of the unknown, the fetid urban alleys and tenements of the towns from which the middle classes were increasingly separated both physically and emotionally. The key figure was the pauper and the condition of pauperism, captured in the abiding concern with overcrowding linked to both emergent medical ideas about contagious diseases and implicit sexual discourses about excess in general and incest in particular.

Philanthropy involved intervention that had two sides: the first was the beginnings of systematic collection of organised knowledge epitomised by Joseph Fletcher's (1847–49) compilations of 'moral and educational statistics'. The other side required a distinctively new form of personal contact, that of 'visiting'. The visit to the homes of the poor was to be the distinctive contribution of an expanding participation by middle-class women, whose hallmark was a 'moral surveillance' that Valverde describes:

> The prying gaze of philanthropy sought to penetrate the innermost selves of the poor, including their sexual desires, which were uniformly conceptualised as vices (incest, illegitimacy, prostitution) (1991: 21).

This emergent philanthropy was structured by a complex engagement with debates about the causes of the ills and evils that confronted the poor. The problem of causes was significant, because whatever the other differences between the protagonists, they shared a belief in the efficacy of positive intervention, in its simplest form, that something could and should be done. The core of the debates was a tangled engagement between moral and social environmentalism. Moral environmentalism emphasised the moral deficiencies that stemmed from an impaired religious faith or a weakened capacity for self-restraint. In contrast, social environmentalism viewed moral deficiencies as resulting from adverse social conditions, poor housing and sanitation, lack of education, and – more radically – low wages.

These contrasting positions rarely presented themselves in a simple opposition between social and moral environmentalism, but generally manifested themselves in various admixtures of these elements. As a rough approximation we find a shift from evangelical philanthropy to 'scientific charity', but it is important to the argument, in this and subsequent chapters, that concern with the condition of the poor involved a recurrent eruption of moral elements within the discourses of social interventionism. Both strands exhibited a tension between coercion and improvement that played itself out both within organisations and in the debates between them.[2] Classically the tension was ever present in rescue work among prostitutes; while some favoured a harsh disciplinary regime, others insisted on providing friendly and humane conditions. The body of this study will demonstrate that, while individual reformers may have had a predisposition to one view or the other, these two elements were already present in moral regulation movements. Two other key features of philanthropy should be noted. The variant embodiments of philanthropy all exhibited an abiding apprehension about urban life. The other general feature of philanthropy was that middle-class women secured a significant space of public engagement that is captured by Harrison:

> Victorian women could derive from philanthropy all the excitements and dangers of penetrating or observing the unknown while at the same time securing that change of scene and activity which is the essence of recreation (1966: 360).

It now remains only to establish the range and diversity of philanthropic projects that emerged during the period under consideration. The Philanthropic Society (founded 1789) was significant for reinforcing the widely employed distinction between the industrious poor and the idle poor. These binary classifications, Foucault's 'dividing practices', were instituted by "private agencies of moralisation" in the discourses of philanthropy (Garland 1985: 40). The Society for Bettering the Conditions of the Poor (founded 1796) was not only important because of the range of its projects, but its very name epitomises the condescending spirit of so much middle-class philanthropy. The culmination of early nineteenth-century philanthropy was the founding of the London Society for Organizing Charitable Relief and Repressing Mendicity in 1818; it became the Charitable Organization Society in 1869, the pioneer of the casework method of household visits. Other organisations focused on more selected targets. The Guardian Society (founded 1813) was a non-denominational body aiming to control prostitution and rescue prostitutes, while the Society for the Suppression of Public Begging (founded 1812) and the Society for the Suppression of Mendicity (founded 1818) aimed at specific manifestations of urban poverty. The Society for Prevention of Cruelty to Animals (founded 1824; later adding

'Royal' to its name) significantly predated by sixty years the foundation of the Society for the Prevention of Cruelty to Children in 1884.

Before turning to a more detailed consideration of the Vice Society, it is important to note that projects of moral regulation had not died out with the demise of the Societies for Reformation of Manners around 1738 and suddenly sprung to life again with the Proclamation Society in 1789. Martin Ingram (1996) has demonstrated that a more or less continuous series of moral regulation projects in England, varying in intensity, can be traced back to the late middle ages. Certainly there were significant moral reform elements in many of the civil and philanthropic associations reviewed above. But there was also a series of full-blown moral regulation projects. In 1757 a strenuous effort was made, largely under Methodist inspiration, to revive the Societies for Reformation of Manners, styling itself as the 'Revived SRM' and restricting itself to the prosecution of Sabbath violations; John Wesley claimed 10,000 prosecutions in a five-year period ([1763]).[3] Similarly, members of the Society for Preventing the Profanation of the Sabbath (founded 1775) combed London on Sunday mornings to report Sabbath violations to the Justices. Other bodies, such as the Society for the Reformation of Principles, were active in the 1790s but left few traces.[4] From the mid-1780s there is evidence of considerable local anti-vice activity directed variously at blasphemy, intemperance, idleness, vagrancy and crime, that in some cases led to the formation of local moral reform societies. These projects seem to have been the work of activist mayors, Justices and other local officials.[5]

I have chosen to explore the Vice Society in detail because it epitomises a link between the earlier prosecution strategy of the Societies for Reformation of Manners and the more multifarious strategies of the late nineteenth-century social purity movements. Further, the activities of the Vice Society spanned the greater part of the nineteenth century and, significantly, it ended its activities only when it was silently absorbed into the leading sexual purity movement, the National Vigilance Association, in 1885.

REFORM OF MANNERS BY PROCLAMATION

The Vice Society had a relation with a precursor, the Proclamation Society, but the details of the link have not been fully clarified. Accordingly it is necessary to examine the Proclamation Society to lay the basis for a fuller consideration of the Vice Society. Some accounts attribute the whole process to the intervention of the influential figure of the High-Church evangelical reformer, William Wilberforce, who argued that what was needed was

> some reformer of the nation's morals who should raise his voice in the high places of the land; and do within the Church, and near the throne what Wesley had accomplished in the meeting and amongst the multitude (R. & S. Wilberforce 1838 II: 130).

The hierarchical nature of his project is evident in his commitment to the "grand law of subordination" – that everyone should know their allotted place in the social order (1797: 405–6). The reactionary politics of Wilberforce were particularly clear. In the debate on the *Habeas Corpus Suspension Bill* in 1817 he warned of the danger that

> the lower orders . . . [might] be tempted by the delusive and wicked principles instilled into their minds, to direct their strength to the destruction of government, and to the overthrow of every civil and religious establishment.[6]

I will show that while he had an important initiatory role he played little or no part in the activities of the Vice Society.

One expression of late eighteenth-century concern about social order took a very traditional form. In association with a number of peers and Church dignitaries, Wilberforce persuaded the Crown to issue a Proclamation against vice and then proceeded to organise an association to further the enforcement of this Proclamation. George III issued such a Proclamation in 1787, entitled *For the Encouragement of Piety and Virtue and for Preventing and Punishing of Vice, Profaneness and Immorality.*[7] It was modelled on an earlier Proclamation from the reign of Queen Anne.[8] Much of the wording of the earlier Proclamation was directly imported into the new one. It complained that the existing laws on vice, profanity and immorality were not being enforced, and invoked a traditional providential doctrine on the necessity to avoid divine wrath and to secure divine pleasure by suppressing immorality. It proceeded to a more legislative mode, asserting prohibitions on the playing of dice, cards, or any other game in public or private on the Lord's Day, and called for the suppression of all gaming houses, and all licentious prints and books. It also required Church attendance, and ordered Justices of the Peace to enforce laws on drinking, blasphemy, lewdness and swearing. The Proclamation was widely circulated to County Sheriffs, Lord-Lieutenants and Mayors and was accompanied by a letter from the Home Secretary urging immediate and vigorous compliance.[9]

The Proclamation against vice was itself part of an emerging project of moral regulation. In 1786 William Wilberforce, then MP for Yorkshire and a recent evangelical convert, adopted two major causes, the abolition of the slave trade and reformation of manners.[10] Although he is remembered primarily for his anti-slavery activities, the reform of manners was probably his major campaign at the turn of the century. He approached a number of senior ecclesiastical figures about the possibility of a new proclamation on vice and the formation of a society along the lines of the earlier Societies for Reformation of Manners. Beilby Porteus, Bishop of Chester, and Shute Barrington, Bishop of Salisbury, were key supporters of Wilberforce's project; it was Porteus who persuaded the Archbishop of Canterbury to approach George III and the Proclamation was issued.

Wilberforce's plan was that after the publication of the Proclamation, a reformation society with branches throughout the country was to be established.[11] Wilberforce sought out prominent Establishment figures to sponsor a society to promote the Proclamation. His success manifested itself in the early membership which included the Archbishops of Canterbury and York, seventeen bishops, fifteen peers (many with close links to the Royal family) and thirteen commoners (two ex-Prime Ministers and eleven MPs). By the launch of the Proclamation Society in 1789, membership had risen to 149, and now included twenty of the twenty-four bishops and thirty peers. The Society never sought to expand its membership; it started out and remained an elite fraternity that brought together evangelical Anglicans from the worlds of politics and the Church. The Society survived until 1808 when it fused with the Vice Society, but its main period of activity had come to an end by 1792.

The Proclamation Society located itself in the same theological critique of society that had motivated the Societies for Reformation of Manners. "The experience of all ages has been that increasing wealth, luxury, and refinement, are attended with a decay in religion and morals" (Proclamation Society 1800: 19). Its targets revealed the impact of a widening literacy: obscene books and prints were the chief target and, especially, blasphemous publications of which Thomas Paine's *The Rights of Man*, that "pernicious work", was a perennial concern. It was not only popular radicalism, but also popular culture that incited concern. Places of public entertainment were condemned for "the most shocking indecency", as were public houses, whose number had been increasing "shockingly" (Proclamation Society 1800: 12). The political thrust of the project to reform popular culture was perhaps most clearly articulated in Joseph Livesey's temperance journal, *The Moral Reformer*:

> Unless the people are morally improved, being now brought into large masses, and possessing increased facilities for mischief, the result . . . may sooner or later, be internal commotion if not a national wreck.[12]

The Proclamation Society seems to have set out to avoid the hostility that had been encountered by the SRM resulting from their informing and entrapment tactics. The Society was not only a child of the Establishment, but was much concerned to ingratiate itself with the religious and political establishment. This had profound implications for its strategy. It sought to stimulate the existing law enforcement agencies towards a more rigorous application of the extant law. This required a shift in the governmental practices of the magistracy who, as we saw in connection with their hostility to SRM activities, employed discretionary prosecution as a means of relating to and securing their local hegemony. To this end the Proclamation Society organised a widely attended convention for magistrates in 1790; the main thrust of the report and resolutions stressed the need for systematic enforcement of the laws relating to Sunday observance and immorality (Proclamation Society 1790).[13] In addition there was discussion of prison government and the regulation of vagrancy. The Society issued several circular letters addressed to JPs. Their wording was suitably deferential, but their substance reminded Justices of those laws that the Society was keen to have enforced: for example, to prevent employers paying out wages in public houses and to prohibit unlawful race meetings.

A second strategic goal significantly differentiated the Society from the SRM. It was explicitly concerned to promote the enactment of new laws. This legislative strategy reveals a most interesting paradox about both the Proclamation Society and the Vice Society, namely, that despite their close links to the Establishment they seem to have been remarkably unsuccessful in securing new legislation. I will consider this issue more fully in connection with the discussion of the Vice Society below.

The Society's litigation strategy was cautious. Cases were brought in order to clarify points of law, in particular with respect to technical points about licensing laws. There was, however, no attempt to emulate the SRM's mass prosecutions. Rather its prosecutions were symbolic but seem to have intentionally been directed against relatively uninfluential individuals. The attack on obscene or seditious literature was directed against vendors, not against publishers or authors. When in 1797 the Society initiated the prosecution of Thomas Paine's publisher, Thomas Williams, it secured the flamboyant Whig barrister, Thomas Erskine, to lead the prosecution, but he withdrew when the Society insisted on pressing for the imprisonment of the ailing Williams. This intransigence resulted in considerable hostile publicity.

The reasons for the decline of the Proclamation Society remain unclear. By 1899 it had run into difficulties and it was admitted that the Society had not met that year because of the sudden withdrawal of its Secretary. There was subsequently a brief revival; thirty-seven new members were reported between 1800 and 1803 probably reflecting an upsurge in anti-Jacobin sentiment. But it seemed to have lost both confidence and a clear sense of direction. This vacuum was filled by a new project of moral regulation that emerged from a different social base.

THE SOCIETY FOR THE SUPPRESSION OF VICE

That the formation in 1802 of the Society for the Suppression of Vice, generally referred to as the 'Vice Society', had occurred while the Proclamation Society was still in existence needs some explanation.[14] The founding documents of the Vice Society make no reference to the other body, but neither, as far as I have been able to establish, did it ever express any criticism of the older organisation. After 1802 the Proclamation Society and the newly formed Vice Society expressed mutual sympathy and support. However, there seem to have been few direct links between the two organisations.[15] Rather it seems probable that the new project was conceived as a different kind of organisation from the somewhat remote and Establishment-orientated Proclamation Society. It was concerned to draw the respectable metropolitan classes into concerted action at a time when fear of impending national disaster was widespread. While there was no sharp break between their strategies, there was a shift of emphasis. The Vice Society was less content to leave the enforcement of morals to the authorities and more prepared to intervene where it detected a lack of resolve from the authorities; but at the same time it continued to make use of its connections with the political and religious establishment.

The experience of the late eighteenth-century prosecution societies and loyalist associations had accustomed the respectable classes to organised voluntary political action.[16] The Vice Society was formed in a climate of patriotic fervour and anti-radical wartime trepidation. An increased emphasis upon the idleness and criminality of the lower orders was articulated through discourses of degeneration and demoralisation. This repudiation of the lower orders expressed itself in both a preparedness to use coercion, as epitomised in the deployment of sedition charges to suppress radicalism, but also in the intervention of 'rational philanthropy'. It is significant that the two most representatives figures of this hard-headed philanthropy, Patrick Colquhoun, whose work focused on the links between poverty, crime and policing, and Thomas Bernard, founder of The Society for Bettering the Conditions of the Poor, both became Vice-Presidents of the Vice Society. The key figure in the formative period of the Vice Society was John Bowles, who had earlier been associated with the anti-Jacobin Society for the Reformation of Principles. He epitomised respectable anxieties about social order in the aftermath of the French Revolution and in the face of the independent radicalism of the London working class. He has been described as "professional propagandist of state and Church party" (Quinlan 1941: 203). He was probably the author of the Vice Society's major early tract, *An Address to the Public from the Society for the Suppression of Vice* (1803).

In contrast to the Proclamation Society, the Vice Society attracted no peers or members of Parliament. Its early members included Anglican vicars, five lawyers, two booksellers, two surgeons and a number of clerks.[17] The Vice Society aspired to a wider membership than had the Proclamation Society; it reported having 200 members in 1802, 561 members by early 1803, 1200 by the end of 1804. As its membership expanded, it came to represent the urban professional and commercial classes with a sprinkling from the lesser gentry. Significantly, given the active exclusion of women practised by most organisations, the Society showed enthusiasm for enrolling women, who formed thirty-three per cent of the membership by 1804. However, the Society was sectarian in restricting membership to adherents of the Church of England, probably in order to ensure that no hint of religious dissent or political radicalism would sully its reputation at a time of patriotic wartime conservatism. The Society seems to have remained a largely centralised body, but there is evidence of at least twelve local bodies bearing the same name, although there is no evidence that local activism was sustained.[18]

The activities of the Vice Society underwent distinct shifts over time, but these do not seem to have been the result of conscious reflection or, perhaps more accurately, they are not visible in the Society's publications. In the early years its project for the reformation of manners was concerned with wide-ranging aspects of popular culture within the context of patriotism linked to aims of 'improving' society. This mix of patriotism and improvement expressed itself in the prosecution strategy, which targeted two significantly different groups, Sunday street-traders and political radicals. These apparently disparate targets were united in the evangelical discourse of moral reform to which the Society subscribed. This link lay at the heart of the critique of conventional Anglicanism that required little more than periodic church attendance. The Society associated national misfortunes, manifest in political radicalism, with the decline of religion and of morals. The preoccupations with Sunday observance and blasphemy were coherent expressions of the general contestation in which the evangelicals saw themselves as being engaged against the forces of secular rationalism; hence they perceived an intimate connection between religious blasphemy and political sedition.

After 1807 the Society went into a steep decline; in 1810 it announced a temporary suspension of its activities.[19] Between 1810 and 1812 only three members remained active. The Society survived this decline; by 1812 it had resumed activities, albeit on a reduced level, and without pretensions to securing a mass membership. In the period after the Napoleonic Wars its attention became increasingly focused on blasphemy and obscenity. These two categories provided a means of linking two distinct targets. The first was the publishers of radical texts and papers; the second was the street-sellers and booksellers of sexually explicit prints and songs. Thereby political radicals were tarred with the brush of obscenity that was furthered by the emergence of the common-law offences of seditious libel and seditious blasphemy. In pursuing these dual targets, the Society came to act as an auxiliary to government. It mounted a series of prosecutions against the Paineite freethinker Richard Carlile, publisher of Paine's books and pamphlets and editor of *The Republican*.[20] Carlile himself was imprisoned between 1819 and 1825, during which time the Vice Society brought prosecutions against his wife, his sister and his employees, who, despite periods of imprisonment, kept the journal alive. Thus it was the rise of political radicalism that elicited the reactive response of the Vice Society between 1815 and 1820 and then again in the late 1830s. Yet it decisively shifted its orientation. While it retained the rhetoric of moral reform, it had become a demonstrably partisan organisation, more concerned to suppress radicalism than everyday immoralities.

In the third phase of its existence from the 1830s until its lingering demise in the 1880s, the Society largely disappeared from public view and became a pressure group concerned to stimulate the legislation of morality. It retained some of its prosecutorial functions, becoming a semi-official enforcement agency on behalf of literary decency, but without seeking to secure the kind of notoriety that had attended its battle with Richard Carlile.

The role of moral legislation in Victorian England raises some interesting questions. While considerable effort was expended on seeking parliamentary action on a variety of legislative proposals, the return on that investment was small. The only notable achievement was in securing the passage of Lord Campbell's *Obscene Publications Act* in 1857 (Manchester 1988).[21] The *Times* enthusiastically endorsed this statute as the "purification of public morals" (14/8/1857). At first it was used against street pornography, but there was a series of prosecutions of artistic and scientific works between 1869 and 1880.[22] Perhaps more significant than this important piece of legislation was the Society's failure to secure legislation on the many other Bills which it promoted. Projects of moral legislation encountered diverse but powerful opposition. In Parliament traditional conservatives, who were suspicious of any extensions of the state's policing powers, joined with radicals, who were increasingly vocal against attacks on popular liberties, while outside Parliament mass action opposed measures that were viewed as attacks on working-class life and leisure. For example, in 1854 and 1855 attempts to restrict Sunday drinking were abandoned when they stirred mass demonstrations.[23]

Less easy to establish is the extent to which governmental parties and ministries became increasingly reluctant to lend active support to projects of moral regulation. It will be necessary to return to this issue later, when many of the late Victorian moral reform projects similarly encountered significant obstruction from the centre of the political and governmental system. An irresistible political demand that involved support from both significant elites and broad endorsement from the middle class became increasingly necessary before central assistance was forthcoming in securing moral legislation.

TARGETS AND TACTICS

The Society defined its targets as crimes injurious to public morals. However, it recognised that the enforcement of such offences, perceived as victimless crimes, could result in accusations of officiousness and generate popular opposition. Yet its evangelical enthusiasm often got the better of such sober calculation. Its main targets were obscene books and prints; but as we have seen this often shifted into attacks on political and theological texts in periods of mounting anxiety about social order.[24] More generally, it evinced the persisting concern of the respectable classes that can be traced back to the Elizabethan period, if not earlier, with two closely related issues, popular recreations and Sunday observance. Places of public entertainment and public houses persistently elicited outrage at the indecencies they flaunted. As a result of the diffusion of wage-labour, Sunday became the occasion for recreational and family activities. The Society launched periodic attacks on the London fairs as sites of unrestrained popular recreation.[25]

There were other targets that the Society set out in the variants of its manifesto: profane swearing was always an extension of Sunday observance and blasphemy; it launched periodic assaults on gambling and lotteries, but seemed unable or unwilling to mount a sustained attack.[26] It included in its list false weights and measures, but there is no evidence that it acted on this matter.[27] It is important to note that, while the Society included the suppression of disorderly houses and brothels, it launched only occasional prosecutions and its rhetoric about the immorality of the age made only passing reference to sexual transgressions.[28] It fulminated against nude bathing, launching some prosecutions in Brighton in 1807. The Society successfully pressed for the inclusion of a clause extending offences against sexual modesty (public urination, naked bathing, courting couples) and another providing hard labour for the public exhibition of indecent prints in the vagrancy statutes of 1822–24.

The Vice Society operated primarily as a prosecuting society; members' subscriptions were used to fund agents who brought these prosecutions. The Society's *First Report* itemised 678 prosecutions, the overwhelming majority, 623, for Sabbath violation.[29] However, the Society was concerned to avoid the accusation that it was preoccupied with prosecuting offenders. It claimed to avoid the direct prosecution tactics of the SRM; thus John Scott claimed that before initiating prosecution, it became the practice to issue a warning to potential targets, who were given one month's notice before prosecution for Sabbath offences. Scott was satisfied with this tactic and went so far as to claim that "the evil was done away with" ([1807]: 13). He claimed, for example, that the Society had been successful in banning Sunday trading in Edmonton, Tottenham and Enfield.[30] He cites a letter from Ware claiming that labourers' wives had praised the Society for its help in keeping their husbands sober on Sunday. The Rochester and Chatham Society reported that its area was now "decent and orderly" on a Sunday. In Gloucester, Sunday trading was eliminated (Scott [1807]: 59).

Further evidence about the Society's tactics emerged when its full-time agent, George Pritchard, was cross-examined about the Society's work before the Police Committee of the House of Commons in 1817.[31] He described its method of work as being to send out agents to inspect an area for Sunday trading and to distribute admonition notices, and only if these failed were prosecutions instigated; even then Pritchard claimed that the Society always sought remission of any fine imposed. He admitted the existence of a conflict of interest with many labourers, who did not get paid until Saturday evening. His evidence is the primary source of the story that was subsequently widely repeated that "a band of over sixty Italian hawkers" sold obscene publications at residential boarding schools for young ladies. He was a little more precise in detailing the prosecution of one James Price for trying to sell snuff boxes with indecent engravings at a boarding school for girls.

It was against obscene publications that the Society focused attention after the initial campaign against Sunday trading. By 1807, the Society claimed credit for the confiscation of 129,681 prints, 16,200 illustrated books, five tons of letterpress, 16,005 song sheets, 5503 obscene artifacts and a "large quantity of infidel and blasphemous publications" (Thompson 1994: 14). With the emergence of regular police forces in the metropolis, the periodic waves of prosecution of traders in obscene publications gradually passed out of the orbit of the Society, and, as we have seen, its attention increasingly shifted to political radicals and then to French novelists.

The Society had to defend its strategy against attack from disparate sources. Its concern to sustain relations with the political establishment led it to seek to deflect the conservative criticism, epitomised by William Cobbett's objection that the Society was a voluntary organisation acting independently of the traditional and proper authorities of the Church and the State. It was, he alleged, "a standing conspiracy against the quiet and tranquility of society" (Roberts 1983: 168). On the other hand the Society confronted a more radical criticism, also expressed by Cobbett, but most famously by Sydney Smith, who suggested that the Vice Society rename itself the "Society for Suppressing the Vices of persons whose income does not exceed £500 per annum" (1809: 342). Sydney Smith drew on the long-standing hostility towards informers and, in the context of attacks on trade unions as illegal combinations, dubbed the Vice Society a "combination to inform". His substantive criticisms distinguished between outward compliance that could be secured by prosecution with the "inward reform" that was essential to any real moral reform. He challenged the hypocrisy of the Society's justification for not prosecuting rich profligates on the grounds that the poor commit their vices in public, while the rich do so in private.

The familiar objection to the use of *agents provocateurs* was widely invoked. This use of 'spies' had wider political ramifications and was a sensitive issue among Foxite Whigs and radicals mobilised around issues of 'liberty'. The use of informers caused internal conflict within the Society. For example, Zachary Macaulay, a key figure in the evangelical movement, cited scriptural authority, holding that it was never permissible to do evil to secure good (Roberts 1983: 169). Preoccupation with the regulation of outward behaviour could not guarantee a lasting reformation of manners. Despite some opposition from within the Executive, the Society formally renounced the use of 'artifice' to secure prosecutions, but the practice probably continued, since subsequent prosecutions of radicals relied on the evidence of agents.

Something of the flavour of the debate over the techniques of moral reform can be gleaned from an anonymous letter addressed to members of the Society published in 1804. The author, who was evidently close to the Society, argues that it would be suicide for the Church of England to become too closely involved with the Society's activities. He insists that the repressive enforcement of Sunday observance is likely to drive away many worthy people who have a generalised faith, but do not regularly attend Church services. The clergy and not the law should be the proper guardians of the Sabbath. The author repeats the objection to the "detestable system of espionage" employed by the Society and suggests, disparagingly, that the next step would be rewards for servants who inform against their masters. He warns against fanatics who are "blinded by their own zeal" (Anon *Letter* 1804: 61).

However, the tactic of suppression through legal prosecution was not without supporters. As late as 1862 we find the Revd W. T. Tuckniss urging that "the only wonder is that the Society does not carry on its operations with greater publicity, vigilance and efficiency" (1862/1967: xxxi). The Vice Society responded vigorously. John Scott mounted a distinctively paternalistic defence of the prosecution of the poor on the grounds that the Society's aim was "to extend the happiness and comforts of the poor by checking their destructive excesses" ([1807]: 18). It is those that lead the poor astray who are guilty of violating their liberties, not the Society that seeks to save them from vice. Scott rejected the charge of 'busybodyism' on the ground that it is not enough to lead a good life; it is also necessary to promote the spiritual good of one's fellow men. The charge of 'informer' is rejected on the ground that 'informers' gain no personal benefit, thus their conduct benefits both society and the individual informed on. Those who object to the work of the Society are "the friends of vice". He dismisses the "fears of the pusillanimous" and the "indifference of the lukewarm" (1807: 40). Yet this type of energetic defence of the prosecution strategy fades after the Society's early years and its activities become largely focused on efforts to influence legislative and enforcement practices.

It should not be thought that the poor were the passive recipients of the paternalistic moralising of their betters. They relished the scurrilous broadsheets reporting the marital adventures of those wealthy enough to afford the promotion of divorce petitions. Symbolically they took to their heart 'Queen Caroline'. When George IV ascended to the throne in 1820, his estranged wife Caroline sought to claim her crown. Popular representations, in melodrama and farce, rather than trivialising the affair, politicised it and provided the urban poor with a vehicle for their own caustic moralising through which the poor turned the moral order upside down and sat in moral judgement on their betters (Clark 1990: 52).

BEYOND COERCIVE MORAL REFORM?

The Vice Society was a project devoted to moral reform from above. As an elite organisation it made little attempt to recruit a mass membership, to mobilise potential middle-class activism or to address those whom it sought to reform. There is a marked contrast between both the Proclamation Society and the Vice Society and their predecessor the SRM. The earlier body had devoted great efforts both to fostering the ideological commitment and intellectual combativeness of its members and to addressing the targets of its reform projects. This ideological work was, as we have seen, couched within an exclusively theological discourse by means of sermons and a massive volume of publications. The SRM mobilised an undoubted intellectual energy in striving to engage the urban populace. In contrast, the Proclamation Society and the Vice Society made only perfunctory efforts to legitimate their project and to address the targets of their reform endeavours. Their tracts were content to assert the moral deficiencies of the nation and to repeat the self-evident necessity of suppressing immorality. They had no hesitation, during periods of heightened political instability, in becoming an extension of the coercive apparatus of the state.

Two inferences can be drawn. First, that the target which preoccupied the Vice Society was the political establishment, which was approached through personal communication rather than through the published word. Second, the failure to address its regulatory targets confirms that the lower orders were to be compelled to virtue rather than to be persuaded of the desirability of moral reform. Thus moral regulation in the early Victorian period was a narrowly conceived coercive strategy. Although the participants had links to the flourishing and expanding philanthropic movement, they remained distinct and largely unconnected projects. As a result, the Vice Society remained dependent upon the political elite, which would use it in times of political unrest as a spearhead against radical dissent, but never embraced the Society's wider project for a more extensive package of moral legislation.

The moral regulation projects of the second half of the Victorian period exhibited a more complex engagement with and reflection upon the relationship between moral reform and philanthropy. The purity movements of the later Victorian period, while they never fully succeeded in escaping from a paternalist relationship with those they sought to regulate, did attempt to build mass movements that penetrated more deeply into everyday life and consciously sought to communicate with their targets. At first, like the Vice Society, these new movements did so in the language of evangelical Protestantism, but struggled to find a new popular secular voice in which to generalise the project of moral reform. The new activists for purity were to grapple with the proper attitude to adopt towards the role of law and state regulation. Issues of interventionism and regulationism were to be central to the politics of the moral reform, which must now be explored.

CHAPTER 3

FROM SEXUAL PURITY TO SOCIAL HYGIENE, 1870–1918: VICTORIAN AMERICA AND BRITAIN

CONVERGENT AND DIVERGENT DYNAMICS OF MORAL REFORM PROJECTS

Moral regulation underwent major transformations at the end of the long nineteenth century, between the last quarter of the nineteenth century and the First World War.[1] In order to emphasise the general character of these changes, this chapter traces developments in both Britain and the United States; Chapters 4 and 5 explore the specificity of these national contexts. Behind the significant national differences and their discrete temporal dynamics, there was an overarching symmetry that spanned the Atlantic.[2] This chapter advances a number of general themes about the transformations of moral regulation movements in the United States and in Britain. This will serve not only to situate the national trajectories, but the approach also has a methodological dimension, that of focusing attention on the important underlying pattern that runs the risk of being concealed beneath the historical specificity of diverse social movements.

The decisive trajectory of moral regulation in the late nineteenth century saw the rise of a distinctive sexual purity movement characterised by a pronounced feminist component; this feminist purity current was then absorbed into a medicalised version of moral reform in the form of the social hygiene movement. This core process was thus to be identified as a transition from sexual purity to social hygiene. The term 'purity' designated more than premarital chastity and marital fidelity; it also encompassed a more generalised sense of sexual restraint and self-control and stigmatised all forms of non-marital sexuality, in particular prostitution. The prime target of regulatory activity shifted from prostitution, conceived as a moral question, to venereal diseases viewed as a medical problem. A subsidiary, but important, hypothesis is that this absorption, of purity into hygiene, cannot be understood simply as a victory of medicine over feminism, of expert men over activist women.

Paradoxically the account which comes closest to the thesis that there occurred a mutation from sexual purity to social hygiene is to be found in the radical feminist account advanced by Sheila Jeffreys (1985). But there is an important difference. Jeffreys contends that the radical feminism that was at the heart of the purity movement that fought valiantly against heterosexual oppression was only to become disorientated and subverted by the 'sex reform' movement in the opening years of the twentieth century. This, she claims, paved the way for the takeover of the purity movement by male doctors and a medicalisation which focused on venereal disease in such a way as to relegitimise male sexual oppression by seeking to make prostitution 'safe' for its customers.[3] This account depends on the conflation of 'sex reform' and 'social hygiene', that one group of male experts (sex reformers) can be equated with another group (doctors). I will show that these were in fact not only distinct, but often opposed projects.

My contention is that the shift from projects of sexual purity to social hygiene projects did not extinguish the discourses of sexual purity. Rather they lived on within the medicalised model that is perhaps best characterised as a medico-moral project. With the emergence of the medicalised social hygiene phase, women were again to play a supporting role, providing the moralising chorus to the main programme, and there were only occasional glimpses of a distinctive feminist position.[4] This important shift was not the result of any conscious plan on the part of any of the participants; neither male conspiracy nor feminist vacillation can account for the transformation. Rather it emerged out of a bewildering complexity of plans, projects, debates and controversies. It will be important to attend to the rich empirical texture of these changes without losing sight of their overall direction.

It is important to comment on my choice of the term 'sexual purity'. Most recent scholarship has adopted the self-selected terminology employed by nineteenth-century moral regulation movements. They used the term 'social purity'. It is significant that little or no attention was given to specifying what the term designated. This was not accidental; rather, I suggest, it was a manifestation of the prevalent euphemisation of the public discourses of sex and sexuality. The key phrase from which the term derives was the euphemism 'the social evil', used to designate prostitution. 'Social purity' was the normative response to 'the social evil'; it self-consciously differentiated itself from the other pervasive strategies for the governance of prostitution, namely, 'suppression' and 'regulation'. It is worthwhile taking the time to unpack the multiple levels of meanings and associations of the concept 'the social evil'. First, it enshrined the contention that prostitution was not one among many social ills; the emphasis was firmly on 'the social evil', stressing prostitution as the primary social evil, thereby insisting on the primacy of the moral agenda. In this respect it is significant to note that, in Britain in particular, the phrase implicitly marked the displacement of the long-standing preoccupation with poverty and 'the poor' as the primary 'social problem', which had been at the centre of attention. In important respects prostitution displaced poverty as the ill which characterised, symbolised and thematised mid-Victorian society.[5]

Second, 'the social evil' designated a distinctively urban phenomenon, one that marked out urbanisation as the problematic consequence of rapid and visible social change. One dimension of this social change, alongside urbanisation and industrialisation, was the diffusion of conspicuous consumption by the newly wealthy and an escalating class militancy from below. It was in this environment that the respectable classes sought to secure a semblance of social and moral order. Prostitution was made flagrantly palpable by street soliciting, brothels and red-light districts. The 'social evil' sexualised urban social disorder. The evil of prostitution was distinctly 'social' in that it ceased to be a private vice of 'fallen women', but came to be perceived as a vice that was both commercialised and organised, a feature that would later take on even greater significance as 'white slavery'. Third, the term 'social evil' captured a whole complex argument about prostitution as being 'social' in marking another feature of the traditional discourses of private vice in that it was the emblematic encapsulation of gender difference and inequality. As the discourses around the social evil reiterated, it was men who created the demand and women who provided the supply. The term was thus already available to take on a profoundly feminist inflection. Thus prostitution was especially important because it provided the primary context within which discourses of sexual purity developed.

In order to achieve some conceptual separation from the contemporary discourses and in order to be able to attend to the meanings and linkages which were enfolded within those discourses, I employ the term 'sexual purity' rather than 'social purity'. This has the added benefit, not merely of avoiding the euphemisms of the period under consideration, but in marking out the profound sense that, I believe, was known to all who used the term, that sex was not just at the core of prostitution itself, but encompassed the way in which the ills which beset society were perceived. The Victorians were not unique in seeing the troubling presence of sex as being at the root of social problems and anxieties. Other periods have grappled with their society and its perplexities by identifying sex as having something significant to do with their deepest tribulations. While I have some reservations about Foucault's dismissal of the view that the Victorians repressed sexuality (I will discuss this more fully below), he was right to draw attention to the proliferation of sexual discourses, even though he failed to attend to the significance of their euphemised form. More importantly, Foucault was correct to draw attention to the link between sexual discourses and truth-telling: "we demand that sex speaks the truth . . . and we demand that it tell us our truth, or rather, the deeply buried truth of that truth about ourselves" (1978: 69). As Carroll Smith-Rosenberg observes, "the radically unharmonious sexual and medical languages which nineteenth-century women and men constructed constituted an intense sexual discourse" (1985: 47). In order to keep to the fore the connection between sex and the forces that stimulate projects of moral regulation, I have chosen to speak of 'sexual purity' as the defining feature of late Victorian discourses of moral regulation.[6]

There have been other classificatory categories used. Most of them take a single dichotomous form, for example, pro-sex *versus* anti-sex or repressive *versus* non-repressive (Marcus 1964); an alternative suggestion is sensualism *versus* anti-sensualism (Mason 1994). I have avoided these dichotomies on the grounds that they have the effect of forcing the material into polarised moulds and inhibit attention to interactions and crossovers between currents that run within social movements. Alongside the shift from sexual purity to social hygiene there are a number of other general features of the moral regulation projects under consideration that distinguish them from their predecessors and which should be noted. First, they aspired to and, in significant measure, succeeded in becoming mass movements that mobilised the sentiments and action of significant sections of the middle class and even sections of the organised working class. Second, women energetically inserted themselves into moral reform politics and by the end of the century became the decisive intellectual and organisational leaders of most of these movements. I will go further and argue that the intellectual and political formation of modern feminism was inextricably bound to the ideology of sexual purity. This contention will acquire additional significance later when consideration is shifted to current moral regulation projects; then the earlier connection between feminism and sexual purity will play a substantial role in understanding our own times.

CONSTITUTING WOMEN, MEN AND SEX

Before considering the emergence of sexual purity it is necessary to consider the way in which its major elements – women, men and sex – were constituted in discourse. There was no unitary discourse, but rather a tangled set of elements out of which came together temporary and always unstable discursive formations which framed contemporary thought and practice. Great intellectual energy has been expended on the way in which women and sex, and to a lesser extent men, were constituted in Victorian discourses. Here I propose only to draw on this work to provide a composite of visions of women, men and sex.

The separate spheres ideology articulated a pervasive set of markers for both masculinity and femininity. To demonstrate its enduring role it is worth quoting at length the entry under the heading "Men and Women" in *Encyclopaedia Britannica,* one that held its place until as late as 1942:

> The man, bold and vigorous, is qualified for being a protector; the woman, delicate and timid, requires protection. Hence it is that man never admires a woman for possessing bodily strength or personal courage; and woman always despises men who are totally destitute of these qualities. The man, as protector, is directed by nature to govern; the woman, conscious of inferiority, is disposed to obey. Their intellectual powers correspond to the destination of nature. Men have penetration and solid judgment to fit them for governing, women have sufficient understanding to make a decent figure under a good government; a greater portion would excite dangerous rivalry between the sexes, which nature has avoided by giving them different talents. Women have more imagination and sensibility than men, which make all their enjoyments more exquisite; at the same time they are better qualified to communicate enjoyment. Add another capital difference of disposition: The gentle and insinuating manners of the female sex tend to soften the roughness of the other sex; and wherever women are indulged with any freedom, they polish sooner than men (1942: 577).

It will be noted that this classic proclamation of the doctrine of the separate spheres encompasses every dimension, physical, mental, emotional and even, somewhat coyly, touches on sexual difference.

Constituting Women

The nineteenth century exhibited extraordinary productivity in attempts to construct gendered identities. It is important to stress that what resulted were contested ideological constructions of the nature and character of women and gender. There was no unitary content to the notions of 'woman' that were generated; the images made use of diverse elements, some new, others reworkings of existing elements. As a result, what emerged never fitted coherently together and thus contained tensions and conflicts. However, out of these complex processes emanated a dominant, but never an exclusive discursive formation within which the persistent talk about women was located.

The construction of gender cannot be separated from the construction of class. A significant dimension of Victorianism was the self-formation of the middle class. F. M. L. Thompson goes so far as to characterise the whole Victorian epoch as the 'respectable society' (1988). Not only did the middle class grow significantly, but it became more thoroughly urbanised with the emergence of suburban lifestyles, undergoing occupational diversification with new forms of administrative, managerial and professional occupations. The middle class acquired for itself and identified itself by means of specific delineations of distinctions. Distinction is here used in the sense pioneered by Bourdieu (1984), with its double sense of distinguishing itself from others, from both the upper classes and the working classes, and accumulating marks of distinction, valued attributes that defined that identity. Perkin identifies the rise of respectability as "a radical effort to impose a new morality designed to support a new society; this was the revolutionary aspect of the moral revolution" (1969: 281).

By mid-century the cult of respectability had percolated into sections of the skilled working class that came to be designated as the 'respectable working class' and opened up a cultural and political cleavage between the respectable working class and the mass of working people. The percolation of respectability is evidenced in the expanding productivity of advice manuals; a significant increase in those directed at middle-class women occurred from 1830, and by 1880 ever larger numbers of such texts were directed at the respectable working class (Ehrenreich & English 1977). As we will see, many of the publications of the purity movement were cast in the form of advice manuals. Respectability provided not only the hegemonic lens through which gender relations were viewed, but it also congealed into the codified etiquette and euphemised discourses which have come to form the twentieth century's image of the late nineteenth century.

The key component of the self-formation of the middle class was enshrined within the ideal of respectability, which in turn played a crucial role in the construction of femininity. The cult of respectability came into being already stamped with a strongly gendered nature. The close associate of respectability was the idea of 'separate spheres'.[7] The ideology of separate spheres looks back nostalgically to an imagined natural division of sexual labour of the farm or artisan household. The work the Victorians had to perform was to translate those 'natural' distinctions into an urban and a bourgeois world. Thus respectability emerges strongly gendered. The masculine attributes of respectability counterposed an ethic of application, work, self-discipline and deferred gratification to idleness, indolence and self-gratification. As Ehrenreich and English argue, the ideology of the separate spheres that "carried to an extreme the demand that woman be a *negation* of man's world left almost nothing for women to actually *be*: if men are busy, she is idle; if men are rough she is gentle; if men are strong, she is frail; if men are rational, she is irrational; and so on" (1977: 98).

It is female respectability that primarily concerns us here. It had at its core a special relationship to the construction of womanhood encompassed by the ideal of respectable femininity and "the cult of true womanhood" (Ginzberg 1990; Welter 1966). True womanhood was characterised by the interlocking ideals of domesticity and motherhood. And here resided the deep enigma of the respectable woman, who on the one hand was valorised for the simplicity of her biological destiny, home and children. This primitive woman was conceived as close to nature, a healthy and natural being. Yet, on the other hand, middle-class female respectability manifested itself in a being that was fragile and sickly, a victim of nervousness given medical respectability as neurasthenia, that was viewed as resulting from the demands imposed by modern society.[8] Such a being was already available for presentation as a sexual victim. The coexistence of these dual elements allowed an enormous range of variation to the discourses on womanhood thereby facilitating a range of possible representations of 'woman'.

It is of special significance to an understanding of the emergence of sexual purity that the doctrine of the separate spheres designated the moral realm as the special arena within which female respectability manifested itself. Women were deemed more emotional and more sensitive, and at the same time were charged with the duties of bearing and rearing children. These elements come together in the idea of woman as the moral housekeeper; one significant component of this role was the task of being the moral guardian of the male soul. On women was bestowed the role of civilising the tendencies of men towards amoral acquisitiveness and immoral sexuality. Women's responsibility for the reformation of men was a central feature of what Elias has called the 'civilising process' (Elias 1978). In this way, the dualism inherent in the separate spheres mirrored the primary gendered distinction with regard to both sexual desire and economic values: male acquisitiveness, and female altruism. One significant result was that it injected a profound conflict into the heart of the family for, on one hand, it placed the mother rather than a father at its centre, but it did not displace the patriarchal headship of the father. In brief it installed 'the war over the family' at the heart of the nuclear family. Although it opened a fleeting glimpse of the 'companionate marriage', it could not envisage the democratic partnership.

Thus women were at one and the same time conceived as more civilised, more moral and more virtuous than men, but also weaker, more fragile and more vulnerable. Their female identity was pivoted around this duality of weakness and strength. They were credited with the capacity for shining moral strength, saintly devotion and exemplary virtue. Thus they were deemed to be both incompetent and competent, broken and whole, pitiable and commendable. This unstable dichotomous set of traits made possible endless nuance and variation in the discourses on women.

The central space within the creed of respectability was occupied by ideals of domesticity and motherhood and thus provided the explanation of why it was that prostitution formed such a persistent and evocative point of discursive reference in Victorian sexual politics. The prostitute was the radical 'other', counterposed to the domestic maternal ideal. The private world of domesticity was the reflex of the 'public' character of the prostitute who was 'public' in the double sense of being visible soliciting in public spaces and also public by virtue of her accessibility to a multiplicity of men. The 'fallen woman' was the counterpoint to the 'domestic angel'.

What Victorian feminism did was to extrapolate this pre-existing duty of moral guardianship that was conferred by the separate spheres ideology into the basis for a radical critique of male immorality. Central to an understanding of the rise of sexual purity is the fact that Victorian feminism operated within the discourses made available by the doctrine of the separate spheres. It harnessed the construct of 'true womanhood', and in particular the theme of woman as moral housekeeper, to the project of challenging male privilege. Lasch captures this paradox:

> It is an irony that the ideas about woman's nature to which some feminists still clung in spite of their opposition to the enslavement of woman in the home, were the very clichés which have so long been used to keep them there. The assumption that women were morally purer than men, better capable of altruism and self-sacrifice, was the core of the myth of domesticity against which the feminists were in revolt (1965: 53–4).

In a different register, Freud presented 'civilised morality', articulated through the ideals of chastity and innocence, as the expression of the "drastic measures" employed to repress female sexuality ([1908]). While for Freud this frequently led to traumatic sexual experiences in marriage and thus to frigidity, we also need to attend to the presence of other voices. Peter Gay's attention to letters and diaries provides evidence that the bourgeois experience was often sensually and emotionally richer than its public expressions attest (1984). In the United States Clelia Mosher's early sex survey revealed a divorce between the private experience of sexual pleasure and a reticence about its public discussion

(1980). It is important to insist that sexual practices and sexual discourses were distinct; what people did and what they said were different, as they are today. The encapsulation of both dimensions of sexuality within the doctrine of the separate spheres rendered sexuality problematic in different ways for women and for men. The absence of viable alternatives to marriage for middle-class women made radical demands for sexual freedom an unattractive prospect for any but the most personally and economically independent. Only monogamy or chastity were practical alternatives for most. In this respect caution is needed about imposing labels such as 'anti-sexual' or 'conservative' on Victorian feminism.

The discourses of the separate spheres provided the hegemonic discursive formation within which 'woman' was constructed. It was hegemonic among both middle-class women and middle-class men. This dominant motif of the separate spheres existed alongside an alternative and more radical tradition grounded on claims of equality. It is not that equality feminism is more radical in some absolute sense, but it was in the Victorian world because it was incompatible with the dogma of the separate spheres and the ideal of female respectability which it generated. One version of the history of feminism can be written in terms of an oscillation between the principles of equality and difference; the Victorian version of the difference principle was enshrined within the dogma of the separate spheres. It will be necessary to explore in Chapter 6 how the return to a doctrine of feminist sexual purity in the late twentieth century is underpinned by the resurgence of the difference principle along with an equivocation about equality in second-wave feminism. For present purposes the important point to note is that Victorian feminism mobilised a central feature of the dominant ideology of separate spheres through which to challenge male privilege.

Constituting Men

In important respects the discursive construction of masculinity was not constrained within the simple dichotomies of the separate spheres doctrine. Masculinity was not just a set of attributes and capacities; it was a project of self-formation. To be a man was to 'make' oneself into a man, of which the economic 'self-made' man was only one version. While this was often conceived in economic terms of entrepreneurial undertakings, it had a much more general sense of a striving for self-realisation and self-sufficiency; man as a private moral agent is engaged in the project of mastering his circumstances. While the quest for respectability was projected at men as well as women, respectability was a necessary, but not sufficient, condition for the realisation of the masculine ideal. The form taken by male respectability was less preoccupied with the prescription of conduct, rules of etiquette, dress, speech and deportment.

The key form of male respectability was the pursuit of 'character' (Cominos 1972). Character was defined by reference to a set of more or less fixed attributes which could be acquired through application and training: effort, self-restraint, perseverance and courage. Regimes built around strenuous team sports, cross-country runs and cold showers, that Collini describes as "exercising the muscles of the will", could develop capacities for fortitude, loyalty and other masculine virtues (1985: 35). Character formation and the work ethic require not only application but the expenditure of physical and mental energy directed towards enhancing the capacity for self-control. As Cominos observes, "continence in sex and in work were correlative and complementary virtues" (1963: 37). It is in this context that the condemnation of both masturbation and 'marital excess' begins to make sense as a dissipation of 'vital' energy that Barker-Benfield captures in the phrase "the spermatic economy" (1973).[9]

It should be noted that the image of man that emerged juggled with contradictory dimensions. On one hand, masculinity was outward looking: a 'man of the world', self-assertive and self-confident. On the other, man was a being beset by potential weakness, needing to keep his energy under careful self-management. He was a sexual being, expected to manifest a strong but controllable sexual 'instinct', yet at risk from sexual 'indulgence'. The ever-present danger of male immorality and sexual lust was a testament to this unstable dualism. Thus respectability was always potentially insecure, a surface of conformity, concealing the failure of self-control, lust and indulgence.

The significance attached to male self-formation resulted in the elevation of projects of self-control. J. S. Mill argued that the victory of civilisation required the victory of self-control over instinct. "Nearly every respectable attribute of humanity is the result, not of instinct, but of victory over instinct" (1964/1874: 46). Self-control required deferred gratification; and here again we encounter the mix of economic and personal virtue. The salient feature was the control of appetite, since weakness in any form led to immoral appetite and indulgence. Hence the place of food in reformation of manners and its association with politeness, respectability and cleanliness. There occurred an extension from conduct to bodies, with the gendering of delicacy in the female body and female governance of male appetite in its widest sense. As we have already noted, this conferring of female domestic responsibility had to negotiate the prior male authority as paterfamilias.

Female domesticity resulted in the transformation of the home into a place of comfort. Middle-class men were to take within the home the comfort and leisure that they had previously enjoyed in the clubs, inns and public house. Social intercourse became increasingly heterosocial; men enjoyed the comforts of home in the company of women within forms of sociability ordained by women. The rise of domesticity did not extinguish the older forms of public spaces. Men were able to move between the two realms, the traditional homosocial worlds of work and leisure and the new sites of heterosocial respectability.

Female moral responsibility for men took many practical forms. In its simplest form, respectability required women to avoid putting 'temptation' in the way of men's fragile self-control and obliged them to rebuff inappropriate sexual advances. Purity activists urged a further extension of female moral guardianship: with women increasingly in control of domestic sociability, they were urged to exclude immoral men from the cycle of reciprocal visiting. There was a marked reticence in some quarters about the implications of inhibiting male sexuality; the ideals of manliness and purity were potentially contradictory and there was much talk of the danger of 'effeminacy'. In a period when in Britain there were anxieties about its imperial capacity and in the United States there was concern about the national ability to shoulder a new quasi-imperial role, 'effeminacy' was much feared.[10] The preoccupation with 'nervousness' in the late nineteenth century was addressed by ubiquitous prescriptions against a "menacing effeminacy" that was to be alleviated by regimes for young men built around strenuous sports, cold showers and "the vigorous reassertion of male superiority" (Gay 1986: 337). As we will see in subsequent chapters, efforts were made by purity propagandists to reconcile purity and manliness. These tensions surrounding masculinity were of special importance with respect to the Victorian construction of sexuality.

Constituting Sex

There has been a remarkable productivity of work on Victorian sexuality and sexual discourses over the last two decades. In large part this interest has been prompted by the discovery that sex has a history. While this is part of a broadly based historical shift within social theory that has focused attention on the sociology of everyday life, more dramatically this sociological interrogation of sexuality has been prompted, or perhaps more accurately, provoked, by Foucault's *The History of Sexuality* (1978). Central to Foucault's initial project was his concern to displace the 'repressive hypothesis', which had come to form much of the historical self-consciousness of the twentieth century, namely, that the nineteenth had been an era of mounting sexual repression and that the twentieth century was engaged in the project of lifting that repression that was encapsulated in the term 'Victorianism'.[11] According to this orthodoxy it had become possible by the 1960s to celebrate a successful, though still incomplete, sexual revolution. The great significance of Foucault's intervention was that its revisionist disruption of the taken-for-granted forced a re-examination of the evidence on which the repressive hypothesis was grounded.

The reinterrogation of sex, sexuality and sexual discourses was Foucault's real achievement. Far from the repression of sexual discourses, he insisted that what occurred was a "veritable discursive explosion" with a multiplication of discourses concerning sex (1978: 17). This claim he supports by reference to opposing transgressive sexual discourses exemplified in the pornutopic vision of *My Secret Life* ('Walter' *c.* 1880/1966). It is axiomatic that no single discourse ever has absolute dominance and that every discourse requires the presence of other discourses to stimulate its expression. Where Foucault errs is in the inference that the existence of parallel or competing discourses refutes the idea that the Victorian sexual discourses were repressive. For while the discourses of sexual purity took many forms (pamphlets, sermons, tracts, advice manuals, medical textbooks, etc.) and circulated into every pore of the social body, texts such as *My Secret Life* circulated privately and probably reached an extremely small readership. Similarly Havelock Ellis failed to find a British publisher for his *Studies in the Psychology of Sex*; it appeared first in the United States (1899).

While I endorse Foucault's general theoretical objective of disrupting the equation of power with repression, this does not entitle him to refuse recognition to the fact that one of the results of "the incitement" to sexual discourse that he identified is that some discourses achieve a dominant or hegemonic position.[12] Once secured, such a discourse is then able to marginalise or exclude competing discourses and in so doing to become the common sense that 'everybody knew' about the truth of sex – a truth that was remarkably similar in the doctor's consulting room and in the drawing room of the middle classes. And yet this common sense was never entirely consistent. An important instance of the inherent instability in sexual discourses revolved around the issue of the consequences of male sexual continence. One major strand of both popular and medical knowledge held to the view that men 'needed' sex and that abstinence had harmful consequences for male potency. This position played an important part in sustaining the 'double standard' since, while women could remain chaste, men were deemed to require some form of sexual outlet. It is significant that, while one strand of the purity movement challenged this doctrine, another component gave it a different inflection by insisting that this 'fact' did not justify young men resorting to prostitutes, but demonstrated the desirability of early marriage.

The merit of the concept of hegemonic sexual discourse is that it carries with it the reminder that the formation of such a discourse always involves links with and borrowings from other related discourses whether sexual, moral or medical. Discourses change through processes of interpenetration by which new elements become added and others fade or are jettisoned. During this filtering process an emphasis may change, with the result that a different theme comes to the fore and becomes dominant, only to join with and be gradually submerged by some other component and some new line of development. In other words, discourses are never complete and self-sufficient or do battle to the death; rather they haggle, steal and swap elements. Yet for a time some stability may be achieved that, in turn, may be solidified by securing intellectual, political or theological legitimation. This complex process manifests itself in the late Victorian period when the hegemonic sexual discourse became gradually loosened from its earlier theological foundations and became predominantly a medico-moral discourse. For these reasons it is always necessary to identify from within the proliferation of discourses those that are dominant or hegemonic, without ever forgetting that such discourses can only reproduce their primacy in competition with alternative discourses. It is for these reasons that I defend a version of the contention that the hegemonic sexual discourse within which Victorians thought and spoke of sex was a repressive one.

One strong justification for the retention of this modified version of the repressive hypothesis is to be found in the difficulty encountered by an important strand within the purity movement that saw sexual ignorance as incompatible with purity and urged that young people be given sex education. Despite this realisation, they were so locked into the refusals and repressions of the dominant discourse that they were literally unable to write or speak the necessary words. For example, the leading American advocates of pure sex education Benjamin Grant Jefferis and J. L. Nichols open *Light on Dark Corners* ([1894]) with a polemical attack on books on sex that are so preoccupied with keeping the reader 'pure' that no useful information is provided. They promise "vital truths" that may safely be placed in the hands of any boy or girl. They provide a chapter on genital anatomy, with medical diagrams of reproductive organs, but are completely silent about the active processes of sexual intercourse, conception and birth. The sex advice manuals, produced in vast numbers in both Britain and the United States on either side of the century, were nothing more than purity tracts overwhelmed by repetition of the prescription of chastity. The repressive sexual discourse, suffused with sexual euphemism, prevented them from discharging their self-declared mission. Young people must still have picked up their sexual knowledge through the vernacular or entered marriage in ignorance. Peter Gay captures the plight of these sex educators as one

> compromised by a pervasive inconsistency: these calls for frankness are reticent; condemning euphemisms, they use little else. The hesitations of the reformers about their mission often overwhelmed them. They extolled purity and excoriated lust. They wrote about sex as a duty, with barely masked embarrassment (1984: 321–2).

In defending the thesis that the hegemonic discourse was repressive, we are still left with the question of how best to identify the content of Victorian sexual discourses. We should note the existence of a minority position, authors who saw themselves as sexual advocates who were forced to accept the label of 'free love' with which their opponents labelled them. For example, they engaged in a "battle over words" in an attempt to roll back the discursive sexual boundaries (Battan 1992; Sears 1977). But this does not justify characterising sexual discourses as simply opposed. For this reason I avoid the use of such binaries as have been variously proposed as pro-sex/anti-sex, sensualist/anti-sensualist, pessimists/optimists. I reserve the designation anti-heterosexual for the brief emergence just after the turn of the century of a radical feminism advocating that women refuse heterosexual intercourse. While the next chapter will argue that this position was not of great contemporary significance, it has assumed a greater import because of the appearance of a sustained anti-heterosexism in the more recent past.[13] But care is needed not to conflate anti-heterosexism with a more diffuse current, early exemplified by Mary Wollstonecraft (1792/1967) and recuperated by later purity authors, that promoted an ideal in which sex would play only a small part in relations between the sexes.

The Victorian hegemonic sexual discourse was never absolute or unequivocal; rather it was constituted of a number of elements assembled with differential emphasis along with occasional omissions or additional elements. The elements variously assembled were never merely the product of an inquiry into the differences between the sexes. Yet we do need to consider how it came to be that the nineteenth century witnessed such an obsession with sexual difference. The attempt to understand sex and the sexual body was always a commentary upon a wider set of social problems that came into sharper relief. It is useful to emphasise how large a part was played by an imagined natural relation between the sexes found in a natural sexual division of labour that was increasingly being disrupted by the transformations that may for convenience be grouped around the image of the Industrial Revolution, of urbanism, industry, consumption and domesticity – the whole stirred by a profound sense of the disruptions set in motion by an accelerating pace of technical and social change. This experience of problematic acceleration was epitomised by the mix of fear and excitement that was unleashed as the railways marched across the land and penetrated into the cities.[14]

In the imagined natural sexual economy, sex and gender were in harmony. Sex was always a set of social roles constituting what, in a different context, Roper has captured as the 'holy household' as a natural co-operative but hierarchic relation between husband and wife (Roper 1989). This relation is disrupted by the separation of economic activity outside the home, and as the home loses its economic significance, it is invaded by an ideology of domesticity. It is under these conditions that the differences between male and female became problematic and stimulated inquiry.[15]

One important feature was noticed by, among others, Elizabeth Blackwell, pioneer of women's role in medicine and major representative of feminist sexual purity. She presented the distinctive feature of human sexuality as being that men and women were freed from the rigid reproductive imperative of animals (1880). What is significant about this starting point is that it pointed in a number of possible directions. It would later ground an approach to sex which, freed from biological necessity, opened up sex as a realm of pleasure. For Blackwell herself, the significance of this biological fact was that it allowed the exercise of reason to control the sexual function and thus rendered it not merely a 'moral issue', but more significantly an arena of moral regulation. For others it served to stimulate the elaboration of the differences between male and female; and for many it made available both social and technical means to render sexual reproduction subject to conscious control.

It should be stressed that it was female sexuality that was the fertile soil on which sexual discourses were constructed. Male sexuality was less problematic. As we have seen, the male sexual instinct was regarded as natural, albeit beset by the moral imperative to exercise self-control. Female sexuality was viewed as much more complex and was, at the same time, much more closely connected with the doctrine of respectability. Women were regarded as having a natural inclination to desire children and it was motherhood even more than the married state which provided a meaningful, if limited, role at the core of the burgeoning domestic ideal. It was also regarded as natural for women to love and admire their husbands as prescribed by the separate spheres ideology. Yet women were deemed to be ambivalent about the sexual intercourse that was both a marital duty and the means to the status of motherhood. However circumscribed the roles of respectability and motherhood, confined within the domestic sphere, may have been, the ideology of motherhood and the 'domestic angel' echoed back and forth through bourgeois culture.[16]

The notion of respectable femininity was endemic, but it was taken up in a variety of different discourses in the promotion of a range of different projects. For this reason it is necessary to unpack the divergent elements of the sexual ambivalence with which women were shrouded. The ideal of respectability and domesticity held out the prospect of fulfilment in a warm and close relationship between husband and wife; but it was a displaced sexuality, not for the wife's pleasure, but taking vicarious pleasure from the giving of pleasure to her husband – an idea captured in William Acton's renowned pronouncement that "as a general rule, a modest woman seldom desires any sexual gratification for herself. She submits to her husband, but only to please him" (1862: 112).[17] Yet even here there were divergent currents. A discourse of sex as a wifely 'duty' carried overtones of a natural 'distaste' that the refined feminine sensibility experienced in the marital embrace. In contrast, such self-sacrifice was itself constructed as a pleasure central to woman's role. Thus Elizabeth Blackwell could assert, without straying outside the ideal of respectability, that women could find sexual pleasure within marriage (1885).[18] In an important respect modesty and sensibility did not simply inhibit or discourage sexuality, but rather titillated it as the coy prize of the decorous chase.

The ideals of respectability and domesticity lent themselves to an emphasis on the sexual innocence, purity and 'passionless' disposition of the 'domestic angel'.[19] Physical frailty became a visible sign of female respectability. The genteel wife, too weak to rise from her *chaise-longue*, not only displayed her own delicacy, but served to mark the vicarious consumption, to use Veblen's phrase, for her husband's capacity to support a household replete with servants in which his wife need do no more than manage the domestic economy (Veblen 1899/1967).[20] The case of invalidism illustrates what I term moral legibility, through which character can be read from signs provided by demeanour, dress and appearance. It is in this context that the polarisation of the images of the domestic angel and the prostitute should be understood. The roles provided by invalidism and sexual quiescence are ambiguous. It is undoubtedly true that many women secured more attention and may even have achieved more power within marriage as the agents of the cult of domesticity, but paradoxically these roles carried a certain sexual charge in that they heightened the pervasive consciousness of sexual difference by highlighting male vigour and female frailty.

Underlying these dichotomous conceptualisations of sexuality there is a reverberation of the responses to evolutionism. There was generalised adoption of an evolutionary view of social and economic progress. But the influential evolutionary ideas were only loosely those of Darwin; instead a Lamarckian view focused on the heritability of acquired characteristics that expressed itself in persistent ideas about the potential harmful effect on offspring of sexual lust on the part of one or both parents. These ideas, in association with a strong dose of Malthusianism, would surface as eugenics and, as we will see, were strongly to influence the social hygiene movement. But at the same time there was a refusal of Darwinian sexual selection. The equation of respectability and civilisation posited a radical separation of the animal from the human realm. The persistence of the medieval view that nature exists for the benefit of man and that God had ordained that man have dominion over nature found expression in a belief that equated sexuality with animality. The march of civilisation, widening the gulf between human and animal, would thus be manifest in a decline in sexual passion.[21] This struggle was also played out within every individual in the contest between the higher and the lower realms of human nature, between 'reason' and 'appetite'; the watchword became the quest to achieve control over the passions. It was to this theme that Freud gave a radical turn insisting that "civilisation is built up on the suppression of instincts" (Freud 1908: 186).

As we will see, this theme was picked up by the anti-heterosexual current within the purity movement while the mainstream of social purity insisted on a distinction between the proper function of sex for procreation and the improper use of sexual indulgence for pleasure.[22] From this period on there is a widening divide between purity discourse and an emerging discourse linking individual fulfilment with sexual pleasure that is most clearly manifest in the emergence of sexology (Birken 1988). Both Birken and Laqueur (1990) link this shift to a wider societal change from productionism to consumerism. Resistance to this change may play a significant part in explaining the re-emergence of prostitution as both a social policy issue and as a metaphor for sexual disorder that is captured in Simmel's account of the link between prostitution and exchange (Simmel 1971). Prostitution epitomises the negative construction of sexual consumption, while sexology began to affirm a positive image of sexual consumption. In Peter Gay's optimist account there emerged a divorce between the private experience of sexual pleasure and public discussion. He argues that it is not so much anti-sexual attitudes that dominate, but rather a petty bourgeois elevation of domesticity which comes to define the public discourse on marriage and the family (1984: 95). It is in the context of these shifting discourses that the sexual purity movement arose.

THE BIRTH OF SEXUAL PURITY

The distinguishing feature of the late nineteenth-century sexual purity movement was the feminist transformation of a traditional moral discourse founded on monogamy and heterosexuality. In effecting that transition some strands came very close to disrupting its heterosexism in the process of replacing the traditional 'double standard' by a 'single standard' of sexual morality. It is important to note that this 'single standard' was the restricted standard which had previously been enjoined upon women, namely, premarital chastity and sexual continence within monogamy. As Cominos demonstrates, both "virtue and vice were integrated in a comprehensive system of celibacy, marriage, the double standard, and prostitution" (1963: 228).

While this basic transition occurred in both the United States and in Britain, it did so within a significantly different chronology, the key difference being the different sequence whereby women came into the leadership of purity politics. For this to occur, spaces had to be won for the autonomous role of women in the public sphere. It was not enough that women be allowed to fill symbolic or mundane roles in forms of politics dominated by men, but movements had to emerge in which women filled roles as leaders, organisers and activists. In the United States women came to the fore early in the 1830s, but the proto-feminism that they espoused was never able to separate itself from the traditional discourses of the 'separate spheres' and of maternal feminism. The Female Moral Reform Society (FMRS) that was founded in 1834[23] attracted much opprobrium from the fact that respectable women should even be discussing the improper question of prostitution.

As will emerge in the next chapter, the FMRS slid slowly into a disciplinary form of philanthropy in running 'rescue' homes for reformed prostitutes. The result was that, when the sexual question presented itself again more sharply in the guise of obscene publications and urban prostitution later in the century, the predominant form of sexual purity politics that came to the fore was grounded in a traditional Protestant moral code that only underwent a secularisation with the rise of the medicalised social hygiene that came to the fore in the early years of the twentieth century. When these transitions are explored in more detail, it will be important to account for a second significant feminist strand with the sexual purity work initiated during Frances Willard's leadership of the Women's Christian Temperance Union (WCTU). Although Willard, through her slogan of 'do everything', attempted to integrate a range of feminist and temperance politics, the temperance focus was always primary and impeded not only the feminism of the WCTU, but also its influence on the purity movement.

In Britain temperance never became a central preoccupation of the main strands of reform activism that brought middle-class women into active engagement in the public sphere. The moral regulation movements in Britain in the early nineteenth century had permitted no place for women. As noted in Chapter 2, while women had eventually been admitted to membership of the Vice Society, they never entered into its inner circles. Women were to find a variety of routes to an expanding participation outside the home; the fertile mix of Protestant evangelicalism and philanthropy was probably decisive (Ginzberg 1990; Prochaska 1980). Aside from the important part that philanthropic activity played in providing an opportunity for engagement in public social action, it also left a strongly maternalist stamp upon early feminism by virtue of the patronising manner in which middle-class women related to working-class women, and in particular, to prostitutes. It will be important to attend to the significant but ambiguous ways in which feminist activists came to relate to other classes of women and especially to prostitutes.

In both Britain and the United States there was a discernible elective affinity between Protestantism, anti-slavery, temperance and moral reform. These considerations of the contributions of the cross-cutting currents of early Victorian life suggest that it is not necessary to choose a unique or privileged pathway to expanded female participation in the public sphere. In each of these fields there occurred a decisive transmutation of the doctrine of separate spheres which had long reinforced a rigid gender division of labour. Its major manifestation was an assignment of women to a private (domestic) realm and men to a public (economic and political) realm. The separate spheres doctrine both endowed women with being nearer to nature and conferred on them more developed emotional and moral sensibilities.

The association of women and morality was readily linked back to the more prosaic domesticity when women were ordained to have responsibility for the moral training of the young. Yet this distinctive moral identity of women also offered a form of intervention in the public realm on condition that the public dimension be conceptualised in religious or moral terms. This is the connecting thread that links religious revivalism, abolitionism, temperance and philanthropy. Each of these fields would be decisive for some groups of women and would operate more intensely in different periods and different contexts.

There is thus no need to assign priority to one route to participation in reform activity over the others. What was crucial was that the ideology of separate spheres, which superficially seemed to do nothing more than consign women to domesticity, provided both the impetus and the legitimation of an expanding engagement with the public life of the wider community. The activation of this potential had material conditions of possibility to which a daily routine not overfilled by domestic labour and child-rearing was crucial. This space was provided by some combination of urbanisation, changes in fertility and the availability of domestic servants for the middle classes. What needs to be stressed is that the presence of middle-class women in public spaces and public roles was a dramatic social change and that participation in moral regulation politics was but one of its significant manifestations. As Smith-Rosenberg observes, it was "through reform organisations, that bourgeois women escaped their home and familiarised themselves with urban and commercial realities" (1985: 156). In their turn, these changes gave rise to wide-ranging anxieties for both women and men about gender roles; these concerns would themselves become central preoccupations of the moral regulation movements by the end of the century.

Women secured an expanded sphere of action in arenas of social action that were linked to moral reform, such as the abolition of slavery and urban philanthropy. But it was, I contend, only in the British sexual purity movements that women secured, if only for a short period, a predominant role. The importance of the purity movements was not that they were mass membership movements, as were the trade union and labour movements of the period, but rather because of the influence they mustered at moments when moral politics coincided with episodes of heightened political or economic instability; this argument will be developed in Chapter 5.

FROM MORAL REFORM TO SEXUAL PURITY

The eighteenth- and early nineteenth-century moral reform projects considered in Chapters 1 and 2 undertook the reform of the morals or manners of troublesome strata of the urban classes in the name of an assumed moral and theological orthodoxy that was already beginning to fracture. In their early phases the sexual purity projects of the nineteenth century were similar. In the early nineteenth century the 'suppression of vice' was the talismanic form in which moral reform was couched and whose discourses drew on a presumed religious consensus even though there was no longer any denominational unity. They spoke the language of the providence of a deity whose wrath descends on individual sinners and immoral nations. The distinctive Protestant form of that doctrine was one which increasingly laid responsibility at the doors of the laity. It is not that sexual purity projects were in any simple sense secularised; indeed it is important to stress the predominant part played by evangelical Protestantism in providing not only the language, but also the wider frame of reference for purity reform.

What seemed to happen was that the religious framing of moral regulation discourses became increasingly conventional. Religion continued to provide the language in which morals were thought and spoken. The activists almost certainly remained motivated by intense evangelical sentiments, compelling them to an active concern with their own moral condition and that of their fellow citizens, in particular, those beneath them in the taken-for-granted social hierarchy which was presumed to mesh with a hierarchy of moral worth. Of particular relevance, the revivalism of the early Victorian period in Britain, but more intensively in America with the Second Great Awakening, placed special emphasis on women as moral agents. It was but a small step within an intermingled religious and feminist discourse that women's moral energy be directed against irreligious and sinful men.

The substance of moral reform projects came to depend less and less upon their religious framing and became by the end of the century couched in the language of philanthropy and social welfare. The passing of the centrality of religion in moral reform is epitomised by the displacement of projects of Sunday observance to the margins. By the mid-nineteenth century clashes emerged between projects to stimulate 'rational recreation' for the masses by organising outdoor concerts, sporting activities and the like, and traditional Sabbatarian objections. Although active Sabbatarian movements survived, the issue never again became central – not so much because religion became less important, but because it came to be treated as a personal matter rather than a collective definition of social cohesion.

The shift away from the suppression of vice to the rise of sexual purity occurs almost imperceptibly, but marks a new stage in which the moral domain becomes separated in important respects from the realm of religion. The project of 'suppression' proved remarkably tenacious; it defined the character of mid-century anti-prostitution and anti-obscenity activity and, significantly, it returns at the beginning of the twentieth century with the endeavour to 'suppress organised vice' and, especially, the 'white slave trade'. Thus the path to 'sexual purity' was uneven, but it is important to trace its rise because it marks a profound change not only in how moral reform was understood, but also in the politics through which it was pursued.

At the heart of the shift from 'suppression' to 'sexual purity' lies a fluctuating tension between attempts to coerce the conduct of others and undertakings seeking to promote the governance of the self. As the detailed accounts of national purity movements will reveal, strategies shifted uneasily between projects relying on coercive deployment of legal mechanisms and those aimed at eliciting attempts at self-formation. Earlier forms had revolved around a theologically inspired inspection of conscience.[24] During the Victorian epoch these practices shifted towards forms of working on the self that manifested themselves in the exhibition of self-control and character formation. Such practices also generated the experience of the "pleasures of self-fashioning" (Barker-Benfield 1992: 82). The demonstration of such capacities provided moral authorisation for attempts to impose external controls over others, whether it be the disorderly poor or the morally fallible prostitute.

A classic expression of pleasure of self-fashioning was in the multiple variants of 'the pledge'. Borrowed directly from the temperance movement, the purity pledge was initiated in England by Ellice Hopkins in 1883 through the White Cross Army. In 1885 Benjamin DeCosta took this proposal back to the United States, establishing a White Cross Army, and the Social Purity Department of the WCTU sponsored a purity pledge in the same year and coined the slogan 'The White Life for Two'. This use of personal pledges drew on the moral suasion tradition of the temperance movement that had used teetotal pledges since the 1830s.

At the heart of purity ideology was the critique of the double standard that authorised differential standards of sexual morality for men and women: chastity for women and sexual adventure for men. This was the element which gave the purity movement its distinctive feminist content. Most significantly it shifted the focus of moral discourse away from the immorality of wayward women and, I will argue, turned the spotlight on to the sexual immorality of men, and, in particular, on to men of the upper and middle classes. The purity movement did not advocate sexual freedom for women, but rather insisted on sexual restraint for men. It was in significant respects less interested in the sexuality of the lower classes. It is a quite remarkable feature of the Victorian purity campaigns that they were directed at the middle and upper classes themselves. In contrast, as we have seen, their forerunners had directed projects of moral regulation at the lower classes. I will seek to demonstrate in the next two chapters that the primary targets of the Victorian purity wars were upper- and middle-class males, and that the main thrust in both Britain and the United States was directed at fostering the self-regulation of the respectable classes. This feature has been largely ignored by commentators, who have insisted that the purity movement was, like earlier moral reform movements, directed primarily against the lower classes. Frank Mort is most insistent the working class was "the real target of purity action" (1985: 210).[25]

Care is necessary to avoid misunderstanding my claim. It is not that the lower classes were never targeted by the sexual purity movements. I will seek to show in subsequent chapters how the rise of a concern with juvenile prostitution and the age of consent from the 1880s marked an important displacement of the attack on the double standard towards the regulation of the working-class family. I will also show the significant role played by a distinctively feminist appeal to the organised working class in both the United States and Britain. Frances Willard's expansion of the purity work of the WCTU depended on a collaboration with the Knights of Labor. Similarly in Britain both Josephine Butler and Ellice Hopkins devoted much energy to appeals to the organised working class. The key point is that the significance of the campaign for a single standard of sexual purity was first and foremost directed at upper- and middle-class men. It should also be noted that the appeal to sexual purity was an instance of a 'dividing practice', serving to construct and reinforce the boundary between the respectable and non-respectable classes (Foucault 1982: 208–9). In this sense, purity discourses indirectly addressed the working class, but only in so far that they were on the other side of the dividing practice.

The purity pledge movement was directed predominantly at men. The sexual purity analysis viewed the impurity of men as the cause of prostitution and led naturally to the feminist repudiation of the traditional strategy of punishing prostitutes. It followed that prostitution could only be eradicated when men committed themselves to chastity and marital fidelity.[26] A central feature of the sexual purity project was thus directed towards the civilisation of male sexuality, the taming and curbing of the beast, bringing under self-control the lower animal instincts.[27] One characteristic articulation of civilised sexuality was the call for a marital continence that restricted sexual intercourse to the purpose of reproduction. John Harvey Kellogg was not alone when he enthused about the possibility that in future there might be "less animal love, but more spiritual communion; less grossness, more purity" (1877/1974: 265).

A critical issue in assessing the trajectory of the purity movement was its relationship to the overarching sexual division of labour that was given ideological expression in the doctrine of the separate spheres. If the attack on the 'double standard' was likely to undermine the 'separate spheres', then the whole network of the relations of family, marriage and gender would be destabilised. If, on the other hand, the attack on the 'double standard' was itself part and parcel of the traditional sexual division of labour and served to reinforce it, then its transformative potential was blunted. It would not matter if the critique of the 'double standard' merely invoked the familiar and thus safe grounds of the separate spheres as a rhetorical tactic. I will argue that the attack on the double standard relies so heavily on key elements of the separate spheres, namely, female moral superiority and female domestic sovereignty that far from breaking with the doctrine of the separate spheres, nineteenth-century feminism buttressed and reinforced this traditional non-feminist ideology. It is not that there were no voices that sought to escape from that doctrine, but they remained a minority voice with relatively little contemporary impact.

Men were not the only targets of the purity campaigners. Since adult males were likely to be already corrupted by their adherence to the double standard, much purity pledge activity was directed at boys, on the principle that if they could be persuaded to commit themselves to purity at a young age, they might maintain it into adulthood.[28] The attention devoted to boys meshed with the discovery of adolescence at the end of the nineteenth century. Not only did this produce serious studies like those by G. Stanley Hall (1904), but it also produced a veritable industry of advice manuals about the rearing and training of boys (Bederman 1995; Demos & Demos 1973).[29] It was also the period of the great expansion of the boys' club movement (Macleod 1983; Mangan and Walvin 1987; Springhall 1977). The most intensive focus of the quest for juvenile purity was directed at youthful masturbation; while this was tinged with concern about homosexuality, its major target was to establish the sexual self-control deemed essential for adult sexual self-restraint, and it was upper- and middle-class boys who were subjected to incessant moralisation and close surveillance (Hunt 1998).

It is important to stress the instability of the 'pledge' tactic. As with the moral suasion tradition in the temperance movement, it was always in danger of lapsing into a coercive response, just as temperance gave way before prohibition. As we will see, the purity pledge tradition was swamped in both the United States and Britain by more coercive strategies of moral regulation; the appeal to moral suasion survived only as a rhetorical gesture in movements promoting repressive legislation.

Another important feature of the purity movements was their shift from religious essentialism located in discourses of 'sin' and 'immorality' to a more secular environmentalism. In its most secular manifestations, moral reform merged into the broader stream of 'social environmentalism' epitomised by movements for housing and sanitary and recreational reforms. This broader strand of the social reform movement was in turn linked to the transformation of philanthropy into social work by the turn of the century. Yet it should be noted that moral discourses never disappeared, nor did the distinctive quasi-feminist content vanish. First charitable work and then reform work became a distinctive expression of respectable femininity. This constructed a role for middle-class women to extend the techniques of domestic surveillance beyond the middle-class home and into the lives of those lower on the social ladder.

With the mutation in moral discourses from a focus on 'personal immorality' and a fixation with the urban location of social problems came a preoccupation with 'commercialised vice' and 'commercial recreation'. One important consequence was the perennial, but fluctuating, anxiety about prostitution. In addition to its exemplification of the double standard, male immorality, urban disorder, it came to articulate a wider concern with social and economic conditions that forced women to resort to prostitution. This discursive transmutation was not just a shift of focus from the individual to the aggregate, but was part of a wider reconfiguration that has come to be identified as the 'discovery of the social'.[30] It is for this reason that one finds significant lines of filiation between the emergent social sciences and moral regulation activism. Thus Frances Willard actively sought out the co-operation of the American Social Science Association with campaigns around prostitution and the age of consent. In Britain important early victories in the campaign against the *Contagious Diseases Acts* were secured in debates in the Social Sciences Association. The early years of the new century witnessed the distinctive American sexual purity strategy of the 'vice commission' that spread from city to city and state to state. These documents freely mixed old-style sermonising with social science presentation of tables and statistics. In their turn they produced a new breed of 'experts' like George J. Kneeland, who went on to play a role in the shift from sexual purity to social hygiene that was in part an expression of the professionalisation of moral reform. A new form of expertise was also beginning to emerge proximate to but distinct from both medicine and the social sciences, namely, sexology. Attempts at the systematic study of sexual behaviour and the place of sexuality in society got underway in the 1880s with self-consciously academic tomes from George Drysdale, Edward Carpenter, Havelock Ellis and others. Their impact on the discourses of sex were to have little impact until the 1920s and 1930s. They were voices waiting in the wings, but ones that had little impact on any of the forces involved in the reconfiguring of moral regulation that was taking place.

The transition from projects to suppress personal immorality to the central preoccupation of the late nineteenth century with prostitution involves one of the most important paradoxes of the moral regulation movements of the long nineteenth century. The distinctive governmental rationality associated with the discovery of the social was the increasing reliance on regulatory strategies. The great urban reforms of the nineteenth century were invested in a mounting volume of legislative activity whether in the form of factory acts, public health acts, housing acts or the multiplicity of major and minor projects of subjecting problematic social arenas to conscious and purposive control under the imprint of a commitment to progress, reform and improvement. Yet while attitudes towards prostitution were within the same socialised rationality, perhaps the most distinctive feature of moral regulation was its deeply anti-regulationist stance. Anti-regulationism first emerged in Britain as a response to the belated discovery that the *Contagious Diseases Acts* (CDA 1864, 1866, 1869) gave police and local magistrates powers to order compulsory medical inspection of those deemed 'common prostitutes'. This legislation was typical of the 'scientific legislation' of the 1860s and 1870s: for example, legislation had required compulsory vaccination of infants against smallpox and made certain diseases notifiable. Yet it was the 'anti-regulation' campaign led by Josephine Butler that was to provide the momentum which made moral regulation projects a force to be reckoned with on both sides of the Atlantic.

It is significant that both in Britain and in the United States the activists called their anti-regulationist stance 'abolitionism'. Not only did this draw on the prestige of the anti-slavery movement, but it implied a positive goal, namely, a world without prostitution. At the same time they differentiated themselves from the earlier and more coercive movements for the 'suppression' of prostitution. Yet they never articulated a strategy to abolish prostitution that went beyond the call for male renunciation and 'rescue' work among prostitutes. For these reasons the term anti-regulation more accurately describes these movements than does the self-ascription of 'abolitionism'.

It is important to draw attention to the contradictory dynamic of the politics of the anti-regulationists. They succeeded in 'breaking the silence' and thereby allowed prostitution to be spoken of in polite company. They displayed contradictory attitudes to the role of legislation in general and criminalisation in particular. They advocated legislative repression of brothels, but seemed unaware that this could only have adverse effects for prostitutes themselves. In contrast, their anti-regulationism imported an anti-statist response which was, in principle, suspicious of all state intervention. They insisted that any legislation on prostitution was tantamount to state recognition of prostitution. Anti-regulation politics involved some mix of these disparate and ultimately unstable elements.

This intermingling of disparate ideological elements stands out as a distinctive feature of moral regulation politics. I will argue that a general feature of moral politics is that it can only be successful when some specific social problem is articulated in such a way as serves to mobilise an array or umbrella of different social forces. This condition for effective moral politics tends to involve a mix of conservative and traditional ideologies along with radical and libertarian elements. This feature is, I will seek to show, characteristic not only of the purity wars of the nineteenth century, but of the twentieth century as well.

The sexual purity movements of the final quarter of the nineteenth century present a fascinating tapestry of contradictory elements. Practices and discourses drawn from religious revivalism, a conservative commitment to a traditional view of the sexual division of labour in terms of 'separate spheres' and, at the same time, a radical critique of at least some components of the traditional gender order. As the next two chapters seek to demonstrate, these themes worked themselves out in distinct national contexts.

FROM SEXUAL PURITY TO SOCIAL HYGIENE: THE GOVERNMENTALISATION OF MORAL REFORM

The anti-regulationist movements of the 1870s, significantly feminist, became the base on which emerged the diverse purity movements of the 1880s and 1890s. The differing trajectories of these movements will be traced in the next two chapters. Here I want to draw attention to the extent to which these broad moral reform movements, organised around the slogan of purity, were already undergoing a significant transformation. By the 1900s an uneasy alliance between purity and a new force, the social hygiene movement, was in place. This alliance was struck under the banner of 'moral hygiene'. Its central characteristic was the displacement of the feminist core of the purity movements by a medical expertise that came to play an increasingly dominant role.

Although discursive invocation of an abolitionist rhetoric continued to be evident, the new alliance marked a dramatic, but often unacknowledged, mutation that had occurred towards a renewed regulationism. In both Britain and the United States the First World War hastened a process which resulted in the formation of an hegemonic alliance between the medical profession, the military and the state health administration, focused on the prevention and treatment of venereal diseases. By the end of the War the purity element remained as a discursive veneer, but in substance a full-blown regulationism was back in place. The question to be posed is not so much why this shift occurred, but rather how the sexual purity dynamic was so silently displaced.

However, before seeking to offer an account of this displacement of sexual purity, it is essential to stress that this process was occurring at the moment of the highest level of activity of the purity movement embodied in the 'white slave trade' campaign. This was a mass campaign in both towns and cities throughout much of Europe and North America. It was grounded in the supposition that there was an internationally organised trade which by fraud or coercion captured young women and sent them to work in brothels in distant cities. This phase of the purity campaigns also marked the highest level of influence secured on both the national and international stage. Major legislation was secured in both Britain and the United States and an international convention on the suppression of the white slave trade was signed by most major powers in 1904.[31]

The dynamics of the white slavery campaign were somewhat different in Britain and the United States. White slavery came to light in Britain in 1879–81 when complaints surfaced that English women were held against their will in Belgian brothels. It quickly became part of the campaign to repeal the CDAs and for the enactment of the *Criminal Law Amendment Act* in 1885. The campaign continued to build momentum and became increasingly internationalised; further criminalisation around prostitution offences was secured in 1912, including the symbolically important reintroduction of whipping as a penalty for male offenders. The 'white slavery' issue had passed quickly across the Atlantic.[32] It reached its peak in the United States with the passage in 1910 of the *White Slave Traffick Act* ('Mann Act').[33]

The imaginary edifice of the 'white slave trade' was actively endorsed by the medical profession and became fused into the social hygiene movement. The existence of the 'trade' had rapidly acquired the status of a self-evident truth. For the purity activists it confirmed the status of prostitutes as victims and pointed the finger at an emotionally powerful symbol of evil men, 'foreigners' to boot, who preyed on young women. For the social hygiene advocates it reinforced the danger of sexually transmitted diseases as a foreign importation. Its most immediate effect was to justify increasingly harsh immigration regimes of inspection and quarantine, particularly in the United States.

It should be noted that the white slavery campaign reached its climax, particularly in the United States, just at the time when the impulse that was to coalesce around social hygiene began to feel a strong urge to know more about prostitution. This was the age of the 'vice commissions' and the first attempts to apply social science techniques. The reports that resulted varied as to whether they made any claim to uncover the existence of some 'big chief' with international tentacles pulling young women into prostitution. This belief was so strongly grounded that absence of supporting evidence did not undermine belief in the truth of so powerful a myth. Its power derived from the centrality of the long-standing belief in female sexual *naïveté*. The dogma of the existence of malevolent prostitution rings made it possible to refuse to address the complex of economic, social and sexual elements that led women to engage in prostitution.

The crucial result was the displacement of sexual purity by social hygiene did not occur because of any overt hostility or even competition.

The doctors, epitomised by Prince A. Morrow in the United States, who worked to unite the two strands, viewed them as part of one overarching project of moral reform that was also a strategy to advance the national health and population. Rather it was the different rationalities of the two tendencies, which sometimes brought them together, but which in the long run would tear them apart. Sexual purity could pursue either a project for the self-governance of male sexuality or a coercive restriction on all forms of illicit sexuality. Social hygiene took a different course, which in an important sense lay in the middle of the two options that confronted purity advocates. Medicine in the service of a national health and population strategy functioned most comfortably within a regulatory regime.

Underlying this strategic difference were incompatible attitudes to sex. The pre-feminist purity movements were wedded to the essentially conservative project of a nostalgic protection of sexual 'innocence'. Keeping young people, in particular young women, away from any exposure to knowledge that might inflame dangerous sexual passion was the essence of the strategy. This strategy was embodied, for example, in projects to provide accessible 'improving literature' as an alternative to mainstream novels, which increasingly alluded to sexual themes. A distinctive feature of purity feminism was its recognition that sexual ignorance flew in the face of an informed and sustainable sexual purity; in addition it was incompatible with the important theme of middle-class purity feminism, that women should be able to control their own fertility and thus limit the number of children they bore. One important dimension of this question was feminist ambivalence with respect to contraception (Banks 1954; Gordon 1974).

Particularly significant was the attitude of the purity movement to sex education. In general the purity movement supported the idea of sex education and condemned 'the conspiracy of silence'. But it insisted that sex education must also be moral education. Here was a challenge that it was never able to meet. Large numbers of tracts were published in both Britain and the United States that were either written by purity activists or endorsed by purity organisations. Not one of them was able to get beyond the 'birds and the bees' to provide useful information about sexual intercourse, conception and related matters (Porter & Hall 1995). Dr Mary Wood-Allen, doctor and superintendent to the purity department of the WCTU, insisted that "the purpose of the Creator in the institution of marital relation can be fulfilled only when the two parties in the relation are agreed to make no provision for the flesh in thought, desire, or practice" (Wood-Allen 1901: 196–7). This sexual reticence reached even into the medical establishment: in 1885 the *Lancet* insisted on the priority of the "cultivation of purity" over sex education. Thus tensions existed between social hygiene and purity over what type of sex education should be provided. Purity authors focused on moral training at home and on the suppression of 'bad thoughts'. Some key figures in the social hygiene movement actively supported the purity discourse: Dr Prince A. Morrow, American founder of the Society of Sanitary and Moral Prophylaxis, came to the aid of the purity message by stressing that sexual continence is compatible with health (1904).

A similar tension existed with respect to sexually transmitted diseases. Effective medical prevention required accessible treatment. Yet both purity and hygiene strands practised a politics of fear and stigmatisation. Morrow and other medical experts were prepared to lend their authority to alarmist figures about high infection rates among men. These figures were further inflated by the anti-heterosexual elements in British feminism. Christabel Pankhurst, in her dramatic *The Great Scourge and How to End It* (1913), presented the majority of men as bearers of venereal diseases infecting their innocent wives and children. Purity voices promoted a view of venereal diseases as 'the sins of the fathers' and the inevitable consequence of male impurity, employing a rhetoric that was to be rehearsed again in the 1980s, this time around AIDS.

A significant contribution to the displacement of purity by social hygiene resulted from the increasing centrality in feminist politics of the suffrage demand. This marked not only a politicisation of feminism, but at the same time a marked secularisation of the movement. This process was much more clearly delineated in Britain; in the United States the culmination of the prohibition movement kept alive the association between feminism and moral reform. Less immediately evident in both countries was the extent to which purity politics came to be perceived as either an impediment to or at least a diversion from what had become the primary goal, that of securing votes for women. In the United States the persistent declarations that the very purpose of securing the franchise was to vote in prohibition served to reinforce male resistance. In Britain it was probably the heightened political radicalism of the suffrage movement that resulted in purity feminism appearing dated and conservative. Whatever weight may be attached to these factors, it is important to recognise that the victory of the social hygiene forces was a result of the tensions inherent within purity feminism.

The process whereby social hygiene displaced sexual purity was long drawn out. By the end of the first decade of the new century in the United States, the collaboration between the purity and hygiene strands led to the dramatic termination of 'segregated districts' in most cities. Yet the medical advances of the same period that were achieving effective tests and viable treatment resulted in greater emphasis on a treatment approach.[34] Particularly in Britain the movement for free and anonymous clinics made rapid progress during and immediately after the First World War.[35]

It was the change in the balance of active forces occasioned by the War that was the most decisive element in effecting the shift towards an administrative and medical model. In both Britain and the United States the military exigencies of restricting the number of troops lost to active service as a result of venereal diseases led to a revival of regulationist strategies. The vehicle was a partnership between social hygienists, drawn from voluntary associations, and representatives of the military and the federal government. The result was that the 'American Plan', formulated under powers created by *Army Appropriations Act* 1916, effectively reintroduced regulated prostitution, medical inspection of prostitutes and medical treatment of STDs. Similarly the regulatory system introduced in Britain under the *Defence of the Realm Act* 1916 (in particular Regulation 40D) effectively reintroduced a system of medical inspection and powers of detention almost identical to those first introduced under the CDAs of the 1860s. By the end of the War the balance had swung decisively in favour of the social hygiene movement, and this continued in alliance with public health authorities as mixed voluntary and state bodies. The social hygiene campaigns were classic exemplars of 'Progressive' social reform in the United States and welfarism in Britain: conservative in content, cautious in spirit, and fostering directed social change from above.

However, it is important to avoid a one-dimensional view of a transition towards a governmentalisation of moral regulation. Rather these processes involved a complex of different alliances and deployments of expertise. Alongside the increasing preoccupation of state institutions with the viability of national population policies, we should remember the other major alliance that centred on the family that sought to harness married women, with the assistance of the medical profession, who were invested with the task of rearing healthy self-regulating citizens. Underlying this governmentalisation and medicalisation of families was an intellectual technology concerned with 'race degeneration' that was manifested in concern about declining birth-rates (especially of the middle and upper classes) and infectious diseases (not only VD, but also TB). Its most extreme expression was in the eugenics movement. The concerns over the linked issues of population and degeneration had their ramifications on the purity movement and on feminism; the concern with health and population reinforced emphasis on women's nurturing functions. Concern, for example, with VD reinforced a perception of the dangers of sex; it reinforced the emphasis on female asexuality and relegated voices raising the possibility of sexual liberation to the outer darkness as dangerously radical ideas.

The shift to 'social hygiene' parallels a more pervasive shift from 'moral environmentalism' to 'social environmentalism'. Moral environmentalism focused on the possibility of perfectibility through self-control and the control of the passions. Particularly influential was a Lamarckian version of evolutionism, which held that immorality produced physical and mental changes that were transmissible through heredity. Social environmentalism shared a different version of perfectionism that insisted that under the right social conditions manifest defects of poverty, disease and immorality could be ameliorated. But these environmental traditions intermingled. Increasingly moral environmentalists came to favour programmes of environmental and social improvements through ameliorative legislation. Yet in contrast, the eugenicists in their ranks adhered to a much more geneticist view of evolution and rejected environmentalism since they denied that such changes could impact on genetic inheritance; indeed they held such environmental changes could exacerbate the problem by increasing the proportion of genetically inferior stock that bred. It will be necessary to consider the working out of these tensions within environmentalist, purity and social hygiene approaches in their specific national contexts. For the present it is sufficient to stress the complex dynamic that was at work in the transition from sexual purity movements to the social hygiene forces which pushed them by the early 1920s to the margins.

This chapter has sought to throw light on the dynamics of nineteenth-century moral regulation movements by viewing them through a comparative approach. This serves to lay the groundwork for an examination of the movements in the United States and Britain. It may be useful briefly to summarise the similarities and the differences between these national contexts.

Nineteenth-century moral reform movements in United States and Britain shared common features. A strong revivalist and evangelical Protestantism stimulated a preoccupation with sexual immorality focusing predominantly on the goal of suppressing prostitution; in particular this project focused on the dangers inherent in rapid urbanisation manifested in the commercialised vice of brothels and red-light districts. This focus was exemplified in the rise of a distinctively feminist social purity committed to an abolitionist or anti-regulationist stance. Distinct new targets came to the fore: juvenile prostitution and the age of consent revealed a central concern with adolescence. White slavery campaigns and their link to venereal diseases exhibited a recognition of greater mobility and massive shifts of population through emigration and immigration. The end result was a distinctive secularisation and a weakening of the feminist content as a social hygiene movement came to dominate.

In the United States the conjunction of revivalism and temperance stamped distinctive features not only on purity movements, but more generally on feminism. The critique of urbanism articulated by these movements was firmly rooted in a rural or small-town resistance to urbanism and industrialism mingled with a nativist and anti-immigrant inflexion. Furthermore, the anti-urban current was a reflection of the central question of municipal government, corruption and related issues.

In Britain there was a different set of features that left their mark on the specific content of the moral regulation movements. The minimal impact of temperance made purity a much more central focus for feminist activism; British religious evangelicalism had a significantly different dynamic from American revivalism. Purity politics were structured by the more stable form of party politics and greater political centralisation that focused action on the magnet of Parliament. Municipal government was much more a reflex of national politics, as was a party politics in which a labour and a socialist movement were coming to national prominence during the same period. The purity movement was a much more strongly urban project, or at least one which revealed only minor elements of a rural–urban tension. The links between the anxieties articulated in purity politics about national or racial degeneration were sharper in Britain; developments of colonial destabilisation, particularly in India, and then the emergence of inter-imperialist rivalry with Germany heightened these concerns. These comparisons serve to lead into a consideration of purity movements in the United States.

CHAPTER 4

MORAL REGULATION IN THE UNITED STATES: FROM SEXUAL PURITY TO SOCIAL HYGIENE

THE ROOTS OF AMERICAN MORAL REFORM

The early colonists brought with them from Britain a tradition which unproblematically linked moral and legal regulation.[1] Offences against sexual morality, such as fornication[2] and adultery, along with offences against religion such as working on the Sabbath, blasphemy and swearing, were part of the legal framework,[3] as also were a range of consumption offences such as drunkenness, tippling[4] and a wide range of sumptuary wrongs.[5] Two significant differences between this melding of law and morals in the New World and in Britain should, however, be noted. In Britain some division of labour existed between the common law and ecclesiastical law, but because of the role the ecclesiastical courts had played in suppressing religious heterodoxy, the colonists had no desire to re-establish a religious jurisdiction.[6] The legal enforcement of morality in the colonies was beset by the paradox that the colonists proclaimed the ideal of a separation between the political and the religious sphere, yet moral offences were subject to legal enforcement. However, the famous 'Massachusetts Code' of 1648, while distinguishing between the laws of God and those of men, contained a considerable number of religious and moral offences.

It was significant that the colonists arriving at the end of the seventeenth century brought with them knowledge of attempts at concerted action to enforce moral rules such as those practised by the Societies for Reformation of Manners, discussed in Chapter 1. Indeed the influential Cotton Mather recommended the establishment of societies for the reformation of manners along similar lines.[7] A few such societies were formed in Boston, but they remained small and died out by 1715. But this effort is significant in drawing attention to the social class dimension of attempts to impose a moral order; the early colonists brought with them a hierarchic view of social life. Much early moral regulation was directed at reinforcing existing class distinctions.[8] The Puritan goal of self-responsibility for conduct and thus hostility to prescriptive regulation existed in tension with a belief in a natural society of rank. However, the formation of civil society was one that exhibited a broad, if not always substantive, openness to projects of moral regulation.

During the nineteenth century the United States experienced two major phases of concerted moral regulation projects that, like so much else, were separated by the trauma of the Civil War. The first major wave during the 1830s was intense but short-lived. Probably the most significant moral reform movement spawned by religious revivalism, the Female Moral Reform Society, brought middle-class female activism to the fore long before any comparable movement elsewhere and laid the seeds of a proto-feminist commitment to sexual purity that would reverberate later in the century.

After the dislocation occasioned by the Civil War the next major manifestation of moral reform emerged in the 1870s. It was significant in that it existed in two distinct forms that coexisted in significant tension. The first was the movement associated with the name of Anthony Comstock and the Society for the Suppression of Vice (SSV, and in particular the New York SSV). Comstock sought to impose moral regulation from above through the coercive use of the criminal law. The second strand was a more diffuse network of temperance, sexual purity and urban reform movements. This revived sexual purity movement never developed the same mass basis or coherence that its sister movements in Britain were achieving during the same period and, as a result, was more short-lived. Yet much of the same intensity of female moral fervour that was channelled into the temperance movement manifested itself in the purity work that was an adjunct of temperance agitation. The distinctively purity components became fused with a medicalised social hygiene tradition. While the quest for sexual purity had been forged around opposition to projects for the regulation of prostitution, the outcome was one of the most sustained projects for the regulation of prostitution in the guise of the 'American Plan', which came under military-medical leadership during the First World War.

One distinctive feature of moral regulation in the United States that distinguishes it from parallel movements in Britain was the different class configuration of its participants.[9] In both countries the leaderships of key Protestant denominations played significant roles throughout the nineteenth century. Distinctive is the fact that at the same time a key role in the United States came to be played by the new capitalist plutocracy. The very wealthy not only financed a wide variety of moral regulation movements, but publicly associated themselves with purity projects. This distinctive feature is epitomised by the significant participation of John D. Rockefeller Jnr.

American moral regulation movements have received a distinctive treatment at the hands of social historians. There are a number of excellent studies of individual movements. Much attention has been given to the Female Moral Reform Society (Ryan 1979; Smith-Rosenberg 1971; 1985; Whiteaker 1997). Comstock and the SSV have been thoroughly scrutinised (Beisel 1990; 1997; Boyer 1968). The feminist influenced purity movement in the later part of the century has been less well served although the purity work of the Women's Christian Temperance Union (WCTU) has been thoroughly explored (Bordin 1981; 1986; Epstein 1981; Parker 1997). Much sustained attention has been lavished on the anti-prostitution movements (D'Emilio & Freedman 1988; Gilfoyle 1992; Hill 1993; Stansell 1986). The transition from sexual purity to social hygiene has been the subject of two significant studies (Burnham 1973; Pivar 1980). The 'white slave trade' campaign has also received careful attention (Grittner 1990; Langum 1994).

The literature that engages with an overview of the wider history of moral regulation in the United States is problematic. Two substantial studies exist (Pivar 1973; Boyer 1978). They are both marked by the strange omission of any substantive treatment of Comstock and the SSV. Pivar seeks explicitly to elevate the significance of the Philadelphian Quaker, Josiah Leeds, over Comstock, perhaps because Leeds' project was more 'positive', in that he promoted worthy literature rather than suppressing the obscene. Boyer's neglect of Comstock probably stems from his concern to stress a long-run transition from 'coercive moral regulation' to 'environmental regulation'. Plausible though this goal is, it is undermined by the remarkable longevity of Comstock's flagrantly coercive campaigns, which endured from the early 1870s through to his death in 1915. I suspect that both Pivar and Boyer's omission was motivated by a desire to demonstrate that there was more to nineteenth-century moral regulation than was encompassed by the derisory label 'Comstockery', with which many had been content to dismiss the whole movement.

There is a parallel tendency in most studies of American moral regulation movements not to attend to the relationships or their absences between the multitude of purity and social hygiene organisations that were active towards the end of the century. That the almost exclusively male SSV coexisted with the WCTU's turn to purity work deserves attention, as does the relationship between Comstock's projects for the suppression of vice and the anti-regulationism of most other purity organisations. Because the treatment of the individual moral regulation movements is so much stronger than the treatment of the overall trajectory of moral regulation, this chapter will focus attention on seeking to make sense of the multidimensional currents running through the proliferation of organisations and campaigns that rose and fell during the long nineteenth century.

REVIVALISM AND FEMALE MORAL REFORM

The waves of religious revivalism that swept back and forth across the expanding domain of the United States in the eighteenth and nineteenth centuries activated rather different social forces. What was significant about the 'Second Great Awakening' that, with varying intensity, persisted through the first four decades of the nineteenth century (1797–1840), was that it involved a distinctive form of female evangelical engagement. While couched in discourses rooted in familiar themes of maternity and domesticity, it expanded the ambit of these distinctively feminine virtues to the public sphere. Significant numbers of middle-class women were encouraged to see themselves as moral agents with a duty to purify a social realm that was perceived as becoming increasingly secularised. In its most militant articulations women came to perceive themselves pitted against irreligious men.

The emergence of the New York Female Moral Reform Society (FMRS) in 1834 was significant for its self-conscious feminism epitomised in the promotion of women in all of its activities, including its bookkeepers and its printers. This mix of feminist consciousness with militant and uncompromising Protestantism stamped the FMRS as a movement that broke new ground well ahead of any comparable movement. It should be noted that, given the difficulties associated with sustaining such movements, its survival for nearly twenty years was in itself a major achievement. It should be borne in mind that in England the evangelical revivalism was more pietistic and did not provide a platform from which women engaged with the male public sphere until the 1870s. Even more distinctive was the fact that the FMRS could deploy a distinctive anti-masculine rhetoric. It should also be noted that a similar distinctive feminism was manifest in the next major phase of revivalism after the Civil War that gave rise to the 'Women's Crusade' that launched the WCTU in 1873–5; the focus on closing saloons again pitted women against a dominant feature of male culture and sociability.

In focusing attention on the FMRS it is important to note that it was a more militant form of a complex set of other activities through which women came to engage with projects concerned with the reform of others which brought them into the public sphere. Revivalism, preoccupied as it was with personal piety and with the conversion of others, engaged in many forms of religious salvation intermixed with forms of social philanthropy. The bulk of activity undertaken was narrowly religious. This was the age of the tract societies and the Sunday school movement. These projects sought to awaken inner checks on behaviour to replace the community checks of a rural society. The messages disseminated in both rural and urban locales were full of a rural nostalgia that confirmed their conservative social message.

However, the belief that every sinner could be saved led some to engage with the prostitute as a biblically significant exemplification of 'the sinner'. But the majority adopted more prosaic targets for attention, of which the most characteristic form was the 'visits' made by middle-class women into the communities and homes of the poor. Christine Stansell captures both the adventure and the disciplinary character of these "voyeuristic journeys into the heart of darkness, the enthralling, 'unimaginable' sinfulness of working-class life" (1986: 201). Another outlet that was to have special significance for American women was provided by their entry in large numbers into the temperance movement during the course of the 1840s. Temperance work had a double significance for women touched by revivalism. On the one hand, it was another form of voyeurism, but one that allowed them a measure of identification with lower-class women whose plight was attributed to the drinking habits of their husbands. On the other hand, temperance impacted closer to home, stimulating and reinforcing their own sense of moral superiority over their own fathers, husbands and brothers.

What was perhaps most significant about these varied forms of activity would have been their impact not upon the lower classes who were their immediate targets, but on the female volunteers themselves as they forged institutional and ideological supports for their moral interventionism in a social environment that they perceived as unsettling and even threatening. Such activities raised problems not only about class relations and rural–urban relations, but also about gender relations. In Marx's words, the advent of modern capitalism disrupted "all the fixed, fast-frozen relations" in the course of which "the bourgeoisie has torn away from the family its sentimental veil" (Marx & Engels 1848/1976: 487). One result was that the household was left with only personal biological and consumption activities – eating, sex, sleeping, children-rearing and death. The unsettled conservatism of the social message of revivalism endowed domesticity with the protective ideology of the separate spheres of males and females and of 'true womanhood' (Welter 1966). Yet at the same time it tugged at women to take the message of this sanctified domesticity to the lower classes who scarcely had the means to sustain its comforting conformity.

The immediate roots of the first female reform effort lay in two more traditional moral reform movements. In 1833 the American Society for

Promoting the Observance of the Seventh Commandment ('Seventh Commandment Society') was formed by males of the extreme wing of the evangelical movement, supporters of Charles Grandison Finney.[10] Arthur Tappan, wealthy backer of revivalist causes, had founded the New York Magdalen Society in 1831, to 'save' prostitutes through religious conversion.[11] The tactic of men approaching prostitutes proved problematic and women, often the wives of revivalist preachers, took over this role. Thus it was that the FMRS was established with Lydia Andrews Finney, the wife of Charles Grandison Finney, as Director and John R. McDowall as agent.

Starting out from a narrow concern with 'saving' prostitutes, the FMRS pioneered the tactic of visiting brothels to hold prayer meetings. Realising that such activity discouraged male patrons, the FMRS repeatedly threatened to publish the identity of customers. The furthest it seems to have gone was to publish in its journal, *The Advocate of Moral Reform*, the initials of patrons and their home towns. It also opened a rescue home for reformed prostitutes, but like so many other such ventures it soon foundered largely because the FMRS was unable to envisage a role for such women other than as domestic servants, which was so often the restrictive role that the women had left for the precarious advantages of the brothel. Despite this inauspicious early experience, the FMRS was to become the dominant moral reform organisation of the early Victorian period. The membership base of the FMRS was widely dispersed through New York State. Much early effort was devoted to the formation of auxiliary societies. By 1835 there were five in NYC and twenty-eight outside the city; this pattern persisted with seventy-five per cent of auxiliaries in rural areas. By 1841 there were 555 auxiliary societies with 50,000 members and a circulation of *The Advocate* of 30,000 bi-monthly across New England (Ginzberg 1990: 230).

In order to understand the role of the FMRS, it is necessary to note a tension between its discourses and its practices. Its discourses were directed against the double standard and 'licentious men'. There was much emphasis on the necessity of wives and mothers controlling sociability through their ability to exclude licentious males from respectable society. A second theme concentrated on the moral education of the young with an emphasis on the key role of 'mothers'. This education had a stern Puritan tone:

> Teach them self-denial, by mortifying as far as possible, the desire of the flesh, or the propensity to seek happiness in the gratification of the senses . . . by inspiring them early with a love of plainness and modesty and a contempt for finery.[12]

The general tone of *The Advocate* revealed a deep bitterness and hostility towards the power, privileges and immorality of men.[13] The FMRS encountered much criticism on the grounds that these women were stepping outside their proper sphere. It responded by insisting that moral reform was pre-eminently the concern of wives and mothers, making them responsible for the moral tone of society. In substance it worked within an ideology of the separate spheres while expanding its boundaries.

A significant glimpse of early local activity of the FMRS can be glimpsed from Ryan's (1979) study of the chapter in Utica, Oneida County, NY. Involving both upper- and middle-class women, it focused its energy on adultery and seduction. Utica was growing rapidly with an influx of young unsupervised men and women seeking employment in nearby factories. The presence of many single young women living away from their homes prompted the concern with seduction; the chapter successfully brought a male employer to trial for sexually exploiting a young female employee. It was instrumental in securing the adoption of anti-seduction laws in New York and Massachusetts.[14] Anti-seduction laws resulted in a paradoxical reversal of the double standard; it was males who were the villains to be penalised, while their consenting partners were treated as innocent victims. The most enduring targets were young male clerks and apprentices who were frequently accused of seducing innocent young women. The FMRS tried to impose responsibility on employers for overseeing the private lives of their clerks. Significantly the clerks rallied against attempts at paternalistic surveillance and the zealotry of female reformers.

This concern with the sexual behaviour of the young and unmarried was not just directed at incomers. Ryan is probably correct in thinking that the anxieties of the FMRS activists also spoke of their concern to 'protect' their own children. Their discourse shifted focus from efforts to impose external controls on sexuality to the promotion of an internalised repression of physical drives and the eradication of all unchaste feelings and licentious habits. Elsewhere local FMRS focused attention on prostitution in a distinctly repressive manner; for example, the Rochester local FMRS informed on prostitutes to the authorities and complained when insufficient action was taken. While the social base of the FMRS was rural, the societies increasingly turned their gaze and then their activity towards the cities. Observed from the small towns of rural New England, the large cities transgressed their most cherished values. They looked like "Sodoms and Gomorrahs of sexual excess and sybaritic indulgence, Babels of conflicting languages, religions, and customs, chaotic, ungovernable, the great cities epitomised the foreign, unknown, and the dangerous" (Smith-Rosenberg 1985: 172).

The moral reformism of the FMRS had faded by the mid-1840s as it became entangled in the contradictions of its own propaganda. In challenging the 'double standard' it came to celebrate a domestic feminine stereotype and a belief in female moral superiority. The preoccupation with sexual propriety in the end prescribed complete reticence about sexual matters. Women were deemed to be sexual victims, morally virtuous, but strangely handicapped when it came to withstanding onslaughts on their purity; men were the personifications of animality and lust. The moral code they promoted imposed stringent sexual repression on their own sex. One manifestation of female moral superiority left women stranded in the isolated private sphere of domesticity which they had themselves done so much to cultivate. "In the last analysis, Victorian women were guided into domestic confinement by members of their own sex" (Ryan 1979: 82). But this same claim opened up a route to engagement with a world outside the home; for while their moral strength was focused on their familial roles it also extended, as Elizabeth Blackwell expressed it, "to all the weak and suffering wherever found" (1885: 6). It was this facet that was taken up by women reformers in projects of moral and social regulation of prostitutes, poor women, abandoned children and others of the weak and suffering.

The practices of the FMRS underwent a gradual but profound shift. It launched a radical onslaught on the sexual dangers that came along with the rise of capitalism and the urbanism and wage-labour it brought with it. As Smith-Rosenberg notes, the activists "rationalised their experiences of radical economic and institutional change, the emergence of a new class structure, and the rise of cities in the language of female protest against male sexual exploitation" (1985: 21). Yet by the end of the 1840s they ended up as little more than a subdued domestic missionary version of philanthropy, a maternal feminism directed towards the urban working-class and immigrant communities.[15] In the larger towns and cities they pursued domestic missionary work among the poor. Gradually there occurred a shift towards rendering aid to the 'deserving' poor through the provision of food, clothing and aid in finding employment. It should be noted that the 'deserving' tended to be constructed in a sectarian manner, being limited to those with evangelical Protestant backgrounds. Important though this transformation was for the growth of social welfare in the United States, it is significant that in little more than a decade the high hopes for a moral revolution had been put aside. This change was exemplified in the change of name to the American Female Guardian Society in 1849. With the fading of the FMRS in the late 1840s no significant moral reform movement emerged until after the Civil War.

DIVERGENT PROJECTS: ANTI-OBSCENITY CAMPAIGNS AND THE RISE OF SEXUAL PURITY MOVEMENTS

The Obscene and the Prostitute

There occurred a significant bifurcation in morality movements in the period after the Civil War. They are most easily separated by their different targets. One side is focused upon projects to suppress obscenity. Its most important embodiment was Anthony Comstock's Society for the Suppression of Vice that attacked the publication of obscene images and went on to attack contemporary European novels through remorseless campaigns of prosecution frequently relying on blatant entrapment tactics. In another manifestation the attack was directed at a broader range of popular literature, in particular newspapers, and sought to promote 'pure literature'. The key figure was Josiah Leeds, who targeted the popular press and crime and policing reporting. The most significant and far-reaching development occurred when the WCTU's 'Purity in Literature' department mounted a successful campaign to impose self-censorship on newspapers and publishers which culminated in the 'pure press code' entered into by the National Editorial Association in 1895.

It should also be noted that Leeds, Comstock and others launched a broad 'reform of popular culture' campaign directed against the popular recreations of the urban masses: campaigns succeeded in stopping most prize-fighting, and had some success in restricting gambling and horse-racing, and also in controlling vaudeville. It should not be thought that Comstock's tactics were exclusively coercive and that Leeds was more moderate; there was a significant convergence, for while Comstock attacked high culture in the form of the female nude, Leeds sought to indict ballet on the grounds that its costumes were tantamount to nudity.

The project of suppressing obscenity is a powerful demonstration of the moral implications of the revolutions brought about by the advance of print technology. Ever cheaper print costs greatly expanded the range of literature available for mass consumption. This expanding range included works which catered to scandal and sensationalism especially when embellished with a dose of sexual material. This association between sexual material and print was enhanced by what Walter Benjamin so appropriately termed 'mechanical reproduction' that made possible the mass production of images (1936/1969: 217–51). One significant form was reprints of classic nudes that had previously been confined to the preserve of the art gallery. Comstock revealed the class content of his project by differentiating the response of cultivated eyes that he argued viewed a nude quite differently from the untutored eyes of common people (1887: 8–9).

The second strand, mirroring parallel developments in Britain, was focused upon the problem of prostitution. From the late 1860s a series of campaigns taking a variety of organisational expressions resisted the spread of regulated prostitution. Its discourse drew on the abolitionist experience of the anti-slavery struggles. Anti-regulationism came to exhibit an increasingly explicit feminism and large-scale middle-class female activism which increasingly broadened its targets during the 1880s to emerge as a wide-ranging and diverse sexual purity movement.

Following hard on the dislocations and population movements of the Civil War, urban prostitution had become more visible. This in itself does not explain why it should have become the focus of moral political concern. From the late 1860s, with fluctuations in intensity, prostitution persisted as a target of concern until the end of the First World War. Urbanisation brought with it a series of pervasive social changes – in particular changes that made towns and cities more anonymous and populated them with increasing numbers of unattached young women and young men, and housed a growing proportion of the population in tenement buildings. At the same time significant shifts were taking place in gender relations; these had different effects in different social classes. For the middle classes and increasingly for the 'respectable' working class, the cult of domesticity came to its fullest development. As long as there was a ready supply of female domestic servants, middle-class wives were separated from productive activity both inside and outside the home, only to be imprisoned within the domestic realm, while acquiring greater control within the household as the gulf between the public and private spheres widened. The doctrine of the separate spheres, social respectability and the moral superiority of women were direct results of these changes in gender relations, and in their turn reinforced, valorised and institutionalised them.

Prostitution thus invoked and resonated with these themes of urban disorder, the separation of male and female fields of activity, and increasingly differentiated moral discourses. These elements, when mixed with powerful evangelical preoccupation with the saving of sinners, made the prostitute and the social spaces she occupied generate an eroticisation of public space (Stansell 1986: 184). The prostitute became a powerful and emotive symbol of these worrying changes in social and gender relations; she became "a master symbol, a code word for a wide range of anxieties" (Connelly 1980: 6).

One response of the upper- and middle-class political elites, who were of course almost exclusively male, tended to be sympathetic to efforts to regulate prostitution. This involved a resignation to the inevitability of prostitution under urban conditions and shifting populations. The core of regulationist thought was to minimise urban disorder and to view prostitution not so much as a moral question, but as a social order and health issue that could be addressed by a combination of two elements: first, the spatial regulation of prostitution (for example, in 'red-light districts') through the registration of prostitutes, which was a prerequisite of the second element, an inspection strategy whose logic focused exclusively on the prostitute as the bearer and disseminator of venereal diseases and thus as the target of medical inspection.

The anti-regulationist movement drew a sharp distinction between strategies designed to control prostitution and those directed at the elimination of prostitution. The social and moral discourses which found their sharpest articulation in revivalism generated a perfectionist frame of mind. Not only could the prostitute herself be saved, but the social and moral environment could be transformed such that a society without prostitution was achievable. Thus a significant shift had occurred in the underlying presuppositions about the nature of prostitution. Traditional moral regulation projects spoke of "suppressing prostitution" in a quite literal sense: prostitutes were the primary target; prostitutes were sinful women who were the primary cause of prostitution.[16] Prostitutes were to be given the option of disciplinary reform in austere rescue homes or punished (or, at least, driven away) by means of a complex battery of criminal sanctions.[17] The anti-regulationists gradually came to distinguish themselves from the suppression strategy; but for a long time the term suppression was used to refer to the suppression of the conditions that engendered prostitution. Two key changes were involved: first, if prostitutes were the supply side it was the demand generated by male sexuality that was primary, and second, prostitution, like so much else, was becoming increasingly commercialised, with the result that attention was increasingly shifted to the brothel-keepers, madams, pimps and cadets, who were the primary commercial beneficiaries. This shift led naturally to a view of the prostitute as victim and in particular to a focus upon the conditions which impelled women to sell their bodies. Thus the discourses of prostitution shifted towards a preoccupation with 'seduction', false promises of marriage, entrapment and, at the end of this line of thought, the victims of 'white slavery', with its image of capture, torture, imprisonment and sexual coercion.[18]

It was this double shift, the focus on male sexual exploitation and commercialisation, that caused the discourses of prostitution to take on a distinctive feminist content and opened up a transformed moral regulation project centred on sexual purity. One of the most important consequences of these transformations in the construction of prostitution was that middle-class female reformers faced the challenging task of reinterpreting the link between their own prized respectability and the victimised prostitute. It is important to stress the ambiguities in this relationship. There was a courageous solidarity, that in the twentieth century would be called sisterhood, which flew in the face of euphemisation of all matters sexual and drew hostility to any mention of prostitution, 'the conspiracy of silence'. On the other hand, however, there was a strong sense of class distinction that stood between the feminist reformers and the prostitutes. It manifested itself sharply in the rescue projects that were a part of so many reform projects; a middle-class maternalism could imagine nothing other than training as domestic servants for ex-prostitutes. Only very occasional voices included tentative calls for better pay for the young women who came to the cities in search of jobs. Class respectability asserted itself again over the contentious issue of the part played by the 'love of finery' as an explanation for entry into prostitution. Elegantly, if severely, dressed matrons viewed the quest by working women for some escape from everyday cheerless clothes as a symptom of idleness and moral laxity (Valverde 1989). This issue came to the fore after the discursive invention of 'charity girls', who engaged in sexual activity in return for presents and treats; such behaviour was soon recoded as 'casual prostitution' (Peiss 1983).

The Suppression of Obscenity

Comstock has been the target of much justified vilification, but has only recently received serious attention (Beisel 1990; 1997). Nicola Beisel's work has been directed at seeking to understand why it was that obscenity provided a target for campaigns of coercive moral regulation that secured significant support from the urban upper and middle classes in the late nineteenth century. Beisel's key claim is that class support for anti-obscenity projects in Victorian America manifested a concern to protect the sons of the upper and middle classes (1997: 9).[19] She pays relatively little attention to the significance of the challenge posed by the expansion of the print medium discussed above. Her focus is on explaining the source of the anxieties which focused on obscene materials.

Beisel makes good use of the expanded account of the cultural dimensions of class reproduction advanced by Pierre Bourdieu. The family reproduction of class position requires parents to concern themselves with securing the socio-economic position of their offspring (Bourdieu & Passeron 1977). This family reproduction was both material and symbolic: the middle classes, in contrast to the upper class, had limited economic capital to pass to their children, and were thus much preoccupied with the transmission of cultural capital ('character', 'respectability' and qualifications). As a result they experienced persistent anxiety about their children; at home they sought to subject their children to disciplinary controls and in the wider social context were concerned about anything that might affect the life-chances of their offspring. It was here that exposure to obscenity (and to allied urban dangers such as gambling and billiards) might lead their sons away from a secure economic future and social respectability. These anxieties were represented by obscenity, perceived as a threat to social and sexual respectability, and were articulated alongside a fear of growing immigrant populations, who were a powerful reminder of the problematic changes sweeping the country and who, in the rhetoric of Comstock and other reformers, were represented as the cause, rather than the symptom, of these changes.[20]

Many facets of the activities of the SSV suggest that it was something of an historical anachronism. I suggest that it shared much in common with the earlier Societies for Reformation of Manners in Britain, with its heavy reliance on a coercive conception of the project of suppressing vice through the use of legal coercion against relatively weak and vulnerable targets. It was this conception of suppression, rather than any defect in Comstock's character, that stamped the strategy of the SSV as a coercion to virtue. In an important sense, the *ante bellum* FMRS was in significant respects more 'modern' than Comstock's SSV. It is significant that the SSV made no effort to draw women into its work despite the success of the campaigns initiated by the FMRS in earlier decades and the contemporary success of the WCTU in extending women's role from moral guardians in the home to the policing of public morality.[21] Although Comstock himself remained active into the twentieth century in seizing and prosecuting obscenity and, increasingly, materials advocating contraception, his activity relied on his ability to mobilise official resources and lacked the popular support he had once commanded. By the turn of the century the new wave of distinctively purity forces avoided offers of help from Comstock.

From Anti-Regulationism to Sexual Purity

In addition to the attempts to introduce regulated prostitution in a number of cities, the stimulus for an anti-regulation opposition in the United States cities owed much to developments across the Atlantic. Starting in 1864, a series of *Contagious Diseases Acts* had been introduced, gradually expanding compulsory medical inspection of prostitutes in areas surrounding army or naval bases. By 1869 a vigorous female opposition had emerged that will be examined in the next chapter. With remarkable rapidity the movement was internationalised; emissaries toured Europe, North America and Australasia, leaving behind them anti-regulationist movements.

Proposals to regulate prostitution in the United States had emerged in the late 1860s. In 1867 the New York state legislature debated a Bill proposed by Judge Charles Folger to regulate prostitution; the first significant opposition came from the leading women's suffrage campaigner Susan B. Anthony. A critical turning point proved to be the introduction in 1870 in St Louis of a scheme to introduce regulated prostitution. This local ordinance, the 'Social Evil Ordinance', provided for the registration and inspection of prostitutes with provision for the compulsory confinement of women with venereal diseases. A handful of other cities passed regulation ordinances but avoided the battles that beset St Louis. Opposition was led by William Greenleaf Eliot, who emerged as a national figure, and the battle over St Louis became a key reference point (Burnham 1971). Anti-regulation campaigns sprang up in Chicago and New York in the early 1870s. By 1877 anti-regulationists had established a national co-ordination body with Aaron Macy Powell, an old abolitionist, as leader. By the early 1880s local movements had staved off the introduction of regulated prostitution in most of the country. The anti-regulation movement pursued the significant legal tactic of seeking what came to be called 'red light abatement' laws that permitted private citizens to initiate actions against brothels as 'private nuisances'. This allowed anti-vice activists to act when they deemed local officials and police to be reluctant to act against prostitution.[22]

The anti-regulationist movement itself lacked an alternative strategy. This gap was most immediately filled by the already existing practice of the 'rescue' of prostitutes which, as we have already seen, fitted the preoccupation of evangelicalism with saving souls. Yet 'rescue' was already a failure; great efforts were made to bring 'fallen women' into homes, but the success rates always disappointed the reformers. It is a classic instance of the persistence of failure leading not to the abandonment of failed projects of governance, but to renewed attempts; as Rose observes: "whilst government is a perpetually 'failing' activity, the will to govern is eternally optimistic" (Rose 1994: 378). The literature of the moral reform movement was full of reports of the opening and early closure of rescue homes.[23]

AMERICAN SEXUAL PURITY MOVEMENTS

The most important extension beyond rescue work was the emergence of a sexual purity theme. It is not that sexual purity directly gave rise to a policy platform; rather its significance was that it launched a critique going to the core of gender relations within the middle and upper classes which was at one and the same time radical and conservative. It was a condemnation of the prevailing ideology of the separate spheres, while at the same time drawing upon precisely that same ideology. The critique of the 'double standard' that licensed male sexual promiscuity and demanded female chastity struck at the soft underbelly of the doctrine of the separate spheres.[24] Yet the solution that emerged was not the quest for some new egalitarian standard, but was to impose the restricted standard required of women upon men. It was the coexistence of these radical and conservative dimensions that explains the considerable influence of this critique on the sexual politics of the late nineteenth century.

The set of themes and policies that formed the sexual purity discourse was one of the two key strategic ideas which gave birth to modern feminism. The other was the equal rights project, which focused on a set of legal reforms clustered around marriage and divorce reform and educational access, and led up to the rights struggle for the female franchise. Sometimes these two strands intersected, and at other times they took their separate paths as two great strategic alternatives, and sometimes they clashed. For example, in the United States Elizabeth Cady Stanton (1898) was conscious that the moralisation of alcohol by the WCTU engendered hostility to female suffrage; the anarcho-feminist Emma Goldmann denounced sexual purity as a smokescreen that diverted public attention from the great social wrongs of exploitation and lack of autonomy suffered by women (1972: 157). While sexual purity demands did not go unchallenged, their great strength was that they were articulated in ways that sat comfortably with the doctrines of the separate spheres and of female respectability.

It is much more difficult to achieve an appreciation of the scope and impact of the sexual purity movements in the United States than in Britain, where, as we will see, the events of 1885 produced a more or less organisationally coherent mass movement. In the United States the purity movements were diverse and, despite a number of efforts to achieve national co-ordination, no stable pattern of organisation or leadership was achieved. When it did arrive, the political form of the organisation had become professionalised and focused on the federal political process and, in doing so, undermined concern to build a mass movement. Significantly, this professionalisation of moral reform politics was paralleled by the displacement in the temperance movement of the mass-based WCTU by the increasingly professionalised Anti-Saloon League (Blocker 1989).

I will not seek to track the complicated course of the many purity organisations that came into existence in the last decades of the century; this task is adequately covered in Pivar's (1973) study that covers the whole of the nineteenth century and, as a consequence, rather rushes over the complex shifting alliances and conflicts within the purity movement. There is as yet no study of purity movements in the United States to parallel those for Britain (Bland 1995; Bristow 1977) and Canada

(Valverde 1991).[25] I will concern myself with a sketch of American purity movements in order to focus on their interrelations and the overall failure to produce a coherent mass purity movement, despite the fact that by the late 1880s purity organisations seemed poised for a major purity reform offensive.

By the early 1880s attempts to introduce the regulation of prostitution had been repulsed. Aside from Comstock's Society for the Suppression of Vice, the scene was open for new initiatives. Efforts to co-ordinate purity work emerged in 1877, of which Aaron Powell and Abigail Gibbon became the national leaders.[26] Powell's report to the 1877 Geneva 'new abolitionist' congress was the first publication with a national circulation (Powell 1878). The journal *The Philanthropist*, originally the organ of the New York Committee for the Prevention of State Regulation of Vice, under Powell's influence became from around 1885 the voice of the whole purity movement; it published reports from a wide range of reform activities from 'saving' prostitutes to Comstock's prosecutions, and much news about purity work in Britain and elsewhere.

It is significant that the first attempt to launch an explicit purity campaign emanated from the WCTU. In 1883, as an instantiation of Frances Willard's 'Do Everything' programme, the WCTU established a 'Purity Department' that quickly became one of the most successful WCTU ventures.[27] The department played a key role in the WCTU's legislative work, with a major focus on the age of consent; by 1894 twenty states had raised the age to sixteen. Without the same success, the WCTU advocated the criminalisation of male patrons of brothels. In 1885 Dr Benjamin DeCosta, a New York Episcopal Minister, brought over another British initiative, introducing Ellice Hopkins' White Cross Army, modelled on the one founded by the Church of England Purity Society; he secured sponsorship from both the YMCA and the WCTU, and DeCosta himself entered the inner circle of purity leaders. The primary target of this project was the 'double standard'; of particular significance is that the specific target of the White Cross Army was men, in particular young men, who were encouraged to pledge themselves to sexual purity and a single standard of morality. In 1890 DeCosta launched the National Christian League for the Promotion of Social Purity in a first attempt at national co-ordination of purity movements, but it never achieved substantial support.

The most concerted effort to co-ordinate the disparate purity organisations occurred in October 1895 with the convening of a 'National Purity Congress' at Baltimore.[28] This brought together a representative set of platform speakers under the chairmanship of Aaron Powell and under the watchful eyes of key figures from the British purity movement, whose significance was underlined by Frances Willard's eulogy to

William T. Stead, who had "made every little girl in Great Britain more safe from brutal men" (1896: 124).[29] It was as a result of Willard's efforts that there was significant working-class backing for the Baltimore Congress, exemplified by the participation of Terence Powderly, the Grand Master of The Knights of Labor. Emily Blackwell, herself the epitome of transatlantic purity feminism, delivered a classic statement of the feminist purity case on "The Responsibility of Women in Regard to Questions Concerning Public Morality" (1896). She attacked the double standard as "the last trace of the slavery of sex" and urged that, if women brought all their influence to bear to bring about "a higher and juster moral attitude towards vice, their influence would be irresistible" (1896: 80).

At the Congress John Harvey Kellogg, who had become a key figure in advancing a medical case for purity, marshalled medical evidence to show that chastity for men was compatible with health. He brought his own preoccupations with diet reform into play in insisting that "the exorbitant sexuality of civilised people is not natural", but is "due to the incitements of an abnormally stimulating diet" (1896: 265). Anthony Comstock differentiated himself from the rest of the platform with his demagogic attack on obscene literature as "the devil's kindling wood with which he lights the fires of remorseless hell in the soul" (1896: 420). The differences within the movement can be read between the lines of the text; in contrast to those who urged chastity and innocence the prolific author of female advice tracts, Mary Wood-Allen, who generally dealt with sexual matters euphemistically, launched a spirited defence of co-education (1896).

The Baltimore Congress thus succeeded in broadening the base of the purity movement. Significant was the support from liberal Catholics and Jewish leaders. The Congress adopted the classical purity slogan 'A White Life for Two' and issued a 'Medical Declaration on Chastity'. The upshot of the Baltimore Congress was the formation of the American Purity Alliance under the presidency of Aaron Powell; on his death in 1899 he was succeeded by Dr O. Edward Janney. The movement's intellectual orientation occupied an uneasy attempt to link an ideal of respectability through the internalisation of sexual control, with a more paternalistic governance through external control and intervention over others, particularly young men and women of their own class, as well as over the urban poor and the mass of immigrants.

Yet the American Purity Alliance was never able to mobilise its broader potential; it continued a widespread publicist role but never put together a coherent campaign. The central theme of 'purity' had the capacity to bring about a linkage between diverse fields of moral regulation and environmental social work. But significantly, the Alliance never succeeded in unleashing the potential feminist activism to parallel the earlier Female Moral Reform Society. The WCTU had provided the major point of entry for women into the public arena. Under Willard's leadership it broadened the scope of its activities: her slogan 'Do Everything' led them into suffrage, prison reform, the eight-hour day, kindergartens, non-alcohol recreations, education for women, purity and prostitution. By the 1880s the WCTU was the largest organisation of women in American history; it was undoubtedly "the cutting edge of the feminist cause in the nineteenth century" (Bordin 1981: 116). The WCTU had for long been more influential than the female suffrage movement that appealed to a feminism of rights. The conjunction was that both Willard's WCTU and the Purity Alliance mobilised around a feminism of fear epitomised by Willard's influential slogan 'Home Protection'.[30] This important and emotive slogan was the key manifestation of maternal feminism, which consecrated women exclusively in the roles of wives and mothers.

Yet by the time the American Purity Alliance came into being, the WCTU, although still powerful, was in decline. In temperance work it was being displaced by the pragmatic politics of the Anti-Saloon League. Suffrage feminism attracted increasing numbers of female activists and was cautious about too close an identification with either temperance or sexual purity. The reform impetus at the turn of the century was more powerful than ever, but it was to take off in directions which, while not alien to purity politics, produced results that departed from its central core. On the one hand, purity became subordinate to the municipal reform movement and more generally to the distinctive phenomenon of American progressivism. On the other hand, the continuing preoccupation with prostitution was to travel the root of legislative coercion that culminated in the 'white slavery' campaign and the Mann Act of 1910. Within these dual yet intersecting trends, the purity lineage continued to find expression within the vice commission movement. Thus, in order to trace the fate of the American purity movement, it is necessary briefly to track these strands. It should be stressed that what fades, or at best becomes a rhetorical residue, is the preoccupation with self-governance and sexual respectability.

A central feature of American moral regulation projects was the centrality of municipal reform. This manifested itself in the rapidity with which movements concerned with temperance issues and prostitution came to focus their energies on projects of municipal reform. The New York Society for the Prevention of Crime, founded in 1877, and led from 1891 by Dr Charles H. Parkhurst, focused on the twin evils of alcohol and prostitution. In an important sense, Parkhurst skipped the purity stage of development in that his organisation rapidly became immersed in battles with the police in New York over the enforcement of morals laws and became a significant force in the municipal reform movement. For the next twenty years the history of urban reform movements can be read in terms of the tactical question of whether to oppose the police and the municipal authorities, or whether to seek their co-operation in advancing reform projects. A full consideration of urban reform movements and American progressivism lies outside my present task. I will concentrate on the question of the nature of the connection between political progressivism and the moral reform movement: can and should they be distinguished? Undoubtedly both strands were engagements with the problems of rapid modernisation, epitomised in urbanisation and commercialisation. The significance of the dual preoccupation with the brothel and the saloon was that they provided the most immediate coded encapsulation of the larger social dangers inherent in the modern city. In so doing they encompassed everything else about urban life that disturbed the middle and upper classes, whether it was dance halls, theatres, billiards, skating rinks or the multitude of other topics that excited concern.

One of the most sustained inquiries into the relationship between moral reform and progressivism has been provided by Paul Boyer (1978). He employs a distinction between 'coercive' projects, directed towards the suppression of some specific evil, and 'environmental' projects, directed to improving some physical or social condition. He further refines his conceptualisation by distinguishing between 'negative environmentalism' (removal of the brothel and the saloon) and 'positive environmentalism' (improving the urban environment with parks, playgrounds, etc.). His general conclusion is organised around differential class support for these reform projects:

> If the prohibition and anti-vice crusades energised the middle and lower-middle classes in the drive to achieve urban moral homogeneity, positive environmentalism was the characteristic mode adopted by commercial elites to achieve the same goal (1978: 281).

Aside from the considerable simplification of the class profile of these movements, I have a more general difficulty with the way in which Boyer draws this distinction between varieties of environmentalism. He views campaigns directed at popular leisure and recreations as being 'positive environmentalism'; this, I suggest, misses the extent to which most projects for the 'reform of popular culture' exhibited an overriding moralisation of popular urban life. The differential emphasis on providing alternatives to morally suspect practices as against seeking their direct suppression was a significant but largely tactical issue.

More fruitful for understanding the complex tensions between progressivism and purity reform movements is to explore the different conceptions of 'progress' that were embodied. Progressivism was at its core an expression of civic idealism; the growing pains of rapid urbanisation were serious, but it was not the modern city itself which was at fault, but its unregulated expansion that had to be corrected through civic paternalism or what Rothman has usefully called 'the state as parent' (1978). Similarly for progressivism, it was not commercialisation that was the cause of social ills, but rather its distorted forms with monopolies and cartels. Purity reformers were not, as has been suggested, rural Puritans who were being passed over in the onward advance of economic progress. There were large numbers exhibiting all the symptoms of *ressentiment* who supported the purity movements. But by the 1880s the core of the movement was thoroughly urban, economically secure and part of the new professional and bureaucratic elite. Purity reformers referred persistently to the idea of progress, not perhaps with such enthusiasm as the progressivists, but neither can they be dismissed as conservatives who looked back to simpler days when men and, in particular, women, knew their place, when sons obeyed their fathers and daughters their mothers. However, purity activists were not inhibited from employing discursive appeals to traditional values. As I have argued above, the feminism of the purity movement mobilised the hegemonic ideology of the separate spheres, domesticity and respectability.

The progress envisioned by the purity reformers was unswervingly nationalist and nativist. Couched in terms of the 'future of the race', progress was conceived as problematic and endangered. There were two distinct elements to these anxieties, both of which found expression in concerns about the threat of degeneracy. The first strand was concerned about the future of the respectable classes and the other focused on the moral condition of the lower classes. The respectable classes were threatened by the risks inherent in urban culture, which could undermine and deflect their own future. Fathers might fall victim to the demon drink or bring home the scourge of venereal disease, sons might succumb to the temptations of 'self-abuse' or of gambling, and daughters might risk their virtue among the dangerous pleasures of the city where degeneracy in every form flourished. The danger of the internal degeneration of the respectable classes reveals a deep nationalism in the frequency of references to the decline and fall of nations and empires – a message fiercely articulated in William Sabine's address to the Baltimore Purity Congress (1896) where he stressed the "indisputable" link between vice and degeneracy. In the more conservative versions of this message, all manifestations of modernity carried the seeds of degeneracy (Nordau 1895). Of particular significance was that, within purity discourses, the sexualisation of marriage itself was regarded as sowing the seeds of degeneracy. Too much marital sex resulted in feeble offspring. Talk of sexual degeneracy had two key points of reference, first to juvenile masturbation and then to non-procreative sex in marriage; both were perceived as routes to race extinction.

The second strand of degeneracy concerns articulated the persuasive but flawed inductive reasoning that came to ground the appeal of eugenics, namely, that with the reduction of the middle-class birth-rate, the lower classes, both native and immigrant, were breeding more rapidly and posed the danger of swamping the best national stock. Yet there was a strange paradox here, for on the one hand, the respectable classes viewed themselves as physiologically superior but, on the other, were preoccupied by their own weakness and debility, especially the nervousness and fragility of middle-class women. This tension was rarely, if ever, acknowledged, and in practice discourses of degeneracy were predominantly concerned about the danger of moral rather than physiological degeneracy of the urban masses. They were concerned to secure social order and maintain socio-cultural class boundaries that were more difficult to sustain in the fluid 'world of strangers' that was the modern city (Lofland 1973; Wiebe 1967).

The progressive and the purity movements were often closely intertwined with a concern with urban conditions and urban politics. Involvement with municipal reform led purity activists into a more narrowly political field of action. Its major form involved participation in often diffuse municipal reform alliances. It is significant that these movements were often initiated by the urban elite, bringing together financial and industrial capital with the new professional elites. These elites provided much of the financial backing for both moral and political reform movements. This feature goes a long way to explain a distinctive difference between the social composition of moral reform movements in the United States and in Britain. While British moral reform movements attracted considerable support from the Church hierarchies, the traditional political classes in the main kept a wary distance from moral reform. The purity movement secured only scant support in Parliament and this did not significantly increase until the leadership of the purity movement passed into the hands of medical and related professionals.

Purity and municipal reformers struck alliances in many American cities. Early models were the Chicago Civic League (founded 1891), Philadelphia Law and Order Society and the City Vigilance Society in New York (founded 1892). These organisations embraced the link between prostitution, saloons and police corruption most clearly articulated by Charles H. Parkhurst. In New York the purity movement secured an ally in Theodore Roosevelt, first as Police Commissioner and later State Governor. Moral reform candidates ousted machine politicians after populist campaigns in many of the larger cities. There was a politicisation of urban morality, which gave the movements increasingly explicit class and ethnic characteristics; they were urgent expressions of the self-assertion of upper and middle classes, who both feared the consequences of rampant urbanism and yet were committed to the accelerated economic development which caused precisely the social problems that they feared. At first these movements were restricted to individual cities; not until 1894 was there an effort to co-ordinate urban reform through the establishment of the National Municipal League. Urban danger was frequently conceived in terms of discourses of infection and plague. This theme forms the core of the influential report of the Chicago Vice Commission of 1911, *The Social Evil in Chicago*, that embodied the discursive association of plague and prostitution:

> Prostitution is pregnant with disease, a disease infecting not only the guilty, but contaminating the innocent wife and child in the home with sickening certainty almost inconceivable; a disease to be feared with as great horror as leprous plague; a disease scattering misery broadcast, and leaving in its wake sterility, insanity, paralysis, the blinded eyes of little babies, the twisted limbs of deformed children, degradation, physical rot and mental decay (1911/1970: 25).

The reform response exemplified an ever-shifting mix of moral environmentalism with an ever-present tendency to resort to more coercive strategies. For example, the provision of public parks as sanitised urban space was an environmentalist response to urban squalor and the street life of the poor, but they were soon perceived as dangerous because they provided a heterosexual social space that threatened middle-class children's future respectability. The middle classes became persuaded that only comprehensive, systematic and orchestrated efforts could stave off moral decay and social disintegration among the urban masses. Environmentalist campaigns resulted in municipal parks, bandstands, civic pageants, municipal art, playgrounds, garden cities and town planning. Such projects aroused enormous enthusiasm and great hope for their reformatory capacity. But no sooner were they in place than they elicited the demand for moral surveillance and for regulation of parks, dance halls, skating rinks, ice-cream parlours, excursion boats and later movie houses.

One of the most distinctive alliances between purity and municipal reform found expression in the vice commission movement, which spread rapidly through the major cities and many states during the first decade of the twentieth century and persisted into the 1930s.[31] The origins of the vice commissions are to be found in the New York Committee of Fifteen, an independent investigative commission established by key figures in the business community, supplemented by influential academics and religious leaders. The report which resulted, *The Social Evil* (1902), provided the prototype for other vice commission reports (Committee of Fifteen 1902). Subsequently vice commissions were established in many cities with membership reflecting a balance of forces between municipal, commercial, purity movements, social reformers, and the religious establishment, of which the most important was the Chicago Vice Commission.

The diverse alliance brought together in the vice commissions determined that their reports were constructed around an amalgam of discursive styles and substantive contents. Their texts deserve fuller attention than is possible here, but some features may be noted. They combine large doses of traditional theologically inspired moralisation against the immorality of the age, buttressed by classical sociological theses concerning the links between rapid urbanisation, individualisation, hedonism and social disorganisation. They frequently incorporate the moral prejudices of their members without making any attempt to sustain their assertions: for example, the Chicago Vice Commission asserted that it "after exhaustive consideration of the vice question, records itself of the opinion that divorce to a large extent is a contributory factor to sexual vice" (1911/1970: 41), even though the report contains no statistics on divorce trends, let alone any analysis thereof. At the same time they are full of empirical detail, typically in the form of abbreviated case reports that were accorded technical citation, for example 'Case X985c', but provide virtually no general presentation of their findings nor any analysis derived therefrom. To this are added elements of eugenicist demands for restrictions on marriage of diverse categories, or demands for better working conditions for young women.

The differences between the vice commission reports are interesting. There is considerable variation in the accounts offered of the causes of prostitution. Some stress the social disorganisation of city life leading women in a search for luxury and idleness and hence into immorality. Others insist that the supply side is only a response to male lust and depravity. Some reports mix both versions. Many reports take up the question of whether there is a link between low wages and prostitution. Some strenuously deny such a connection, but the majority make a plea to employers to increase the wages of female sales clerks and factory workers. Another key variable is the relationship between the vice commission and the municipal authorities; while some explicitly place themselves alongside the authorities, others use their reports as indictments of political corruption and police collaboration with the social forces that sustain quasi-regulated vice. On other occasions there are decisive shifts in relations between the anti-vice forces and the authorities: for example, the New York Committee of Fourteen (successor from 1905 to the Committee of Fifteen) abandoned the objective of 'suppressing' prostitution and entered into alliances with the police, municipal authorities and brewers in order to ameliorate the social conditions that promoted prostitution.

The vice commissions were significant in that they generated a new species of experts, private agents of moralisation, who were commissioned to execute and write the reports.[32] The vice commissions opened up a distinctive role for the emergent social sciences as technicians of the quantification of morality. Recognition has been accorded to the role of late nineteenth-century reform movements, in particular the settlement movement, epitomised in the connection between Jane Addams and sociology in Chicago in providing stimulus to empirical social inquiry (Deegan 1988; Ross 1991), but little attention has been given to the relationship between moral reform and the rise of the social sciences.[33] A second category of moral experts was state attorneys, who specialised in both prosecuting and publicising moral offences.[34] The trend towards the harnessing of these new forms of expertise tended to separate these professionalised moral reform projects from any potential mass base. The vice commissions were often a response to new styles of popular journalism and their findings were frequently amplified by such journalism. Of particular note were the writings of George Kibbe Turner in *McClure's Magazine*. His exposé of Chicago vice helped pave the way for the appointment of the vice commission (Turner 1907). His populist assault on New York prostitution mobilised not only the imagery of the daughters of the poor being sacrificed to the lust of the wealthy, but also deployed an explicit anti-Semitism.[35]

One surprising feature of the vice commission reports is how little substantive attention they gave to the contemporary preoccupation with the 'white slave trade'. This classical moral panic persisted between 1900 and 1914; it was constructed around the theme of the entrapment into prostitution of white women by 'foreigners'.[36] What is significant is that the vice commissions implicitly accepted the founding presupposition of the white slavery myth that women as sexual innocents never entered into prostitution voluntarily and must, by definition, have been coerced or manipulated. It should also be borne in mind that the white slavery discourses were suffused with a nativism which placed the responsibility for the immorality of American cities upon non-Anglo-Saxon immigrants. The majority of vice commissions accepted an expanded version of white slavery which equated it with 'commercialised vice' or 'organised vice'. Such views, while implying the familiar large-scale organisation of capitalist enterprises, in all probability involved little more than co-operative relocations of prostitutes as market conditions changed and local recruitment fluctuated. However, it is significant that those vice commissions which explicitly pursued the question of white slavery failed, with obvious regret, to find any evidence to sustain the mythology of syndicates and 'Big Bosses'. Yet these failures did little or nothing to dent the grip of the white slavery construct, which had by now been disseminated in the popular imagination in a long line of popular novels and movies.

The period of the vice commissions was an important component in the transformation of the purity movement into an increasingly centralised and professionalised project. Little space was left for forms of mass participation that had been so prevalent in the earlier period when the WCTU took up the cause of purity, in contrast to the movement in Britain to be examined shortly. The final stage in this transformation of the form of moral reform politics came with the occupation of the central role in sexual politics by strata of the medical profession, as the preoccupation shifted from the figure of the prostitute to what was seen as the primary consequence of prostitution, namely, venereal disease. The previous chapter traced the general form of this shift from sexual purity to the medicalisation of venereal disease; it is here necessary to attend to the specifically American form of this important shift.

THE RISE OF THE SOCIAL HYGIENE MOVEMENT

The rise of the social hygiene movement was prepared in the last decades of the nineteenth century by the dual re-presentation of prostitution not as personal immorality, but on the one hand as 'commercialised vice' and on the other as a health problem. It was their combined articulation that gradually downgraded the moral message of chastity, purity and self-control promoted by the purity campaign; these did not disappear but came to play the role of supporting discourses. For the next decade or more there persisted an uneasy alliance between 'purity' and 'social hygiene'; they coexisted under the banner of 'moral hygiene', stressing the need to challenge the 'conspiracy of silence' that impeded frank discussion of sex and the continuing repudiation of the 'double standard'.

The social hygiene movement had emerged among fairly conservative medical specialists associated with the rise of 'public health' medicine and concerned to press forward with the advances that were just beginning to emerge with respect to the diagnosis and treatment of a number of venereal diseases. From the beginning there existed a potential for conflict with purity forces over the practically and symbolically significant issues of sex education and the medical inspection of prostitutes. A key role in constructing and preserving the medical–moral alliance was played by Dr Prince A. Morrow, a venereal disease specialist who had published one of the first medical texts on venereal diseases, and also had excellent credentials as an anti-regulationist. In his own contribution, Morrow combined morals and medicine. His influential text *Social Diseases and Marriage* (1904) not only presented current medical research on venereal diseases, but also emphasised the importance of sex education and stressed the moral dimension by allocating to married men the major responsibility for the spread of sexually transmitted disease.

Morrow set about establishing an American Society of Sanitary and Moral Prophylaxis in 1905; he sought to include prominent laymen as well as doctors, but it remained heavily medical in its membership. He stressed its key role as being that of public education, with the focus on insisting that male sexual continence was compatible with health. Increasingly the social hygiene trend influenced social purity thinking; by 1906 the purity journal *Philanthropist* was urging support for social hygiene societies and emphasising sex education issues. The medical–moral alliance was further strengthened by the formation in 1906 of the National Vigilance Committee; while retaining much of the terminology of the purity movement, it achieved policy influence in the corridors of government.[37] By 1908 the American Purity Alliance had endorsed sex education and preventive aims alongside its moral purity goals.

The social hygiene aspects came increasingly to the fore and again Prince Morrow was the key figure in the establishment of the American Federation for Sex Hygiene in 1910, of which he was the founding President. This organisation was significant in influencing the medical establishment; it successfully submitted a resolution to the American Medical Association in 1910, condemning the 'double standard' and declaring that prostitution constituted a grave menace to both individual and national health. The hegemony of social hygiene was confirmed by the establishment in 1911 of the Bureau of Social Hygiene, founded and funded by John D. Rockefeller Jnr., who had earlier directed his resources to the purity movement. Rockefeller was also at the hub of the establishment in 1913 of what was to be the most important social hygiene organisation, the American Social Hygiene Association (ASHA).[38] The ASHA sought to keep alive the alliance between purity and medicine. In the lead article in first issue of the ASHA journal, *Social Hygiene*, its lay figurehead Charles Eliot, ex-President of Harvard, linked the ASHA to the purity tradition in stating that it would assist in the prosecution of obscene literature and the suppression of prostitution. His advice against "sexual perversions" reproduced traditional moral prescriptions by promoting exercise, moderation in diet and abstinence from alcohol, tobacco and hot spices, while commending coeducational sex instruction (1914).

In this union of purity and social hygiene tensions remained, in particular, as to what kind of sex education should be advocated. Authors focused on purity training at home and suppression of 'bad thoughts', and their sex education had a traditional religious flavour premised on linking sex to a marital obligation to reproduce. The substantive content remained locked within the genre of 'the birds and bees'. The purity activists remained very cautious, fearing that the provision of further instruction might encourage sexual experimentation; similarly they feared that offering treatment for venereal disease would encourage vice.[39] They divided sharply over proposals to provide soldiers with contraceptives. Yet out of these tensions there emerged, haltingly, a new concern with the idea of 'fulfilment' in life and in marriage; this theme first found expression in debates over divorce, which again exposed differences between the two constituencies. This tension revealed a wider cultural conflict over the place of sex in conceptions of marriage as a romantic and intimate relationship. The separation of sexuality and reproduction ushered in by improved contraception was soon to reshape the dominant conceptions of marriage towards the 'companionate marriage', dependent on mutual compatibility and sexual satisfaction. By the 1920s marriage manuals were emphasising foreplay, female orgasm and sexual satisfaction, but retained injunctions requiring premarital chastity and marital fidelity.

With the entry of the USA into the First World War, an overt alliance was formed between social hygiene and the military that generated the 'American Plan' for dealing with prostitution and venereal disease in the military. By the end of the War the purity element remained present only as a discursive veneer, but in substance a full-blown regulationism was in place. The 'American Plan' was formulated under powers created by *Army Appropriations Act* of 1916. An 'Interdepartmental Board of Social Hygiene' was established, with representation from the Secretaries of Treasury, War, Navy, the US Public Health Service and the Surgeon General, and included Major William Snow, representing the ASHA. The Plan gradually abandoned any emphasis on moral suasion and education; increasingly morality was to be enforced through the police powers of the state, which were increasingly directed against prostitutes. The regulations issued designated 'pure zones' of a five-mile radius around military camps, and established VD clinics in many camps.

Women suspected of prostitution could be arrested, subjected to compulsory medical inspection and sent to detention centres on indeterminate sentences.[40] By 1917 the social hygiene movement had become largely absorbed into the military apparatus and the early leaders of the voluntary associations had lost their influence. Opposition, particularly to the distribution of contraceptives to soldiers, could still be mustered, but did not seriously impact upon the increasingly bureaucratic implementation of policy. The policies pursued under the American Plan were cautious; significantly infection rates did not fall as rapidly as they had in Britain after the introduction of a system of free and anonymous clinics.

THE HIBERNATION OF MORAL REGULATION?

The two great coercive moral regulation campaigns that persisted into the twentieth century were directed at doing battle with the saloon and the brothel. These terms became evocative codes for the complex disruptions inherent in the profound transformations of urbanisation and industrialisation occurring alongside mass immigration. This latter context accounted for the temporary abandonment of assimilative social policies and reinforced the tendency to rely increasingly on coercive reform strategies, to be prepared to impose their norms on those who either denied them or promulgated some other image of urban life. Hence there was an increased preparedness to employ the coercive edge of law in support of the imaginary reconstruction of American society. This multi-layered project was never simply conservatism, nor was it just Protestantism, although, as elsewhere, images of the past are often more vivid than the hazy contours of the future. The environmental movements that yielded municipal parks, bandstands, civic pageants, art galleries, museums, playgrounds and garden cities were just as much moral reform movements. Yet it would be wrong to view the most conspicuous coercive 'success' of implanting prohibition in the Constitution as representing a final flourish of the coercive strategy. Rather it is necessary to view both coercive and environmental strategies as coexistent tendencies within the overriding projects of the reform of popular culture. Yet it remains central to the history of moral regulation in the United States that its twentieth-century profile is overdetermined by the central place of alcohol prohibition. Not only did this provide direction for diverse constituencies, but it also accounts for the limited resistance to the medicalisation of projects of sexual regulation. Opposition to the saloon was always so closely tied to anti-prostitution and social purity politics that no clear line of separation can be drawn. Indeed an interesting project, outside the scope of my broader comparative concerns, would be to chart the interrelationship between sexual purity movements and the temperance–prohibitions movement.

American moral regulation exhibits a significant circular trajectory. The abolitionism and anti-regulationism of the mid- to late nineteenth century, heavily influenced by feminist themes, becomes by 1910 an uneasy alliance between 'purity' and 'social hygiene', coexisting under the banner of 'moral hygiene', with medical regulatory strategies coming to play an increasingly dominant role and exhibiting strong regulatory urges. With the entry of the United States into the First World War, an overt alliance was formed between 'social hygiene' and the state, while the sexual purity tradition was sustained only as a discursive supplement. Yet it is significant to note that the purity strand was never extinguished. Its persistence was exemplified in the long career of the Mann Act, which not only survived the repeal of prohibition, but was so strongly ensconced that it faced little overt opposition and remained as a potent reminder of the coercive legislation of morality until the recent period, by which time it had been, as it were, replaced by even more draconic legislation directed at what is perhaps the distinctive twentieth-century target of moral regulation, the consumption of psychoactive drugs.

There has been a distinctive pattern to the influence on American moral reform movements of explicitly feminist forces. The early nineteenth-century movements had a distinctive proto-feminist character, exemplified by the Female Moral Reform Society. This was firmly constrained within a maternal feminism which, despite anger at the double standard, was rooted in precisely the same attitudes and assumptions that underpinned the doctrine of the separate spheres. Having early manifested its influence, the feminist contribution to the whole range of moral regulation projects, whether temperance, anti-regulationism or sexual purity, remained imprisoned within this proto-feminist form. Thus during the crucial years at the end of the nineteenth century and the opening of the twentieth century, feminism was to make a much less decisive impact than, as we shall see in the next chapter, was the case in the parallel movements in Britain. But this does not mean that feminist influences were absent. Critically important was the comprehensive platform launched by Frances Willard and the WCTU; yet the primacy of temperance as the mobilising issue ensured that political and sexual feminism remained underdeveloped and always a potentially disruptive force. Even Willard's charisma could not guarantee the assent of the major female forces unleashed by the WCTU. Other feminist voices linked sexual purity issues to political feminist demands: for example, Susan B. Anthony early insisted that the prevalence of prostitution and sex crimes proved the immorality of men, for which a cure could be found only through women's economic independence and political equality. "The roots of the giant evil, intemperance, are not merely moral and social. Financial and political power must be combined with moral and social influence, all bound together in one earnest, energetic, persistent force" (1875/1968: 160).

The contrast between the United States and Britain was that, while American women entered the fray much earlier than their British sisters, only in small numbers did they go beyond the horizons presented by the coexistence of the temperance and sexual purity movements. In contrast, British sexual purity politics occurred in conjunction with the period of mass franchise movements. Those links can next be explored.

CHAPTER 5

SEXUAL PURITY, MATERNAL FEMINISM AND CLASS IN LATE VICTORIAN BRITAIN

FEMINISM AND MORAL REGULATION IN BRITAIN

The distinguishing feature of late nineteenth-century moral regulation in Britain was that it had at its core from the beginning of the major revitalisation of the 1870s a distinctively feminist content. It was the campaign against the regulation of prostitution, culminating in the defeat and repeal of the *Contagious Diseases Acts*, that led smoothly into a campaign for the criminalisation of a variety of sexual offences which peaked with mass mobilisations in 1885 and the enactment of the *Criminal Law Amendment Act* 1885.[1] Although such a high point was never reached again, an indisputably feminist presence pervaded the field of late Victorian sexual politics. Furthermore, the themes derived from the sexual purity campaigns became fused into an increasingly militant struggle for 'the Vote'. Although not all suffragists agreed with the slogan, the intimate connection between sexual purity and suffrage is enshrined in Christabel Pankhurst's famous slogan "Votes for Women, Chastity for Men" (1913).[2]

However, it should not be thought that feminism dominated moral regulation movements in nineteenth-century Britain. There were many movements that were unambiguously not feminist. And more importantly, it was throughout supremely ambiguous as to what was designated by the label 'feminist', which was coming into use by the end of the century. As with all other terms in whose name important social and political projects are launched, feminism is an 'essentially contested concept' (Gallie 1955–6). Thus while avoiding any idea of stipulating a 'correct' definition, substantial attention needs to be paid to the complex and shifting content that the term feminism embraced.

My concern is to understand how it was that Victorian feminism, which courageously challenged an increasingly defensive ideological orthodoxy, should come to espouse a sexual politics in the form of 'sexual purity' that was unambiguously both conservative and authoritarian, and was to bequeath a problematic legacy to twentieth-century feminism.[3] In order to grasp what it was that was new in the purity politics that emerged from the 1870s, it is important to stress that during the long nineteenth century traditional moral regulation movements set much of the tone and the agenda. For this reason I start with a brief recapitulation of traditional moral politics; but before doing so one other introductory point should be mentioned.

It will be important in assisting our understanding of Victorian reform movements to identify the targets at which their projects were aimed, in particular, which social groups or classes were their targets. It will soon become clear that there was no class symmetry to the purity campaigns. This will justify the rejection of the conventional thesis that purity projects were directed against the working classes. Broadly I will seek to show that the working class and 'lower orders' were generally not the exclusive targets of the purity movement. It is certainly true, for example, that the Social Purity Alliance (SPA) directly addressed the morals of the working class, whose lax morals were alleged to be caused by "overcrowding" (a coded reference to sleeping arrangements that led to early sexual experience and incest). However, the SPA argued that better housing for the poor was not enough; it would require a "moral force" to root out the behaviour and attitudes that lead to sin (SPA 1884a). But the purity campaigns were also concerned with the self-formation of the upper and middle classes. Thus we find the Bishop of Durham addressing his appeal "To the Men of the Upper Classes", arguing that idleness, although itself a comparatively venial fault, leads to sin, which pollutes the moral atmosphere and manifests itself in adultery among the upper classes.[4]

TRADITIONAL MORAL POLITICS

The persistence of traditional moral politics is captured by the longevity of the Vice Society, which, as noted in Chapter 2, sustained some level of activity until it merged itself and its assets in the National Vigilance Association when it was formed in 1885. It had secured the passage of the *Obscene Publications Act* 1857 which was invoked by the Vice Society to seize 250,000 indecent photographs between 1868 and 1880 and to prosecute 'indecent' publications.[5] In the 1880s the Vice Society launched an attack on the 'immoral' European novel that culminated in the prosecution in 1888 of the publisher Henry Vizetelly for translations of the works of Zola, Flaubert, Balzac and others (Hyland & Sammells 1992).

More generally, the mid-nineteenth century was marked by a proliferation of projects of moral reform pursued by expanding numbers of societies and associations focused on the reform of popular culture. So diverse was this activity that any summary runs the risk of concealing the diversity and complexity of these regulatory projects. However, two distinguishable projects are identifiable. The first involved attempts to institute direct bourgeois leadership over an increasingly identifiable working class. The second was aimed to foster the creation of a 'respectable' working class (Storch 1977). In practice the main result was to open up a cultural and political rift between the respectable working class and the mass of working people.

The increasingly active agents of bourgeois culture were the expanding middle classes. Their targets and methods varied. Much energy was expended on the suppression of the recreations of the poor (ratting, prize-fighting, bear-baiting) while other pastimes were sanitised and subjected to regulation (public houses, gambling, music halls). Some sought to revive the enforcement of religious observance, while others engaged in the increasingly important work of 'domestic missionary' activity, distributing Bibles and tracts, and in another important strand opening Sunday schools and promoting youth organisations, aimed at an urban population whose lives had become increasingly secular (Laqueur 1976; Springhall 1977).

For present purposes it is important to attend to the ways in which reform activism facilitated the participation of middle-class women in the public sphere. Women found a variety of routes to participation outside the home. The rich mixture of Protestant evangelicalism, charity, philanthropy and moral reform projects generated a distinctive gendered expression of class relations.

> Victorian moralising fused ideological currents with varying degrees of affinity to capitalism – moral Protestantism, Enlightenment, and utilitarian theories of progress, notions of individual and social 'improvement', an imperial sense that Britain had global moral responsibilities, and regime fear of the 'dangerous classes' below (Mann 1993: 481).

Philanthropic and moral reform activities had a distinctive imprint of maternalism, which was a variant of the more authoritarian paternalism that embodied an earlier phase of class relations. Wilberforce provides a pristine example of a doctrine of social order, what he called the "grand law of subordination", in which classes had to keep to their allotted station (1797: 405–6). The grave danger posed by radicalism was that it could lead to the lower classes becoming restless over their subordinate position. Since he shared the belief widely held by the propertied classes that the propertyless were inherently prone to rebellious disorder, he had no reservations about the adoption of coercive tactics when confronted with turbulent political and economic conditions.[6]

The maternalist ideology that middle-class women took with them when they engaged in that key domestic missionary practice of 'visiting' prostitutes or working women was full of self-confidence and showed no recognition that these women had fashioned viable survival strategies for themselves. From such visits, "Victorian women could derive from philanthropy all the excitements and dangers of penetrating or observing the unknown while at the same time securing that change of scene and activity which is the essence of recreation" (Harrison 1966: 360). Most importantly, such visits were class relations; an imperious and condescending tone pervaded the advice given by middle-class female visitors.[7]

It is important to get a sense of the scale and reach of maternal reformism. The scale of the resurgence of traditional Anglican social action can be glimpsed through two Church of England 'family organisations'. The Girls' Friendly Society (founded 1874) by 1900 had nearly 200,000 members in over 800 branches that fostered a semi-maternal relationship between Anglican ladies and working-class girls, especially in rural areas. The Mothers' Unions (founded 1885) had 157,668 members by 1889 (Harrison 1973). While such organisations fostered a patriotic religiosity, others harnessed the environmentalist spirit of progress as exemplified in the Leeds Rational Recreation Society (founded 1835), which organised cheap concerts on Saturdays and Sundays and thereby came into conflict with local Sabbatarians. Of more lasting significance were bodies like the Ladies' National Association for the Diffusion of Sanitary Knowledge (founded 1857), which was to be a major force for urban sanitary reform.

Maternalism was an ideology well adapted to projects to reform the lower orders, to make them respectable through the transfer of the rules and protocols of bourgeois domesticity to working-class women. Maternalism provided a means of giving the central dogma of bourgeois respectability, the moral superiority of women, a class dimension. For middle-class women the language of virtue and respectability counterposed to vice and disorder was a class code. It provided the framework for intrusive visits to the homes of the poor and for pressing a variety of projects of protective surveillance over working-class women and girls, in particular over their sexuality. The significance of maternalism is that it was precisely this ideology which was colonised by the overtly feminist currents that emerged in the 1870s to ground the 'maternal feminism' to be discussed below. This ideology was to suffuse the whole of the purity movement. There was nothing inherently feminist about maternalism. Yet it had a short-term tactical advantage: the espousal of these conservative views on gender and female sexuality gave feminists the ability to employ an acceptable public rhetoric which, at the price of locking women into child-bearing and domesticity, allowed them to attack the 'double standard'.

One key ingredient from the mid-century discourses of maternal reformism remains to be considered. The sexual question was to become central. It is important to consider how this came about, since what came to be called the 'conspiracy of silence' vigorously policed the discursive latitudes of female respectability so as to exclude any but the most euphemised reference to the sexual. And yet attempts to discipline sexuality were to provide the distinguishing mark of moral reformism. We can trace something of this critical transformation in the history of one of the important fields of philanthropy, the 'rescue' of prostitutes. When the London Society for the Protection of Young Females (LSPYF) was established in 1834, the Patrons and Committee Members were all male. In order to protect the sexual reputations of the worthy gentlemen, a 'Ladies' Visiting Committee' was established to make contact with "those unfortunate victims who have fallen prey to the machinations of licentiousness" (LSPYF 1839: 2). The LSPYF ran a rescue home where its maternalist ideas were revealed in the decision that its inmates were to remain in the home "until the Committee are fully satisfied as to their moral conduct and their fitness for service" (LSPYF 1839: 16). The reformers had great difficulty in differentiating between their desire to protect young women from moral danger and their desire to control them. The key insertion of sexual politics into the reform agenda came with the protracted struggle against the *Contagious Diseases Acts.*

PROSTITUTION, SEXUAL POLITICS AND ANTI-REGULATIONISM

Much has been written about the struggle waged by the Ladies' National Association for the Repeal of the Contagious Diseases Acts (hereafter LNA), under the leadership of Josephine Butler, that only a summary account is necessary here (McHugh 1980; Smith 1971; 1990; Walkowitz 1980).[8] I will then explore the question: how did English feminist sexual politics become so enduringly linked to an anti-regulationist politics of prostitution?

The *Contagious Diseases Acts* (CDAs) were an offshoot of a wider movement for sanitary regulation exemplified in 'scientific' legislation to regulate food adulteration and noxious trades aimed at the eradication of hazards to health through the incorporation of expert knowledge and increasing central regulatory controls.[9] The CDAs had their origin in concerns within the British military about the health and efficiency of the armed forces, which became focused on the incidence of venereal diseases. The legislation incorporated contemporary medical views on the transmission of disease and the link to the inheritance of degeneracy. Opponents of regulation extrapolated ideas of contagion to the realm of vice: for example, Edith Ward advanced an explicit contagion theory of vice. Since she viewed incontinence within marriage as a vice, she allowed herself to conclude that the children of such marriages are "born into the world with tendencies to sexual vices" because "the growing brain of the unborn child is impregnated with the deadly poison of sexual passion" (1892: 15). Others attributed many illnesses to venereal diseases, but medical knowledge not only lacked effective diagnostic tools, but had no reliable methods of treatment; the major breakthroughs would not come until shortly before the First World War.[10] The legislation gave effect to the view that infected prostitutes were the major active agents in the transmission of venereal diseases; with multiple sexual partners, prostitutes transmitted sexually transmitted diseases to large numbers of men.

Opposition to the legislation emerged only slowly. By the time the third Act was under consideration and there existed an active medico-military lobby pressing for the extension of these laws to the whole of the civilian population, opposition was beginning to be articulated.[11] The 'Social Science Congress' (Bristol 1869) carried a resolution against CDAs and led to the formation of the overwhelmingly male National Association for the Repeal of the Contagious Diseases Acts. By the end of the year a 'Women's Manifesto' signed by 130 women, including Josephine Butler, Harriet Martineau and Florence Nightingale, was published in *Daily News* (31/12/1869). In the meantime Josephine Butler launched the LNA.[12]

The two bodies, the largely male National Association and the LNA, existed side by side, co-operating most of the time. The LNA spearheaded the public campaign, while the men focused their efforts on gathering medical and other evidence to prove the ineffectiveness of the CDAs and thereby to influence Parliament. They largely seemed to have accepted this subsidiary role, a reversal of wives making sandwiches and tea while the husbands involved themselves in public affairs.

The formation of the LNA was greeted with much public abuse; that women should be so immodest as to speak of such improper subjects as prostitution and venereal disease was widely condemned. There is no doubt that the LNA did much to breach the taboo against public discussion of sexual matters. After prolonged agitation the culmination of the campaign came in 1883 when James Stansfield MP successfully moved a motion in the House of Commons that "[t]his House disapproves of the compulsory examination of women under the

Contagious Diseases Acts". Thereafter the enforcement of the Acts was suspended; formal repeal was secured in 1886. After repeal of the CDAs in England, Butler and many others took up the anti-regulation cause in India (Ware 1992).

What was significant about the sustained campaign waged by the LNA between 1869 and 1883 was the combination of discursive elements that were mobilised. This weaving together or enfolding of discursive elements is significant in that it accounts for the emergence of a broadly based coalition; some participants were attracted to traditional talk of the 'suppression of vice' embedded in the theology of evangelical Protestantism, while others were fired by the unambiguously feminist critique of the 'double standard', and still others by the liberal hostility to the extension of state powers. From this perspective, the significance of the personal role of Josephine Butler, whom Judith Walkowitz assesses as the "great founding mother of modern feminism" (1980: 255), aside from her undoubted skills as an orator and organiser, was that she embodied all of these strands in her personal intellectual formation. Indeed it was this combination that overcame some of her less frequently discussed weaknesses; since the approach adopted here is not biographical, some features that stand out from her speeches and correspondence should be noted as a corrective to the eulogistic treatment she has often received. She was uncompromising in the assertion of a personal mission to an extent that marred her judgement, making her tactically rigid, and making her rhetoric one that was untroubled by details of evidence and consistency.

While it is important to avoid being too schematic in constructing neat sub-divisions of the elements of complex discourses I will take such a risk and identify four distinguishable elements in the politics of the campaign to repeal the CDAs; schematically these were evangelical Protestantism, the critique of the double standard, anti-regulationism or liberal anti-statism and, finally, a radical populism.

Butler's speeches against the CDAs were structured by a religiosity which, while evangelical in its intensity, also appealed to a more traditional Protestant vision of the battle between virtue and vice. Victorian evangelicalism expressed itself as a self-confident mission; it exuded an air of self-righteousness coupled with an overwhelming sense of duty (Bradley 1976: 93). In one of her major addresses to the LNA, Butler argued that the CDAs were enacted to test

> the faithful and uninterrupted efforts of the servants of God to establish the supremacy of conscience . . . [that] will finally be crowned by an act of the Divine Will whereby the original principle of evil itself will be expelled from the earth, and the reign of righteousness will be established (1871a: 5–6).

Such traditional ideas about the struggle between good and evil found expression in the conviction that there existed a divinely inspired link between 'moral laws' and the 'law of nature'. This led directly to the traditional theological conclusion that the 'cure' for the social evil of prostitution was 'moral' rather than 'physical'. This made possible the dual strategy of 'rescue' work to 'save' prostitutes, and political action to repeal laws that condoned if not promoted that evil. In its simplest form, the stress on the link between morality and nature allowed a conservative invocation of the idea that venereal diseases were the just deserts for immorality. But the implication that no steps should be taken to prevent or to cure the infected was undercut by the fact that, while dissolute men were punished by such diseases, they passed disease to their 'innocent' wives and children.[13]

Here we see a characteristic link that connected to the second component, a distinctively feminist discourse. The Christian invocation of 'innocence' resonated through the critique of 'the double standard', but this took on a specifically feminist content when it targeted the unequal gendered morality that imposed chastity on women and condoned male sexual licence. Something of the flavour of the justification of the double standard is found in the report of the Royal Commission on the working of the CDAs:

> There is no comparison to be made between prostitutes and the men who consort with them. With the one sex the offence is committed as a matter of gain; with the other it is an irregular indulgence of a natural impulse (Great Britain 1871: col. 408).

This inequality is inscribed in the CDAs that imposed the medical inspection and detention of women labelled 'common prostitutes' while imposing no sanctions on their male customers.[14] Butler broadened the critique by pointing out that one section of womanhood is "kept strictly and almost forcibly guarded in domestic purity" while the other section is "set aside . . . to minister to the irregularities of men" (1881: 8). "It is unjust to punish the sex who are the victims of vice, and leave unpunished the sex who are the main cause" (1896: 18).

A similar discursive shift from religious to feminist discourse is apparent in the degree of sympathy, even identification, between middle-class reformers and working-class prostitutes as "fallen sisters" or as "daughters of the people". As 'daughters' they were in need of the maternal authority of middle-class ladies over unruly working-class girls. Butler linked the treatment of prostitutes to the denigration of all women.

> The degradation of the poor unhappy women is not degradation for them alone; it is a blow to the dignity of every virtuous woman too (1913: 30–1).[15]

This thesis that 'degrading of one, degrades all' has been a persistent feature of feminist discourses. But this should not be thought of as an expression of solidarity, an early version of 'sisterhood is powerful'. Rather it connotes, not so much solidarity, but a paternalistic dimension at the heart of maternal feminism. It exhibits itself as condescension in which gender is unable to displace an ever-present class consciousness. I suggest that it is useful to recognise this characteristic as a 'paternalistic maternal feminism'. Aside from its clumsiness, the merit of this concept is that it draws attention to the fact that middle-class women exercised authority over working-class women (and often over working-class men), in that they derived their authority from their location within class relations. This patronising relation is exemplified in Ellice Hopkins' calls for "the greater utilisation of the increasing culture of upper-class women to bring light and higher influence as well as brightness and beauty, to the 'dim populations' of our great factory towns, especially the toiling working women and mothers" (1882a: 52).

Thus the concern for 'fallen sisters' embodies a reprise for the ideology of the separate spheres with its emphasis on female weakness and vulnerability, in which prostitutes are viewed as victims of male lust and perfidy. Butler added a feminist inflexion to an essentially evangelical campaign against 'sin' with the focus on women as victims. But it is important to note that the acceptance of the 'separate spheres' itself created an opening for the very 'double standard' which the moral reformers otherwise rejected. There is an inevitable tension between the insistence on the difference between men and women and the call that they be subject to a common standard of morality. This tension is also present in commentaries that claim that female moral reformers rejected both the 'double standard' and the 'separate spheres' (Jackson 1994, Jeffreys 1985, Kent 1987, Levine 1990). Rather the acceptance of the ideology of separate spheres impeded the capacity of Victorian feminists effectively to challenge the double standard. Despite the LNA's emotional talk of 'poor sisters', this did not apply to recalcitrant prostitutes. Elizabeth Blackwell insisted that "the tenderest compassion may be shown to the poor creature who ceases to be a prostitute; . . . but do nothing to raise the condition of prostitutes as such, any more than you would try to improve the condition of murderers and thieves" (1886: 54).

The campaign against the CDAs provided a point of entry to a wider critique of gender inequality. It facilitated the means for identifying the 'feminist' content of the discourses of Victorian moral regulation. It will be noted that feminism thus conceived as a critique of inequality does not involve any necessary commitment to an egalitarian strategy and certainly not one that is premised on the liberation of women from traditional gender roles. The dominant strand within Victorian feminism was a maternal feminism that advocated the interests of women based on an acceptance of the primacy of sexual reproduction and the culturally stipulated maternal and domestic functions. Maternal feminism thus sought to advance the interests of women within an acceptance of an ideology of separate spheres that modified rather than challenged the delineation of male and female roles and, more importantly, sought to change the social value attached to these gendered activities.

The typical expression of maternal feminism was the demand for 'purity', that men be made subject to the same moral code founded on chastity and monogamy to which women had long been subject. The most significant consequence of this conception of feminism is that it can be used to make sense of the multiple dimensions of Victorian discourses on women, sex and morals. It serves to focus our attention on the contradictions between the discursive content of maternalism and that of egalitarian feminism, the latter being incompatible with the discourse of the 'separate spheres' and its close associates, the doctrines of female respectability, domesticity and moral superiority.

The campaign against the CDAs gave a significant inflexion to the ideology of 'separate spheres'. The traditional version of this ideology, which sought to make a virtue of women's implicit inferiority to men, emphasised female weakness and emotionality. The feminist variant staked out a more positive claim to female moral superiority. Butler built this into an evolutionary framework:

> The history of human life is encouraging, inasmuch as it shows that men are not generally slow to come up to the mark of what the women around them require, whether it be in folly or in goodness. See then what a responsibility rests on us! (1871c: 16).

There was, however, a tension at the heart of the claim for female moral superiority over men. The paradox was that women were somehow less able to withstand designs on their chastity; their sexual ignorance was construed as 'innocence' and was itself eroticised (Cominos 1972); Elizabeth Blackwell rhapsodised the "special mission of young women to make virtue lovely" (1884: 99). Women were raised within a paradigm in which innocence enhanced their desirability; the same paradigm instructed men as to the kind of women they should desire. Thus both female vulnerability and desirability were linked to ideals of female innocence and frailty. Frequently sickly, temporarily insane, and always susceptible to mental and physical derangement, women were nevertheless presented as possessing great moral strength and saintly devotion.

If women were to be able to resist the snares and pitfalls of the male seducer, they had in some way to be prepared. In large measure the main preparation was precisely the discourse of seducer–victim itself.

The traditional variant held that sexual ignorance/innocence had the effect of inhibiting sexual desire and this in itself was the best defence of female virtue. But increasingly there was a shift to the view that it was the 'conspiracy of silence' and sexual ignorance which rendered young women vulnerable and that some sex education was desirable, especially in the context of the trauma of the wedding night that beset young brides reared within the cult of innocence. However, what that instruction should be was fraught with difficulties. Trapped in the refusals and euphemisms of the dominant discourse, they were literally unable to write the 'facts' that they knew were necessary. Thus many Victorian sex education manuals were almost indistinguishable from the moral homilies that they sought to go beyond.

Much has been written about issues surrounding the history of sexual advice and sex education (Porter & Hall 1995). I am concerned only with the part played by the sexual purity movement and in particular by feminist currents within it. Edward Lyttelton's writings on sex education carried weight by virtue of his role as the Headmaster at Eton during the 1880s. In his *The Training of the Young in the Laws of Sex* (1900), he urged the necessity of sex instruction by parents and schools, since children will otherwise pick up "vicious ideas"; these can only be countered by "wholesome teaching" (1900: viii). He tackled the vexed question of the method of presentation, laying down as the first principle that "there is nothing in natural law which may not be spiritualised in its presentation to a child" (1900: 71). This resulted in his recommended account of conception being that "the seed of life is entrusted by God to the father in a very wonderful way, and that after marriage he is allowed to give it to his wife" (1900: 85), adding that, with boys, it may be necessary to indicate what portion of his body is entrusted with this function. He suggests that there is no need for sex education for females until they are about to be married; even then he is hesitant about what should be included: he seems content that knowledge of the "suffering" of childbirth is sufficient. This style is typical of myriads of books and tracts produced by the purity movement in the late Victorian period. As late as 1913 Lyttelton is still arguing, in a letter to *The Times*, the inherent dangers of juvenile sexuality.

> In regard to sexuality two facts stand out. First, that in proportion as the adolescent mind grows absorbed in sex questions wreckage of life ensues. Secondly, that sanity and upright manliness are destroyed, not only by the reading of obscene stuff, but by a premature interest in sex matters, however it be excited (*Times* (22/11/1913) 11).

The first feminist sex education book, *Counsel to Parents on the Moral Education of their Children*, was written by Elizabeth Blackwell, but as Lucy

Bland wryly comments, "one may be forgiven for wondering how her feminism informed her text" (1995: 139).[16] For Blackwell sex education is essentially a moral project; she advances a passionate advocacy of purity as chastity in defence of a single moral standard that is located within a eugenicist and imperialist problematic of race degeneration and national decline.[17] Her argument is directed towards mothers, whose duty it is to educate their children in "physiological truths" – but these turn out not to be physiological, but moral – the indispensability of chastity (1885: 88). This special duty devolved upon women, as mothers, to secure the purity of their sons and daughters: "it is only by securing mental purity that young women will unconsciously address themselves to the higher, rather than the lower, instincts of their male companions" (1885: 104). The alternative is "licentiousness" that is given an alarmist treatment with the contention that sexual indulgence leads to the deterioration of the brain, spinal marrow and lungs (1885: 39). Despite her insistence that women need knowledge of sexual physiology, Blackwell seems to condemn any explicit sexual instruction. "It is a sign of something wrong in education, or in the social state when matters which concern the subject of sex are discussed with the same freedom and boldness as other matters" (1885: 55).

In her *Early Training of Boys and Girls*, Ellice Hopkins urged the middle class to get involved in reaching out to women of the lower classes, because it is working-class girls who are most at risk from men. Since it is "modesty and decency which are the outworks of a girl's chastity" (1882b: 19), she proceeded to lay out a plan of instruction intended to help mothers raise their children in purity. It is light on positive sex education, but strong on homely moralisms such as "tub [bathe] the girls before the boys" (1882b: 23) and "let me speak most earnestly to you about little girls' under-clothing" (1882b: 25).

While each has its own nuances, these three variants of purity education never move beyond the moralising injunctions of purity and chastity. Some purity feminists continued to advocate silence; Louise Creighton claimed that "for most people the wisest and safest plan is to concern themselves as little as possible with the things of the body . . . the sensual desires, the flesh, are what have to be *kept in subjection*, and to do this the wisest plan is to think . . . and speak of them as little as possible" (1914: 74).

When authors provided more explicit information about conception and childbirth, they ran into the contradictions inherent in sexual purity ideology. This is well illustrated in the case of Dr H. Arthur Allbutt, whose *Wife's Handbook* (1886) was an important and informative sex education manual, more explicit than most in its content. Its publication was greeted by the Leeds Vigilance Association successfully petitioning the General Medical Council to have Allbutt, who was a Fellow of the College of Physicians, Edinburgh, struck off the register for "infamous conduct". The verdict included the significant finding that his offence was to publish his book "at so low a price as to bring the work within the reach of the youth of both sexes, to the detriment of public morals" (Hynes 1968: 199).

The third component of the anti-CDA campaign was perhaps the most distinctive. It went beyond the criticism of the content and administration of the provisions of the Acts to a more general objection, namely, that it was wrong in principle for the state to seek to regulate vice. It was this element that gave the movement its most settled self-conception, namely, the objection to the 'state regulation of vice'. I want to suggest that its importance derives from the fact there are two distinguishable elements present which embody very different political stances. On one hand, it embodies a deeply conservative or traditional response that to regulate vice is to condone it; it follows that since prostitution is self-evidently immoral the only permissible objective is the suppression of prostitution. The other strand revolves around the objection to any expansion of state powers (Butler 1879). This argument brought together the traditionalist opposition to the state as infringing upon the historical prerogatives of the dominant landowning class and the distinctively liberal view that counterposes state powers and individual rights:

> Since the beginning of our crusade I had been convinced in my conscience and understanding of the folly, and even wickedness, of all systems of *outward repression* of private immorality, for which men and women are accountable to God and their own souls, but not to the State (Butler 1896: 174).

Butler and the LNA pressed the liberal claim that the police powers created under the CDAs were not only an infringement of the individual rights of prostitutes, but also exacerbated gender inequality, since compulsory medical inspection applied only to women.[18] This line of argument paralleled the widespread sense of outrage that divorce law permitted a husband to obtain a divorce on the grounds of his wife's infidelity, while a husband's adultery was not alone sufficient for a wife to obtain a divorce. Butler argued that, because of their gender inequality and their infringement of civil rights of prostitutes, the CDAs were unconstitutional (1871b).

The important point to be made is that opposition to the CDAs could create a broad alliance because its arguments appealed to a range of both conservative and liberal sentiments. Butler's more radical-liberal position on individual rights was pursued by the parallel organisation she set up in 1871, the Vigilance Association for the Defence of Personal Rights (better known by the name adopted in 1886, Personal Rights Association), which not only opposed the criminalisation of prostitution, but also rejected state censorship of literature. Butler's anti-regulationism led her to oppose 'protective legislation' that imposed restrictions on hours of employment of women, which she argued was designed "not to protect, but to oppress women" (Butler 1874: 8).

The fourth general feature of the campaign against the CDAs, marking a dramatic shift from the moral politics of the early nineteenth century, was the espousal of distinctly radical populism. Its major expression was directed at working-class men, warning that "the daughters of the people" were being sacrificed to the lechery of the rich (Stead 1885: 2). "A Parliament of rich men is unfit to legislate for the poor" (Butler 1874: 8). The purity activists even invoked the risk of revolution from below, warning that the workers would not long tolerate the violation of their wives and daughters. It is significant that the first thing that Butler did in launching her campaign was to address a mass meeting of railway workers in Crewe, the centre of the rapidly expanding railway industry, and then to go on a speaking tour around the industrial north.[19] The other side of this radicalism was that the rhetoric of the reformers pointed at "the guilt of the men of the upper and educated classes" (Butler 1881: 18).

The campaign against the CDAs was marked by a high level of organisational initiative. Butler and her associates put together a crusade that involved many thousands of public meetings with women as the keynote speakers, the production of uncountable tracts and leaflets, and mass petitions along with concerted parliamentary action. Their success in forcing the suspension and then the repeal of the legislation was the last great victory of an alliance between evangelical Protestantism and liberalism against the expansion of state regulatory power. But this victory in vindicating female purity was secured at the price of reinforcing the continued acceptance of the delicacy of women, their need for protection. While it is difficult to be certain of its wider impact, it is probable that it reinforced opposition to suffrage.[20]

For all the energy unleashed in the campaign against the state regulation of vice, it was beset by a deep contradiction. The activists never seem to have confronted the question of what policy on prostitution should be pursued once the detested state regulation had been defeated. The platform rhetoric generally implied that to repeal the legislation would somehow bring an end to prostitution. However, the probable outcome, particularly because the LNA condemned the criminalisation of prostitution, was that prostitution would remain entirely unregulated or, more likely, would be subject only to the existing assortment of legal provisions and a large element of police discretion, which had been the situation before the CDAs were passed.

The absence of any positive strategy had serious implications that have not been picked up by previous commentators. The orthodox view has been that the purity reformers were divided between the anti-regulationists and those who relied upon a criminalising strategy. This view is misleading. True there were those who were loath to rely on coercive techniques. But it is precisely the absence of a viable anti-prostitution strategy that generated a deep dilemma. Within a matter of two or three years the overwhelming majority of the female activists from the anti-regulationist struggles found themselves supporting the campaigns for the criminalisation of vice and immorality. To understand this shift, it is necessary to explore the relationship between the anti-regulation movement and the sexual purity movement.

THE SEXUAL PURITY MOVEMENT

The conventional account is that the proto-feminist battle successfully pursued by Josephine Butler, the LNA and its allies was subsequently suffocated by the more conservative and less feminist purity movements of the 1880s and 1890s.[21] I will offer a different account, one that rests on the argument already presented that the tensions which give the appearance of 'two wings' were present within the anti-regulationist movement from the beginning. Rather than there being 'two camps', the history of moral regulation in the late Victorian period is one of an ever-present tension that is present in varying configurations between coercive and transformative impulses in all versions of the projects of moral regulation.

The 1880s marked the high point of the British sexual purity movement; it increased its momentum, and broadened its demands, and became a mass movement that was able, if only temporarily, to impose itself on the political establishment. In so doing it secured for itself deep lines of affiliation throughout respectable society, the police and the civil order institutions of the state that were to prove surprisingly resilient. For most of the 1870s Parliament had treated the anti-CDA movement as an external irritant, but one that finally had to be accommodated by abandoning the CDAs. In the early 1880s pressure on Parliament from the moral reform movement to pass a wide-ranging sexual offences statute had been frustrated; then in the summer of 1885 the purity movement secured national attention and then imposed itself on Parliament. The key incident in this transformation was the publication in the populist journal, *Pall Mall Gazette*, of the 'Secret Commission' report on the "Maiden Tribute to Modern Babylon". The serialised account provided an assemblage of accounts of juvenile prostitution, the most dramatic being the detailed account of how the editor, W. T. Stead, 'purchased' a thirteen-year-old virgin. This led in a matter or weeks to the passage of the *Criminal Law Amendment Act* (CLAA) 1885, which raised the age of consent from thirteen to sixteen, increased police powers and penalties for offences associated with brothels, and criminalised homosexuality.[22]

The 1880s was a tumultuous period; it saw deep economic crisis, cyclical recession, high unemployment and turbulent social action by an increasingly assertive and organised working class. With the major extension of the franchise to include the great bulk of middle-class men in 1884, the propertied classes consciously strove to reform working-class culture and to cultivate 'respectability'. While the respectable classes were wooed, the poor – the dangerous classes – were policed more coercively and subject to greater intervention.

The social and ideological basis for the purity movements of the 1880s had been laid down over the previous decade. The core feature was the promotion of a governance of the self that was epitomised by the centrality accorded to 'chastity'; it took the distinctive form of sustaining the traditional injunction of female chastity and seeking to institute male chastity as the new and reforming component. The theme of self-governance, or "self-culture", was articulated with great clarity by the great Victorian ideologue, Samuel Smiles:

> It may be of comparatively little consequence how a man is governed from without, whilst everything depends upon how he governs himself from within (1859/1958: 36).

A great part of the significance of the nineteenth-century purity movements lies in the mundane and everyday forms of the government of the self that were promoted. They contributed a distinctive component of a more general project of self-governance. Valverde has argued that projects of moral regulation are not so much concerned with changing behaviour as with the inculcation of "ethical subjectivities" (1994: 216). The distinctive feature of the subjectivity promoted is one which requires constant self-monitoring and self-supervision. Its most general form, which permeates the economic, social and moral discourses of the nineteenth century, is the quest for 'self-control'. I do not take issue with Valverde's invocation of ethical subjectivity, but I emphasise the mundane features of self-governing; hence I define the governance of the self as those voluntary practices by which people not only set for themselves rules of conduct, but seek to modify the social presentation of their selves.[23]

Self-governance for those who were the targets of moral regulation during the nineteenth century involved the acquisition of certain behavioural practices that were socially visible. They were manifest in the acquisition of that most important form of social and moral capital called 'character'. Character was never simply external conformity – although that was a major component; it also involved what the most important early nineteenth-century practitioner of moral regulation, Hannah More, captured in the wonderful phrase "an habitual interior restraint" (1830 II: 319). There is a complex connection between the 'interior restraint' – the disciplining of the will through practices of self-monitoring – and external conformity. The acquisition of character requires the internal victory over 'bad thoughts' and 'bad habits', but dissimulation could generate the approved external conformities. This, I suggest, is the root of the conventional accusation that the Victorians exhibited hypocrisy. Pretensions to piety and purity made the affectation of prudery a safe response to anxiety about sensuality and sexuality. Such prudery often involved an obsessive preoccupation and vicarious enjoyment of the forbidden: for example, the separation of male and female authors on bookshelves revealed what the Victorian novelist Charles Reade spoke of as "prurient prudery" that was marked by resort to a euphemisation of all things sexual.

Character was the visible outward sign of inner moral qualities. To 'build character' involved a form of caring for the self that was based on a striving for conformity with a set of public virtues requiring a display of stylised manners, theological orthodoxy and sexual probity that generated a specific type of 'truth-telling'. The acquisition of character required individuals to assemble a set of traits which included self-control, perseverance, honesty, loyalty, bravery, diligence, application and manners (Collini 1985; Susman 1984). Individuals were conceived as being creatures of 'habits'; the problem was to instil 'good' habits and to eradicate 'bad' ones (Burnham 1993: 7). The key mechanism in the struggle to fashion a self that could provide public testimony to the acquisition of character was the exercise of will-power in order to achieve self-control. As the influential psychiatrist Henry Maudsley insisted, the "strong or well-formed character which a well-fashioned will implies is the result of good training applied to a well-constituted original nature" (1884: 110). The results of self-discipline and training were realised in the acquisition of 'moral fibre' that is externally confirmed, for example, by an upright stance.

Projects to instil self-control impacted especially sharply on middle- and upper-class children. In this respect, stern disciplinary regimes sought to instil 'character education'. Character, like so much else, was strongly gendered; in some discourses only men had character, whose key feature was the "inner connection between masculine identity and a sense of self-control" (Seidler 1987: 87). In other discourses females could acquire character, one that was marked by a different set of dispositions and behavioural traits at whose core were passivity and chastity. Character had a history; the late Victorian period marked the high-water mark of projects of character formation; by the beginning of the twentieth century it was being transformed into an emphasis on 'personality', a more individualistic and individuated project.[24]

Purity movements contributed a distinctive content to Victorian character-building projects. Aside from the ever-present injunction to chastity, they promoted a regime of everyday self-disciplinary practices designed to suppress sensuality; in the main these projects were directed at boys and young men. The Revd Richard Armstrong of the Social Purity Alliance argued that "God has given you many good things, that will help you beat down the foe. Plenty of cold water, plenty of brisk exercise, plenty of occupation of the mind, plenty of honest purpose in life" (1887: 88). Elizabeth Blackwell urged that "hard exercise in the open air is, in most cases, an efficient remedy against vicious tendencies" (1879: 65). In similar vein Robert Bullen, Secretary of the Social Purity Alliance, proposed 'Eight Rules for Daily Life' that were a mix of disciplinary practices and moral injunctions: a cold bath every day; regular and vigorous exercise; sleep on a hard bed; moderation in eating and drinking; avoidance of all "unhealthy excitement"; never consult doctors who advertise; regular prayer; perform an act of kindness every day (1886: 21).[25]

Much less specific techniques were suggested for women. They were urged to preserve their chastity and virtue. Occasionally they were advised about personal hygiene and to avoid all unnecessary touching of their bodies.[26] Women were more often addressed as potential agents of moral regulation. They were charged, over and over, with the duty of instituting a social ban on licentious men, who were to be excluded from polite society (Blackwell 1879: 119).

I will now focus on presenting a synoptic view of the organisational forms, policies and politics of the more important purity movements. My criterion of inclusion is whether the movements are significantly implicated in the sexual purity movements which I treat as the core of late nineteenth-century moral reform projects in Britain.

I start with the National Association for the Promotion of Social Purity (founded 1870) which dedicated itself "to maintain purity as the law of individual and social life" by prescribing that "the law of purity is of universal obligation on all men and women alike" (NAPSP 1870). It was reborn in 1873 as the Social Purity Alliance (SPA) under the inspiration of Josephine Butler. In addition to the campaigning work of the LNA she saw the need for an organisation directing its activity at uniting young men for the maintenance of purity.[27] However, it seems likely that Butler herself left the organisation possibly because it fell under the influence of Laura Chant, who was one of the most vociferous advocates of the use of law to stamp out immorality (Chant 1883). However, the SPA was significant because it highlighted what was to become the central theme of purity discourses, namely, 'the Law of Purity' as a universal obligation for all men. To abolish prostitution required eliminating the demand and this necessitated a great advance in male purity. The SPA's main target was young men, not yet corrupted by the sexual licence of their elders.[28] The Secretary of the SPA, Robert Bullen, identified his specific target as the "men of the upper classes" who resorted to prostitutes.

> The man who thus enslaves one woman implicitly tells every other woman that she is entitled only by accident, not by right, to be spared the same degradation (1880: 17).

The SPA remained active until 1910, when it organised the important 'National Purity Conference', which was significant in securing substantial 'official' representation from state and Parliament. The conference resolved to press for the age of consent to be raised to eighteen. The SPA was a major participant in the purity movement's revival of the anti-masturbation panic (Hunt 1998).[29] It was also much preoccupied with the protective surveillance of young women and campaigned for the provision of safe lodgings for single women (Chant 1902).

In 1879 the Association for the Improvement in Public Morals (AIPM) came into existence.[30] Its major role was to offer co-ordination among the moral reform organisations; it published *The Sentinel*, which was the major vehicle of the British purity movement. *The Sentinel* survived the demise of the AIPM in 1881 and was published until at least 1900. The next organisation to emerge, in April 1881, was the Moral Reform Union (MRU). Its most significant member and sustaining force was its Secretary, Mrs R. A. Browne, and its members included Elizabeth Blackwell. On the ground that it had a largely female membership, Jeffreys describes the MRU as "staunchly feminist" (1982: 634). However, its gender composition and feminist status seem largely a result of the fact that its main form of activity was holding 'drawing room meetings'. The MRU's main project seems to have been the promotion and publication of approved 'purity' titles – books that were often written by men with decidedly traditional views. For example, an MRU pamphlet written by James Hollowell presented morality as chivalry and "purity as a young man's training for marriage" (1887: 4). Further doubt is cast on the MRU's feminist credentials by its policies. Its first handbill's formulation on purity is at best ambiguous:

> If chastity is a law for women, it must be so for every woman without exception; and if it is a law for every woman, it follows, necessarily, that it must be equally so for every man (MRU 1883: 4).

The slogan "in the interest of pure family life" was carried under the main logo in all MRU publications; they gave voice to one of the distinctive tactics of the purity movement by calling for the ostracism from polite company of all profligate men. In 1886 the MRU adopted decidedly conservative policies. It decided to target male public figures as part of a demand for 'moral Members of Parliament'. It opposed the remarriage of divorcees and any extension of divorce, and called for a law against seduction and the prosecution of seducers. The MRU did, however, register its objection to the exclusion of women from the Church of England Purity Society and the Central Vigilance Committee for the Repression of Immorality. It would be wrong to view the MRU as in any significant sense feminist.

The first stirrings of what was to become the 'white slave traffic' campaign arose around reports that English girls were being held against their will in Belgian brothels and that girls under twenty-one had been registered with the connivance of the '*police des moeurs*' (Borel 1880). Frederick Dyer, with assistance from his brother Alfred and Josephine Butler, managed to secure a Parliamentary Select Committee and Butler was instrumental in establishing the Society for the Suppression of the Traffic in British Girls in 1881.[31] Although it attracted some publicity, the 'Belgian scandal' was short-lived, probably because the young women complainants were full-time prostitutes who had voluntarily gone to Belgium even though conditions were not necessarily to their liking. The moment of 'white slavery' had not yet arrived.

Organised religion had largely avoided getting involved with the campaign against the CDAs. But as that particular battle reached its climax, explicitly denominational purity organisations were established. In February 1883 the White Cross Army, with close connections with the Church of England, was established on the initiative of Ellice Hopkins with the assistance of the Bishop of Durham (Hopkins 1883). Although her name is less well known today than that of Josephine Butler, she was undoubtedly a major figure, active in a wide range of moral reform and purity activities that paralleled those of Butler; the two were rarely in the same organisation or shared the same platform, but both were public speakers who could attract large audiences and hold their rapt attention.[32]

The 'White Cross' movement was significant in two respects. First, it was explicitly addressed to the working class; it sought to mobilise the respectable working class in favour of the dissemination of the values of the bourgeois family, which had gradually been percolating into the working class. Second, it borrowed the technique of the 'pledge' pioneered by the temperance movement to ground a participatory ethic. The purity pledge was couched in the imagery of medieval chivalry, King Arthur and St George and the dragon, and nationalism.[33] The 'White Cross Pledge' required adherents to "treat women with respect, put down bad language and coarse jests; the law of purity as equally binding on men and women; keep oneself pure".

In the same year Ellice Hopkins also played a key role in the founding of the Church of England Purity Society (CEPS; also referred to as the 'Purity Society'). Its first meeting attracted official endorsement, with the Archbishop of Canterbury in the chair. From the fact that the annual subscription was five shillings we can infer that it was aimed at the middle classes; and in its early years it excluded women on the grounds that the matters under discussion were not suitable topics for respectable women. Its aims were male purity, chivalrous respect for womanhood, preservation of the young from contamination, rescue work and a higher tone of public opinion. Something of the flavour of CEPS propaganda can be gleaned from a tract directed at young men. "God has endowed a certain part of your body with very wonderful powers and desires" (CEPS 1885: 3). These powers were only to be used later in your life, in marriage; until then they present grave dangers. "Many young men die in the prime of life from nothing in the world but disease brought on by sad habits of impurity" (CEPS 1885: 5).

The nonconformists were quick to establish their own Gospel Purity Association (GPA) in 1884, with James Wookey as its General Secretary.[34] The GPA employed a pledge very similar to that of the White Cross. The discourses of the GPA were characteristically class orientated; they highlighted the sacrifice of the daughters of the people to the lust of the powerful. Wookey toured the country tirelessly; his speeches invoked a mix of class rhetoric along with medical and religious arguments for chastity. He stressed that purity involved a personal strategy of self-improvement, requiring self-discipline and thrift along with the 'class' demand for the chastity of the upper classes. The class argument and the evocation of helpless womanhood were an evocative mix. Alongside the appeal to self-governance, the GPA was uncompromising in the demand for state action. "The true function of the state is to repress not to regulate vice" (GPA 1886: 37).

In the same year, 1884, an attempt was made to achieve some co-ordination between the rapidly multiplying purity organisations. A Central Vigilance Committee for the Repression of Immorality was established under the chairmanship of the Revd H. W. Webb-Peploe, but his style and orientation were too conservative to capture the allegiance of the new wave of purity agitation.[35] Another more enduring trend was formally constituted in early 1885, with the establishment of the Travellers' Aid Society that had begun railway station work under the auspices of the YWCA. Its aim was "to meet the country girl at the threshold of our wicked city" (quoted in Bristow 1982: 328). Such activities provided a popular form of activity that combined purity work with more traditional forms of female philanthropy.

The decisive event for purity reform activity in Britain was to come later in 1885. The three key moments were the publication of "A Maiden Tribute to Modern Babylon", in *The Pall Mall Gazette*, in July, the formation of the National Vigilance Association, in August, and the passage in the same month of the *Criminal Law Amendment Act* 1885. This conjuncture is considered in the next section; here it is sufficient briefly to consider its organisational expression in the National Vigilance Association (NVA). It was conceived as an activist organisation bringing together existing organisations and establishing local branches to cover the whole country. The founding meeting was held at St James' Hall on the afternoon before the mass rally in Hyde Park on 22 August to demand the passing of the criminal law Bill currently before Parliament. Once established, the NVA gradually absorbed the majority of the other purity organisations under its umbrella, capably organised by its Secretary William Coote. The NVA constitution defined its general stance:

> The NVA is an association for men and women to enforce and improve the laws for the repression of criminal vice and the protection of minors.
>
> The Association recognises the principle that the moral law is the same for all men and all women (NVA 1887: 3).

The NVA was to be the heart of the purity movement for the next two decades. It undertook a wide range of campaigns. It produced a mass of leaflets and tracts promoting chastity directed mainly at young men, and called on women to ostracise 'rakes'. It undertook a series of national crusades, such as the 'Social Purity Crusade' led by the Revd James Marchant, who alongside William Coote provided the movement's leadership. It concentrated on the suppression of prostitution, pursuing collaboration with police and local authorities to prosecute brothel-keepers in what in many areas amounted to local vigilantism. It launched the second white slavery campaign directed at securing greater legal powers with respect to prostitution. The NVA also promoted 'rescue' work among prostitutes and 'travellers' aid' to 'protect' single women in the cities. It undertook campaigns against popular entertainment; the popular music halls were a special target, as was high culture through prosecutions for obscenity in art and literature.

What is significant about the range of activity undertaken by the NVA and its allies is that it transcends any attempt to impose a division between coercive and non-coercive techniques; every available tactic was employed. Any attempt to impose a coercive or non-coercive, feminist or non-feminist classification fails to grasp the politics of late Victorian moral reform. However, it is important to recognise the remarkable shift in alignment involved in the campaigns which followed the anti-regulationist battles. These new campaigns relied significantly on using the state to promote legislation, having previously condemned state legislative intervention.

The promotion of moral reform through legislation generated a debate that would often raise its head over the next two decades. It was encapsulated in the question of whether it was possible to 'make men moral by law'. Elizabeth Blackwell eulogised the moral role of legislation, but insisted that it did not 'make men moral', rather it could 'protect' chastity and other virtues (1884: 115). She proposed wide-ranging legislative projects, including increased wages for women, improved housing for the poor and rational recreations (1884: 119). Ellice Hopkins confidently defined law as the chief agency for enacting God's work. William Coote directly confronted the objection against the legislation of private morality:

> There is a very popular cant phrase that you cannot make men good by Act of Parliament. It is false to say so . . . You can, and do keep men sober simply by Act of Parliament; you can, and do, chain the devil of impurity in a large number of men and women by fear of law . . . While human nature is so weak and yet capable of so much wrong-doing, we must by every means in our power, by the administration of just and equal laws, do all we can to enslave vice and give the utmost liberty and freedom to all that is pure and good (1902: 69–70).

Herbert Everitt, of the White Cross Army, justified legal coercion by posing the rhetorical question: how far is it our duty to "interfere with another's liberty to live his own life"? This was resolved by use of the analogy of the duty to save a drowning man; we should respond similarly to those drowning in "the flood of evil" (1906: 12); he failed to notice the weakness of the analogy in that the drowning man is in no position to give or withhold consent to such interference. Bramwell Booth, leader of the Salvation Army, defended such intervention robustly, if not persuasively. He recognised that the legal enforcement of morality involved "a considerable infringement on the general liberty. . . I feel it is high time that liberty was infringed. Liberty to do the Devil's work should be restricted!" (1910: 255).

It is in the context of this debate that Josephine Butler most clearly revealed her libertarian instincts, which separated her from most other participants, but there is an ambivalence in her position, as revealed in her letter to Mary Priestman:

> I continue to protest that I do not believe that any real reform will ever be reached by outward repression . . . [L]et individuals alone, nor . . . pursue them with any outward punishment, do not drive them out of any place, so long as they behave decently.[36]

If liberty is conditional on "behaving decently" it leaves immense scope for legal repression. While Butler sought to argue from principle, other opponents were more pragmatic. Havelock Ellis declaimed against the unanticipated consequences of legislating morals:

> So gross is the ignorance of the would-be moral legislators – or, some may think, so skillful their duplicity – that the methods by which they profess to fight against immorality are the surest methods for enabling immorality not merely to exist – which it would in any case – but to flourish (1912: 299).[37]

These exchanges missed the way in which law is itself productive in defining and redefining shifting forms of both normal and dangerous or deviant sexuality. Matrimonial law valorised heterosexual reproductive relations (for example, by granting annulment for non-consummation) and by allocating shifting rights and duties to husbands and wives. Similarly legal constructions of prostitution legitimised some forms and penalised others (for example, street solicitation was increasingly criminalised as were a variety of relations deriving economic benefit from prostitution). Legal intervention thus played a role in organising the cultural experience of sexuality, of legitimating or delegitimating specific forms of sexual pleasures and desires (for example, by valorising heterosexual relations while stigmatising homosexual relations). Debates couched in simple normative terms about which arenas of sexual conduct should be regulated missed the more complex productivity of law.

1885, THE "MAIDEN TRIBUTE" AND CRIMINAL LAW REFORM

The purity movement had made a number of efforts to promote what would later come to be called 'white slavery' scandals. The Belgian affair of 1879–81 protested against the fate of 'English girls' held in 'foreign' brothels. But the campaign failed in its major aim to promote legislation criminalising the procuring of women for brothels at home or abroad. The decisive shift occurred when attention was shifted to focus on child prostitution, where the designation of young girls as 'victims' and their male associates as 'villains' worked more successfully. It was the question of the 'age of consent' that provided a unifying issue, even though there was little evidence that there had been an appreciable increase in the incidence of child prostitution. The shift of attention to child prostitution provided the purity activists with a less ambiguous signifier. The young readily fitted into the discourses of innocence, and in addition they offered a distinctive class dimension, with working-class girls victimised by upper-class men. But girls and women did not figure in the purity politics only as victims. Maternal relations were also relations of authority and thus projects to 'protect young girls' also involved surveillance and control of juvenile sexuality.

Much of the radical and working-class support for purity campaigns was generated by the images of upper-class sexual depravity, wealthy old men violating the 'daughters of the people'. This line of thought involved a problematic reinforcement of working-class patriarchalism, which summoned respectable working men to defend the honour of *their* wives and daughters. A more coercive form of protective surveillance had been embodied in Ellice Hopkins' successful campaign for the *Industrial Schools Amendment Act* 1880 (the 'Ellice Hopkins Act') that gave JPs the power to commit any child under fourteen to an Industrial School when in 'moral danger', and in particular those under sixteen found living in a brothel. As Bristow observes, "interest in raising the age of consent came as much from a desire to civilise the poor and protect them from themselves as from the devils of the West End [upper-class rakes]" (1977: 92).

The first opening of the purity campaign in 1885 was the prosecution of a Mrs Jeffries, accused of running a string of high-class brothels. There were allegations that thirteen-year-old girls were whipped and violated by high-placed clientele: the Prince of Wales and King of Belgium were rumoured to be involved. Josephine Butler, along with Benjamin Waugh and Robert Scott, found two ratepayers to initiate proceedings and obtained a writ alleging the keeping of a disorderly house. The prosecution was led by William Shaen, legal adviser to the NVA, but before any evidence was presented Mrs Jeffries, flanked by Guards officers, turned the trial into a demonstration; she pleaded guilty and was fined £200 which was paid on the spot by her admirers, and drove off in triumph with an escort of Guards (Petrie 1971). Wookey and others tried to expose Mrs Jeffries' clientele, but their efforts fell flat, only succeeding in getting *The Sentinel* banned by the major retail distributor.

Stead subsequently retold the Jeffries affair as part of the "Maiden Tribute" series. None of the evidence against Jeffries collected for her trial directly supported the story promoted by Stead about child-procuring and sadistic practices. The 'evidence' subsequently relied on by Stead came from a servant who had left Mrs Jeffries' employ thirteen years before (Playfair 1969). Stead, Butler and the other purity activists were frustrated by their inability to generate public reaction to what seemed to them a classic instance of upper-class depravity. This played a decisive role in determining Stead's next major project.

Stead set out to prove that it was possible to 'purchase' a young virgin in London. His report was published in the name of a 'Secret Commission', but it would seem that this never functioned in the organised way that the title suggests. Rather Stead used his contacts in the purity movement; Frederick Charrington put Stead into contact with an ex-brothel-keeper from Mile End who had stories of how he 'lured' country girls to prostitution in London. While most attention, both at the time and subsequently, has focused on the story of 'Lily', there are many other 'stories' in the three parts of "A Maiden Tribute". It seems probable that these stories were collected by Stead and his informants in bars and coffee-houses; they have an apocryphal feel to them, lack convincing detail, are too peremptory and have none of the narrative drama of the 'Lily' story.

A brief account of the events surrounding the story of 'Lily' starts with Josephine Butler introducing Stead to Rebecca Jarrett, an ex-prostitute living in a home run by Josephine Butler. Jarrett promised to acquire one or more virgins for Stead. After a series of unsuccessful ventures she approached a friend, Nancy Brougham, in Marylebone, who introduced her to a Mrs Armstrong.[38]

From this point on the accounts of the participants diverge. Jarrett claims that Mrs Armstrong knew that her quest was for a virgin for immoral purposes. Mrs Armstrong maintained that Jarrett stated that she was looking for a girl for a position in domestic service and for this reason suggested her thirteen-year-old daughter, Eliza Armstrong (who appears in Stead's account as 'Lily'). Jarrett purchased new clothes for Eliza and paid a sum of money to Mrs Armstrong.

On 3 July Jarrett collected Eliza, taking her to a boarding house, which Stead describes as a house of disrepute, where Eliza was chloroformed and examined by a midwife, Mme Mourez, who confirmed that Eliza was a virgin. She was put to sleep in a bedroom. Then, in the most extraordinary scene in the whole episode, Stead disguised himself as an old rake using makeup and false moustache; he entered Eliza's room, she awoke terrified and Stead promptly retreated. She was then handed over to Bramwell Booth of the Salvation Army and Mme Combe, of the Swiss Salvation Army, who took her to France. Thereafter Stead and Bramwell Booth seem to have been intent on 'saving' Eliza from her mother. Eliza wrote to her mother from France, but Stead persuaded Bramwell Booth not to deliver the letter to Mrs Armstrong.

The "Maiden Tribute" was published in *The Pall Mall Gazette* in three episodes between 6 and 8 July 1885 (Stead 1885). By the third instalment there was rioting outside the *Gazette* office as members of the public struggled to get copies; by the end of July a pamphlet version had sold 1.5 million copies. It was the journalistic sensation of the century. However, things were soon to go wrong for Stead and his associates. Stead was roundly attacked from a number of different directions. The Establishment reaction was to brand his revelations as obscene; others began to attack the credibility and veracity of Stead's allegations. Interestingly Stead's mode of defence was to place the issue of the truth of his account before an "independent inquiry" composed of Archbishop Benson (Canterbury), Bishop Temple (London), Cardinal Manning (Westminster) and Samuel Morley MP; they pronounced the "Maiden Tribute" story "substantially true" and brushed aside "trivial errors in points of detail".

Meanwhile not having heard from her daughter, Mrs Armstrong invoked the assistance of *Lloyd's Newspaper*, a rival to the *Gazette*. The efforts of Marylebone magistrates and the police started to unravel Eliza's disappearance, but were impeded by the fact that Stead refused for the next month to acknowledge any link between 'Lily' and Eliza Armstrong. Mrs Armstrong was persuaded to attend the opening session of the 'independent inquiry', where she denied that she had 'sold' Eliza and pleaded with the dignitaries for the return of her daughter. The search for the whereabouts of Rebecca Jarrett led to Josephine Butler, who claimed that her membership of the 'Secret Commission' was the reason for refusing to give information concerning the whereabouts of Eliza, but she did refer the police to Bramwell Booth, who handed over an address in France where Eliza was being held. Eliza was moved to Stead's home in Wimbledon over the weekend of the big NVA rally on 22 August; she was finally returned to her parents on 23 August.

The *St James Gazette*, fiercely critical of *Pall Mall Gazette*, picked up the story and raised the question of whether the purity activists had the right to decoy thirteen-year-olds from their parents and suggested that Stead was guilty of the crime of abduction. By now Stead's position was becoming precarious, not only was there a danger of prosecution, but if the story of 'the sale of virgin Lily' collapsed, so did the whole "Maiden Tribute" campaign. But the purity movement stuck loyally behind Stead and he became a popular hero. It does not seem to have occurred to Stead that others might see as unpardonable arrogance his assumption that, because his motives were good, he had the right to abduct a thirteen-year-old girl. After her release Eliza Armstrong was taken before the public prosecutor and a warrant was issued for the arrest of Rebecca Jarrett and charges laid against Jarrett, Stead, Bramwell Booth and other minor participants. They were charged with 'abduction' (the unlawful taking of an unmarried woman under the age of sixteen out of the possession of her father and mother) – the irony being that it was under the provisions of the *Criminal Law Amendment Act* 1885 that Stead had done so much to force through that he was charged. The other charge, tried separately, for assault, arising from the medical inspection of Eliza, was brought against Stead and Mme Mourez.

When the committal proceedings opened in September, Stead and his collaborators underwent rapid transmogrification from heroes to villains. The hearing lasted three weeks; all defendants were committed for trial to the Old Bailey where they appeared in October 1885. The central question of fact around which the whole trial revolved was whether Mrs Armstrong had 'sold' Eliza into prostitution or to go into domestic service. Mrs Armstrong's husband, Charles Armstrong, was a chimney-sweep; he came to play a critical part in the final act.[39] When he discovered that his wife had let Eliza go and had not obtained an address, he admitted to beating up his wife. This confession of patriarchal violence was the testimony that clinched the fact that Stead and Jarrett had abducted Eliza without the consent of the father, which was a criminal offence. Charles Armstrong now displaced Stead as the hero, an albeit rough patriarch defending his 'daughter of the people' against the arrogance of middle-class 'do-gooders' like Stead and his associates.

Stead conducted his own defence; he sought to call the Archbishop of Canterbury and Cardinal Manning. The judge refused permission on the grounds that they would only be able to attest to Stead's motives, which were not in dispute. On the same grounds he was refused permission to deliver a lengthy speech justifying his actions in exposing child prostitution.[40] Stead and Jarrett were found guilty of abduction, Mourez of indecent assault, and Stead and others of aiding and abetting an assault. Jarrett and Mourez were sentenced to six months imprisonment and Stead to three months. He went off to jail still convinced of the legitimacy of his action and was welcomed in triumph on his release by the purity movement. It is clear, however, that both then and now his tactics sharply polarised public opinion. It is surprising, if not shocking, that Stead's tactics can still receive endorsement in the name of feminism, as when Gorham accepts the veracity of the "Maiden Tribute" as telling "an irrefutable story of sexual exploitation that is as horrifying today as it was in the 1880s" (1978: 362).

What is undoubtedly true is that without the sensation of Stead's publication the legal changes introduced in the *Criminal Law Amendment Act* (CLAA) 1885 would not have been achieved so quickly. The main thrust of successive attempts to pass a *Criminal Law Amendment Bill* had been to raise the age of consent from thirteen to sixteen. Along with this were an assortment of other demands, to increase penalties for indecent assault, and to create a new offence of procuring any woman, irrespective of age, to enter an overseas brothel. The opposition was varied and mixed, but underlying it was a long-standing reservation that was shared, in varying degrees, by the reformers about the creation of increased police powers. The reformers sought to confront this objection in the 1885 version which, alongside increased police powers, provided a space for private enforcement; but this did nothing to limit police powers, it merely created scope for legal vigilantism. In the Act that passed in 1885 the purity movement got most of what it had wanted, but with significant extensions of police powers. Aside from raising the age of consent, the Act provided that brothels could be searched on information sworn before a JP by any person acting on behalf of a 'missing girl'; it created powers to remove young girls from immoral parents. It introduced a new offence, that of inducing any female under sixteen into prostitution, and any female by force. Section 1 created an offence of inducing a female of any age to leave the UK for the purpose of entering prostitution abroad; s. 4, the 'white slave' clause, made it an offence to procure a woman into a brothel "within or without the Queen's dominions". Clauses to make soliciting a crime had been dropped. The introduction of summary procedure against brothel-keepers and landlords whose premises were used for prostitution was to provide a major focus for local activism of vigilance committees, who took to 'informing' against prostitutes and the establishments from which they worked. The achievement of the major objective of raising the age of consent to sixteen was tempered by the inclusion of a defence of "reasonable cause to believe" that the female was over sixteen.[41] It should also be noted that s. 11 created an offence of 'gross indecency' in private between consenting males; it became a misdemeanour and subject to two years hard labour and thus effectively criminalised all homosexual activity.[42]

It was the demand for raising the age of consent that was the cement that held the campaign together. It did so because there was a consensus that young women were sexual innocents liable to seduction and in need of protective surveillance. Thus, despite her earlier concern with the rights of the individual, Butler had no qualms about the age of consent. Only Charles Hopgood MP, who had been an active opponent of CDAs, opposed the CLAA 1885 on the grounds that "repressive legislation of this kind is not calculated to improve public morals".[43]

After the repeal of the CDAs and the passage of the CLAA 1885, moral reform movements expanded the range of their campaigning. It would make analysis of the complex of movements much simpler if it were possible to identify some clear pattern, for example, if some organisations limited their activity to the promotion of further criminalisation of moral wrongs, while others promoted projects of self-regulation intended to secure male chastity. There was some specialisation resulting from the specific aims of individual organisations; thus the White Cross Army promoted purity pledge drives among working-class constituencies. Similar campaigns were also pursued by the NVA, while it also promoted legislative campaigns for the criminalisation of incest and for stronger powers against prostitution. Despite efforts by earlier commentators to distinguish between coercive and non-coercive strands (Bristow 1977; Levine 1990; Mort 1985) or between feminist and non-feminist projects (Jackson 1994; Jeffreys 1985), these neat classificatory grids simply do not mesh with the diverse projects pursued by late nineteenth-century moral regulation movements.[44]

My contention is that there occurred an ineluctable drift from anti-regulationism to legislative coercion. It can be illustrated by considering the case of Josephine Butler herself, who was, undoubtedly, the most committed and sophisticated anti-regulationist. If she wavered and veered towards coercion it is little wonder that the rest of the movement did. The historical record is far from clear. What is not in dispute is that she played, as we have seen, an active role in orchestrating the first 'white slavery' movement in the Belgian scandal of 1879–81. She associated herself with the more overtly coercive demands for anti-procuring powers promoted by the Society for the Suppression of the Traffic in British Girls, which represented the 'problem' of prostitution as an organised conspiracy of evil brothel-keepers. And this despite the fact that she had expressed the view that:

> My motto is *no* legislation at all on prostitution . . . The very fact of leaving the State to do it by its laws will lessen the sense of personal responsibility and weaken the fervour of charity in all, the best of us, so that our hands will hang down and we shall leave it to the State to do this deep, difficult, holy work (quoted in Bell 1962: 109).

Yet her position, as we have seen, was not as unambiguous as it at first appears. "The principle of the Federation has always been to *let individuals alone* . . . but to attack *organised prostitution.*"[45] Thus she dramatically curtailed her injunction against legislation on prostitution so long as it was directed against 'organised' prostitution. The claim to attack some vice on the grounds that it was an 'organised' vice was a common legitimation tactic.[46]

When the NVA was founded in the immediate aftermath of the publication of the "Maiden Tribute", Butler became a member of its Council in full knowledge that the major policies of the NVA were to press for the criminalisation of a wide range of prostitution-related practices. It is also undeniable that subsequently Butler expressed her disquiet with the coercive strategy of the NVA. But it was not until 1897 that she pronounced against coercive legislation in the name of purity:

> Beware of 'Purity Societies' . . . ready to accept and endorse any amount of inequality in the laws, any amount of coercive degrading treatment of their fellow creatures in the fatuous belief that you can oblige human beings to be moral by *force*, and in so doing . . . promote social purity (quoted in Bland 1995: 99–100; emphasis in original).

Perhaps it was even more significant that, although her role in the NVA declined, she never seems to have resigned.

If, as I have argued, there was no clear separation between feminist and non-feminist or between repressive and non-repressive moral reform movements, an important consequence follows. The tensions within moral reform projects are *internal* in the sense that the governance of the self and the governance of others are not two alternative strategies, but always exist in combination. The next section explores the slide towards an increasing reliance on attempts to impose morality through legislation, one that failed to sustain the mass support achieved in the late 1880s and rendered the purity movement vulnerable to being enveloped by projects organised around the medicalised discourse of social hygiene.

SEXUAL PURITY AND FEMINISM

If there was no straightforward distinction between repressive and non-repressive strategies, there is no readily identifiable distinction between feminist and non-feminist versions of sexual purity politics. In particular it soon became clear that there was no simple distinction between the repression of brothels and the repression of working prostitutes; to close brothels made the latter more heavily dependent on street soliciting and on pimps. The local branches of the NVA that had been set up sought to collaborate with police and municipal authorities to close local brothels, but the most immediate brunt of this purity onslaught was felt by individual prostitutes who understandably did not welcome the purity activists. In 1888 a campaign to close brothels in the garrison town of Aldershot resulted in prostitutes taking to the streets marching behind a drum major in protest.[47]

In order to understand the connection between feminism and sexual purity, it is necessary to return to the issue of how we should understand the sexual politics of late nineteenth-century feminism. It will be recalled that in Chapter 3 I expressed reservations about the distinction between pro- and anti-sex, sensualist and anti-sensualist tendencies within feminism. For example, Bristow sets up this opposition by contrasting Butler's anti-regulationism with Ellice Hopkins' anti-sexual purity; his characterisation of the social purity movement was as an "alliance between puritans and feminists" (1977: 230). Aside from the inherent difficulties with all such binary oppositions, there is a more significant reason for this reservation, namely, that it presumes that attitudes to sex and sexuality formed the starting point for feminist positions. The espousal by middle-class women of the cult of respectability had its roots in the older tradition that linked femininity and sensibility. This certainly gave rise to a predisposition to dissociate feeling and sensitivity from the physicality of sexuality, but in itself was not sufficient to account for the values espoused by nineteenth-century feminism.

The dominant feature of late nineteenth-century feminism was, as I have suggested, organised around a maternal feminism. This never entirely submerged 'egalitarian feminism', as the importance of campaigns for legal equality, the reform of matrimonial law and for educational opportunities attests.[48] But maternal feminism did much to constrain these movements within an ideology that was grounded in an acceptance of the rigid gender polarity inscribed within the doctrine of the separate spheres. From this perspective women were characterised by their reproductive role, which was construed as endowing them with a preoccupation with the domestic realm and with the moral responsibility for child-rearing; this in turn expressed itself in the discourses of female moral superiority that promoted the ideal of female moral guardianship of both home and nation.[49] This reflected the pervasive preoccupation in nineteenth-century science to demarcate a clear distinction between the human and the animal realms; one of its major manifestations was the preoccupation of the scientific and medical community with 'sex difference' (Geddes & Thompson 1889).[50]

There was a deep tension embedded in the dominant conceptions of male and female sexuality. Women were dominated by their reproductive function and, as such, were closer to 'nature'. Men inhabited the realm of calculation and reason, yet the male sexual drive was conceived as 'lust', a drive that, while serving a necessary reproductive function, was associated with the animal realm. Thus we have two incompatible lines of thought that coexisted with an inevitable instability. Men manifested reason and civilisation, women were the bearers of nature and biology. Yet men were animal, while women represented morality and civilisation. The latter strand expressed itself in a marked anti-sensualism; sex was to be contained and restrained as the means to the maternal role, but never an end in itself. Its classic expression was epitomised in William Acton's oft-quoted dictum: "The majority of women (happily for them) are not very much troubled with sexual feeling of any kind"

(1865: 112).[51] Thus maternal feminism urged the importance of restraining anything that might stimulate erotic feelings, attacking everything from romantic novels to tea, coffee, alcohol and meat.[52]

The preoccupation with refusing any form of sexual hedonism was encapsulated in the policing of a dividing practice that distinguished between marital sexual reproduction and sexual pleasure as the central vision of sex that was shared by both conservatives and purity feminists. The only role that was permitted for sexuality was for reproductive purposes, a view expressed most clearly by a correspondent, Mrs P. Sherwen, in *The Freewoman*, normally a vehicle of advanced views on sexual matters: "sex relationships and sex organs should be held absolutely sacred to the production of children, and never be degraded to minister to lustful pleasure" (25/1/1912). Elizabeth Blackwell could only approve "natural occasional intercourse" (1885: 51). Henry Varley appealed to husbands to reduce the frequency of marital intercourse by "control of the passions" because 'excessive' sex weakens men (1884: 10). Frances Swiney also wanted sex confined to procreation; she opposed sex during pregnancy, alleging that it resulted in the species being "diseased by sexual vice, overpopulated with degenerates, imbeciles and malformed individuals" (1907: 54). Edith Ward went one step further by criticising wives who were complicit in 'excess':

> Many women are but too willing partners in excessive intercourse and their debasement is as great as that of any wretched prostitute who walks the streets (1892: 13).

Incontinence in marriage results in the children of such marriages being "born into the world with tendencies to sexual vice in every form" (1892: 14). Elizabeth Blackwell gave the demand for marital continence a specifically feminist inflexion: "the wife must determine the times of union" (1888: 55), and motherhood must be voluntary with "the full assent of the mother in the joint creation of superior offspring" (1879: 24). Such an approach resonated with her concern that sexual reproduction bears more heavily on women both with respect to the risks associated with pregnancy and a growing consciousness of the desire to restrict the number and frequency of pregnancies. Thus despite an apparent consensus on the immorality of contraception, middle-class marriages were changing, as was revealed in a marked decline in fertility.[53]

These concerns with the specific risks and dangers of sexual activity were expanded to cultivate a more general sense of sex as inherently dangerous. Elizabeth Blackwell gave an alarmist account of the physical and moral dangers of sexual indulgence that she alleged could result in the deterioration of the brain, spinal marrow and lungs (1884: 39). She cited Queteletian statistics and insurance tables to demonstrate the high mortality of bachelors between eighteen and twenty-eight and concluded that "'Died from the effects of fornication' would be the true warning voice from these premature graves" (1884: 41).

It should be noted that the preoccupation with marital sexuality marked a movement away from a fixation upon prostitution. While prostitution lurked in the background as the troublesome deviant and non-reproductive form of sexuality, deep social concern about the destabilisation of gender relations was abroad. This was clearly evidenced in the voluminous response to the debate initiated by Mona Caird around the question 'Is marriage a failure?' (Caird 1888; 1897). It was significant that a majority of the published correspondence was critical of the institution of marriage, but what was striking then, as now, was that while the tone was critical, the great majority of participants had high expectations of marriage. Peter Gay's account of the experience of the Victorian middle class is helpful. He identifies a specific form of 'bourgeois anxiety' that was both diffuse and endemic (1984: 57). We might not wish to follow Gay's Freudian terminology in using the term 'repression', but it is a useful marker for a class culture that exhibited such a powerful capacity for self-control and sublimation. It was a culture that blended a spirituality that denied the body with a respectability that demanded the most intense self-consciousness about bodies.

The sexuality that was unable to speak for itself save through euphemisms existed alongside a readiness to account for a great arrays of ills, social and physical, as sexually driven. The Victorian plague of nervousness seems readily comprehensible; the demands for an external self-control and an inner self-monitoring while in search for an expanded sensitivity and sensibility must indeed have been a very demanding existence. The Victorian middle classes, at least in their public discourses, dissociated love from sex. In so doing they made love ethereal yet at the same time trivial, marked externally by the exhibition of domestic respectability and deferential affection. And, more importantly for my immediate purpose, they failed to provide any other socially approved role for women than that of domestic respectability, thereby reinforcing the imagery of woman as the maternal guardian of the home.

There also existed another perception of female sexuality which did not deny female sexuality, but rather distinguished it from male sexuality. This position was also represented by Elizabeth Blackwell. "Physical passion is not in itself evil, on the contrary, it is an essential part of our nature" (1884: 52). She even denied that the sex drive is stronger in men than in women; they have equal, but different, sexual powers, although the "physical functions of sex weigh more imperiously upon the woman than the man" (1885: 47). But women's passion fits with ideas of female moral superiority; it is not an expression of sexual pleasure, but of her desire for motherhood. "The profound depth of the passion of maternity in woman extends not only to the relations of marriage, but to all the weak and suffering wherever found" (1885: 6). Note the significance of her extension "to all the weak", which encapsulates a pervasive current that provided legitimation for middle-class moral or protective surveillance of working-class women. Blackwell constructed her maternal feminism by pointing to the distinctive feature of human sexuality as being that humans were freed from the rigid reproductive cycle of most animals. This biological fact allowed the exercise of reason to control the sexual function. "Chastity is the government of the sexual instinct by the higher reason or wisdom" (1885: 63).

Maternal feminism, in its variant forms, was trapped within its preoccupation with sexual difference and thus allowed itself to be tied to ideals of domesticity, respectability and separate spheres, leading not to a transformation of gender relations, but rather to a reinscription and relegitimation of those beliefs and practices which sustained female subordination. The centrality accorded to maternity led Victorian women back into the home rather than liberating them from domesticity. It is not so much anti-sexual responses that dominate, but rather a petty bourgeois elevation of 'domesticity' which comes to define public discourse of sex, marriage and family, the important implication being that we should reject two related analyses of the late Victorian period. The first account presents 'feminism' and 'purity' as two parallel strands with the purity version coming, by the end of the century, to dominate the 'feminist' dimension. The second conceives a non-repressive feminism succumbing to the more repressive strategy inherent in the purity tradition. My account of the moral regulation organisations confirms that no such separations can be sustained. While maternal feminism was never the only form of feminist thought and practice, it was the dominant one and it involved an ideology and political tactics that found their most coherent expression in the project of sexual purity.

FROM WHITE SLAVERY TO SOCIAL HYGIENE

The dramatic 'success' of the "Maiden Tribute" campaign led the purity reformers to become preoccupied with a search for new targets. New targets they certainly found, but never again was there to be the unity of purpose that the movements around the CDAs and the age of consent had exhibited. Instead we encounter a number of overlapping interventions. Much effort was devoted to the enforcement of the legislative gains of 1885. In particular the provisions in the CLAA 1885, facilitating prosecutions for brothel-keeping, resulted in many local campaigns to close down brothels and to disrupt the tacit red-light districts, which many police forces had found to be the easiest way of regulating prostitution. In these campaigns there were fruitful grounds for co-operation by local branches of the NVA and other purity organisations with the police and municipal authorities. The specific configuration varied: in some cases purity groups had close relations with the police, while in others the police were the enemy accused of condoning prostitution, but these conflicts with the police never reached the sharp antagonisms that transected American urban politics in the late Victorian period. It was easy for such crusades against 'organised vice' to spill over into attacks on prostitutes, who were subject to increased surveillance and harassment. Most contemporary reports note a marked decline in the visibility of prostitution, but it is likely that what occurred was a dispersal rather than a reduction of prostitution.

Others in the purity movement continued to press for the strengthening of legislative provisions for a range of sexual issues. Many urged a further increase of the age of consent; some pressed for an increase to eighteen and a few to twenty-one. Although such demands never made much progress, they were significant in making it clear that the 'protection' of young women was being broadened into an attempt to criminalise non-marital sexual relations, since the ages proposed were above the legal age for marriage. Other legislative projects pursued by the NVA sought a tightening of the statutory rape provisions by removing the three-month limit on prosecutions and by the repeal of the 'reasonable cause' concerning the age of female involved. Another quick legislative victory for the NVA was the passage of the *Indecent Advertisements Act* in 1889, directed against quasi-medical adverts, and this attests to the continuing strength of the anti-contraception stance of both maternal feminism and purity traditions.

A new legislative project sought the criminalisation of incest. Millicent Fawcett raised the demand in 1892 (Fawcett 1892). The LNA, which after 1885 added 'and the Promotion of Social Purity' to its title, took up the criminalisation of incest in 1894.[54] The NVA also adopted incest and organised the first of a number of unsuccessful parliamentary Bills in 1896. The attack on incest was an explicit attack on the disorderly sexuality of the working classes and, by implication, of their threat to social order (Wohl 1978). The moralisation of the working classes is explicit in Ellice Hopkins' plea: "I implore you again, keep the girls and the boys apart at night *somehow*" (Hopkins 1882b: 22). Even the Fabian socialist Beatrice Webb articulated this moralising theme: "to put it bluntly, sexual promiscuity, and even sexual perversion, are almost unavoidable among men and women of average character and intelligence crowded into the one-roomed tenements of slum areas" (Webb 1926: 310).

After a number of parliamentary failures the *Incest Act* finally became law in 1908 and the purity movement celebrated a further strengthening of its legislative armoury (Bailey & Blackburn 1979).[55] The NVA inherited and reinvigorated the long-standing anti-obscenity tradition by launching prosecutions of both literary and visual representations of sexual themes. The English publisher of translations of Zola was successfully prosecuted in 1889 and an exhibition of Rabelais' pictures was cancelled in 1891. The attacks were not limited to high culture. The popular music halls that thrived on a ribald sexuality were major targets of the purity campaigners. Frederick Charrington attacked the music halls as a major source of moral contagion, raising the alarmist claim that "young men and young women were soon sent to a premature grave, but also that many hitherto happy couples were cruelly separated in these infernal dens" (1885: 15). Laura Chant (1895) made herself a butt of popular derision for her attempt to close the Empire Theatre. Sir James Marchant revealed a deeply repressive response when in condemning 'living statues' in the music halls, he argued that female performers should be prosecuted (Bailey 1978: 147–68).

An interesting feature of the English purity project was the failure of its attempts at a more general criminalisation of non-marital sex under the guise of 'seduction' laws, which, as we have seen, were significant components of the American purity agenda that were successfully legislated in a number of states.[56] In England seduction was never given legal recognition beyond the context of its association with the action for breach of promise to marry, which had long been regarded by even respectable opinion as very dubious. Many of the original anti-regulation activists stayed with the issue in a number of colonial contexts, especially India, where a form of regulation associated with the presence of British troops generated the opportunity for British women to espouse the interests of their Indian sisters (Burton 1995).

While much of the energy of purity activists was directed to the parliamentary arena, it should not be forgotten that the form of purity campaigning which reached the largest number of the population, the purity pledge campaigns, continued. There was a series of crusades launched in the early 1900s. James Marchant, major figure in the NVA, launched a 'National Purity Campaign' in 1902; it was reincarnated in 1904 as 'Forward Movement for Purity' (Marchant 1904). These campaigns mounted hundreds of public meetings attracting large working-class audiences, and employed the new technology of lantern shows and films, presenting sex as profoundly dangerous and largely reprehensible thoughts and practices; they issued large numbers of tracts and pamphlets that probably reached millions of adolescents and young adults. It is difficult to assess the significance of these appeals. I have been surprised to find that no attempts were made to count the number of pledges made; this suggests that the purity pledge had none of the symbolic power of the temperance pledge. Similarly it is difficult to get a sense of the impact of the purity rhetoric, with its mix of moral uplift, incitement of sexual anxieties and warnings of national catastrophe that were likely to have compounded feelings of sexual trepidation, especially when linked to the enforced sexual ignorance that afflicted so many. In addition it probably fuelled the mounting sense of national apprehension.

The feature of sexual purity activity that had the most enduring impact in the build-up to the First World War was the white slavery campaign. While, as was noted in the previous chapter, the American white slavery campaign has been extensively studied, the English version of white slavery has been almost entirely neglected.[57] Possibly the first usage of the term was in 1837 by Dr Michael Ryan, who gave what can serve as a definition:

> [T]he infernal traffic in question is still carried on to a great extent, principally by Jews. These white-slave dealers trap young girls into their dens of iniquity, sell them to vice and debaucheries (Ryan 1837: 14).[58]

The 'white slavery traffic' referred to a system of 'commercialised vice' that was believed to be a highly organised international operation whereby young women were trapped or forced into prostitution after having been transported to some foreign destination where they were friendless victims of those who ran and profited from organised prostitution.

Mention has already been made of the first wave of 'white slavery' allegations, when in 1879 Alfred Dyer and William Coote initiated the 'Belgian scandal'. Josephine Butler was also active in Paris, coming into conflict with the '*police des moeurs*'. What emerged were convictions in both Belgium and France for registering young women under the official age of twenty-one, and a complex of practices that placed young inexperienced prostitutes in debt to brothel-keepers. After Dyer's exposé, Butler took up 'white slavery' and formed the London Committee for Suppressing the Traffic in English Girls (1880–81). With the passage of time the term 'white slavery' became a synonym for prostitution, reflecting the belief that no woman would voluntarily enter such a trade and must therefore be the more or less innocent victim of male manipulation or coercion. Thus the white slavery discourses never distinguished between 'exploitation' and 'coercion'.

In 1881 a House of Lords Select Committee was established, which concluded that while most British women in Brussels were professional prostitutes, they were subject to serious abuses. The report recommended raising the age of consent from thirteen to sixteen, the creation of police powers to search for under-age prostitutes, and raising the age of 'abduction for immoral purposes' from sixteen to twenty-one. It recommended the creation of a crime of procuring a woman to leave her usual place of abode for the purposes of prostitution. These recommendations became the basis for many of the provisions of the CLAA 1885, but by this time the focus was primarily on internal prostitution.

A second wave of the white slavery campaign was launched in 1899. The key role was played by the NVA Secretary, William Coote, who formed the British National Committee for the Suppression of the White Slave Traffic. There was an explosion of white slavery tracts, books and novels that achieved wide circulation.[59] While some purity activists were concerned that this material played on prurient interests, the flow continued. These texts took a common narrative form, that of the apocryphal melodrama.[60] The tracts are consistently apocryphal, using scantily identified sources. Significantly, many informants were reported as having been encountered at that most important of Victorian social settings, the railway station. Descriptions of individual undocumented cases are common; they were presented in a typically apocryphal style, "an innocent country girl", "a young woman of good family". The vagueness and elusiveness of the characters blended with a story line in which small errors and ill-chosen companions led rapidly to the brothels of Buenos Aires and an early death. Only rarely is the true melodramatic resolution of salvation permitted.

From the beginning this campaign was internationalised, with the holding in the same year of the first 'International Congress on the Suppression of the White Slave Trade' in London; thereafter there was close interchange between the British and the American campaigns. Immediately a 'white slavery' Bill was introduced in the House of Commons. But progress was slow. It was not until 1912 that W. T. Stead was again to play a role in British purity politics, but this time from the watery grave as one of the victims of the sinking of the *Titanic*. His memory was honoured with another *Criminal Law Amendment Act* 1912 that was widely referred to as the 'White Slavery Act'.[61] The Act gave increased police powers against procurers and brothel-keepers, providing for the arrest of suspected procurers without warrant. Landlords were required to evict any tenant who had been convicted of using the premises for prostitution with penalties for failure to do so. Symbolically significant and testifying to the repressive instincts of the purity movement was the provision that allowed judges to impose whipping on procurers and male brothel-keepers. As with the CLAA 1885, the practical result of the 1912 Act was to intensify the persecution of prostitutes.

The NVA organised a 'Pass the Bill' campaign and there was a brief flurry of mass action, with street demonstrations and mass petitions. The 1912 campaign had a different class resonance from that of the 1885 campaign. The 'daughters of the people' were displaced by a generalised threat to all women and xenophobia was more evident as the guilty became explicitly identified as Jews or 'foreigners'. The South London Free Church Council that had been active in purity politics since the mid-1890s in 1903–04 highlighted what it called 'the Alien Question', the connection between aliens and an increase in brothels and crimes of violence; it cited Polish Jews, Greeks, Italians and Germans as persistent traders in vice.[62] The white slavery movement manifested a condensation of different discourses and different fears into a single image. The themes that had been present in earlier discourses around prostitution were conjuncturally synchronised – fears of non-marital sexuality, prostitution as symbol of urban disorder, a xenophobia elicited by the fears of the coming European conflict. These elements, along with a nostalgia for an imaginary simpler time when gender roles were firmly in place, reinforced images of innocent and fragile women in need of protection. The 1912 campaign exhibited the hallmarks of a 'moral panic', a concept which I have earlier suggested should be used with caution. Nothing had changed in the conditions and practices of prostitution; indeed the streets of London and most other cities had largely been purged of prostitutes. There was no substantive evidence of organised export or import of prostitutes, although large-scale involuntary migration from eastern Europe contributed to a visible foreignness and large numbers of unattached young women in the urban landscape.

The Bill met with little opposition in Parliament, but it was significant that what opposition there was came from feminist quarters.[63] The prominent suffragist Teresa Billington-Grieg expressed scepticism about the whole white slavery construct by dismantling the discourses that inflamed the panic. Not only did the numbers of alleged victims strain credulity, but she noted the repetition of the same stories with minor variations: one of the most often repeated was of a man who visits a brothel only to discover that the prostitute was his daughter or his sister. She pressed the authors of the white slavery tracts for details of the cases they cited and demonstrated their flimsy basis. One involved two girls who had been observed at Sheffield Station with a woman dressed as a rescue worker, but no further evidence was adduced. In another, an informant saw two girls picked up by a car in Richmond, but had no names or registration number. Those asserting the truth of their allegations kept referring to each other for authority. Billington-Grieg concluded that "the truth is that the structure erected by the neuropaths and prudes is reduced to ashes. They are convicted of getting legislation by false pretences" (1913: 445). She particularly objected to the fact that, while presenting men as vicious, they held that women were "impotent and imbecile weaklings incapable of resisting him", and in so doing provided arms and ammunition for "the enemies of women's emancipation" (1913: 445–6).

In the anxious years before the outbreak of war the purity crusades betrayed a deep sense of national and imperial anxiety (Hyam 1990). This is revealed in the manifesto of 1911 addressed to the 'People of Great and Greater Britain' that was published by the National Council of Public Morals:

> We, the undersigned, desire to express our alarm at the low and degrading views of the racial instinct which are becoming widely circulated at the present time, not only because they offend against the highest ideals of morality and religion, but also because they therefore imperil our very life as a nation.[64]

Similar sentiments were voiced by the editor of the influential journal, *The Spectator*:

> Unless the citizens of a State put before themselves the principles of duty, self-sacrifice, self-control, and continence, not merely in the matter of national defence, national preservation, and national well-being, but also of the sex relationship, the life of the State must be short and precarious. Unless the institution of the family is firmly founded and assured, the State will not continue.[65]

It is significant that these discourses linked individual self-formation to national state-formation or preservation. Such linkages that straddled what were otherwise separate fields gained effectivity precisely because of the fusion of everyday individual preoccupations with grander issues of national destiny. They served to endow otherwise mundane projects for the reform of popular culture, such as boys' clubs and useful recreations, with national and imperial themes. These concerns with the fate of the nation and the empire were frequently couched in the narrative form of a 'decline and fall' thesis that took its motif from Gibbon's study of the Roman Empire (1910).[66] The expansion of these themes explains the transition away from a feminist orientation and led to the project of the purity movement being transformed into a social hygiene movement. It was almost as if the participants did not notice the change that was taking place and if they did, they did little or nothing to resist the transmogrification of their movement. It is to this process that I now turn.

The purity authors increasingly incorporated into their discourses a concern with 'race degeneration', a discourse which took more overtly eugenicist forms as the influence of Francis Galton grew around the turn of the century.[67] It is significant that from the beginning Galton himself gave eugenics a strongly moral content in defining it as concern with the improvement of the "inborn qualities of a race with regard to health, energy, ability, manliness and courteous disposition" (1904: 47). Soon purity discourses were suffused with the ambivalent conception of 'race', signifying both the 'human race' and the 'white race'.

The ready adoption of eugenic discourse not only by purity and feminist movements, but by many other strands of social thought, deserves comment. My suggestion is that the espousal of eugenics was an aspect of the secularisation of moral discourses. The self-justifying appeals to God's law and God's wrath suddenly became less persuasive to the rapidly secularising working classes and the middle class, whose religious commitment increasingly approached an occasional conformity. As religion became less self-evident, the prestige of science rose. Yet eugenics reflected a similar intellectual style to that of evangelicalism in that it acquired a categorical form in which the dictates of nature replaced the dictates of God. Its popularity was facilitated by the fact that it reflected back as 'science' that which is familiar (class and sex difference) and justified what its audience already believed (that the working class is a lower order, and women's role is defined by their reproductive organs). Eugenics was common sense, but 'bad sense' in scientific guise. For much feminist thought in the period, confined as it was within the structures of maternalism, eugenics confirmed what was already pleasant to hear, the valorisation of maternity not just as personal duty, but as national destiny. Ellice Hopkins typifies what may be called this familial nationalism:

> When shall we learn that whoever touches the higher life and well-being of a family still more vitally affects the wider family of the State, and threatens its disintegration . . . the State is an organised polity, capable of embodying, preserving and promoting the higher life of the nation (1899: 160).

Marchant, in similar vein, insists that the 'sex instinct' should be called the 'racial instinct' since sex is not primarily for individual pleasure, but for the benefit of the race (1917: 162).

It is important to stress that turn-of-the-century eugenics had a much more benign face than the late twentieth century allows, because eugenics came to be seen as harbouring the germs of genocide and totalitarianism. It is important to draw attention rather to the fact that eugenics provided an important instance of the rise of Foucault's biopolitics of population. Eugenics provided a way of breathing substance into the long-standing connection that purity politics had insisted on between immorality and national peril, and endowed it with the growing prestige of science in general and medicine in particular. Josephine Butler was typical of many evangelicals in insisting on the unity of moral and physical laws. For present purposes, my interest in eugenic thought is restricted to its intersection with the purity movement.

In 1904 Sir James Marchant, who had been an influential and full-time worker in the NVA, left that organisation to found the National Council of Public Morals (NCPM), which was established with the aim of constructing an alliance linking purity advocates, eugenicists and doctors associated with work on venereal diseases (Marchant 1909). The NCPM absorbed many but not all of the existing purity organisations.[68] In 1911 the NCPM issued a 'Manifesto on Public Morals', stating its aims as "the regeneration of the race – spiritual, moral and physical".[69] It called for a renewed morals campaign in order to inculcate "the great truth that the racial instinct [i.e. sexual instinct] exists not primarily for individual satisfaction but for the wholesome perpetuation of the human family".[70] The extent of the shift in thinking is exemplified by the fact that in the same year Havelock Ellis, whom we have previously encountered as a sex reformer pouring scorn on 'moral legislators', had his book, *The Problem of Race-Regeneration* (1911), published by the National Council of Public Morals with an Introduction by James Marchant. He presented eugenics as a profoundly moralising discourse:

> These [unfit] classes, with their tendency to weak-mindedness, their inborn laziness, lack of vitality, and unfitness for organised activity, contain the people who complain that they are starving for want of work, though they never perform any work that is given them (1911: 44).

The NCPM was orientated to work in close alliance with Parliament and state institutions; it had no aspirations to become a mass movement. Its focus of attention shifted decisively towards concern with venereal disease. It is a significant feature of the medicalisation of moral reform that 'the problem' with which it engaged was no longer prostitution. The moral discourses of the purity movement became blended with the medical concern with the prevention and treatment of sexually transmitted diseases; Frank Mort captures this shift with his concept "the medico-moral complex" (1987: 4).

At the beginning of the twentieth century, feminist inspiration became more intently focused on the question of suffrage. It was not that purity and suffrage were in any significant sense opposed, although in Britain, as in the United States, there were suffrage campaigners who resisted too close a relation to purity themes, fearing that the espousal of purity demands would generate increased resistance from men who might otherwise have supported demands for equal political rights.[71] Rather it was that the women who were drawn into active political involvement in the 1870s and 1880s had been inspired by purity politics, while in the 1900s it was suffrage that was the active agent of politicisation.

The outbreak of war in 1914 brought a rapid change to the political terrain on which moral regulation politics operated. Military concerns came to the fore. There was a growing concern with venereal diseases among military personnel. It was for this reason that a 'Royal Commission on Venereal Diseases' was appointed. It was centrally concerned with the issue of prevention, but its debates were strongly influenced by the classic anti-regulationist objection that nothing should be done by the state to promote or accept vice. It was for this reason that the proposal that contraceptives should be issued to soldiers was summarily rejected, but this objection did not hold sway against the key recommendations for the establishment of accessible treatment facilities for both military and civilian personnel. The commission's report, published in 1916, was constructed of a mix of moral and medical discourses, but its recommendations were overwhelmingly concerned with military and medical matters (Great Britain 1916). It led to the establishment of the semi-official body, National Council for Combating Venereal Disease (NCCVD), supported by grants from both central and local government. By now even the Association for Moral and Social Hygiene (the successor to the LNA) declared that "the attempts to suppress vice by penal legislation can accomplish very little" (1920: 13). By the end of the War a widely dispersed system of 'VD Clinics' existed, even though there was a considerable degree of stigmatisation associated with them. Located in the most unattractive facilities, they provided treatment, but at the price of an environment of stern moralisation and harsh discipline.

The most important practical consequence of the Royal Commission was the introduction in 1917 of 'Regulation 40D' under emergency powers created under the *Defence of the Realm Act* 1916. These made it an offence for a woman affected with a transmissible form of VD to solicit or have sex with a member of the armed forces. An attempt was made to make these changes permanent. A 'Criminal Law Amendment Bill' was introduced in Parliament; it sought to reintroduce medical examination for prostitutes, make transmission of a communicable VD an offence and increase penalties for soliciting. However, the Bill was dropped as a result of opposition, which for a while reignited the memory of the struggles against the CDAs. In 1920 a package of moral regulation and regulationist Bills was sent to a Joint Committee of Parliament, from which came a final victory for the purity forces. The *Criminal Law*

Amendment Act of 1922 abolished the "reasonable cause to believe" clause with respect to statutory rape of females under sixteen; in addition it further increased penalties for brothel-keepers.

At the end of the War purity voices were still vociferous, but probably commanded less attention. The purity contention was still heard that to provide readily available treatment for VD was itself an encouragement for vice, since it removed an important deterrent against immorality. The National Council of Public Morals persisted with the imperial and racial rhetoric: "as the world-war revealed, the whole of the white races must, in the end, stand together to maintain their position in the world, or they will be overwhelmed in racial competition" (NCPM 1921: 41). Mary Scharlieb, of the London Council for the Promotion of Public Morality, sustained a fiery condemnation of birth control as a "general relaxation of the moral fibre" (1920). But James Marchant's tone had changed considerably: on birth control his position was now that the desire to control the number of children "cannot be described as a sign of depravity or frivolity" (1917: 144). By 1924 the wartime NCCVD had become the British Social Hygiene Council (BSHC) and broadened its objectives to encompass a mix of family welfare issues and some older purity themes such as an equal standard of sexual morality, and 'racial improvement'. But tensions between 'moral' and 'medical' discourses continued well into the 1920s; despite significant official backing, the BSHC tended to lose out to projects more narrowly focused on medical approaches and came to avoid the moralisation of sexually transmitted diseases.

While the infrastructure of the pre-War purity organisations remained in place, they slowly declined, losing members and financial support. Increasingly their tone and message lost the hegemonic potential that it had gained in certain conjunctures in the previous period. They came to sound 'old fashioned' and were more and more frequently met with an amused rejection of their 'prudery'. The underlying cause of this falling-away was that the predominant response to social problems had taken a welfarist shift. This is most evident in responses to mass unemployment. Climactic events like the General Strike of 1926 manifested deep anxieties among the respectable classes over the threat to social order. However, the underlying common sense was that for an individual to be unemployed was not evidence of moral fault, but was a structural socio-economic problem. While there were deep political divisions about both the degree and form of state intervention in social and economic matters, few continued to believe that seeking to impose moral regulation had any significant contribution to make. Of particular importance were important shifts in the discourses of marriage and sex in which the ideal of companionate marriage and mutual sexual satisfaction came to the fore (Holtzman 1982; Van de Velde 1928). Purity rhetoric became increasingly marginalised and purity organisations were unable to sustain significant campaigns. Yet they continued to be heard as the background chorus to the continuing battles over literary and theatrical censorship in which the work of D. H. Lawrence has a special place, up to and including the famous trial of *Lady Chatterley's Lover*, originally banned in 1928 and not reprieved until 1961 (Thomas 1969, Rolph 1961). Between the Wars the purity themes became increasingly ideologically conservative, existing largely as sectional interests within conservative political and religious organisations.

PURITY, MATERNAL FEMINISM AND CLASS

How should we understand the remarkable proliferation of discourses and organisations that congregated around the theme of sexual purity in the period between 1870 and 1914? I will elaborate and defend the view that the moral regulation movements of late Victorian Britain were manifestations of a distinctive 'governmentalisation of the sexual field'.[72] By 'governmentalisation' I demarcate first those discourses and practices whereby something comes to be regarded as a proper and suitable object to be governed and, second, the means of governing which are deployed through a complex of more or less rationalised programmes, strategies, tactics and techniques directed towards acting upon the actions of others. I will insist, that 'acting on others' includes all external forms of action (surveillance, constraint, coercion) and these forms are directed to stimulate and incite the governance of the self. It should be stressed that I intentionally employ a broad conception of what it means to be governed; Proudhon captures this with his remarkable definition:

> Being governed means being under police supervision, being inspected, spied upon, directed, buried under laws, regulated, hemmed in, indoctrinated, preached at, controlled, assessed, censored, commanded, . . . noted, registered, captured, appraised, stamped, surveyed, evaluated, taxed, patented, licensed, authorised, recommended, admonished, prevented, reformed, aligned, and punished in every action, every transaction, every movement (1923: 294).

The governmentalisation of the 'sexual field' was, of course, not invented by the Victorians, but as Foucault argued, they produced a "veritable discursive explosion" (1978: 17). The sexual is not confined to 'sexual acts', but includes the way in which gender is sexualised, as when male and female authors were reputedly segregated on library shelves, and the way in which gender attributes such as feminine frailty were eroticised. The governmentalisation of the sexual is crucially concerned with the way in which it is rendered into something that can potentially be governed. A crucial part is played by classifying practices that distinguish between different sexual acts and desires which are not merely ranked but differentiated into normative categories such as 'natural' and 'unnatural', 'licit' and 'illicit'. The sexual becomes governed through the deployment of mechanisms of prohibition and incitement. Prohibitions include the criminalisation of specific acts (e.g. before the CLAA 1885 made 'gross indecency' between males a criminal offence, 'buggery' had long been a felony) or types of relationships (e.g. incest, adultery). But prohibitions also include informal sanctions imposed on those who breach the rules of conduct (e.g. appropriate and non-appropriate touching and gestures) or violate the normative framework of gender relations (e.g. ridicule of effeminate males and masculine females). Incitement is rooted in the sexualisation of difference through which individuals are prompted, nudged, pushed into 'appropriate' expressions of sexual desire. But incitement also includes more overtly governmental action as, for example, when tax benefits accrue to the married and are denied to the unmarried or same-sex partners.

For present purposes I am concerned with the way in which the governance of the sexual changed its form and its techniques in Victorian Britain. What was distinctive about Victorian moral regulation was the important role played by social movements and how such non-governmental bodies entered into complex connections with the state in the transformation of the sexual field. The purity reformers were active participants in the production of new sexual identities; they stressed the link between extramarital sex and venereal disease, and highlighted adolescent sexuality, especially that of young unattached women in the cities; not only were such sexualities identified, but they were then tracked down, exposed, tamed or eradicated. Purity forces endorsed and participated in attempts to regulate extramarital sex via the imposition of what Nancy Wood has identified as a specific "regime of domesticity" (1982: 76).[73]

The purity reformers were active in the production of targets for regulation by means of discourses that served to create or reinvigorate distinctive 'dividing practices'.[74] Distinctions were sustained between 'respectable' and 'non-respectable', between 'pure' and 'impure', between 'self-control' and 'self-indulgence', between the 'racially superior' and 'the degenerate'. These dividing practices percolated into a whole range of official knowledge.

What is of significance is that these practices are double-sided in that they bring together two fields, that of 'sex/gender' and that of 'class'. The problem of how to theorise the coexistence of multiple structural divisions, with sex, class and race being the three most frequent points of reference in contemporary debates, in a way which does not accord some *a priori* causal priority to one or the other remains one of the most difficult tasks confronting social theory. For this reason I end this chapter with some reflections on the way in which moral regulation projects in Victorian Britain were interventions in both sexual politics and class politics; the discourses on sexuality always had distinctive class articulations. It will be recalled that in Chapter 3 I took issue with the view that nineteenth-century moral reform was directed primarily against the working class. In its place I suggested that, for both the United States and Britain, the primary targets of the Victorian purity wars were upper- and middle-class males, and that the main thrust in both Britain and the United States was directed at fostering the self-formation of the dominant classes, in which the expanded middle classes had come to play an important if subaltern role. In this chapter I have demonstrated that some components of the moral reform projects in Britain were unambiguously targeted at sections of the working class; this is true of the campaign to criminalise incest and also of the complex of interventions with respect to juvenile female sexuality epitomised in the legislation on industrial schools. Further, it is important to understand disjunctions between discourses and practices: thus while anti-prostitution discourses were directed against male patrons and economic exploiters, the practices amounted to increased surveillance of street prostitutes.

The central character of the British purity movements was their coupling of two distinct mechanisms of social power, those of gender and class, which came together to produce distinctively gendered forms of class relations and class forms of gender relations. For a first level of presentation we can conceive of these processes as a feminised set of discourses and practices seeking to act upon male sexuality; at its core was the outrage vented against the 'double standard', symbolised by the dividing practices through which women were either 'pure' or 'fallen'. This division was both instantiated and symbolised in the institution of prostitution. Men had a double set of relations with women as 'virtuous wives and mothers' and as commercial sex; it should be noted that this line of thought only had to take a small inflexion to re-emerge as the radical critique that marriage and prostitution were both forms of sexual commerce between men and women (e.g. Caird 1897).

At a second level of analysis we need to insert the idea that, in seeking to act on male sexuality, women moral reformers were also acting upon themselves in self-constituting their own gendered and sexualised identities.[75] They were producing an active maternal feminism which, although built from much of the same material as an earlier patriarchal construction of womanhood, replaced the passive 'angel in the home' with the strong maternal moral guardian of the home. Without suggesting that women thereby secured anything approximating to equality, it is important to suggest that maternal feminism was a significant intervention in the structure of gender relations. The major result was twofold: first, it carved out large dimensions of the domestic field as a domain of female authority and, second, it secured some small but significant sectors of the public sphere as feminised terrain: moral politics, philanthropy, family policy and gradually social work and wider fields of social welfare became legitimate arenas of female intervention.

Thus while the gender politics of maternal feminism sought to act upon aspects of male sexuality, its class dimension was preoccupied with two important arenas of class politics: first, the sexuality of middle-class men and, second, the respectabilisation of working-class men. I suggest the former was the predominant arena of the sexual politics of maternal feminism and that its core was directed to bring male sexuality into line with the wider process of the domestication of male social life. Men were increasingly induced to take more pleasure in their homes, to take their recreations within the 'comfort' increasingly provided there and thus to withdraw from more unruly forms of external sociability. Visiting, receiving, dining and entertainment became increasingly important in middle-class life, and came increasingly under female control. Maternal feminism was a major vehicle of the 'myth of the family' as a yearning for a place of harmony and sociability. The project in so far as it was directed at working-class men was concerned to promote the values of domesticity. One important dimension that was present in both the purity and temperance movements was to induce working men to spend their leisure time at home and not in the pub.

The central demand of purity reformers for male chastity was concerned with both sexual and class dimensions. It was a project that can best be understood as being about the class formation of the middle classes as an increasingly important component of the dominant bloc. This can be seen most clearly in the often radical critique of upper-class immorality. The condemnation of wealthy rakes and metropolitan *flâneurs* was part of a shift, whose full dimensions are too complex to document fully here, in which the middle classes increasingly came to conceive of themselves as the hegemonic force in British society. The industrial and financial bourgeoisie rarely sought to play a direct and public role in political leadership. The old aristocracy was less and less able to secure its role as the natural leader of the Conservative Party. As the middle classes came more and more to equate themselves with 'the nation' and with 'the Empire' they became increasingly concerned about their ability to be the kind of class able to sustain a system with such high self-expectations. This was especially true in a context barely visible at the time, although British supremacy was already waning.

The 'new' middle class was increasingly engaged in professional, administrative and managerial roles, with its leadership located within the increasingly meritocratic civil service and in the new municipal universities (Perkin 1969; 1989). This class was increasingly preoccupied with its own self-formation as a ruling authority, concerned with the self-justification and ethical competence of its aspirations to rule. To this end it was concerned with its technical capacities, the mobilisation of science and ideals of progress, but it was responsive to the thrust, if not always the specific content, of the purity campaigns. The middle class was concerned with its own moral, or perhaps better, ethical capacity for tasks which it conceived as onerous and demanding; thus those who were to govern should themselves be morally regulated so as to secure cultural hegemony (Osborne 1994: 292). If the middle class was to be a new 'ethical class', it required what John Rajchman has called the "ethical subjectivity of power" (1991: 116). It is in this sense, more limited than she herself suggests, that Mariana Valverde is correct to identify moral regulation as being focused on the production of "ethical subjectivities" (Valverde 1991: 216).[76]

I turn to the relationship between the British middle class and the working class. An important component of the project of middle-class hegemony required a new relationship with the working class. In the early nineteenth century the middle class was suffused with a deep fear and disgust when it surveyed the working class: for example, Kay-Shuttleworth spoke of the "volcanic elements, by whose explosive violence the structure of society may be destroyed" (1832/1970: 112). The contemporary debate over the disorderly working class, its increasingly insubordinate disposition, its desperate forms of life and its disorderly leisure, symbolised a whole set of middle-class anxieties run together when confronted with the improvidence, immorality and criminality of the lower orders. Alongside periodic eruptions of coercive responses to the threat, real or imagined, to social order, a more reflective strategy appeared, namely, that of creating a respectable working class that could serve as a 'transmission belt' by which the values of thrift, self-help, temperance and sexual propriety could be diffused throughout the working classes.[77]

Robert Storch posed the important question: how should we account for the perseverance of middle-class moral reform projects after 1850? Why was it that after the profound social crisis, which lasted from Waterloo to the end of Chartism, after the decline of any immediate danger to social order, they became even more energetic in promoting projects of moral reform with its typically bourgeois impulse to mould the inner man, to transform him morally? (1977: 155). And why, I add, was this project so predominantly a moralisation generated and staffed by the middle class in which the upper classes played such a limited role? Storch's answer to his interesting question is that the continued promotion of what he calls the "conventicles of respectability" was simply the other side of the coin of moral environmentalism and sanitary reform. The middle classes were consciously concerned to effect "the reimposition of a system of common morality" (1977: 156–7).

My answer to Storch's question is significantly different. First, as I have argued above, he neglects that whole dimension of reform projects that were concerned with the self-transformation of the middle class itself. Second, with respect to the relationship with the working class, it was not just a quest for a shared morality. The activists were concerned to promote the enlightenment, cultivation and improvement of the people (symbolised by an improved sexual morality), in order to cement the two great modern classes into a 'new' national community under the leadership of the middle class, which deserved and had earned the right to rule. At the core of this strategy was a dual environmentalism, a socio-economic strategy and a moral reform strategy. The socio-economic strategy laid the basis of what by the early twentieth century was coming to be called 'welfare' and subsequently expanded to become the welfare state with its reliance on the provision of a measure of economic security through insurance techniques coupled with interventionist strategies in the fields of education, housing and other arenas. The dimensions of moral regulation of the working class were concerned with the surveillance of youthful sexualities, primarily of females and, more generally, with making the working-class family correspond ever more closely to the middle class's own myth of the family.

The forms taken by such strategies could and did vary considerably. It is for this reason that we should be careful about drawing too sharp a contrast between coercive and non-coercive strategies. As I have argued, British purity movements should not be viewed as an alliance between conservative moralists and non-authoritarian feminists; neither were the purity feminists pushed aside by doctors or sexologists, nor did they somehow lapse from an otherwise liberal concern with individual rights. As I hope to have demonstrated, maternal feminism was always paternalistic, with the consequence that when the targets of its moralising concern failed to transform themselves through active self-governance, resort to coercive legislation was never far behind. The outcome was that the purity feminists were most successful in securing legislation that impinged on the weaker among their targets. This should remind us that the middle classes had not secured leadership within the political system. This helps explain the highly cautious approach to purity demands by those that held political power at the centre not only of the Conservative Party, but within the Liberal Party. These forces rarely took the lead in matters of moral regulation. The general pattern of the purity reform movement, from the abolitionist battles of the 1870s to the Great War, is that it combined the self-formation of the middle classes with a coercion that fell most heavily on street prostitutes, the 'fallen sisters'.

CHAPTER 6

RETRADITIONALISING MORAL REGULATION: MAKING SENSE OF CONTEMPORARY MORAL POLITICS

THE RETURN OF MORAL REGULATION?

The two previous chapters left the sexual purity and hygiene movements just after the First World War; from that vantage point moral regulation movements were on the wane. They did not disappear completely; indeed in one important respect they reached their single most important impact with the prohibition amendment to the American Constitution in 1919. Prohibition was in an important respect the culmination of the long nineteenth century; between 1890 and 1916 sixteen states had gone dry and it was the heightened wartime nationalism that was critical in tipping the balance in favour of prohibition. The focus on alcohol significantly deflected personnel and resources away from other moral reform projects, such that, when the prohibition experiment floundered in the 1920s and was ended in 1933, moral regulation had became increasingly conservative, concerned with a nostalgic 'good old days' of class deference, religious conformity, gender certainty and bourgeois respectability. The old legitimations for prescriptive moral codes couched in terms of social conformism no longer retained much influence over the working classes and sections of the middle classes were restless. In Britain the moral reform forces had dissipated during and immediately after the First World War. It would have been an eminently persuasive prognostication to conclude that such movements would fade away into the margins of conservative politics.

Moral politics did not disappear; rather it underwent a significant change in form. The trajectory was one in which issues of moral reform became deeply imbricated in the shift of social problems into the arena of state action. In this form moral reform became located within increasingly utilitarian discourses. For example, unmarried mothers were still moralised, but their offspring were increasingly channelled into state-administered adoption regimes; they were stigmatised as illegitimate. The results of this socialisation of moralised social problems became encapsulated in 'the welfare state', which reached different levels and forms of state involvement in different jurisdictions. The extension of the range and scope of such governmentalisation of social problems expanded rapidly in the wake of the economic depression of the late 1920s and the exigencies of the Second World War.

To study these developments would require a much closer inspection of state practices, policies and institutions. Such an undertaking would disrupt the focus upon reform movements arising from within society. Accordingly the focus of this chapter is upon moral regulation movements from the 1970s onwards. Thus, as indicated earlier, the present chapter differs in important respects from those that precede it.

It does not purport to offer an analysis of the wide variety of moral regulation movements and projects that have appeared over the last three decades. Instead the focus is consciously restricted to pursue a comparison of recent movements with the sexual purity movements of the late nineteenth century.

By the 1960s 'social welfare' was being perceived by critiques, from both Left and Right, as a system of bureaucratic moralisation and disciplinarity. Welfare had become a profoundly paternalistic set of disciplinary practices operating to expand the production of disciplined bodies wedded to the requirements of the labour market and the reproduction of familial relations that generated useful citizens. In contrast to welfare's paternalism, the new hegemonic discourses of consumerism invoked 'choice', and the individual as 'consumer', to become the heart of the social imagination.[1]

However, moral regulation did not remain encapsulated within this welfarist framework; to play a minor supporting role within the welfare apparatuses was not the final resting place of moral politics. This concluding chapter engages with the striking phenomenon of the rebirth or re-emergence of a vigorous and expanded realm of social movements pursuing a great diversity of moral regulation projects. Even as 'welfare' was undergoing its most rapid extension and expansion in the 1960s, there emerged 'new moralisations' from a fresh crop of social movements springing up from within civil society. At first many of these campaigns were attempts to reimpose sexual respectability, decorum and good manners on the cultural industries through campaigns to revitalise censorship or to implement self-censorship in films and TV, along with the more traditional battles over the theatre and literature. In the United States, Citizens for Decency Through Law pressed for tougher obscenity laws and initiated attacks on sexually explicit literature, symbolised by the court battles over *Lady Chatterley's Lover* and *Tropic of Cancer*. Meanwhile in Britain, Mary Whitehouse and the National Viewers and Listeners' Association pursued a remorseless campaign against the BBC over 'bad language' and the amount of flesh exposed on screen. Such projects were instances of traditional conservative attempts to reinstate an old version of respectability. They sought to revalorise a sexuality confined within marriage that was private in the sense of something not spoken of and practised with the lights out. Explanations couched in terms of status anxiety or petty bourgeois repression are more than adequate to explain this genre of moral politics.

Yet less than two decades later these conservative projects were to re-enter the mainstream in the 1980s when they moved to centre stage as the radical politics of neo-liberalism, and in doing so reactivated the discourses of morality. This was classically exemplified by Margaret Thatcher's linking of individual responsibility and 'family values', which came to encapsulate a whole package of moral projects. In order to understand this revitalisation of moral politics, I draw on Clifford Geertz's interesting contention that such conservative moral ideologies are not simply a return to traditionalism, but rather involve an "ideological retraditionalism" that is "an altogether different matter" from 'traditionalism' (Geertz 1973: 219). Unfortunately he does not flesh out what is distinctive about 'retraditionalisation', but I hope to be able to amplify this concept. I suggest that it should be understood as involving two key elements. First, it involves efforts to provide fresh grounds and justifications for projects to reinstate traditional forms of social relations and to respond to new and disturbing social changes that were exemplified in the demonisation of 'the sixties' and the 'permissiveness' that refused deference to religious authority or to social hierarchy. Second, and I suggest more important, is that 'retraditionalisation' advances a new configuration of social values.

The operation of this mechanism of retraditionalisation can be illustrated by examining Margaret Thatcher's reintroduction of 'family values'. While this process can be observed in other neo-liberal discourses, Thatcher has the advantage of being more explicit than others in her politics. This retraditionalisation is particularly evident in Thatcherism, more so than in Reagan's politics, because of her explicit assault on the traditional institutional power located within the quasi-aristocratic rulers of the Conservative Party (Letwin 1992). It is in this context that her espousal of 'enterprise culture' highlighted individual responsibility rather than faith in the blind forces of the market. We can make sense of one of Thatcher's most famous pronouncements: "There is no such thing as Society. There are individual men and women, and there are families" (1993: 626). She constructs 'families' as the primary social unit, voluntarily entered into by autonomous parties equally capable of exercising responsibility and capable of cultivating robust virtues and initiative. The family is counterposed to the bureaucratic paternalism of the welfare state. While Thatcher was no feminist, neither did she espouse a return to the traditional family constituted around a male 'breadwinner' with a non-employed wife devoted to maternal tasks. Rather she presumed that marriage partners could work out for themselves the complex mix of parental duties and economic activities. It should be noted that this analysis entirely omitted any recognition of structural features of gender orders or of labour markets. The key feature is that Thatcherism exemplifies a 'retraditionalisation' in that her politics of the family is not reducible to the reinvocation of a traditional family (Wilson 1987).

Matters become more complex when we notice that Thatcher also explicitly invoked the authority of tradition. "Victorian values aren't Victorian; they're really, I think, fundamental eternal truths."[2] The tendency which Thatcher exemplified involved an enfolding of new content within traditional discourses, thereby adding, I suggest, an important component to our understanding of the mechanisms of 'ideological retraditionalisation'. Its importance is that the plausibility and legitimacy of moral discourses were powerfully augmented by the admixture of 'new' and 'old' elements in such a way as to paper over tensions and contradictions. Thatcher's invocation of 'responsible families' and 'Victorian values' avoids endorsing the Victorian sexual division of labour, while at the same time adding the authority of tradition and continuity to her message. This tendency of recent moral reform projects to combine 'old' and 'new' elements that are ultimately incompatible makes it unwise, if not impossible, to impose unidimensional categories such as 'conservative' or 'progressive', 'pro-sex' or 'anti-sex' on these movements.

Nowhere is this political ambivalence more evident than with respect to perhaps the most distinctive feature of moral reform over recent decades. Movements emerged which deployed discourses of moral regulation in the register of 'social transformation'; these movements barely cast a glance backwards over their shoulders. Their organisational forms, political rhetoric and style were unambiguously 'modern'. Most significantly, these movements spoke uncompromisingly in the name of a reinvigorated feminism, its 'second wave', characterised by an emphasis on the limits of formal political equality and on the persistence of continuing inequalities that reproduce gendered structures resulting in the systemic subordination of women.

The main objective of this chapter is to explore the relationships between these different strands of moral reform. They sometimes coalesce and at other times take different trajectories. In order to accomplish this task, I will not attempt to provide a detailed account of the multiple movements that form the topography of contemporary moral regulation. Instead of a detailed examination of a myriad of organisations, I will offer a comparative account of moral regulation projects over the last three decades. My reason, aside from the fact that a full mapping would itself require a book-length treatment, is that much of that map will already be familiar to readers and that this task has been undertaken by others.[3]

EXPLAINING MORAL REGULATION

In turning attention to our own period, we confront two distinct problems, which, though they appear different, are, I will argue, manifestations of the same difficulty. The problem is how to avoid the temptation to lapse into what has rather clumsily come to be called 'presentism', that is, the tendency to privilege the presumed uniqueness of our current circumstances. One aspect is the temptation, that is strongly represented throughout the tradition of social theory, that accentuates 'our' difference from that which has gone before. The most significant manifestation that impinges on my current concerns is the idea that the modern history of 'developed' societies has undergone a process of individualisation which has created the modern subject.[4] The version that has been influential in accounts of the trajectory of projects of moral regulation suggests that there has been a fundamental shift from attempts to impose external codes of behaviour to projects that seek to stimulate self-governance. In short, this view argues for a long-run shift from the 'governance of others' to the 'governance of the self'. Nor should we too readily accept another version of the presentist thesis that claims that the twentieth century has seen morality displaced as a disciplinary technique by the onward march of medicalisation and the 'medical gaze'. As I have argued with respect to both the United States and Britain in the nineteenth century, medical discourses on sexuality did not simply replace moral discourses, but rather distinctive versions of medico-moral discourses came to predominate.

The opposite, but essentially similar, trend is one that focuses attention on the continuity and the persistence of what went before in order to trace it into the present.[5] In its most influential form, such an account invokes the idea that there has been a return or historical reprise. This model takes the form of a thesis that moral regulation movements undergo a sequential transition from attempts at persuasion only to end by promoting coercion; such a model is exemplified by Blocker's (1989) account of the temperance–prohibition movements in the United

States. With respect to accounts of the history of moral regulation, its most common expression is the contention that 'second-wave' feminism has 'returned' to the theory and politics of 'first-wave' feminism in so far as it has pursued a strategy that has revived the purity politics of the nineteenth century.

It is important to insist that neither of these two related explanatory strategies is 'wrong'; there is much evidence that can be adduced to support both views. My point is a rather different one: the alternative approach which I will seek to amplify is one that refuses to adopt either of the two *a priori* explanatory models. Rather I will attend to the complex of ways in which human dispositions have been formed and conduct governed in different historical periods. This involves attention to the interaction between the different forms of authority, of expertise, of truth, and the techniques and tactics employed.

In order to avoid misunderstanding, I distinguish my position from two interpretations of the case being argued which I consciously seek to avoid. First, I am not arguing against any possibility of social explanation by espousing relativism, insisting that everything is contingent, that each and every event has its own unique contextual conditions. Nor do I want to be read as suggesting that 'nothing changes'. Current moral regulation projects are, I insist, different from those of earlier periods. Rather I will defend the claim that they are different because they exhibit a different configuration of components, even though they share features of earlier Victorian movements. Thus, for example, I will stress that the greatly enhanced significance of recent projects of self-governance, which draw their resources from the psychological discourses, does not mean that self-governance is 'new'. As I have stressed in previous chapters, a central feature of Victorian moral politics was less a matter of external coercion, but more significantly directed at the project of 'self-control' of the middle classes. The techniques employed and the discourses mobilised allow us to distinguish between different forms or styles of self-governance.

Projects of moral regulation involve participants who actively seek to chart and engage with social problems perceived and experienced as problematic or dangerous.[6] Moral reformers are social explorers; this was especially the case in the nineteenth century, when they ventured out into the streets and, like their compatriots exploring the jungles of 'darkest Africa', they penetrated the hovels inhabited by the poor, the brothels of the prostitutes and the drinking establishments frequented by the lower orders.[7] Today's research undertakings are not experienced as so dangerous, although participant observation studies of the underclasses still retain a frisson of voyeurism. These explorations generate social topographies whose basic components map morals against the central repertoire of class, gender, criminality and disease. For example, the diverse techniques deployed by the psy complex generate new topographies of conduct and disposition and also make use of new techniques of therapeutic intervention. These techniques of the expert governance of the self are reinforced by claims to scientific justification. The techniques are more extensive than those available to the Victorians, who had to make do with stern regimes of the reading of religious texts and practices of self-scrutiny and introspection that were coupled with doses of exhortation backed by warnings of dire consequences, as when the juvenile masturbator was threatened with insanity and early death. It is important to note that the social location of experts changes. The older forms of authority sustained by unitary professional bodies certified by the state have been undermined by a pluralisation of experts. This process is well captured by Bauman's contention that today's experts and intellectuals cease to be 'legislators' and are now merely 'interpreters' (1987). As a result, individuals are increasingly required to choose their own preferred 'expertise' and to take responsibility and for their own "self-constitution" (1992b: 201–4).[8]

Not only do the discourses and the techniques available vary over time, but so too does their relationship to formal institutions and the apparatuses of the state. It is by now clear that moral regulation has long been predominantly a field of voluntary action coming, if not from 'below', at least from the 'middle'.[9] Such activities were rarely formally co-ordinated, but they were brought together and acquired a semblance of coherence through the generation of discursive formations: for example, in the nineteenth century through the networks formed by projects of 'character' and 'self-control', where the 'will' was trained to exercise restraint over conduct. The changes in the regimes of self-governance did not simply replace some earlier version, but rather injected or enfolded new forms of authority and expertise into the practices of the self. It is for this reason that I have insisted that moral regulation is not simply a matter of social control of the dangerous classes, by stressing that such projects significantly engaged with the self-formation of significant categories such as young middle-class men, professional women and respectable mothers. It should be borne in mind that these projects were far from homogeneous and coexisted with counter-discourses. Thus a plurality of moral discourses and voices is not only an attribute of the present. What is new is that the truths and techniques produced a shift from 'vice' and 'sin' to contemporary concerns with 'addictions' and 'abuse'.

Throughout the nineteenth and twentieth centuries new authorities have gradually colonised the practices and rationalities of self-fashioning, self-formation and self-management.[10] A key feature of the twentieth century has been the 'governmentalisation' of the linkages between the governance of others and governance of the self. Rather than being alternative strategies of moral reform – disciplinary governance of others *versus* the self-reform of the will – the relation between these components is both intentional and linked: for example contemporary anti-smoking strategy employs self-help techniques for 'quitting', medical innovations, dire health warnings from experts, along with disciplinary practices that have shrunk the spaces that the smoker may inhabit. These techniques and tactics come together to produce an intense moralisation of tobacco consumption, one of the most salient features being a class moralisation which increasingly associates smoking with defective self-care and a lack of cultural sophistication. Every area of moral regulation exhibits a distinctive combination of techniques of governance. For this reason I counsel caution before adopting a one-dimensional explanatory model such as that offered by appeal to 'medicalisation' or 'psychologisation'.

More generally it is important to avoid the seductions offered by theorists of modernity. While such theories take a number of forms, a common feature identifies a shift in the form of relations between a deepening individualisation and a weakening or fragmentation of relations with others, an increasing distance between a sovereign individual and community. The most influential versions link modernity and individuality, embracing themes of secularisation, rationalisation, de-traditionalisation and reflexivity.[11] One version of this account pertinent to an understanding of the place of moral regulation is Baumgartner's (1988) thesis that modernism is associated with a "moral minimalism" of the suburbs ('Don't get involved', 'It's not my business'). Such a position makes it extremely puzzling how it comes to be that significant numbers of the relatively secure inhabitants of the suburbs have come to be mobilised by moral campaigns around such targets as child abuse, pornography and sexual choice. There is little mystery about how such issues become part of the lexicon of the modern moral politics of the conservative and fundamentalist religious wings as a manifestation of the revolt against modernism and secularism (Kepel 1994; Marty & Appelby 1991–94).

For this reason, I will focus my attention on the participation of sections of the intelligentsia and the professional and related strata. Not only is this more difficult to explain, but it is from these constituencies that new content and form have been injected into moral regulation projects. However, we should not rule out the possibility that such social groups are affected by some anti-modernist currents. For example, it may help to explain the attraction of the new moral politics for those women, now a declining minority, who are outside the labour market and for whom mothering is a central component of identity, and who have responded to feminist valorisation of mothering since it defends and legitimises that self-identity (Chodorow 1978).[12] But significantly it valorises maternity in a 'new' form; it no longer seeks to ennoble the 'housewife', but rather links such women not only to single mothers, but more importantly to the economic and social interests of working mothers. However, we should, I suggest, rule out the idea that middle-class employed women have been experiencing a significant decline in their social status; thus 'status anxiety' accounts suggesting that declining social groups exhibit symptoms of *ressentiment* will be of little help.[13] Similarly it leads me to reject Bourdieu's thesis that moral revolts can be explained as emanating from "declining fractions of the petty bourgeoisie" (1984: 435). This approach is unable to explain the part played by the core constituencies of what may be designated as the modernist moral reformers, the most important category being the radical feminists, who are so prominent in many of today's moral reform projects. While their rise in academic, administrative and business enterprises has not been without major battles, they are indisputably on the social and economic ascendancy.

These considerations lead directly to the question: what, if anything, is 'new' about current projects of moral regulation? And in particular, what does contemporary feminism contribute to these projects? As I have indicated above, my answer will require me to distinguish my position from a familiar line of thought which argues that the overtly anti-sexual current in contemporary moral politics represents a reversion to the doctrine of separate spheres and the maternal feminism of the late nineteenth century and as such amounts to a 'new Victorianism'.[14] Moral reformers today, both conservatives and feminists, share with the Victorian purity reformers a view of sex as an inherently dangerous force and also share an anti-hedonism in so far as 'pleasure' is not valorised as a significant human aspiration. Relying on a rigid bipolar construction of masculinity and femininity, both strands have become increasingly hostile to liberal values of choice and diversity.[15] This analysis comes in a variety of forms. Its two most commonly encountered variations are one that posits a 'grand regress', a *fin de siècle* rediscovery of Victorian virtues, and another positing an oscillation that has swung from Victorianism to the 'permissiveness' of the 1960s and is now, like a pendulum, moving back towards a period of restraint.

To avoid lapsing into some version of a cyclical account of moral reform projects, I will propose a 'crisis theory' in which the occurrence of an upsurge of attempts to institute moral regulation is a manifestation of some identifiable 'crisis' in some field of social relations or institutions. By crisis I understand the existence of strains or tensions within some social field such that it becomes increasingly problematic for people to continue in the way to which they have been accustomed. This condition is likely to be both a 'crisis of governing', in which it becomes increasingly difficult to continue to rule in the same way, and a 'crisis of authority', in which existing forms of legitimacy of rule are questioned and challenged by those subject to them. The existence of a crisis condition involves a disruption of that which is taken for granted, or, in Gramscian terminology, manifests itself in a crisis of 'common sense' when that which 'everybody knows' is no longer stable. The existence of a crisis expresses itself at the level of the consciousness of social actors as a crisis of identity, since they are no longer able or willing to continue in patterns to which they were accustomed.

Some caution is needed in addressing 'crisis'; there is a risk of crisis inflation, of treating social features that exist in near permanent tension as being in 'crisis' so as to lose the distinctive sense of the periodic and convulsive nature of crisis. As a partial safeguard against this problem I will speak of 'crisis tendencies', disturbances that have the potential to give rise to crisis situations (Offe 1984). Such crisis tendencies will manifest themselves in full-blown crises where some combination of conditions amplifies their impact and where some specific circumstances provide the spark which mobilises social action. The circumstance which ignites action around a combination of crisis conditions may not itself be a direct manifestation of the underlying crisis. On the basis of these general reflections on the mechanism of social crises, it is now time to identify the more important crisis tendencies.

CRISIS TENDENCIES AND MORAL REGULATION

The period from the end of the Second World War to the present has witnessed a profound and wide-ranging reconsideration of the problem of government, one of whose major manifestations has been the crisis of the welfare state. This has been experienced much more sharply in Britain and much of Europe, where the welfarist system of governing had developed more fully, than in the United States. The crisis of welfare should not be understood, as much contemporary political discourse presents it, as a ubiquitously negative phenomenon. The crisis lies precisely in the clash between the aspirations to govern more and to govern less. The expansion of the realm of governmental action stimulated by demands that 'something should be done' is a manifestation of the technical possibility of bringing more aspects of life under attempts of conscious control. The crisis of the welfare state is an expression of the exponential social costs of providing for such an expanding sphere of intervention. This inflation of regulation is not readily reversible and explains the meagre achievements of the political rhetoric of 'deregulation'. Yet strong counter-tendencies have come to the fore that are not reducible to a reversion to an unrestrained economic market. Their general features involve a desire for less bureaucracy and less centralism, for decentralisation, making services and resources more accessible to users, and for autonomy, for greater self-sufficiency and self-fashioning (Rosanvallon 1988). There is a crisis because, while it was once possible to provide an equal access by all to some essential but limited social goods such as health care and education, it is not possible to guarantee unlimited access for all to services that are both more extensive and increasingly expensive.

This crisis expresses itself in wide-ranging conflicts over the scope of social governance. A demand is generated to use the expanded capacity to govern in order to achieve greater social justice, for example, by acting against discrimination on grounds of gender, race or sexual orientation. Yet at the same time resistance manifests itself to such expansions of the aspiration to govern whose major expressions take the form of anti-taxation movements and the desire to restrict the scope and intrusiveness of regulation. In the arena of moral regulation the result has been the angry struggles over what has come to be called the 'culture wars' (Gitlin 1995; Hunter 1991). It needs to be emphasised that the contention that the reprise of moral regulation today is a manifestation of the crisis of governability does not imply that there is a crisis of social order; too often in both historical and sociological literature a 'crisis' has been equated with 'disorder', while in fact disorder is only one of many forms in which crises may display themselves. In late modernity the experience of increased security intersects with heightened perceptions of risk and the experience of anxiety. In this respect 'crises' become a 'normal' part of life, but take on distinctive forms.

The angry struggles of the cultural wars involve a significant distinction between today's moral politics and earlier varieties of moral regulation projects. In previous chapters I have attended to evidence of resistance or opposition to attempts to impose moral regulation. In general resistance was limited and largely inarticulate. Thus, Londoners in the 1790s may have impeded or even attacked the agents of the Societies for Reformation of Manners, but there was little persuasive criticism of their moral reform programme. Similarly in the Victorian period, in both Britain and the United States the ideals of chastity and purity were rarely disputed. But today projects of moral reform are contested and become arenas in which fierce political and cultural battles are fought out, often between erstwhile allies, the most striking illustration being the contest within feminists between pro- and anti-censorship positions. No sooner does a new panic emerge than it is contested; as McRobbie observes, today “folk devils can and do ‘fight back’ ” (1994: 201). One consequence of the contestability of moral regulation is that individual campaigns tend to be short-lived; they arise with often inflammatory and widely dispersed publicity before stimulating opposition and then receding into localised guerrilla wars.[16]

The contested life of recent moral regulation projects is well illustrated by significant phases of the movement around child abuse. Concern with ‘cruelty to children’ emerged in the 1870s as an offshoot of the cruelty to animals movement.[17] Since then there has been an important shift from the focus on ‘cruelty to children’ to ‘child abuse’ (Hacking 1991; Jenkins 1992). The key feature of this transition was that ‘cruelty’ had been organised around a class moralisation; it was the uncivilised lower orders who were cruel to their children. In contrast, ‘abuse’ is stripped of class referents; it is a generic condition of relations between parents and children and, most often, between fathers and children. Action around child abuse has taken many forms. For example, in Britain during 1987, paediatricians in Cleveland using a new and controversial diagnostic technique claimed that a high percentage of young children passing through the health system had been subject to sexual abuse. They were backed by local social workers, who used their powers to remove the children from their parents. There ensued an intense controversy that was taken up in the national media in which local politicians, journalists, doctors, social workers and others lined up on opposite sides. Significantly the parents faced with the accusation of sexual abuse fought back and organised a counter-campaign. The controversy was significant because it generated multiple and incompatible targets: hostility was directed towards ‘abusing parents’, ‘meddling doctors’, ‘do-gooding social workers’ (Ashenden 1996; Campbell 1988; McIntosh 1988).

During the same period in the United States, the controversies over child abuse took a different turn. The controversy over ‘multiple personality’ syndrome, which had attracted considerable interest in the popular media, took a new turn when exponents alleged that ‘multiples’ had frequently been abused during childhood, adding a whole new moral dimension to the diagnostic debate by constructing ‘abusive parents’ as the target. Rival organisations battled for public attention, mobilising competing ‘victims’, so that ‘abused multiples’ and parents who were the ‘victims of false memory syndrome’ were forced to confront one another (Hacking 1995).[18]

These different trajectories in Britain and the United States were to converge for a period when the issue of child abuse merged with charges of ‘ritual abuse’ and ‘Satanism’ that reached their peak in 1989. Significantly these allegations were mobilised by a tacit alliance of Christian fundamentalists and prominent feminists; in Britain the religious Right shared the platform with Beatrix Campbell, who had earlier been a highly visible socialist feminist (Jenkins 1992: Chapter 6). Children had long been significant in moralising discourses because the association between 'children', victimisation and innocence was deeply imbricated in popular culture. They still figure as classic 'innocent victims' in an expanding range of scandals that revolve around abuse of power such as the widespread abuses by Catholic priests, and those involving teachers and administrators in a variety of residential establishments in many countries, and a widening array of sports coaches, youth leaders and others. Most dramatically fitting the model of a 'moral panic' has been the near universal reaction against the possibility of sexual contact between adults and children that has concretised around the label paedophile.[19]

If today's moral reform projects are part of a deep ambivalence about the scope of governance, and this expresses itself in the contestability of such projects, it is not surprising that many of these conflicts will revolve around issues of sex and sexuality. The most important feature that provides a bridge between the late Victorian period and the close of the twentieth century is a profound crisis of gender relations and of family relations. It is around these linked relations of gender and family that the key differences between our two pivotal periods revolve.

CRISES IN GENDER RELATIONS

My account of the changing form of family and gender relations can best be presented as a reformulation of Lawrence Stone's influential periodisation of the family. Stone identifies a transition from a 'restricted patriarchal nuclear family' to a 'closed domesticated nuclear family', characterised by "strong affective ties" between husbands and wives, that comes to the fore in the eighteenth century (Stone 1977). My contention is that the closed domesticated nuclear family, although it existed as the ideal in the earlier period, could not establish itself even in the nineteenth century, because patriarchal relations still dominated family relations and furthermore the exclusion of women from public life was reinforced by the practices and ideology of domesticity. The Victorian crisis of the family involved dual challenges to patriarchal power and exclusion from the public sphere. The Victorian feminist challenge to patriarchy proved to be what Barrington Moore has termed a 'suppressed historical possibility', an unrealised project because it was fought out within the terms of a maternal feminism that accepted the very practices of the separate spheres and the valorisation of the maternal role that sustained familial patriarchy (Moore 1978). Purity feminism, as we have seen, was incapable of mounting a viable challenge. Victorian feminism was much more successful in its challenge to the exclusion of women from the public sphere; painfully slow though those advances were, the struggles for educational and legal rights, and for suffrage, were decisive.

While second-wave feminism learnt that neither education nor the vote automatically ensured that public roles and spaces would open, the core of its struggles has been to explore the territory beyond a gendered 'closed domesticated nuclear family'. The ideal of companionate interpersonal relations between women and men required challenges to the persisting inequalities, structural and attitudinal, that stood in the way of providing the possibility of companionate relations for all.[20] The key substantive arena for feminist politics of the late twentieth century has revolved around an issue that was entirely absent from the discourses of Victorian feminism, namely, the question of domestic violence, sexual violence and rape (Walkowitz 1982). This silence was in itself significant; it certainly did not mean that such violence was absent, nor did it mean that it was simply taken for granted as a prerogative of patriarchal power. The issue that came closest to engaging with the exclusive rights of patriarchy was the question of the frequency of sexual relations within marriage. As we have seen, purity activists, feminist and non-feminist, urged that sex be severely limited and restricted to procreative functions. For the Victorians, the frequency of sex was not about 'marital rape', but was about the control of family size and the frequency of pregnancies, and thus about the assertion of female control of these issues.

The 'modern' question of domestic and sexual violence goes to the heart of the conditions of possibility for companionate relations between women and men. In an important respect it re-presents the question of 'purity' that had been posed by late Victorian feminism, but it raises it in a new form. It addresses individual self-governance by men, not only posing challenges about appropriate forms of conduct, but also problematising attitudes and values. The content of the Victorian purity discourses was about premarital chastity, extramarital behaviour and resort to prostitutes. Until recently the central issues revolved around behaviour within relationships; more recently this has been made more complex as one of the reverberations of the AIDS epidemic.

Feminist interventions have not always presented themselves in the form of challenges to male self-governance. While there has been much attention to the centrality of 'domestic' violence, this thrust has been undercut by the tendency to construct women as 'victims'. This has had two problematic consequences. First, it implies a retreat to the presentation of sexual danger as emanating from the anonymous stranger, the rapist, and this in turn is amplified by radical feminism's presentation of all men as potential rapists (Russell 1993), or, as Robin Morgan famously put it, "pornography is the theory; and rape the practice" (1980: 139). Second, the victim status of women leads to a focus on 'danger' that incapacitates women from realising personal self-determination, whether it be in engaging in sexual relations with men or in being active in the complex array of public places and spaces. In its most significant form this trend beats a retreat from the transformative project of 'liberation' which was the central feature of the revival of feminist politics in the 1960s; instead it retreats to the same political space colonised by Victorian feminism, namely, that of a politics of 'protecting women'. The polarisation within feminism that has resulted from the controversies over the content of liberation led to a similar retreat to the one that had earlier been travelled by purity feminism. This time the move was not back to the valorisation of female passivity and domesticity, but rather to a rejection of sexual liberation itself, as something that merely furthers male sexual licence. Thus one major strand of modern feminism has become profoundly suspicious of the sexual and erotic realm.

As a consequence, one of the most significant areas of contestation has been over sexual representations. Reflecting the changing technologies of reproduction and dissemination, the targets of moral regulation have shifted over time. The main targets had earlier been printed sexual images and words (designated by the term 'obscenity').[21] These targets were superseded, first by photographic images, then by video films and more recently by electronic communications (with a corresponding shift to the term 'pornography'). One of the key differences between the nineteenth-century battles over obscenity and the recent ones around pornography is that resistance to censorship has been vociferous and, in particular, has sharply divided the feminist constituency.

The feminist anti-pornography campaign both replicates and departs from the earlier censorship of obscenity. The replication manifests itself by treating the pornographic image as inherently dangerous. In Chapter 4 we encountered Comstock's imagery of the dreadful consequences that befell the eye of the juvenile beholder; one glimpse of a sexual image would lead the observer into the depths of depravity. While such thinking still resonates in current conservative rhetoric, in the feminist anti-pornography movement there have been two distinct discourses surrounding sexual imagery. First, the danger of the image is rendered more plausible, one glance is no longer sufficient; instead – harnessing the wider preoccupation with addiction – it is a surfeit of pornography which is presented as leading the consumer towards the commission of sexual offences. Such a causal connection is notoriously elusive, its most significant effect – which some have been prepared to treat as confirmatory evidence – being that it has provided the sex offender with an exculpatory discourse of blaming the pornographic image for the offence. A similar mechanism is at work with respect to the contention that pornography itself encourages violence against women; this is exemplified in the 'snuff movie' myth that arose in the late 1970s with claims about the existence of Mexican snuff movies in which women were killed in front of the camera. It was the publicity which this attracted that resulted in a low-budget horror movie that had been made some years earlier being released under the title *Snuff* (1975), with extra scenes depicting the murder of an actress.

The second feminist anti-pornography discourse centres on the claim that the very existence of pornography is degrading and thus damaging to women. It is interesting that the rhetoric of degradation deploys an old theme that sexual desire is itself a degraded condition. This theme is given a supplement with the idea that sex is especially degrading to women. Thus to be an overtly sexual being is degrading; to give and to receive sexual pleasure is to be degraded. The radical feminist discourse provides a modern encapsulation of this theme with the contention that brands heterosexual practices as inherently degrading. In this scenario oral sex has a special place; it is presumed that oral sex is inherently degrading for women.[22] This is, of course, a return to a very ancient view that specific acts can be classified as innately right or wrong. These discourses imply that women share a single sexual nature. As such not only does this misrepresent female sexuality, but it displays a hostility to sexual diversity that amounts to an insistence that 'good girls don't' (watch sex videos, wear high heels, dress sexily, etc.). The rhetoric of degradation is significant in that it operates to create a climate of sexual shame. Carol Smart demonstrates the rhetorical reliance on 'testimony' of experience of pornography of the form: 'after he started using porn, my husband wanted me to do disgusting things'. This naturalises the sense of sexual shame by reinforcing the presupposition that the visual representation of genital sexual conduct is inherently degrading (Smart 1992).[23]

The policing of sexual diversity reached new heights with the 'discovery' of sexual addiction, which renders deviant everything but monogamous sex (Irvine 1995). It is thus not surprising that lesbian feminism exhibits a marked polarity between those whose main focus is to attack heterosexuality and those concerned to celebrate sexual diversity. It is for this reason that the controversy within lesbian feminism over sexual representations has been the most inflamed.

The campaign against pornography took a significant turn in the 1980s with the move, led by Catharine MacKinnon and Andrea Dworkin, to secure municipal anti-pornography ordinances. In Minneapolis in 1983 an ordinance was passed in Council, but was vetoed by the

Mayor. In Indianapolis, a much more conservative purity movement in alliance with MacKinnon feminists secured a similar ordinance.[24] The ordinance strategy showed an awareness of the tactical disadvantages of the strategy of the older tradition of criminalising sexual representations. MacKinnon insisted that anti-pornography ordinances were not an attempt to impose moral laws (MacKinnon 1984). In an astute tactical move, she sought to link her proposed legislation to the influential civil rights discourses involving opposition to discrimination on the basis of race, religion or sex. The ordinances asserted that pornography discriminates against women on the basis of sex by promoting negative images and representations of women. Yet the substantive proposals marked a significant return to an earlier phase of 'abatement' laws that had been used at the end of the nineteenth century against brothels. The proposals would have allowed any female citizen to initiate actions against distributors of pornography. This legal tactic also served to reinforce the ideological claim that pornography was a harm to all women, hence any woman should be able to initiate legal proceedings. The rejection of such legislation by the courts in the United States, invoking the doctrine of free speech, turned the tide against these legislative projects.[25] There was a marked shift of opinion within most feminist constituencies against the censorship strategy. In 1991 the National Organisation of Women rejected a proposal to launch an anti-pornography campaign and Women Against Pornography collapsed.

Meanwhile in Britain, anti-pornography feminism acquired a rather different form of political influence. It secured some support on the left of the Labour Party, but at a time when Margaret Thatcher was at her strongest, Labour was in disarray and had little opportunity for legislative action. It is significant that Thatcher, who made much of the promotion of 'family values', seems never to have been attracted to the promotion of censorship legislation; but there were some minor legislative changes. For example in 1981 an *Indecent Display (Control) Act* was passed, imposing restrictions on the advertising of sexually explicit material and instituting warning labelling on sexual materials. In the late 1980s fresh attempts were made to promote anti-pornography legislation. A key role was played by Clare Short, a Labour MP with left-wing credentials, but the project foundered when her scarcely veiled alliance with the Christian Right became apparent.

In both Britain and the United States the major legacy of the anti-pornography campaigns was a pervasive and strongly moralised hostility to sexual representation. It has more recently sprung back into life, significantly with much more governmental involvement and legislative enthusiasm, over the issue of pornography in cyberspace. The distinctive element in the current anti-pornography movement is the invocation of the protection of children. Appeals to the 'protection of innocence' now, as before, have created a more favourable environment for coercive forms of regulation. Of decisive importance is the fact that children are invoked as being in need of protection in a double sense: as both objects of pornographic depiction and as potential viewers of pornography. This is a classic instance of the power of convergence of multiple targets. Convergence occurs when two or more activities are linked in the process of signification so as, implicitly or explicitly, to draw parallels between them. Where convergence between two or more social elements occurs, the possibility is created for a process of amplification in which the significance of the threat or danger is increased or enhanced, with the result that:

> One kind of threat or challenge to society seems larger, more menacing, if it can be mapped together with other apparently similar phenomena . . . As issues and groups are projected across the thresholds, it becomes easier to mount legitimate campaigns of control against them (Hall et al. 1978: 225–6).

The struggle over censorship has left unresolved important issues surrounding adult sexuality and its representation. Most importantly it has deflected attention from the future of heterosexual desire and its expression. This issue has remained alive within the left wing of feminism exemplified by Ehrenreich et al. (1986) and Segal (1997), and men strongly influenced by feminism such as Connell (1995) and Seidman (1992). A similar concern with what Connell calls the democratisation of sex is evident in the polemical voices of Rene Denfeld (1995) and Marcia Pally (1994), who have challenged the sexual conservatism of radical feminism. The crux of these debates is the conditions for the empowerment of women as agents of heterosexual desire. It is crucial to move beyond the misplaced concreteness of the anti-pornography feminist view that 'ending' pornography would end subordination and sexual violence (Snitow 1986). To do so requires a very different debate about the relationship between sexuality and sexual representation.

Yet the argument that the conditions exist for the democratisation of sex as an important component of the completion of the unfinished project of equality has to note the existence of a line of thought which presents a pessimistic vision of the future of intimacy. There is a bleak one-sidedness to the focus on the retreat into privatism, narcissism and the transitoriness of self-realisation within the monogamous family (Lasch 1975; Sennett 1974). Anthony Giddens offers a more nuanced vision, less bleak but attending to serious impediments to a positive outcome of the crisis of gender relations, whose general form is an erosion and destabilisation of gender boundaries. Modernity produces a transformation of intimacy through the pursuit of and commitment to personal relationships.[26] While such relationships are arenas of doubt and anxiety, they are nevertheless the key to understanding current projects of self-fashioning (Giddens 1991: 186). He subsequently argues that sexuality, once separated from reproduction, is freed – in principle – from the rule of the phallus and the sexual control of women. It is this decline in male control that gives rise to a rising tide of male violence stemming from insecurity and inadequacy; this analysis rejects the idea that there has existed a seamless continuation of patriarchal dominance. Rather violence is a destructive reaction to the waning of female complicity (Giddens 1992: 122). Care is needed to ensure that this line of argument does not become a rationalisation for male violence.[27]

This approach can perhaps most fruitfully be developed by focusing on the governmentalisation of gender boundaries. This requires attention to the multiple ways in which structural aspects of gender are viewed as becoming capable of being governed and are made objects of attempts at their governance by a variety of agents. For example, during the 1980s feminists were successful in both Britain and the USA in making rape and serial murder manifestations of sexual danger and proper arenas for governance action, ranging in scope from street demonstrations to 'Reclaim the Night' and the opening of 'rape crisis centres' to legislative interventions in the field of domestic violence. At the same time there has been a periodic eruption of concern over the link between serial killings and sexual violence. For example, in Britain the multiple murders between 1975 and 1980 of Peter Sutcliffe, the 'Yorkshire Ripper', heightened concern with sexual danger. Further amplifications have occurred because the police had an institutional interest in creating national structures focused on serial murders and child abuse which have led to the establishment of computerised data bases and special units. Such responses have constituted a significant process of the governmentalisation of sexual danger.

At the level of interpersonal relations, changes occur in what participants regard as acceptable expressions of gendered identities; of crucial importance here is Giddens' point about the decline of complicity. This is complex because those limits, while constitutive of gendered identities, are themselves produced by unequal gendered relations. At the level of institutional contexts, the complex of behaviours that stretches from insensitive and blundering conduct to coercive harassment is central to the way in which gender relations are governed in workplaces and other public spaces. These fields have been subject to a long-running process of juridification as rules, procedures and hearings become more formal. The boundaries of what is acceptable and what can be challenged mark out the shifting terrain of the governance of gender relations. It is important to insist that, with sexual relations being substantively divorced from marriage and procreation and from any sense of 'natural' sex roles, the result is that sexuality increasingly becomes 'a mystery' that is revisited and remade in everyday life.

It is only in the context of engaging with these issues of the governance of gender relations that Giddens' hope of the possibilities of the transformation of intimacy involving a "wholesale democratising of the interpersonal domain" might be realised (1992: 3). While it is important to imagine what such relations could be like, we can observe that projects that are directed at the retraditionalisation of gender relations can only work within an already existing set of discursive components characterised by the maintenance of gendered polarities. For this reason many such efforts present themselves as anti-sexual and/or anti-heterosexual. Few have engaged in the transformative imagination which will resolve the content of democratised sexual relations.

CRISES IN FAMILIAL RELATIONS

Alongside and interwoven with the tensions that beset contemporary gender relations is a pronounced set of concerns about relations between adults and children, in particular between parents and their children. Unresolved and often unstable interpersonal relations are further compounded by a set of discourses invoking both a sacralisation and a demonisation of children. A profound paradox lies at the convergence of regulatory projects directed towards the 'protection' of the 'innocence' of children with a conjuncture in which the innocence of children has itself become increasingly problematic. These contradictory manifestations need to be placed within the context of some important social changes that have affected the relations between parents and children. There has been a return to a prolonged period of dependence with the extension of the time spent in education. Yet at the same time the expansion of youth consumerism and the elaboration of youth cultures has heightened the demand for greater economic and personal autonomy.

In the recent period the moral status of children has become more ambiguous. I shall take as emblematic of this destabilisation of childhood innocence the murder in 1993 of the two-year-old toddler James Bulger, who was captured on a shopping mall security video being led away from the vicinity of his mother by two ten-year-old boys; his beaten body was later recovered. The subsequent media and court trial of the two boys, Robert Thompson and Jon Venables, saw the mobilisation of a set of discourses that spoke of a generalised crisis of family authority, maternal responsibility and, hence, of the moral fabric of society (Hay 1995: 206). The case counterposed 'innocence' and 'evil', attributing responsibility to broken homes, irresponsible mothers, the harm of 'video nasties' and the breakdown of traditional morality. A distinctively American version of such parables of innocence and evil is provided by the rash of schoolyard shootings of classmates and teachers by children using lethal weapons.

There is nothing new, as we have seen, in eruptions of social anxiety surrounding childhood and adolescence. It is of course significant that the targets for such concerns have become younger. Two distinctive features mark contemporary misgivings. First is a generalised concern that parents have lost either the will or the capacity to control their children. The second is that those who pose the source of danger to children are no longer dangerous strangers, but treacherous intimates, parents themselves and those in positions of trust such as clergy, youth leaders, sports coaches and the like.

Through a long series of shifting policies 'the family' has remained at the centre of social intervention and social anxiety. By the early twentieth century the state had become centrally involved in the regulation of the family (Donzelot 1980; Rose 1989). Particularly since the Second World War, a web of legal powers, social agencies and practices began to spread around troubled and troublesome families. The general process has been the 'familialisation' of social policy, the central feature being a set of policies that operate "by inciting the family itself to take on board the business of production of normal subjects" (Rose 1989: 156). While powerful social forces induce young people to assert increased autonomy, moralising discourses assert the responsibilisation of parents for the conduct of their children.

There is an inherent tension in projects of familialisation; the family can only serve the expanding objectives of health, education and welfare as a voluntary activity. It cannot work through coercion and compulsion. Thus the focus has shifted to enlisting parents, and in particular mothers, in positive projects of child-raising. On the one hand, the tension is embedded in a contradiction at the heart of social policy, namely, an unstable oscillation between the construction of children as being 'in need of care and protection' and, in contrast, 'beyond parental control'. On the other hand, the family is perceived as the root cause of delinquency because of the inability, unwillingness or refusal of parents to engage in 'proper parenting' – one of the sharpest manifestations being the persistent concern over single mothers.

The family in crisis is less and less reliable as the primary agency for the production of normal well-adjusted citizens. But the celebration of the private family carries with it the difficulty, if not impossibility, of regulating the family through mechanisms of social control and discipline. The only available strategy is one which promotes the self-realisation of responsible families through the mixed techniques of the construction of pleasures and ambitions, and at the same time the activation of guilt, anxiety and disappointment. For those falling outside this capacity for self-government, there remains the increasing deployment of dividing practices which impose disciplinary constraints on those excluded from the 'new respectability'. The content of this new respectability departs from the rigidly prescribed rules of Victorian respectability which was epitomised, but not subsumed by, the dictates of etiquette. The rules of respectability were inviolate and unyielding as exemplified in the rule that illegitimacy damned both mother and her offspring from 'society'.[28]

The modern crisis of familial relations cannot be protected by respectability, since the dangers that threaten it are not only external, but can reside even in the 'normal family'. Nikolas Rose labels the ideal of 'the autonomous responsible family' as the emblem of a new mode of government of the self (Rose 1989: 208). But we must add that the 'autonomous responsible family' is beset by dangers – dangers of 'abusive relations' and a whole expanded array of 'addictions'. This is precisely the significance of the distinctively American discourses about the non-class character of negative relations, epitomised by the feminist contention that both spousal abuse and child abuse are distributed through all segments of society. Some care is needed not to take this contention too literally. Many of the discourses of transgression have a very distinctive class content. Many of the contemporary fields that are subjected to moral regulation have a distinctive class dimension. It is possible to resist John Burnham's conservative normative assessment and yet agree with his observation that 'bad habits' continue to have a distinctive association with the lower classes. The use of tobacco and alcohol, the refusal or inability to restrict food intake, and many other practices of consumption have increasingly become predominantly associated with the lower classes.

It is this duality of the crisis of the family – an endemic crisis of the family institution and an intensified crisis along class lines – which provides the parameters within which contemporary projects of moral regulation need to be approached.

MODERN ANXIETIES AND MORAL REGULATION

There is a widely shared view that the escalation of moral politics at the century's end is an expression of an intensification of 'social anxieties'. Thus, for example, Todd Gitlin (1995) explains the American 'culture wars' as a response to anxieties over American identity. Such arguments reflect a longer tradition, which explains outbreaks of moral fervour as responses to deep social anxieties. For example, Kai Erikson (1966) explained the Salem witch trials as manifestations of the response to intense social anxieties. Richard Hofstadter (1955) accounted for outbreaks of "moral frenzy" over alcohol and prostitution in late nineteenth-century America in terms of the 'status anxiety' of the participants; and this tradition informed Joseph Gusfield's (1963) now classic explanation of the prohibition movement.

Such accounts, offering explanations in terms of 'social anxiety' that stimulates attempts at moral regulation, are attractive, and often intuitively convincing, but suffer from a serious limitation in that they claim to offer more explanatory power than they are able to deliver (Hunt 1999b). Anxiety analyses can only point in the direction of necessary conditions for an upsurge in moral politics, in that they lay the ground for a moral reform project. But an anxiety thesis cannot by itself provide an explanatory account of either the timing or the specific configuration of a moral reform campaign. The limitations of the explanatory capacity stem from the endemic nature of social anxiety; social life in modern societies, if not more generally, is beset by anxieties. The ubiquity of anxiety is one facet of the widely agreed diagnosis that has labelled modern society as a 'risk society' (Beck 1992). Thus anxieties are persistent or background features of social life; they can manifest themselves in a variety of ways, but the important point is that they do not always give rise to projects of moral regulation. In order to explain such occurrences something else, some supplement, is required.

We can, however, learn much from anxiety analysis if it is approached with appropriate caution. Throughout I have been concerned to identify general background conditions of social anxieties, such as the strains or tensions generated by rapid urbanisation, mass immigration and changing gender relations. These strains create the conditions to stimulate and provoke attempts to intervene. But such projects, as I hope to have demonstrated, will not materialise without the presence of the necessary agents of moral reform in the form of some moral regulation movement. Even where such a movement comes into existence, it will make little impact unless it is able to mobilise a discursive formation which has what can be called a combinatory capacity, that of mobilising a combination of elements which bring together (over time, place and field) a number of different strands of moralised discourses and perceptions. It is this capacity to establish linkages between current anxieties and the common sense of the period to produce a strategy which makes sense to a potential political community of activists or supporters. Whether the principal target is the prevalence of Sunday trading in early eighteenth-century Britain or the visibility of prostitution in late nineteenth-century cities in both Britain and the United States, the links between these phenomena and other troublesome features of contemporary life have to make sense to significant constituencies. Only then can moral regulation movements become activated. Moral regulation becomes possible where some specific social anxiety serves to mobilise an array of different issues and alliances of disparate social forces. Thus it would seem that the otherwise paradoxical alliance between radical feminists and religious fundamentalists that has been mobilised around moral reform projects over the last two decades is not some oddity or some betrayal, but is rather a condition of existence for this distinctive form of modern politics.

Moral regulation movements are manifestations of an anxiety of freedom that haunts modern liberal forms of rule. Large urbanised masses live with no evident mechanism of unification and no shared values. Traditional authorities are no longer able to rule in the old way and social deference, whether of class, gender or ethnicity, is fragile. There is no 'natural' system of order. Formal education is conceived within a narrowing remit; projects of Durkheimian 'moral education', whether in schools or the media, have become attenuated. What is perceived as essential is that mechanisms of self-restraint/self-discipline should be generalised and disseminated. The mechanism of first choice is the family, but as we have seen, the family is increasingly fallible, while increasing awareness of social diversity impedes state legislative efforts at producing a public realm capable of and committed to enforcing a moral order which is conceived as a necessary condition for social order. Any such state projects have first to create a sense of alarm and danger, epitomised in the state war against drugs, which itself undermines the sense of social and moral order. Another non-state version of the project of moral order is to be found in the retraditionalisation that marks the most visible face of contemporary feminist moral reform and, less surprisingly, in the authoritarian traditionalism of the political and religious Right. But such projects meet with increasingly vocal opposition that radically distinguishes them from the normative consensus which was the context for the purity politics of the late nineteenth century. However, there is, as has been injected into my account, another mechanism that engages with the goal of moral order, and one that is becoming increasingly important in both its scope and its impact. Modern moral regulation is increasingly embedded within the liberal governance of the self.

MORAL REGULATION AND GENEALOGY OF THE SELF

The distinctive form of contemporary moral regulation is not the high-profile and contentious regulatory projects of the plethora of moral regulation movements, even though they remain a significant force. Today the decisive form of moral regulation is to be found in the pervasive spread of multiple projects of self-governance. In order to grasp the connection between modern self-governance and moral regulation, it is necessary to track the emergence of new forms of self-governance. A decisive feature of the changes in the government of the self during the twentieth century has been a move away from the system of welfare which sought directly to stimulate the self-monitoring and self-governance of citizens (Dean 1991; Donzelot 1980; Rose 1993). The system of welfare has been gradually displaced by a complex system of links between expert knowledge, economic and social resources and the government of the self in which

> the ethical valorisation of certain features of the person – autonomy, choice, authenticity, enterprise, lifestyle – should be understood in terms of new rationalities of government and new technologies of the conduct of conduct (Rose 1996: 320).

These diverse techniques span a range of resources from psychological and other therapies to self-help regimes of dieting and behaviour modification that have infused the practices of many experts and authorities, from school-teachers to marriage guidance counsellors. These in turn have cultivated the moral self-regulation of the modern citizen. In brief, moral regulation is alive and well. It relies less on theology, but is more likely to employ the language of self-health, nutrition, medical science and proliferating forms of expertise ranging from modern quackery to high science. It remains profoundly moral in that its target is focused on the ethical subjectivity of the individual (Valverde 1994: 218).

These changing patterns in the form of the content of the governance of the self are intimately connected to major shifts in the forms of political authority and the rationalities of governing. By the end of the nineteenth century the projects of liberal governance were increasingly targeted at the socio-economic realm that was acted upon by techniques which operated on the 'family economy' in order to reform the habits and morals of men and women, to support its members economically over the course of their lives, and to stimulate the raising of healthy children with a respect for authority. Increasingly these projects were pursued through techniques of 'governing at a distance' (Rose & Miller 1992). Modern liberal forms of government rely less and less on governing through 'society', but rather seek to stimulate and activate the controlled choices of individual citizens. This 'advanced liberalism' involves "the calculated administration of diverse aspects of conduct through countless, often competing, local tactics of education, persuasion, inducement, management, incitement, motivation and encouragement" (Rose & Miller 1992: 175). In the first half of the twentieth century it was the new techniques of the psychological sciences which introduced new forms of expertise such as child guidance, intelligence testing and personnel management into the governance of the population (de Swaan 1990; Rose 1989). My concern is to stress the dimension of moral regulation practised by these experts: for example, the instilling of a work ethic has constructed hard work as a moral and social good which supplements the disciplinary techniques of timeclocks and productivity measures. In the field of social welfare there has been an inexorable growth of surveillance over families, in particular over working-class families.

Valuable though the neo-Foucauldian research conducted under the sign of 'governmentality' theory has been in charting the changing interpenetration and enfolding of the government of others with the government of the self, there remains a major omission that must now be addressed. The agents that are active in these accounts are threefold: governments, experts and individuals. In their present form they provide little opportunity to incorporate the role of social movements. Yet such movements are of crucial importance if we are to grapple with the significant fact that moral reform movements play a decisive part in the marked volatility of the moral politics of our period. What this study has demonstrated is the key role played by organised social movements in advancing and sustaining projects of moral regulation. The important point to be made in connection with the prevalence of moral self-regulation is that here again organised movements continue to play a crucial role.

The new forms of liberal governance have emerged in a period when governing has become increasingly technical and governmentalised, vested in the hands of experts. This tends, despite formal space for participation provided by liberal politics, to effect the practical exclusion of non-experts. Yet expertise is persistently reintroduced through a variety of different mechanisms. Sometimes this involves 'non-experts' training themselves to become experts or hiring experts of their own, as when trade union officers acquire technical knowledge of job evaluation systems. Of particular importance for my present concerns is self-help literature which provides alternative knowledge, as in the case of alternative medicine which allows people to become 'experts for themselves'. Or individuals become 'experts for each other' as in many self-help movements where, for example, rape victims become counsellors; such acquisition and dissemination of expertise is particularly evident in the many versions of the Twelve-Step programmes first developed within Alcoholics Anonymous (AA) (AA 1976; Reinarman 1995).

While there has been much attention to 'self-help', there has been inadequate attention to its moral regulation dimension. Self-help involves an incitement to self-regulation. As I have stressed at each stage, regulation and moralisation march hand in hand. Thus in the nineteenth century philanthropy acted through moralisation; in particular it sought to instil the responsibilisation of men as 'breadwinners' and women as 'mothers'. In self-help movements the voice of the outsider non-expert is reinserted in the form of the 'moral voice' that is such a significant component of the plethora of self-help movements that populate the modern landscape of moral action. The moral voice was present in the discourses of philanthropy when middle-class women instructed working-class women on how to make 'nourishing soups'. Today it is present within the practical advice proffered by advice manuals and self-help movements; the injunction to monitor and record the amount of exercise taken or calories consumed is this quiet nagging voice of moral regulation. Self-help is one of the new techniques that has been invented, or perhaps more accurately, continuously reinvented, for the government of the self. The self-government of subjectivity is effected through the stimulation of sustained and intense self-scrutiny. In one of its simplest forms this self-examination is evidenced through the ubiquitous presence of weighing machines in our bathrooms (Schwartz 1986). More generally the self that is liberated through the exercise of self-control is obliged to live life harnessed to projects of its own identity, its normality, its weight, its mental and physical health.

Modern advice and self-help discourses can be distinguished from the long-lived tradition of 'conduct books', which began to appear from the earliest days of printing (Neuberg 1977). The early forms were dominated by what came to be called etiquette, the laying down of prescriptive rules of conduct to which the individual is exhorted to conform. Increasingly in the long march to modernity, the tone changes and the advice becomes less prescriptive, but rather seeks to engage in a reflexive project of the self which harnesses self-monitoring and introspection to the production of a personality in which authenticity comes to displace conformity. The inculcation of moral self-regulation requires slow, painstaking and detailed work upon ourselves, a continuous and committed self-scrutiny. "The self that is liberated is obliged to live its life tied to the project of its own identity" (Rose 1989: 254). Thus self-help operates though the mobilisation of self-esteem and self-respect. The important point is that moral regulation has come to acquire a new and distinctive form.

Self-help moral regulation generates new forms of expertise. On the one hand, there is an increasing pluralisation of expertise such that individuals are required to choose their own experts; in health care, body maintenance or personal relations a plethora of experts bid for the allegiance and commitment of individuals; complex struggles take place over credentialism, professionalisation and official certification in which all forms of traditional authorities are challenged by clamorous rivals. In being required to choose their own experts, individuals increasingly must become 'experts for the self'. In so doing, subjects engage in a subjectification that is more profound since it seems to originate in an autonomous search for their own identities. Hence it becomes important to attend to the way these new and varied authorities become enfolded within the project of the self and to insert new forms of knowledge and systems of truth. For example, 'Twelve-Step' programmes emanating from AA require both a rigorous practice of confessionalism geared to the exercise of self-control, along with an acknowledgement of a "power greater than ourselves" (AA 1976: 10). These diverse elements are melded into a complex regime for the governance of the self that is an ideological response to the pervasive individualism of modernity while, paradoxically, promoting an individualist vision of recovery (Room 1993). Such techniques coexist with those within the retraditionalisation model such as the promotion of marital fidelity by 'promise keepers', a late twentieth-century version of the earlier purity pledge, while on another front state-sponsored campaigns to 'Just Say No' in anti-drug programmes herald a return to the 'suppression' strategy of early purity movements. Such complex 'multi-track' modes of governance reveal a distinctive combination of different modes of moral regulation, bringing together a variety of forms of legal compulsion and of self-regulation.

Thus modern moral regulation can be understood as a combination of two general strategies, that of retraditionalisation and that of self-help. It is not that one form is superior to or more modern than the other, but rather that they exhibit different modalities of governance.

The outstanding question that arises from this identification of the modalities of contemporary moral regulation is whether they open up the possibility of any transformative political strategies capable of intervening in the crises of sexuality, gender and the family which form the core of the politics of moral regulation. My question generalises the issue that haunts contemporary feminism and which is perhaps most sharply posed by Judith Walkowitz (1983: 437): how can feminists formulate a strategy against sexual violence without playing into the hands of the New Right? As I have sought to demonstrate, we have experienced a resurgence of the inherently repressive strategy that I have characterised as the retraditionalisation of sex–gender relations. Yet it remains far from clear that the strategy underlying the burgeoning self-help movement offers a potentially radical or transformatory prospect. These techniques of self-regulation and personality modification founder upon the construction of the individual as a morally autonomous agent capable of realising the emblematic slogan of the period: 'Just Do It'. How can a strategy be formulated against 'bad habits' and 'bad behaviour', such as male sexual violence or the sexual abuse of children, without playing into the hands of conservatism and religious fundamentalism? How can moral self-regulation touch the most intractable recesses of sexuality within which the 'return of the repressed' harbours the dark secrets of civilisation?

It would be exhilarating if, at the end of this exploration of the social history of moral regulation, a solution to the tension between an intransigent authoritarianism and an implausible individual moral responsibility could be unveiled. But no such rabbit can be plucked from this hat. As Antonio Gramsci insisted:

> The crisis consists precisely in the fact the old is dying and the new cannot be born; in this interregnum a great variety of morbid symptoms appear (Gramsci 1971: 276).

Little has changed in the intervening decades to change this judgement. However, while Gramsci anticipated that social revolution would ease the birth of the new; we can have no such optimism. The most that can be sustained is an insistence that the contending projects of moral regulation be submitted to the processes of democracy, which itself can hold out no guarantee that morally sustainable or practically efficient outcomes will emanate. Contests over projects of moral regulation will continue to provide a significant part of the social and political agenda; the best that we can hope is to restrain the worst excesses while we continue to grapple with the intractable conditions of social life that generate the impulse to subject the conduct of conduct to moral governance.

NOTES

INTRODUCTION

1 The anti-comics campaign is interesting in establishing that projects of moral regulation do not always emanate from the political Right; in the period 1949–55 the British Communist Party was instrumental in launching an attack on American cultural influence.
2 For fuller discussion of the link between 'character' and the governance of the self and the displacement of social discourses of character by those organised around 'personality', see White & Hunt 2000.
3 Note that the specifically moral standpoint is frequently linked to some utilitarian claim that not only is some conduct wrong, but that it causes harm of some kind or another.
4 It is important to note that what is suggested here is a double moralisation of both the active social agents and their targets; for example, in the case of prostitution both moral reformers who sought to 'save' prostitutes and the prostitutes themselves are moralised.
5 It is today uncommon to find moral discourses that link 'wrong' and 'harm', but they are still to be found. The contention that homosexuality is wrong because it is 'unnatural' and that sexual relations with children are inherently wrong are two contemporary instances of exclusively moral discourses.
6 'Experts' should be construed broadly at this stage: priests, social workers, doctors and psychoanalysts are obvious examples, but as we will see this role is also taken by a broader category of activists in the arena of moral regulation as, for example, in self-help movements in which participants become their own experts.
7 This idea of 'umbrella effect' emerged after reading D'Emilio and Freedman's discussion of anti-prostitution movements in the United States; they draw attention to the fact that much of the significance of the anti-prostitution movement was that it secured support from a constellation that spanned from Protestant fundamentalism to socialist unionism (1988: 150 ff.).
8 Frequently the structures of rule and discipline that are imposed through employment institutions are particularly fragile in the most volatile urban areas, where employment is scarce or discontinuous.
9 For discussion of the weaknesses of the moral panic tradition, see pp. 18 ff.
10 For an important discussion of the genealogy of the concept 'reformation of manners', see Ingram 1996.

11 This process is traced with impressive precision in Wrightson and Levine's (1979) study of the Essex village of Terling.
12 It should be stressed that variations in the configuration of forces have been identified: for example, Martin Ingram (1984b) has noted that the model in which the 'middling sort' abandoned popular culture and formed a power block with the gentry was only one among a number of patterns. Much of rural England remained untouched by the 'reform of morals'; a shared culture and rituals remained alive and well. He notes that during the seventeenth century a more organised onslaught, headed by the Church Courts and Quarter Sessions, conducted a new policy of 'moral discipline' on popular culture directed against such targets as unlicensed alehouses, drunkenness, tippling and dancing.
13 This conception of moral regulation mirrors Oestreich's (1982) conception of the forms of social discipline that emerged in early modern Europe. His account involves a dual emphasis on self-discipline of the individual (contrasted with the rule of the passions and emotions) and a social discipline (epitomised by the rise of the police), such that both were part of a project to bring new and expanded fields of life under control. The difference between my conception of moral regulation and Oestreich's conception of discipline is that for him the state is the primary agent, whereas for me the state is only one among a range of regulatory agents.
14 I read Dean's own study of the nineteenth-century government of poverty as making precisely my point. The 'charitable' discourses that promoted the responsibilisation of the male 'breadwinner' had major importance precisely because they denied that they were 'political' (employing a common-sense distinction between the private and the public), thereby providing the basis for what subsequently becomes a new political programme (Dean 1991).
15 For a sustained critique of social control along these lines, see Van Krieken 1991.
16 Or, to be more precise, it is humans in connection with non-humans that act as Latour (1988) demonstrates so brilliantly in his paper on the revolving door.
17 I have elsewhere offered a fuller account of the strengths and weaknesses of social explanations that offer an account of social change as a response to prevailing social anxieties (Hunt 1999b).
18 It should be noted that debates over Sunday opening have undergone a significant discursive displacement; while a rhetoric of Sunday observance carries over, today's controversies are more about control over the working week between employers and trade unions.
19 I will argue that the term 'sexual purity' better encapsulates the content of these movements and avoids the euphemisation that characterised the sexual discourses of the period.

1 COMPULSION TO VIRTUE

1 The absence of the definite article in the organisation's name follows the usage of the Societies themselves.

2 A number of different dates between 1690 and 1695 have been given for the formation of SRM; 1691 or 1692 seem most likely. SRM were active between 1691 and 1708; they went into decline between 1708 and 1714, revived between 1715 and 1725 and gradually declined until the last trace of activity in 1738. A 'revived' SRM, in which John Wesley was heavily involved, existed between 1757 and 1766, when this revived movement came to an abrupt end when the Society was hit by damages awarded against it in a court action (Wesley 1763).

3 One manifestation in some SRM texts was the commitment to a "pure and primitive Christian doctrine" (Barton 1700: 43).

4 Detailed accounts of the political and theological background to the SRM are provided by: Bahlman 1957; Bullock 1963; Overton 1885; Spurr 1990.

5 The ugliness of the neologism 'responsibilisation' is compensated for by its heuristic value. The concept catches the duality of responsibility for the self and for others by drawing attention to the active components of many discourses that assign responsibility to specific categories of agents as is exemplified in the slogan: 'Only you can stop drinking and driving', which individualises the responsible driver.

6 This strand of Christianity continued to play an important role. It surfaces explicitly again in the 'Vice Societies', a successor movement to the SRM (see Chapter 2). Many have also noted its key role in first-wave feminism and the purity movements of the second half of the nineteenth century. It tends to be identified as 'evangelicalism', which involves a unique combination of spirituality, participation and social action captured by the idea of the responsibilisation of the laity.

7 The claim that the SRM were the first lay religious association should be qualified. There is much debate in the literature about another body, the *Religious Societies*, that came into being around 1678. They had a more narrowly evangelical role than the SRM; they sought to find an active spiritual role for the laity aside from passive attendance at services and private prayer. They also engaged in certain limited action in the secular realm through the organisation of charity schools in London and providing bursaries for poor scholars to attend university. Some commentators tend to fuse these Societies with the SRM (e.g. Woodward). Since little hinges on this issue I do not pursue it further.

8 Valuable general accounts of the SRM are to be found in the following: Curtis & Speck 1976; Hayton 1990; Isaacs 1979; Portus 1912.

9 2 Mary, 21/1/1690–91.

10 1 Anne, 25/2/1702.

11 Horton identifies as key pro-SRM figures in Parliament: Colonel Maynard Colchester (Middlesex JP), Sir Humphrey Mackworth (distributed anti-swearing tracts to MPs), Sir John Perry (sponsor of unsuccessful anti-blasphemy and anti-immorality Bills). If these men promoted SRM policies in Parliament, it is strange that the SRM literature, normally quick to acknowledge support from influential quarters, never mentioned them.

12 For example, in 1692 a Bill to 'prevent profanation of the Lord's Day' went to a second reading before disappearing, while in 1695/6 a Bill against

profane swearing and cursing was passed, but never reached the statute book. In 1699 an 'Immorality Bill', passed by 134 to 124, was lost due to adjournments.

13 I use 'civil society' and 'public sphere' to designate all associations that are neither state apparatuses nor primarily economic associations.

14 Woodward hints at the existence of other branches, for example, "a Society of Ministers of the Church of England", but he lapses into conspiratorial silence: "I am withheld at present by some considerations from descending to any further particulars concerning them . . . But I can say that the stated meetings of such persons are as proper and may be more useful for the promoting of this work than any other I have described" (1701: 16).

15 Also referred to are eight other "regulated and mixed bodies of Housekeepers and Officers . . . who differ in their constitution from those beforementioned, but generally agree in the methods of inspecting the behaviour of Constables and other Officers, and going along with them, and assisting them in their searching of Disorderly Houses" (SRM 1699a: 15). The nature of this group remains uncertain; it may well have been local societies which, as the movement grew, functioned in other areas of London. By 1701 these seemed to have swollen to about twenty societies in the London area (Woodward 1701).

16 Portus (1912) identifies over forty local groups, the majority of which were in substantial cities and trading centres.

17 The only extant membership records are those for Bristol; there the membership included many civic leaders, but this characteristic does not seem to have been true in London.

18 One sermon attacked the "excesses and abuses in the several boroughs of the nation at Election Times" (Ollyffe 1709). Woodward (1701) reported action against Sunday horse-racing in Lincolnshire.

19 I have been unable to find further details of this Revd Thomas Bray, but suggest he may have been the same Revd Thomas Bray who was such a powerful sermoniser for the SRM (Bray 1709).

20 Rigby evaded capital punishment because 'attempts' were, under the common law, not felonies.

21 These references are not included in the main statistical breakdown but inserted as addenda, suggesting that sodomy was viewed differently from the standard moral offences which they prosecuted.

22 4 Jac. I, c. 4; *Statutes of the Realm* 4(2): 1141–2.

23 Commentators have advanced a variety of suggestions. Some are clearly wrong; Daniel Defoe has been suggested, but although he advocated a reformation of manners, he kept a suspicious distance from the informing tactics of the SRM (Defoe 1698; 1702). Since I have nothing further to contribute on the question of authorship I follow the British Library catalogue which attributes authorship either generically to the Societies or to Josiah Woodward.

24 The only 'missing' report is the '25th Report'; otherwise these major sources are available either in the British Library or the Bodleian Library. Oddly, the 42nd Report appears to be a republication of the 31st Report and is therefore omitted from my statistical compilation (see Table 1).

25 Some commentators have sought to identify these founders. Craig claims that Sir Richard Bulkeley was the founder of the first SRM in 1691, but unfortunately he gives no evidence to support this view; another strong contender was Edward Stephens (Craig 1980: 21). Other key early figures were Ralph Hartley MP, William Yates (barrister), Col. Maynard Colchester (barrister).

26 The versions of the *Account* attributed to Woodward all carry details of letters of support for the work of the SRM received by the author from many countries in Europe and the American colonies.

27 Presentments were general directions to juries at Quarter Sessions; the one dated 1702 warned against the neglect of duty by magistrates and constables. A set of 'Orders of Sessions' for the years 1691, 1692, 1693 and 1696–1702 explicitly encourages Christians to lay information against "profane and vicious persons"; this suggests that the SRM did not 'invent' its main tactic, but rather deployed it in a systematic manner (SRM 1706).

28 My suggestion is that this text was directed towards the French Protestant community in London.

29 Nine volumes of warrants are in the Bodleian Library [MS. Rawlinson D.1396].

30 There is a sharp contrast between the warrant books analysed by Isaacs and the figures published by the Societies in their Annual Reports. Sunday trading was only ever the second ranking offence in these statistics; on average they were around only a half of those prosecuted for lewd and disorderly behaviour. Isaacs' figures cover a period before the fuller statistical material from the SRM became available in the *Accounts* from 1715. It is possible that there was a marked shift in their targets, but the discrepancy may be accounted for by information not provided by Isaacs, namely, the geographical location of the registers which she examined.

31 This figure of 135 sermons improves on the number located by Portus (1912), who listed fifty-eight, and Isaacs (1979), who identified 104. I suspect there are more in existence since my total (which includes those found by Portus and Isaacs) is derived almost entirely from the collections in the British Library.

32 These two categories can normally readily be distinguished since those delivered by Anglicans were normally preached at St Mary-le-Bow, in Cheapside, and those by Dissenters at Salter's Hall, a fashionable Presbyterian meeting house in Ironmonger's Lane. Other sermons were delivered before local societies outside London.

33 This sermon must have achieved a certain significance because it was reprinted in 1760 under title *A Sermon Preach'd Before the Former Societies.*

34 'Maintenance' was the legal wrong of participating in another's legal action in which one had no legal interest. Opponents frequently used the allegation of maintenance to contend that the SRM project was unlawful.

35 This document published a 'Black Roll' (blacklist) of the names of offenders; it also revealed an interest in the incidence of ordinary criminal offences, not otherwise referred to in SRM texts.

36 I found no indication that the SRM ever considered the possibility of using the ecclesiastical courts which, although much weaker than in the sixteenth century, were still quite active (Hill 1969); but significantly their secular jurisdiction related to those private realms of family and marriage that did not form part of the SRM agenda.
37 Common informers were particularly active between 1550 and 1624; their role was not finally abolished until 1951, although their legal recognition had long been obsolete.
38 Along with the jurisdiction of the Cities of London and Westminster, Middlesex covered the remainder of the London area.
39 Shoemaker (1991) discovered that during the period under examination, Hartley issued only one warrant for a non-moral offence. It seems clear that he equated his judicial role with his enthusiasm for the SRM and its project.
40 Middlesex County Record Office MJ/SBB 490, fos. 58–9 and 493, fo. 53.
41 Most early SRM tracts devoted space to defending Hartley and Bulkeley. Stephens (1691; 1697) devoted the most attention, finding all the accusations false; Fowler (1692) pleaded that Hartley's errors were trivial and stoutly defended his role. The SRM tracts and sermons persistently mounted a general defence of the integrity and honesty of the SRM. In particular there was a strenuous denial that they collected reward money.
42 Sacheverell himself achieved great notoriety when he was impeached before the House of Lords as a result of two sermons (1709a; 1709b). The details of this episode lay outside my present concerns; it is sufficient to note that not only did he attack the SRM, but went further in attacking the post-1688 political settlement involving a compromise between the Whig–Anglican Establishment and the Dissenters. His trial resulted in significant popular riots in his support and contributed to undermining the Whig political supremacy (Holmes 1976).
43 Defoe's motives are far from clear. This 'class bias' thesis has the ring of an opportunist argument of convenience since he was not in other respects a defender of popular grievances.
44 A year later one Thomas Cook was arrested in Dublin; he confessed to Cooper's murder, and was executed on 11 August 1703; all that we learn of Cook was that Cooper had been killed "by the hands of an Atheist" (Bray 1709: 18).

2 MORAL REGULATION FROM ABOVE

1 There is some tentative evidence of a link between loyalist associations and the Vice Society. One of the more important organisations, The Association for the Preservation of Liberty and Property against Republicans and Levellers (1792) was founded by John Reeves, who became one of the early members of the Vice Society.
2 Boyer (1978) seeks to capture this dualism by distinguishing between a 'negative environmentalism' (e.g. suppression of brothels and saloons) and 'positive environmentalism' (e.g. improving the urban environment with parks, playgrounds, etc.).

3 The link with the earlier Societies for Reformation of Manners was kept alive through the republication of some of their major tracts (SRM 1786).
4 The Society for the Reformation of Principles was established by anti-Jacobin Anglicans in the late 1790s. The rules restricted membership to Anglicans, probably because the evangelical wing of the Church of England wanted to prove its loyalty. The leading activist was John Bowles, a prominent pamphleteer against Thomas Paine, who later became a prominent member of the Vice Society.
5 The names of the Revd Henry Zouch JP, William Hey (Mayor of Leeds), the Revd Samuel Glasse of Wanstead, Essex, and William Mainwairing (MP for Middlesex) (Innes 1990; Isaacs 1979) appear frequently. Glasse and Mainwaring later became executive members of the Proclamation Society.
6 36 *Parliamentary Debates* (1817) col. 1120.
7 27 Geo. III, 1/6/1787.
8 *For the Encouragement of Piety and Virtue and for the Preventing and Punishing of Vice, Prophaness, and Immorality* (1 Anne, 26/3/1702). This Proclamation was reissued with minor variations in 1703, 1708, 1715 and 1727.
9 Subsequently a series of further Proclamations was issued against vice and immorality based on the wording of the 1702 Proclamation in February 1820 and June 1837, and the last Proclamation against vice in June 1860. It should be noted that, with the securing of parliamentary legislative sovereignty from the late seventeenth century, Proclamations were less and less significant as legislative mechanisms. Paradoxically they came to take on the characteristics of the early Tudor Proclamations, issued at a time when it had not yet been settled that a statute once passed remained in force until repealed. They called for the enforcement of existing law and reminded justices and other officials of their duties. A number of benches of JPs adopted resolutions for their enforcement and, in turn, further circulated the Proclamation and their own resolutions. The project had all the hallmarks of a well-orchestrated campaign of moral regulation.
10 Wilberforce wrote in his journal in 1837: "God Almighty has set before me two great objects, the suppression of the slave trade and the reformation of manners" (Wilberforce 1838 I: 149). But once the Proclamation Society was launched, Wilberforce seems to have played no further active role, although he continued to insist on the importance of the reformation of manners.
11 The Proclamation Society has attracted little recent attention aside from Innes 1990, and passing comments in Quinlan 1941, Jaeger 1956, and Bristow 1977. It has as yet received no in-depth study.
12 (6/1/1838); the full title of Livesey's journal was *The Moral Reformer, and Protester Against the Vices, Abuses, and Corruptions of the Age.*
13 Another conference was planned for 1791, but I have not been able to trace any record of its being held.
14 The full name was 'The Society for the Suppression of Vice and the Encouragement of Religion and Virtue through the United Kingdom'.
15 Of the twenty-nine people present at the founding meeting of the Vice Society only three had had prior connection to the Proclamation Society (Roberts 1983: 164).

16 The use of class categories during this period involves real difficulties. I avoid the term middle class except in a loose descriptive sense, since the modern sense of the middle class as a large salaried managerial, administrative and technical stratum had not yet emerged. I use, albeit tentatively, the term 'respectable classes' in much the same way as does F. M. L. Thompson (1988); it identifies a process of class differentiation in which each social class was developing distinctive notions of self-respect and its own identity.

17 Among these early members were John Bowdler, who 'bowdlerised' Shakespeare and the Bible; Sarah Trimmer, a leading evangelical publicist; the current Lord Mayor of London; and the publisher Charles Rivington.

18 In December 1806 twenty gentlemen met in Hull to form a Society for the Suppression of Vice; seventy attended a meeting called to launch the Society and a Committee was established. They proceeded to launch prosecutions of some brothel-keepers and 'dram shops' opening on Sundays (Scott 1807). Sydney Smith (1809) noted the spread of local offshoots of the Vice Society to York, Reading and other provincial centres.

19 This cessation of activities was probably associated with a financial scandal in 1809 that disgraced John Bowles, who until that point had been the leading force in the Society.

20 One of the paradoxes of the attack on Carlile was that he himself had openly defended the prosecution of everyday obscenity.

21 The main impact of this statute was to regularise the existing common-law offences facilitating prosecutions and providing increased police powers to search for and confiscate obscene material. The Statute's influence persisted and, linked with the judgment in *R.* v. *Hicklin* (1868) 3 QB 360 that enshrined the test of "whether the tendency of the matter . . . is to deprave and corrupt those whose minds are open to such immoral influences" (at 371), was to form the textual basis of the *Obscene Publications Action* 1959.

22 When the National Vigilance Association absorbed the Vice Society's anti-obscenity role in the mid-1880s it carried on the attack on foreign, particularly French, literary works. It orchestrated prosecutions of Henry Vizetelly who had been publishing English translations of Zola, Flaubert, Gogol, Dostoevsky, Tolstoy and others. In 1887 an obscene libel prosecution was initiated; Vizetelly broke under the strain and allowed his counsel to persuade him to change his plea to guilty.

23 On Sunday, 24 June 1854, 200,000 protested in Hyde Park and Karl Marx applauded.

24 This running together of obscenity and political dissent is epitomised by the attack on the "infidelity and insubordination fostered by the licentiousness of the press which have raised into existence a pestilent swarm of blasphemous, licentious and obscene books and prints which are insinuating their way into the recesses of private life to the destruction of all purity of sentiment and all correctness of principle" (Society for the Suppression of Vice 1803: 15).

25 For a detailed account of the protracted struggle to suppress the fairs, see Cunningham 1977.

26 The Society does seem to have played a key role in preventing the establishment of a national lottery in 1826.
27 The same lack of detailed attention characterised its listed concerns with parish apprentices and fortune tellers. It expressed concern about cruelty to animals, but there seems to have been some division of labour with the Society for Prevention of Cruelty to Animals (1824), which launched systematic attacks on popular recreations such as dog-fighting and bear-baiting, but not deer or fox-hunting, the recreations of the urban gentry.
28 There seems to have been a burst of activity on sexual transgressions between 1815 and 1818 when the Society collaborated with the recently established Guardian Society in a mixed tactic of prosecution of prostitutes and brothel-keepers.
29 Scott [1807] claimed that the impact of prosecutions for Sabbath offences was so successful in subsequent years the number of prosecutions fell to 180, 178 and 70.
30 Towns on the northern fringes of London were being absorbed by the metropolis.
31 That the Society was comfortable with the results of this inquiry is attested by the fact that the Minutes of the hearings were published as an appendix to one of its major publications (Society for the Suppression of Vice 1825).

3 FROM SEXUAL PURITY TO SOCIAL HYGIENE, 1870–1918

1 I will adopt the convention of treating the nineteenth century as a 'long century' that does not end until the outbreak of the First World War in 1914.
2 The same general thrust can be detected in Continental Europe, but the detailed configuration of moral regulation projects in, for example, France and Germany is sufficiently distinct, influenced in particular by differences in religion and in state–Church relations, that it would be beyond the scope of the present project to address moral reform movements outside Britain and the United States.
3 Although it is not developed in Jeffreys' account, it is clear that she views the priority given by feminism to securing the ballot as a major component in the derailment of the strong feminism of the 1890s. According to her account, feminism went into abeyance only to revive with the emergence of 'revolutionary feminism' in the 1970s (1985).
4 Not all women were relegated to the chorus. The increasing number of female doctors were well represented in the social hygiene movement, but rarely as leaders since it, like the increasingly tightly organised medical profession, was firmly in male hands.
5 Of course, poverty never faded from the debates and controversies; Mayhew ([1851–62]/1967) brought it back into focus at mid-century. Nevertheless poverty had to be rediscovered towards the end of the century (Booth 1889; Mearns 1883). In the United States a distinctively rural critique of urbanism was of social disorder; the discovery of poverty had to wait until late in the nineteenth century (Riis 1890).

6 I have pondered whether the contemporary phrase 'social hygiene' should similarly be displaced by 'sexual hygiene'. While venereal diseases are sexual in multiple ways, the prefix 'social' adds the important sense in which the project was not just about the quest for effective medical treatment, which was secured by 1914, but the strong sense in which participants were deeply wedded to a social-environmental approach. It would not impact significantly on my general argument to change this designation and, since the juxtaposition of 'sexual purity' and 'social hygiene' corroborates the significant shift from private sin to public problem, I retain this usage.

7 As Laqueur has demonstrated (1990), the lines of cleavage between the sexes exhibited complex variations as philosophers and doctors tried to work out whether those divisions exist in a one-sex world (female as inverted male) or a two-sex world (incommensurable sexual difference).

8 Nineteenth-century nervous debility was reborn as 'stress' in the late twentieth century and again provided with medical respectability and legitimation.

9 These views were consistent with the vitalist tradition which from the end of the eighteenth century had been displacing a philosophy of the body deriving from Galen's 'humours'. In addition the sex act involved a powerful release, not only of 'vital fluid', but of nervous energy and was thereby linked to the pervasive discourses of neurasthenia (Nissenbaum 1980).

10 For a discussion of the historical roots of anxieties surrounding effeminacy see Barker-Benfield 1992: Chapter 3.

11 By the time the impact of Foucault's first pithy volume was being felt, he himself had dramatically shifted his concerns in the succeeding volumes (Foucault 1985 and 1986).

12 For an extended critique of Foucault's treatment of the repressive hypothesis see Porter 1991; Porter & Teich 1994.

13 This position is paradigmatically represented by Sheila Jeffreys (1985), who celebrates early anti-heterosexual feminists and seeks to reclaim them for contemporary radical feminism.

14 The deeply paradoxical response of fear and excitement to the railways is best captured by Schivelbusch (1979), while Peter Gay (1986: 328) registers the sense of sexual danger and pleasure that the railways brought with them.

15 As many commentators have noted medical inquiry during the mid-Victorian period was preoccupied with charting sexual difference; see Benjamin 1991; Jordanova 1989; Laqueur 1990; Russett 1989.

16 The sanctification of matrimony and motherhood was reinforced by the common belief that prostitutes were barren and that commercialised sex was in a double sense non-productive (Laqueur 1990: 230).

17 As a number of commentators have pointed out Acton's was not the only voice; others recognised female sexual pleasure (e.g. Culverwell [1847]). The existence of alternative voices should not blind us to the extent that they were swamped by Acton's prestige and the widespread citation of this passage.

18 Blackwell argues if wives experience indifference or repugnance for marital sex this resulted from the fear of childbirth or awkward or brutal conjugal

approaches. In these circumstances abstinence and frigidity became an "easy virtue" (1885: 45).

19 The link between respectability and the 'passionless' woman has been explored by Cott (1978), Nead (1988), Yeazell (1989) and others.

20 Dijkstra (1986) studies the cult of female invalidism in the images in Victorian paintings of 'the collapsing woman' represented as a nymph with the broken back.

21 This view has a racialised expression in the belief that the 'lower races' exhibited a more pronounced sexuality than the 'higher races' (Geddes & Thompson 1889).

22 Not only was sexual indulgence both immoral and harmful, sensuality could be transmitted so as to "blight the innocent offspring" (Blackwell 1885: 34).

23 The FMRS rapidly displaced its predecessor, the Seventh Commandment Society, a male evangelical body. As a significant qualification to the 'feminism' of the FMRS it should be noted that its moving force and 'agent' in its early years was John R. McDowall, who insisted on the special affinity of women for moral reform work.

24 Note that the appeal to conscience persisted in the rhetoric of those who explicitly linked moral reform and evangelical religion such as Josephine Butler who appealed to the "supremacy of conscience" (1871a: 5–6).

25 This theme is echoed in most studies of nineteenth-century moral regulation movements (Boyer 1978; Bristow 1977; Pivar 1973; Valverde 1991). The most significant exception is Beisel's study of anti-obscenity movements (1997); she demonstrates how a concern about the social reproduction of the middle-class family manifests itself in anti-urban and anti-immigrant discourses.

26 Purity pledges were not exclusively directed at men. In an early incarnation the New York Female Moral Reform Society (FMRS) sponsored a pledge for women: "We pledge ourselves to observe the strictest rules of chastity, in thought and deed, according to the Bible; and to promote the cause of purity by every laudable means in our power. We will not indulge ourselves in any filthy jestings, songs, anecdotes, or conversation; and we will discountenance all lewd books, poems, and pictures; and, in cases of licentiousness, fully believing the male is equally, and in most cases more guilty than the female, we will withdraw from all unnecessary intercourse with the vile of both sexes, except with a view to reclaim them" (4 *The Advocate of Moral Reform* (15/1/1838) 16).

27 Lucy Bland captures precisely this core theme in the title of her study of the British purity movement, *Banishing the Beast* (1995).

28 The sexual purity message implicitly assumed that it was young men who, in the increasingly lengthy period between sexual maturity and marriage, were most likely to resort to prostitutes.

29 The conjunction of sexual purity and adolescence expressed itself in Baden-Powell's near fanatical concern with adolescent purity in the Boy Scout movement (Rosenthal 1986).

30 Polanyi located the root of this profound change as one in which "pauperism and political economy together form part of an indivisible whole: the discovery of society" (1957: 103).

31 "Agreement between the United States and other Powers for the Repression of the Trade in White Women: Signed May 1904" (October 1908) 2 *American Journal of International Law* 363–6.
32 The publication of a pamphlet by British activist, Ellice Hopkins, was the first to link the issue of coercion of juveniles into prostitution with the call to raise the age of consent (1883).
33 (1910) 36 *US Statutes at Large* 825–7. This federal Act prohibited the transportation of women across state lines for immoral purposes. For a full account of the Mann Act, see Langum 1994.
34 The main advances were the Wasserman test in 1906 and Salvarsan test for syphilis in 1910.
35 Yet the VD clinic movement continued to oppose ready access to condoms as preventive measure. Wartime proposals to provide contraception to soldiers overseas were greeted with much hostility as a measure sanctioning immorality.

4 MORAL REGULATION IN THE UNITED STATES

1 For a general account of early attempts at legal enforcement of morality, see Flaherty 1971.
2 Fornication covered sexual relations between unmarried persons and between a married man and an unmarried woman; sex between a married woman and any man constituted the much more serious offence of adultery.
3 Typical of such legislation was *An act for the more effectuall suppressing the several sins and offences of swaring, curseing, profaincing Gods holy name, Sabbath abuseing, drunkenness, fornication, and adultery* of 1691 in Virginia.
4 Tippling was idle drinking, mere sociability that kept people from work.
5 Sumptuary laws prescribed legal penalties against extravagance, luxury and fashion (Hunt 1996: 38–9, 345–8).
6 It should be noted that in the colonies, congregational churches, including the Quakers, exercised moral jurisdiction over church members and sometimes over family members.
7 The organisation established by Cotton Mather, Society for Suppression of Disorder, sought to suppress brothels in Boston.
8 For example, Connecticut empowered town constables to restrain "all such as they judge to exceed their conditions and ranks" (Foster 1971: 29).
9 While a small number of leading religious figures in both the established Church and the other Protestant denominations participated in the sexual purity movements in Britain, as we will see in Chapter 5, the political and economic leadership in the main kept a considerable distance from the upsurge of moral reform activity that was an expression of the self-formation of the middle classes.
10 The Seventh Commandment Society borrowed from the temperance movement the technique of holding meetings at which men were invited to sign a pledge "to discountenance licentiousness in all its forms, both by precept and example, and to regard this sin in persons of both sexes as equally infamous".
11 Although short-lived, the Magdalen Society brought John R. McDowall into moral reform action; he was perhaps the first professional moral reformer and

was to play a key role in the early years of the FMRS. The Society was short-lived, as its first report, in which McDowall claimed that there were 10,000 prostitutes in New York, generated such a storm of protest against the airing of such an indelicate subject that its members hurriedly closed the Society.

12 3 *Advocate* 197 (15 January 1837).

13 As Ginzberg observes "one cannot exaggerate the hostility toward men in their journals . . . and, most important, discussions of poverty and prostitution. Lust appeared as a disease that had infected the entire male population" (1990: 20).

14 The legislation in New York State, passed in 1848, provided for a maximum of five years imprisonment and $1000 fine.

15 I explore 'maternal feminism' in more detail in Chapter 5.

16 It is significant to note that the sinfulness of the prostitute coexisted with claims about the moral superiority of women, since that superiority involved a vulnerability to personal moral failure; once 'fallen', women had further to fall than men.

17 The most frequently used legal device against prostitutes in the nineteenth century was the refurbished vagrancy laws.

18 The concept of 'seduction' is significant because it was premised on male sexual predation of women who while naturally morally superior were nevertheless vulnerable and thus not responsible for their own sexual conduct.

19 The sophistication of Beisel's analysis lies in her explanation of the differential support for Comstock's SSV in Philadelphia, where it never secured elite support, in contrast to the support he secured in New York and Boston. In Philadelphia with only a small immigrant population, the political elite was secure in its political control, while in New York and Boston the old elites were losing control to political forces relying on the mass support of Irish immigrants.

20 Comstock persistently alleged that immigrants were responsible for the distribution of obscene material.

21 Women were not even admitted to SSV meetings in New York until 1893.

22 Such legislation was secured in Maine 1871; by 1915 seventeen states had statutes; and by 1917 these had risen to thirty states (Mackey 1987: 24).

23 It was not until environmentalist approaches to social problems became more developed and the focus moved away from a single-minded concern with prostitutes, that the more successful and sustained approach of the settlement movement yielded some positive results, even though such movements had strongly disciplinary tendencies (Davis 1967; Platt 1969).

24 The 'discovery' of the double standard predates the Victorian era; Keith Thomas demonstrates the historically shifting concerns of men and women with sexual reputation (Thomas 1959).

25 There are, as I indicate elsewhere in this chapter, excellent studies of individual American moral reform and anti-prostitution movements.

26 Both Powell and Gibbon were 'old abolitionists'. Powell as will be seen played a key role in the purity movement; Gibbon lent her support to the 'new abolitionism' and became President of the New York Committee for the Prevention of Licensed Prostitution in 1876.

27 The department was initially styled 'Department for the Suppression of the Social Evil' and changed to 'Purity Department' in 1885. In 1887 Willard established a closely related 'Department to Suppress Impure Literature'; Deborah and Josiah Leeds, long-time anti-obscenity campaigners, headed the department.

28 The platform speeches were published under Aaron Powell's editorship (Powell 1896).

29 Stead, editor of *The Pall Mall Gazette*, had launched the sensationalist "Maiden Tribute to Modern Babylon" (1885), which, as we will see in the next chapter, had lit the touchpaper for a mass upsurge in purity activity in 1885.

30 For the distinction between the feminism of rights and the feminism of fear, see Marilley 1993.

31 The vice commissions have not been the subject of the rigorous investigation that they deserve. They appear in recent studies only in terms of their part in the 'white slavery' campaign between 1909 and 1914; yet despite their location in the moral regulation tradition they adopted a largely agnostic position about the existence of an organised 'traffic in women'.

32 One key figure was George J. Kneeland; he directed the Chicago Vice Commission investigation having earlier worked for the New York Committee of Fourteen. He was hired by John D. Rockefeller Jun. to produce a report on commercialised prostitution in New York (Kneeland 1913). He subsequently directed the Newark inquiry in 1913–14, and those in Philadelphia and Syracuse.

33 It is one of the ironies of the period that the important Chicago sociologist W. I. Thomas, who had worked on the Chicago vice commission report in 1911, was himself sacked from the University of Chicago on the grounds that he had been arrested under the Mann Act, even though he was never prosecuted under its 'transportation for immoral purposes' provisions.

34 Attorneys specialising in moral offences are exemplified by Clifford G. Roe and Edward W. Sims. Roe was an Assistant State Attorney in Illinois, acting as special prosecutor against procurers in Chicago (1906–09). He was brought to New York by Rockefeller to head his vice investigation (1911–12). He was a leading figure in the Illinois Vigilance Association; Executive Secretary of the National Vigilance Committee; and President of the American Alliance for the Suppression and Prevention of the White Slave Traffic. He was the author of numerous 'white slavery' tracts (Roe 1910, 1911a, b, c, 1914). Reckless (1933) established that Roe fabricated the 'facts' in these white slavery publications by persistently presenting consensual prostitution as coerced white slavery. Sims was a US Attorney in Chicago; he gave sensationalised treatments of 'white slavery' and was primarily responsible for the oft-repeated allegation that American prostitution was controlled by a syndicate led by 'The Big Chief', with clearing houses that held 'auctions' of victims and with agents in Canada and Europe (Sims 1909).

35 "It is an absolute fact that corrupt Jews are the backbone of the loathsome traffic in New York and Chicago" (Turner 1909: 57).

36 The history of the white slavery campaign has been well documented in the

recent study by Frederick Grittner (1990) and on the very specific question of Jewish involvement in prostitution by Edward Bristow (1982). The most significant legislative manifestation, the Mann Act of 1910, has been thoroughly explored by David Langum (1994).

37 In 1910 it changed its name to National Vigilance Society.

38 The ASHA was formed from the fusion of a purity organisation with a medical anti-VD movement, the American Vigilance Association and American Federation for Sex Hygiene. Prince Morrow did much to bring about this development, but died shortly before it came to fruition.

39 William Foster, active in the ASHA, recognised the tension between providing sexual information and the call for chastity; his solution reverted to an older purity tradition by instituting an active, healthy regime for the young with lots of cross-country running and cold showers (1914).

40 The 'Plan' was careful to include elements aimed at limiting opposition to the regulationist strategy. It contained powers to close red-light districts and explicitly rejected the use of 'military brothels'.

5 SEXUAL PURITY, MATERNAL FEMINISM AND CLASS IN LATE VICTORIAN BRITAIN

1 The long title of the *Criminal Law Amendment Act* 1885 makes its content clear: *An Act to Make Further Provision for the Protection of Women and Girls and the Suppression of Brothels and Other Purposes* 48 & 49 Vic., c. 69.

2 My contention that feminism played a more decisive role in moral politics in Britain than in the United States is by no means uncontroversial. For example, Olive Banks (1981: 83) argues that British movements were less feminist than movements in the United States.

3 My problematic is very similar to that posed by Judith Walkowitz in her study of the campaign to repeal the CDAs: "Why did male and female repealers, who were advocates of personal rights, anti-statist in their political ideology, and even knowledgeable of the realities of working-class prostitution, permit themselves to be swept up in a movement with such repressive political implications?" (1980: 248).

4 8 *Sentinel* (July 1886) 7.

5 The Metropolitan Police established an 'Obscene Publications Squad' in 1868.

6 36 *Parliamentary Debates* (1817) col. 1120.

7 Something of the patronising tone can be glimpsed in one of Ellice Hopkins' addresses: "I soon grew to love you working-people"; "I want you to join an association, now that is rather a long word . . ."; "I never knew that women swore" (1869: 5–6).

8 The full title was *An Act for the Prevention of Contagious Diseases at Certain Naval and Military Stations* 27 & 28 Vic., c. 85; officially to be referred to as *Contagious Diseases (Women) Act* 1864. Further extensions followed in Acts in 1866 and 1869; these expanded the geographical range of application of the powers created to require compulsory medical examination of women

deemed to be 'common prostitutes' in areas proximate to army barracks and naval dockyards.

9 Examples of related legislation were the *Food Adulteration Act* 1860, *Vaccination Act* 1861, *Diseased Meat Act* 1863, *Sanitary Act* 1866, *Public Health Act* 1875.

10 Arthur Ingram, the Bishop of London, went so far as to allege that "children in hospitals suffering from rickets, and worse, are the result of the diseased inheritance of their fathers" (1909: 11).

11 The Association for the Extension of the Contagious Diseases Acts was formed in 1868.

12 The largely male 'National Association' rapidly deferred to the LNA, which was henceforth the most visible component of the anti-CDAs campaign; it subsequently changed its name to the Ladies National Association for the Abolition of the State Regulation of Vice. The campaign was soon internationalised; in 1875 Josephine Butler formed the British and Continental Federation for the Abolition of the Government Regulation of Prostitution (which later became the International Federation for the Abolition of State Regulation of Vice).

13 Frederick Binney, referring to the link between sexual immorality and venereal diseases, expressed the view that "it is one of the happiest things for man that Nature is on the side of virtue" (1883: 5). More recently similar sentiments have been expressed about AIDS and sexual morality.

14 This inequality was compounded by the fact that in 1860 the military authorities abandoned attempts to impose genital inspection on serving soldiers and sailors because of opposition from the ranks (Smith 1990). It should be noted that there was also a class dimension, since medical inspection of officers had never been considered. There was, however, some talk of making sexually transmitted diseases notifiable and criminalising their transmission.

15 Note the family resemblance to the major thematic of recent feminist anti-pornography campaigns, that pornography degrades all women.

16 Blackwell constructed working-class women as both victims and sources of moral contagion; there was no feminism in her contention that "unchaste women become a most dangerous class of the community" (1885: 53).

17 Blackwell's chauvinism is striking in the contrast she draws between "the polygamous and sensual East and the monogamous and intellectual West" (1885: 55).

18 As Walkowitz's study (1980) makes clear, there was strong opposition from many prostitutes to the inspection procedures even before their opposition was actively encouraged by LNA members; but paradoxically inspection was often welcomed by prostitutes because it provided them with a valuable clean bill of health (Smith 1990).

19 This was no idiosyncrasy on Butler's part; it is interesting to note that the only woman who rivalled her influence, Ellice Hopkins, launched the White Cross Army in 1883 by undertaking a lecture tour in working-class districts in the North of England.

20 F. Barry Smith goes further in insisting that "this massive campaign helped retard the fuller emancipation of women" (1971: 134). It is certainly true

that there was resistance from important sections of suffrage feminism to becoming involved in the issue of prostitution and some key figures associated with women in medicine movements, in particular Elizabeth Garrett Anderson, sided with the regulationists.

21 Versions of this analysis can be found in most accounts of the English purity movements (Bland 1985; Bristow 1977; Mort 1987; Walkowitz 1980). The radical feminists Sheila Jeffreys (1985) and Margaret Jackson (1994) offer a variant of the orthodox account: they argue that the purity movement had two wings, one conservative and the other feminist. The feminist wing of the purity movement they view as the direct successor to the anti-regulation campaign.

22 Under the CLAA 1885 'gross indecency' became a misdemeanour, triable by magistrates, and subject to two years hard labour; the impact was effectively to criminalise all homosexual activity.

23 The forms of the 'care of the self' with which Foucault was much concerned in his later work added an ethical dimension to everyday self-governance by making of lives a work which incorporates aesthetic and stylistic values; it is not, I suggest, by chance that such practices manifested themselves in the privileged lives of Greek males (Foucault 1986).

24 For an application of the significance of the transition from character to personality with respect to the practices of citizenship, see White & Hunt 2000.

25 Similar lists can be found in Alfred Dyer 1884 and Edith Ward 1892; they add such items as going to bed early and scrupulous personal cleanliness.

26 Edward Kirk advised girls that "there is one thing that may most seriously hurt a girl's body, and that is touching the private parts in any way to make the sensitive nerves give a sensation of pleasure" (1905: 21).

27 Butler wrote *The Hour Before Dawn* (1876) for the SPA, who also published her famous speech on social purity at Cambridge University (1881).

28 Jackson and Jeffreys dismiss the SPA because of its male membership; but since its target was the reformation of male sexuality this is hardly surprising.

29 In *Schoolboy Morality* mothers were urged to "make the fear of the results a deterrence. Tell him that if a boy once begins to give way, it is almost impossible for him to stop himself, so he goes on and on until he becomes the slave of his body, and that it is better to die than become such a slave" (SPA 1884b: 11).

30 Its leading members were Alfred Dyer, George Gillet, Professor James Stuart and Josephine Butler.

31 Other key participants were Benjamin Scott, William Shaen, Henry Wilson MP, George Gillet and Benjamin Waugh.

32 The Alliance of Honour, established in 1901, was another purity pledge movement that aimed at young men of lower middle class and working class; its platform promoted "religion, home, and empire". Important figures included Baden-Powell and Bramwell Booth.

33 The invocation of Arthur and Knights of the Round Table and of patriotism to the cause of self-dedication to purity managed to ignore the adultery that lay at the heart of the Arthurian saga.

34 The founding figures were George Gillet, Alfred Dyer, Robert Morgan and Robert Scott. The year following a parallel women's organisation was established, Women's Union of the GPA, with Mrs E. H. Bradley as Organising Secretary and Mrs Laura Ormiston Chant as Honorary Secretary.
35 Webb-Peploe explicitly drew his inspiration from the model of the Societies for Reformation of Manners (Bristow 1977: 164); and consistent with that found no place for the female activists who were by now such a significant force in the purity movement. The upsurge during 1885 displaced this traditional model of moral reform and Webb-Peploe's committee was rapidly absorbed by the National Vigilance Association (NVA).
36 Letter to Mary Priestman, 5/11/1894 (Butler Collection, Fawcett Library, London).
37 This debate generated much steam, but never reached great depth. It was not to achieve that until the famous exchange over prostitution and homosexual law reform between Patrick Devlin and H. L. A. Hart in the debate over the 1957 Royal Commission on prostitution and homosexuality ('Wolfenden Report') (Devlin 1959; Hart 1963).
38 There are a number of accounts of the events surrounding Stead's acquisition of a young virgin (Bristow 1977; Gorham 1978; Pearson 1972; Playfair 1969; Schults 1972; Stafford 1964; Terrot 1959; 1960; Trudgill 1976). Walkowitz (1992: Chapters 3 and 4) provides a different treatment; she is not concerned with 'the truth' or Stead's sexual psychology, but rather is interested in why the distorted representation of prostitution in the "Maiden Tribute" was so exciting and compelling to a variety of social constituencies. She focuses on a deconstruction of its narrative in order to explore the cultural meanings surrounding sexual danger.
39 It subsequently transpired that the couple was not formally married, but like many working-class people cohabited, and he might not have been Eliza's biological father.
40 Stead subsequently published his speech in self-justification as a pamphlet (Stead 1886).
41 The 'reasonable cause' defence was removed by the *Criminal Law Amendment Act* 1922 (12 & 13 Geo. V, c. 56). The 'reasonable cause' defence remained controversial in the law relating to rape.
42 The origins of s. 11 remain controversial. At the last minute the radical MP Henry Labouchère introduced the clause. Davenport-Hines (1990) claims that Henry Labouchère's amendment was the act of a flamboyant Radical intent on ridiculing the CLAA; see also Smith (1976).
43 *Hansard* (Commons), 3d ser., 300 (30/7/1885), cols. 579–85.
44 One possible exception is the Personal Rights Association (PRA) that opposed the legislative imposition of morality. But once the CDAs had been repealed, it focused its activity in directions which were no longer within the ambit of moral regulation. It was shortly to bifurcate, with the PRA becoming increasingly civil libertarian, while its more conservative components found a home in the Liberty and Property Defence League (1882), which represented the right wing of libertarianism.

45 Letter to Miss Priestman, 5/11/1894, quoted Bell (1962: 174; emphasis in original).
46 It was invoked not only in the cases of prostitution and obscenity in the nineteenth century, but is alive and well today in the cases of 'organised' drug trade and 'paedophile rings'.
47 *Aldershot Gazette* (23/6/1888).
48 Egalitarian feminism was often ambivalent about how far the claim for equality with men should be pressed. For example, Mona Caird pressed the radical contention that marriage was no different in principle from prostitution, since married women were slaves, suffering sexual and household servitude to a man in exchange for a livelihood. Yet she rejected the idea of women pursuing equality in the male sphere of work and business. "It will be a happy day for humanity when a woman can stay in her own home without sacrificing her freedom" (1897: 165).
49 Charles Kingsley gave voice to this idealised conception of "woman as the teacher, the natural and therefore divine guide, purifier, inspirer of the man" (quoted in Houghton 1957: 351).
50 Geddes and Thompson provided one of the most influential late Victorian theorisations of sex differences. They presented a view of males as active and progressive while females are passive and conservative. They argued that a decline in sexual passion is associated with the evolution of the 'higher races'. Yet despite the conservative thrust of their views, they were supporters of women's rights.
51 Perhaps just as significant was Acton's pathologising of female sexuality: "It is too true, I admit, as the divorce courts show, that there are some few women who have sexual desires so strong that they surpass those of men" (1865: 112). One paradoxical feature of Victorian sexual ideology was that, while women were viewed as passionless, once they manifested any sensuality they were deemed to have less capacity than men to control their passions. In its turn this line of thought played an important part in the dividing practices that enshrined a gulf between 'respectable' and 'fallen' women.
52 One component of the Victorian sexual code had deep roots in the long-standing rejection of all forms of 'excess', which grounded the hostility to luxury and self-indulgence (Berry 1994; Hunt 1995). Edith Ward argued that a choice that confronts all great civilisations "as soon as success brought them wealth, and wealth brought luxury and idleness, vice followed in their footsteps" (1892: 7).
53 Peter Gay (1984: 271) argues that the slow but real triumph of contraception was a result of the "pressure of reality" and provides evidence of increasing female sexual enjoyment associated with a reduction of the anxiety over unwanted pregnancies.
54 It is significant that, while large numbers of LNA activists joined the NVA, the organisation declined to merge itself with the NVA.
55 8 Edw. VII, c. 45. The Act imposed between three and seven years imprisonment for incestuous relationships involving male grandparents, fathers and siblings, but did not include stepchildren.

56 Canada, it may be noted, went even further and enacted comprehensive anti-seduction legislation in 1886 (Dubinsky 1993).
57 Even Lucy Bland, who provides the most thorough study of English sexual politics, offers only a few brief pages on white slavery (1995: 297–303). Otherwise there is Terrot's non-academic account (1960), which simply reproduces the assertions of the purity campaigners. This neglect may reflect the fact that the campaign was largely a pressure group campaign directed at Parliament and exhibited few mass movement features.
58 Bristow's (1982) study of the white slavery campaigns and the complex relations between prostitution and immigration establishes that anti-Semitism was a frequent accompaniment, with the finger of blame variously pointed at other immigrant groups; in England not only Jews, but French, Belgians and Italians came in for their share of demonisation.
59 I make no attempt at an inventory of white slavery texts; but the following are a sample of the more widely cited: Boyle 1912; Mackirdy & Willis 1912; Robins 1913; Willis 1910; 1912.
60 Apocryphal melodrama was not invented by the white slavery texts; it had been widely used in temperance and sexual purity discourses, and in particular in anti-masturbation tracts (Hunt 1998). Judith Walkowitz demonstrates the use of melodrama in narratives of the dangers of the city (Walkowitz 1992).
61 2 & 3 Geo. V, c. 20.
62 For example, George Sims (1908) presented an entirely unsubstantiated attack on Germans as pimps to London prostitutes. Arnold White, at the same conference, delivered an outright racist attack on Jews, Russians and Orientals as pimps (White 1908).
63 A speedy passage was assured when the Liberal women's organisation threatened to end support for the Liberal Party after its refusal to include suffrage in its legislative programme; the Bill received government support as a blatant act of appeasement.
64 *Times* (31/5/1911) 5.
65 *Spectator* (20/11/1909) 846–7.
66 For example, the Revd John Morris gave a 'decline and fall' account of the white slave trade (Morris 1885).
67 One symptom of the concern with degeneracy was the recitation of stories of degenerate tribes. The most frequently invoked was the American case, 'the Jukes', who were reputed to have bred legions of imbeciles, criminals and prostitutes. James Marchant discovered a British parallel in the person of one 'Ada Young', among whose 700 descendants there were alleged to have been 106 bastards, 142 beggars, 64 in workhouse, 181 'fallen', 69 'gaol birds', 7 'murderers' (1909).
68 In 1915 Josephine Butler's anti-regulationist Ladies National Association finally changed its name and became the Association for Moral and Social Hygiene, to form an amalgamation with other purity organisations. It is significant that they felt obliged to adopt the now fashionable medico-moral terminology of social hygiene.

69 Signatories included the populariser of eugenics Caleb Saleeby, the Fabian reformer Beatrice Webb and Ramsay MacDonald, later to become the first Labour Prime Minister.

70 *Times* (31/5/1911) 5.

71 Christabel Pankhurst's slogan 'Chastity for Men, Votes for Women' (1913) and Louisa Martindale's 'The Cure for Prostitution – the Vote' (1908) were not always welcomed by suffragists.

72 In a different context Jeffrey Minson has spoken of a "governmentalisation of sexual difference" (1993: 62). I employ the phrase 'sexual politics' to emphasise the significance of the idea that sexual practices and sexualities are appropriate social facts to be made subject to governing. I use the concept 'field', following Bourdieu, to refer to a socially patterned set of practices (1989: 39). The metaphor of the 'magnetic field' is pertinent in that a field exerts a force which connects all that falls within its range.

73 This line of thought draws on Donzelot's account of the forms of alliance formed between state, welfare agencies and mothers in the development of 'welfare' as the distinctive modern form of regulation of gender relations and the family (1980).

74 'Dividing practices' is the concept that Foucault uses to designate all those processes of regulation that work through the imposition of separations and segregations (e.g. sane and insane) (1982: 208–9).

75 It should be noted that this line of argument is incompatible with one of the most paradoxical faces of today's feminism which is seeking to mobilise women to engage in the transformation of themselves and of gendered relations; it first insists that women are and always have been victims acted upon and determined either by men or a generic patriarchy. One of the refreshing features of late nineteenth-century feminism was its vibrant realisation of women's own agency.

76 While my account of this concern of the British middle class with its own self-formation as a class draws largely on the terminology of the neo-Foucauldian 'governmentality' school, I suggest that the same substantive conclusions can be expressed in terms of a Gramscian theory of hegemony.

77 A narrower class interest of middle-class women is present in the persistent concern with 'the servant problem'. Typical was an anonymous article in the purity journal *The Sentinel* (February 1881) that warned of the dangers of too close an association between respectable children and domestic staff, who are accused of levity, profane jesting and sneering at religion. She recommends "reducing [servants'] wages, now so absurdly high . . . thus withholding the means of indulgence in dress and finery unsuited to a servile station".

6 RETRADITIONALISING MORAL REGULATION

1 The new consumerist discourses did not simply displace the prior concerns with aggregate populations, their health and fertility, but these concerns were translated into individualised forms, and work discipline was reborn as 'job satisfaction'.

2 Thatcher in radio phone-in, 1985.
3 Without endorsing any particular account, most of which differ from the argument I will put forward, the following are representative texts. Moral reform movements in the United States are covered by the following: Burnham 1993; Denfeld 1995; Goode and Ben-Yehuda 1994; Nelson 1984; Wagner 1997. For accounts of related movements in Britain see: Jenkins 1992; McRobbie 1994; Matthews 1994; Newburn 1992; Thompson 1994; Wallis 1979.
4 Influential examples of this current of thought are Ulrich Beck's (1992) diagnosis of 'risk society' and Anthony Giddens' (1992) account of the rise of 'intimacy' and the 'pure relationships'. More generally the quest for the uniqueness of the present is central to the grand sociological tradition exemplified in Tönnies (1955), with his account of the transition from *Gemeinschaft* to *Gesellschaft* (community to association), and Weber's quest for the 'uniqueness of the West' (1930).
5 Friedrich Hayek (1973) advanced a sophisticated version of theories of persistence with his contention that a 'spontaneous order', formed by unconscious evolutionary processes, although threatened by misguided attempts at social planning, is still intact.
6 For present purposes Robert Merton's definition is sharp and concise: "A social problem exists when there is a sizeable discrepancy between what is and what people think ought to be" (Merton 1976: 7).
7 The dangers, real or imagined, were frequently captured in the moralised terms of 'dens' which invoked not only evil and vice, but also the risk of contagion.
8 A limitation of Bauman's (1987) 'legislators' to 'interpreters' thesis should be noted. First, the process is perhaps less new than he suggests; from the Reformation onwards individuals have confronted the necessity of religious choice. In emphasising the importance of practices of self-formation, there is a tendency to see such practices as 'new', as manifestations of modernity (Calhoun 1994; Cascardi 1992; Giddens 1991). It must be borne in mind that intense preoccupations with practices of self-governance are also found in ancient societies, as Peter Brown (1988) and Foucault (1985) have demonstrated.
9 The distinctive role of state apparatuses over a long period with various phases of the 'war on drugs' functions as a significant 'exception to the rule', which underlies a persistent distance and hesitation of state institutions in the field of moral regulation.
10 Barker-Benfield makes use of the stimulating notion of 'self-fashioning' (1992: xxv).
11 It is important to note that while such modernist thematics have come under the critical invective of postmodernist thought, postmodernism is itself complicit in reproducing just such a linearity. It differs simply by insisting that the process has moved on further down the line towards the often sketchily drawn vista of postmodernity.
12 Ryan employs just such an account to explain the attraction of the New Right politics of the family, arguing that at a time of major changes in social and

sexual relations some women seek to defend a traditional domestic sphere (Ryan 1979). This current found its major policy ramification in Bowlby's revalorisation of the maternal role through his 'maternal deprivation' thesis (1969). This line of thought not only legitimised and sentimentalised the 'full-time' mother, but also launched a scarcely veiled attack on the 'working mother', which has been taken up by a plethora of conservative political positions.

13 My position is at variance with Wagner's recent account of the resurgence of moral regulation as being stimulated by the economic crises from 1973–74 that undermined the long post-Second World War economic boom and ushered in a significant economic decline in the position of middle America (Wagner 1997). For fuller discussion see Hunt 1999a.

14 A representative cross-section of versions of this argument is presented in: Denfeld 1995; Dubois & Gordon 1983; Ginzberg 1990; Showalter 1990; Wagner 1997; Walkowitz 1983.

15 The rejection of liberal values by radical feminism is the organising principle behind the papers collected in Leidhold & Raymond 1990. Radical feminism had started out making heavy reliance on elements of socialist thought, most distinctive being MacKinnon's analogy that "Sexuality is to feminism what work is to Marxism: that which is most one's own, yet most taken away" (1982: 515).

16 Thus while abortion remains subject to extremist opposition manifesting itself in assassinations of doctors, this confirms that the fundamental social battle for the right of women to terminate pregnancies has been won.

17 In the United States the New York Society for the Prevention of Cruelty to Children was founded in 1874, while in Britain the London Society for the Prevention of Cruelty to Children was formed in 1884.

18 Such contests over victim status are not unusual. Mothers Against Drunk Drivers (MADD) condemns the contemporary "victim culture" and insists on accountability for conduct while speaking in the name of another set of victims, the families of those killed by 'drunk drivers' (Lightner 1996: vii–ix).

19 The ripples created by reports of paedophiles and 'sex rings' have spread widely. In Britain in 1998 there is reported to be a large decrease in the number of males wishing to pursue training as primary school teachers.

20 The ideal of companionate interpersonal relations was more recently extended to same-sex relationships.

21 Other forms of representation have remained as targets of moral regulation. Legal battles over the sexual content of novels continued into the 1960s. And the cinema as a key vehicle of commercial mass culture has continued to provide an arena of contestation.

22 Significantly no comment is made on whether oral sex performed by males degrades them, since it is presumed that the male sexuality is itself degraded by lust.

23 The evidence presented in support of the Minneapolis anti-pornography ordinance (*Pornography and Sexual Violence* 1988) and to the Meese Commission (1986) relied heavily on such testimony.

24 A similar ordinance was rejected in referendum in Cambridge, Mass. Other moves were defeated in Los Angeles, Madison and Suffolk County, NY.
25 *American Booksellers* v. *Hudnut* 475 US 1001 (1986).
26 I avoid Giddens' own terminology of 'pure relationships' because of its ambiguity, but not his definition as a relationship entered into for its own sake.
27 This caution is especially important when linked to the contention that shifts in the division of labour have eradicated many traditional areas of male employment involving forms of heavy manual labour. One important consequence has been the undermining of the ideology of the male role as breadwinner. The negative side-effect of this potential positive change requires the dissemination of some alternative imagery of the sexual division of labour.
28 Sufficiently 'high' connections with blood or money could counterbalance the disadvantages of illegitimacy. The genealogy of 'bastardy' and 'illegitimacy' comes to an almost sudden end after the 1960s and no longer serves as a dividing practice.

REFERENCES

Where authorship or date of publication is uncertain the best available evidence is placed between square brackets; in most cases my usage is consistent with the British Library catalogue, save in a few instances where I have been satisfied that there are strong grounds for so doing. Where no publisher's name or place of publication appears on the frontispiece, no information is given.

Acton, William (1862), *The Functions and Disorders of the Reproductive Organs in Youth, Adult Age, and Advanced Life, Considered in Their Physiological, Social and Psychological Relations* (3rd edn; Churchill: London).

—— (1865), *The Functions and Disorders of the Reproductive Organs in Youth, in Adult Age and in Advanced Age Considered in their Physiological, Social and Moral Relations* (4th edn; J. & A. Churchill: London).

Alcoholics Anonymous (1976), *Alcoholics Anonymous: The Story of How More Than One Hundred Men Have Recovered from Alcoholism* (AA World Services: New York).

Allbutt, Dr H. Arthur (1886), *Wife's Handbook* (W. J. Ramsey: London).

Anon (1804), *Letter to a Member of the Society for the Suppression of Vice in which its Principles and Proceeds are Examined and Condemned* (Cawthorn: London).

Anthony, Susan B. (1968), "Social Purity" in Aileen S. Kraditor, ed., *Up from the Pedestal: Selected Writings in the History of American Feminism* [1875] (Quadrangle Books: Chicago) 159–67.

Armstrong, The Revd Richard [1887], *Our Duty in Matters of Social Purity: An Address to Young Men* (Social Purity Alliance: London).

Ashenden, Samantha (1996), "Reflexive Governance and Child Sexual Abuse: Liberal Welfare Rationality and the Cleveland Inquiry" 25(1) *Economy & Society* 64–88.

Association for Moral and Social Hygiene (1920), *The State and Sexual Morality: Report of the Committee of Inquiry* (George Allen & Unwin: London).

Bahlman, Dudley (1957), *The Moral Revolution of 1688* (Yale University Press: New Haven).

Bailey, Peter (1978), "The Case of the Victorian Music Halls" in *Leisure and Class in Victorian England: Recreation and the Contest for Control, 1830–1885* (Routledge & Kegan Paul: London) 147–68.

Bailey, Victor, & Sheila Blackburn (1979), "The Punishment of Incest Act 1908: A Case Study of Law Creation" *Criminal Law Review* 708–18.

Banks, Joseph A. (1954), *Prosperity and Parenthood: A Study of Family Planning Among the Victorian Middle Classes* (Schocken Books: New York).

Banks, Olive (1981), *Faces of Feminism: A Study of Feminism as a Social Movement* (Martin Robertson: Oxford).

Barker, Martin (1984), *A Haunt of Fears: The Strange History of the British Horror Campaign* (Pluto Press: London).

Barker-Benfield, G. J. (1973), "The Spermatic Economy: A Nineteenth-Century View of Sexuality" in Michael Gordon, ed., *The American Family in Social-Historical Perspective* (St Martin's Press: New York) 336–72.

—— (1992), *The Culture of Sensibility: Sex and Society in Eighteenth Century Britain* (University of Chicago Press: Chicago).

Barton, Dr Samuel (1700), *Sermon Preach'd Before . . . St. Mary-le-Bow, October 2, 1699* (Matthew Cotton: London).

Battan, Jesse F. (1992), "'The Word Made Flesh': Language, Authority, and Sexual Desire in Late-Nineteenth Century America" 3 *Journal of the History of Sexuality* 223–44.

Bauman, Zygmunt (1987), *Legislators and Interpreters: On Modernity, Post-Modernity and Intellectuals* (Polity Press: Cambridge).

—— (1992a), "Legislators and Interpreters: Culture as the Ideology of Intellectuals" in *Intimations of Postmodernity* (Routledge: London) 1–25.

—— (1992b), "A Sociological Theory of Postmodernity" in *Intimations of Postmodernity* (Routledge: London) 187–204.

Baumgartner, M. P. (1988), *The Moral Order of a Suburb* (Oxford University Press: New York).

Beck, Ulrich (1992), *Risk Society: Towards a New Modernity* (Sage: London).

Becker, Howard (1963), *Outsiders: Studies in the Sociology of Deviance* (Free Press: New York).

Bederman, Gail (1995), "'Teaching Our Sons to Do What We have Been Teaching the Savages to Avoid': G. Stanley Hall, Racial Recapitulation, and the Neurasthenic Paradox" in *Manliness and Civilization: A Cultural History of Gender and Race in the United States, 1880–1917* (University of Chicago Press: Chicago) 77–120.

Bedford, Arthur (1705), *Serious Reflections on the Scandalous Abuse and Effects of the Stage* (Bristol).

Beier, A. L. (1985), *Masterless Men: The Vagrancy Problem in England 1560–1640* (Methuen: London).

Beisel, Nicola (1990), "Class, Culture, and Campaigns Against Vice in Three American Cities, 1872–1892" 55 *American Sociological Review* 44–62.

—— (1997), *Imperiled Innocents: Anthony Comstock and Family Reproduction in Victorian America* (Princeton University Press: Princeton).

Bell, Enid M. (1962), *Josephine Butler: The Flame of Fire* (Constable: London).

Benjamin, Marina, ed. (1991), *Science and Sensibility: Gender and Scientific Enquiry, 1780–1945* (Blackwell: Oxford).

Benjamin, Walter (1969), "The Work of Art in the Age of Mechanical Reproduction" [1936] in *Illuminations*, ed. Hannah Arendt (Harcourt, Brace & World: New York) 217–51.

Berg, Barbara J. (1978), *The Remembered Gate: Origins of American Feminism: The Woman and the City, 1800–1860* (Oxford University Press: New York).

Berry, Christopher J. (1994), *The Idea of Luxury: A Conceptual and Historical Investigation* (Cambridge University Press: Cambridge).

Billington-Grieg, Teresa (1913), "The Truth About White Slavery" 14 *The English Review* 428–46.

Binney, Frederick (1883), "Dissipation and Its Consequences" 33 *Sentinel*.

Birken, Lawrence (1988), *Consuming Desire: Sexual Science and the Emergence of a Culture of Abundance, 1871–1914* (Cornell University Press: Ithaca).

Blackwell, Elizabeth (1879), *Counsel to Parents on the Moral Education of their Children* (Hatchards: London).

—— (1880), *The Human Element in Sex: Being a Medical Enquiry into the Relation of Sexual Physiology to Christian Morality* (J. &. A. Churchill: London).

—— (1884), *Counsel to Parents on the Moral Education of their Children* [1878] (7th edn; Hatchards: London).

—— (1885), *The Human Element in Sex* (J. & A. Churchill: London).

—— (1886), *The Purchase of Women: The Great Economic Blunder* (G. Bell: London).

—— (1888), *A Medical Address on the Benevolence of Malthus, contrasted with the Corruptions of Neo-Malthusianism* (J. & A. Churchill: London).

Blackwell, Emily (1896), "The Responsibility of Women in Regard to Questions Concerning Public Morality" in Aaron M. Powell, ed., *National Purity Congress* (American Purity Alliance: New York) 72–80.

Bland, Lucy (1985), "'The Cleansing of the Portals of Life': The Venereal Disease Campaign in the Early Twentieth Century" in Mary Langan & Bill Schwarz, eds, *Crises in the British State, 1880–1930* (Hutchinson: London) 192–208.

—— (1995), *Banishing the Beast: English Feminism and Sexual Morality 1885–1918* (Penguin: Harmondsworth).

Blocker, Jack S. (1989), *American Temperance Movements: Cycles of Reform* (Twayne: Boston).

Booth, Bramwell (1910), "Speech at Public Morals Conference, 1910" in *The Nation's Morals: Public Morals Conference, July 14–15, 1910* (Cassell: London).

Booth, Charles (1889), *Life and Labour of the People of London*, 2 vols. (Williams & Norgate: London).

Bordin, Ruth (1981), *Women and Temperance: The Quest for Power and Liberty, 1873–1900* (Temple University Press: Philadelphia).

—— (1986), *Frances Willard: A Biography* (University of North Carolina Press: Chapel Hill).

Borel, T. (1880), *The White Slavery of Europe* (Dyer Bros.: London).

Bourdieu, Pierre (1984), *Distinction: A Social Critique of the Judgement of Taste* [1979] (Routledge: London).

—— (1989), "Toward a Reflexive Sociology" 7 *Sociological Theory* 26–63.

Bourdieu, Pierre, and Jean-Claude Passeron (1977), *Reproduction in Education, Society and Culture* (Sage: London).

Bowlby, John (1969), *Attachment and Loss* (Hogarth Press: London).

Boyer, Paul S. (1968), *Purity in Print: The Vice-Society Movement and Book Censorship in America* (Charles Scribner's Sons: New York).

—— (1978), *Urban Masses and Moral Order in America, 1820–1920* (Harvard University Press: Cambridge, Mass.).

Boyle, Nina (1912), *The Traffic in Women* (Minerva Publishing: London).

Bradford, Samuel (1710), *Sermon Preach'd in the Parish Church of St. Mary-le-Bow, March 26, 1710* (London).

Bradley, Ian C. (1976), *The Call to Seriousness: The Evangelical Impact on the Victorians* (Jonathan Cape: London).

Bray, Thomas (1709), *For God or for Satan: Sermon Preached . . . 24 March, 1708/09, at the Funeral of Mr. John Dent, who was barbarously murder'd in the doing of his Duty, in the Execution of the Laws against Profaneness and Immorality* (Joseph Downing: London).

Bristow, Edward (1977), *Vice and Vigilance: Purity Movements in Britain Since 1700* (Gill & Macmillan: Dublin).

—— (1982), *Prostitution and Prejudice: The Jewish Fight against White Slavery 1880–1939* (Clarendon Press: Oxford).

Brown, Ford K. (1961), *Fathers of the Victorians: The Age of Wilberforce* (Cambridge University Press: Cambridge).

Brown, Peter (1988), *The Body and Society: Men, Women and Sexual Renunciation in Early Christianity* (Columbia University Press: New York).

Brown, Richard M. (1975), *Strain of Violence: Historical Studies of American Violence and Vigilantism* (Oxford University Press: New York).

Bullen, Robert A. (1880), "Address to the Social Purity Alliance" in Social Purity Alliance, *Laws and Operations and Address* (Inchbold & Beck: Leeds).

—— (1886), *Our Duty as Teachers with Reference to Social Purity Work* (Social Purity Alliance: London).

Bullock, F. W. B. (1963), *Voluntary Religious Societies 1520–1799* (Budd & Gillat: St Leonards-on-Sea).

Burchell, Graham, Colin Gordon & Peter Miller, eds (1991), *The Foucault Effect: Studies in Governmentality* (Harvester-Wheatsheaf: Hemel Hempstead).

Burke, Peter (1978), *Popular Culture in Early Modern Europe* (Temple Smith: London).

Burnet, Gilbert (1700), *Charitable Reproof: Sermon Preach'd Before the Societies for Reformation of Manners, March 25, 1700* (Chiswell: London).

Burnham, John C. (1971), "Medical Inspection of Prostitutes in America in the Nineteenth Century: The St Louis Experiment and Its Sequel" 45 *Bulletin of the History of Medicine* 203–18.

—— (1973), "The Progressive Era Revolution in American Attitudes Toward Sex" 59 *Journal of American History* 885–908.

—— (1993), *Bad Habits: Drinking, Smoking, Taking Drugs, Gambling, Sexual Misbehavior, and Swearing in American History* (New York University Press: New York).

Burton, Antoinette (1995), *Burdens of History: British Feminism, Indian Women, and Imperial Culture, 1865–1915* (University of North Carolina Press: Chapel Hill).

Butler, Josephine (1871a), *Sursum Corda: Annual Address to the Ladies National Association* (Ladies National Association: Liverpool).

—— (1871b), *The Constitution Violated* (Edmonton & Douglas: Edinburgh).

—— (1871c), *Speech on the Contagious Diseases Acts* (Croydon Liverpool).

—— [1874], *Legislative Restrictions on the Industry of Women, Considered from the Women's Point of View.*

—— (1876), *The Hour Before the Dawn: An Appeal to Men* (Social Purity Alliance: London).
—— (1879), *Government by Police* (Dyer Bros.: London).
—— (1881), *Social Purity: An Address Given to Students at Cambridge* (2nd edn; Dyer Bros.: London).
—— (1896), *Personal Reminiscences of a Great Crusade* (H. Marshall & Sons: London).
—— (1913), *The Voice of One Crying in the Wilderness* (Bristol).
Caird, Mona (1888), "Marriage" 130 *Westminster Review* 186–201.
—— (1897), *The Morality of Marriage and Other Essays on the Status and Destiny of Women* (George Redway: London).
Calhoun, Craig (1994), "Social Theory and the Politics of Identity" in Craig Calhoun, ed., *Social Theory and the Politics of Identity* (Blackwell: Oxford) 9–36.
Campbell, Beatrix (1988), *Unofficial Secrets: Child Abuse – The Cleveland Case* (Virago: London).
Cascardi, Anthony J. (1992), *The Subject of Modernity* (Cambridge University Press: Cambridge).
Chant, Laura Ormiston (1883), *Speech at the Annual Meeting of the Social Purity Alliance, June 13th, 1883* (Social Purity Alliance: London).
—— [1895], *Why We Attacked the Empire* (Horace Marshall: London).
—— (1902), "Women and the Streets" in Sir James Marchant, ed., *Public Morals* (Morgan & Scott: London).
Charrington, Frederick [1885], *The Battle of the Music Halls* (Dyer Bros.: London).
Chicago Vice Commission (1970), *The Social Evil in Chicago: A Study of Existing Conditions with Recommendations* [1911] (Arno Press: New York).
Chodorow, Nancy (1978), *The Reproduction of Mothering: Psychoanalysis and the Psychology of Gender* (University of California Press: Berkeley).
Church of England Purity Society (1885), *Paper for Men: Letter of Warning to a Lad of Fifteen* (CEPS: London).
Clark, Anna (1990), "Queen Caroline and the Sexual Politics of Popular Culture in London 1820" 31 *Representations* 47–68.
Cohen, Stanley (1972), *Folk Devils and Moral Panics: The Creation of the Mods and Rockers* (MacGibbon & Kee: London).
Cohen, Stan, & Jock Young, eds (1973), *The Manufacture of News: Social Problems, Deviance and the Mass Media* (Constable: London).
Collini, Stefan (1985), "The Idea of 'Character' in Victorian Political Thought" 35 *Transactions of the Royal Historical Society* 29–54.
Colquhoun, Patrick (1799), *The State of Indigence and the Situation of the Casual Poor in the Metropolis* (H. Baldwin: London).
Cominos, Peter T. (1963), "Late-Victorian Sexual Respectability and the Social System" 8 *International Review of Social History* 18–48 & 216–50.
—— (1972), "Innocent Femina Sensualis in Unconscious Conflict" in Martha Vicinus, ed., *Suffer and Be Still: Women in the Victorian Age* (Indiana University Press: Bloomington) 155–72.
Committee of Fifteen (1902), *The Social Evil: with Special Reference to Conditions Existing in the City of New York*, ed. Edwin R. A. Seligman (G. P. Putnam's Sons: New York).

Comstock, Anthony (1887), *Morals versus Art* (J. S. Ogilvie: New York).
—— (1896), "Demoralizing Literature" in Aaron M. Powell, ed., *National Purity Congress* (American Purity Alliance: New York) 418–22.
Connell, R. W. (1995), "Democracies of Pleasure: Thoughts on the Goals of Radical Sexual Politics" in Linda J. Nicholson & Steven Seidman, eds, *Social Postmodernism: Beyond Identity Politics* (Cambridge University Press: Cambridge) 384–97.
Connelly, Mark T. (1980), *The Response to Prostitution in the Progressive Era* (University of North Carolina Press: Chapel Hill).
Coote, William A. (1902), "Law and Morality" in Sir James Marchant, ed., *Public Morals* (Morgan & Scott: London).
Corrigan, Philip (1981), "On Moral Regulation" 29 *Sociological Review* 313–37.
Corrigan, Philip, & Derek Sayer (1985), *The Great Arch: English State Formation as Cultural Revolution* (Basil Blackwell: Oxford).
Cott, Nancy F. (1978), "Passionless: An Interpretation of Victorian Sexual Ideology" 4 *Signs* 19–36.
Craig, A. G. (1980), "The Movement for the Reformation of Manners, 1688–1715" (PhD dissertation, University of Edinburgh: Edinburgh).
Creighton, Louise (1914), *The Social Disease and How to Fight It: A Rejoinder* (Longmans, Green & Co.: London).
Culberson, William C. (1990), *Vigilantism: Political History of Private Power in America* (Greenwood Press: New York).
Culverwell, Robert J. [1847], *On Single and Married Life, or the Institutes of Marriage* (London).
Cunningham, Hugh (1977), "The Metropolitan Fairs: A Case Study of Social Control" in A. P. Donajgrodzki, ed., *Social Control in Nineteenth Century Britain* (Croom Helm: London) 163–84.
Curtis, T. C., & W. A. Speck (1976), "The Societies for the Reformation of Manners: A Case Study in the Theory and Practice of Moral Reform" 3 *Literature & History* 45–64.
Davenport-Hines, Richard (1990), *Sex, Death and Punishment: Attitudes to Sex and Sexuality in Britain Since the Renaissance* (Collins: London).
Davis, Allen F. (1967), *Spearheads for Reform: The Social Settlements and the Progressive Movement, 1890–1914* (Oxford University Press: New York).
Dean, Mitchell (1991), *The Constitution of Poverty: Toward a Genealogy of Liberal Governance* (Routledge: London).
—— (1994), "'A Social Structure of Many Souls': Moral Regulation, Government, and Self-Formation" 19(2) *Canadian Journal of Sociology* 145–68.
Deegan, Mary Jo (1988), *Jane Addams and the Men of the Chicago School, 1892–1918* (Transaction Books: New Brunswick, NJ).
Defoe, Daniel (1698), *The Poor Man's Plea in Relation to All Declarations, Acts of Parliament, etc. which have been made and published for a Reformation of Manners and Suppressing Immorality in the Nation* (London).
—— (1702), *Reformation of Manners: A Satyr* (London).
D'Emilio, John, & Estelle B. Freedman (1988), *Intimate Matters: A History of Sexuality in America* (Harper & Row: New York).

Demos, John, & Virginia Demos (1973), "Adolescence in Historical Perspective" in Michael Gordon, ed., *The American Family in Social-Historical Perspective* (St Martin's Press: New York) 209–21.

Denfeld, Rene (1995), *The New Victorians: A Young Woman's Challenge to the Old Feminist Order* (Warner Books: New York).

de Swaan, Abram (1990), *The Management of Normality: Critical Essays in Health and Welfare* (Routledge: London).

Devlin, Patrick (1959), *The Enforcement of Morals* (Oxford University Press: Oxford).

Dijkstra, Bram (1986), *Idols of Perversity: Fantasies of Feminine Evil in Fin-de-Siecle Culture* (Oxford University Press: New York).

Disney, John (1708), *An Essay Upon the Execution of the Laws Against Immorality and Prophaneness* (Joseph Downing: London).

Donzelot, Jacques (1980), *The Policing of Families: Welfare Versus the State* (Hutchinson: London).

Drew, Robert (1731), *A Sermon Preach'd to the Societies for Reformation of Manners at St. Mary-le-Bow, January 5th, 1730* (Joseph Downing: London).

Dubinsky, Karen (1993), *Improper Advances: Rape and Heterosexual Conflict in Ontario, 1880–1929* (University of Chicago Press: Chicago).

Dubois, Ellen C., & Linda Gordon (1983), "Seeking Ecstasy on the Battlefield: Danger and Pleasure in Nineteenth-Century Feminist Sexual Thought" 9(1) *Feminist Studies* 7–26.

Durkheim, Emile (1973), *On Morality and Society: Selected Writings* (University of Chicago Press: Chicago).

Dyer, Alfred S. (1884), *Facts For Men on Moral Purity and Health* (Dyer Bros.: London).

Eden, Sir Frederick M. (1797), *The State of the Poor: A History of the Labouring Classes in England from the Conquest to the Present Period*, ed. A. G. L. Rogers, 3 vols. (Routledge: London, 1928).

Ehrenreich, Barbara, & Deirdre English (1977), *For Her Own Good: 150 Years of the Experts' Advice to Women* (Anchor Press: New York).

Ehrenreich, Barbara, Elizabeth Hess and Gloria Jacobs (1986), *Re-Making Love: The Feminization of Sex* (Doubleday: Garden City, NY).

Elias, Norbert (1978), *The Civilizing Process* (Basil Blackwell: Oxford) Vol. I: *The History of Manners.*

—— (1982), *The Civilizing Process* (Basil Blackwell: Oxford) Vol. II: *State Formation and Civilization.*

Eliot, Charles W. (1914), "The American Social Hygiene Association" 1(1) *Social Hygiene* 1–5.

Ellis, H. Havelock (1899–1928), *Studies in the Psychology of Sex*, 7 vols. (Random House: New York).

—— (1911), *The Problem of Race-Regeneration* (Cassell: London).

—— (1912), *The Task of Social Hygiene* (Constable: London).

Emlyn, Thomas [1698], *Sermon Preach'd . . . in Dublin, October 4, 1698* (William Marshall: Dublin).

Encylopaedia Britannica (1942), "Men and Women" Vol. XIII: 577.

Epstein, Barbara (1981), *The Politics of Domesticity: Women, Evangelism, and Temperance in Nineteenth Century America* (Wesleyan University Press: Middletown).

Erikson, Kai (1966), *Wayward Puritans: A Study in the Sociology of Deviance* (John Wiley: New York).

Everitt, Herbert (1906), *'Manners Makyth Man': Dedicated to the Gentlemen of England by the White Cross League, Church of England Society* (White Cross League: London).

Fawcett, Millicent (1892), *On the Amendments Required in the Criminal Law Amendment Act 1885* (Women's Printing Society: London).

Flaherty, David H. (1971), "Law and Enforcement of Morals in Early America" in Donald Fleming & Bernard Bailyn, eds, *Perspectives in American History* (Harvard University Press: Cambridge, Mass.) Vol. V: 203–53.

Fletcher, Joseph (1847–49), "Moral and Educational Statistics of England and Wales" 10 *Journal of the [Royal] Statistical Society of London* 193–233; 12: 151–76; 12: 189–335.

Foster, Stephen (1971), *Their Solitary Way: The Puritan Social Ethic in the First Century of Settlement in New England* (Yale University Press: New Haven).

Foster, William Trufant (1914), *The Social Emergency: Studies in Sex Hygiene and Morals* (Houghton-Mifflin: Boston).

Foucault, Michel (1978), *The History of Sexuality* (Pantheon Books: New York) Vol. I: *An Introduction.*

—— (1980), "Prison Talk" in *Power/Knowledge: Selected Interviews and Other Writings 1972–1977*, ed. Colin Gordon (Harvester Press: Brighton) 37–54.

—— (1982), "The Subject and Power" in Herbert Dreyfus & Paul Rabinow, *Michel Foucault: Beyond Structuralism and Hermeneutics* (University of Chicago Press: Chicago) 208–26.

—— (1985), *The History of Sexuality* (Viking Press: New York) Vol. II: *The Use of Pleasure.*

—— (1986), *The History of Sexuality* (Pantheon Books: New York) Vol. III: *The Care of the Self.*

—— (1989), "The Concern for Truth" in *Foucault Live: Interviews 1966–1984*, ed. Sylvère Lotinger (Semiotext(e) New York) 293–308.

[Fowler, Edward] (1692), *A Vindication of an undertaking of certain gentlemen, in order to the Suppression of Debauchery and Profaneness* (London).

Fowler, Edward (1699), *Sermon Preach'd Before the Societies for Reformation of Manners, 26th June, 1699* (London).

Freud, Sigmund [1908] "'Civilized' Sexual Morality and Modern Nervous Illness" in *The Standard Edition of the Complete Psychological Works*, trans. & ed. James Strachey (The Hogarth Press: London, 1953–1975) Vol. IX: 177–204.

Gallie, W. B. (1955–56), "Essentially Contested Concepts" 56 *Proceedings of the Aristotelean Society* 167–98.

Galton, Francis (1904), "Eugenics: Its Definition, Scope and Aims" in Sociological Society, ed., *Sociological Papers* (Macmillan: London) 43–50.

Garland, David (1985), *Punishment and Welfare: A History of Penal Strategies* (Gower: London).

Gay, Peter (1984), *The Bourgeois Experience: Victoria to Freud* (Oxford University Press: Oxford) Vol. I: *The Education of the Senses.*

—— (1986), *The Bourgeois Experience: Victoria to Freud* (Oxford University Press: Oxford) Vol. II: *The Tender Passion.*

Geddes, Patrick, & J. Arthur Thompson (1889), *The Evolution of Sex* (Walter Scott: London).

Geertz, Clifford (1973), "Ideology as a Cultural System" in *The Interpretation of Cultures: Selected Essays* (Basic Books: New York) 193–229.

Gibbon, Edward (1910), *The History of the Decline and Fall of the Roman Empire* [1776–88] (Dent: London).

Gibson, Edmund (1723), *Sermon Preach'd Before . . . St. Mary-le-Bow, January 6, 1723* (2nd edn; Wyat: London).

Giddens, Anthony (1991), *Modernity and Self-Identity: Self and Society in the Late Modern Age* (Polity Press: Cambridge).

—— (1992), *The Transformation of Intimacy: Love, Sexuality and Eroticism in Modern Societies* (Polity Press: Cambridge).

Gilfoyle, Timothy (1992), *City of Eros: New York City, Prostitution, and the Commercialization of Sex, 1790–1920* (W. W. Norton: New York).

Ginzberg, Lori (1990), *Women and the Work of Benevolence: Morality, Politics, and Class in the Nineteenth Century United States* (Yale University Press: New Haven).

Gitlin, Todd (1995), *The Twilight of the Common Dream: Why America is Wracked by Culture Wars* (Metropolitan Books: New York).

Goldmann, Emma (1972), "Victims of Morality" in Alix K. Shulman, ed., *Red Emma Speaks: Selected Writings and Speeches* (Random House: New York) 126–72.

Goode, Erich, & Nachman Ben-Yehuda (1994), *Moral Panics: The Social Construction of Deviance* (Blackwell: Oxford).

Gordon, Linda (1974), *Women's Body, Women's Right: A Social History of Birth Control in America* (Penguin Books: Harmondsworth).

Gorham, Deborah (1978), "The 'Maiden Tribute of Modern Babylon' Re-examined: Child Prostitution and the Idea of Childhood in Late-Victorian England" 21 *Victorian Studies* 353–79.

Gospel Purity Association (1886), *The Purity Crusade: Its Conflicts and Triumphs* (Morgan & Scott: London).

Gramsci, Antonio (1971), *Selections from the Prison Notebooks of Antonio Gramsci*, ed. and trans. Q. Hoare & G. Nowell-Smith (Lawrence & Wishart: London).

Great Britain (1810–28), *Statutes of the Realm*, ed. Alexander Luders et al., 11 vols. (Dawsons: London).

—— (1871), *Report of the Royal Commission on the Administration and Operation of the Contagious Diseases Acts 1866–69* (Parl. Papers, vol. 19).

—— (1916), *Report of the Royal Commission on Venereal Diseases* Cd. 7475.

Grittner, Frederick K. (1990), *White Slavery: Myth, Ideology and American Law* (Garland: New York).

Gusfield, Joseph R. (1963), *Symbolic Crusade: Status Politics and the American Temperance Movement* (University of Illinois Press: Urbana).

Hacking, Ian (1991), "The Making and Molding of Child Abuse" 17 *Critical Inquiry* 253–88.

—— (1995), *Rewriting the Soul: Multiple Personality and the Sciences of Memory* (Princeton University Press: Princeton).

Hall, G. Stanley (1904), *Adolescence: Its Psychology and Its Relations to Physiology, Anthropology, Sociology, Sex, Crime, Religion and Education*, 2 vols. (Appleton: New York).

Hall, Stuart, Chas Critcher, Tony Jefferson, John Clarke & Brian Roberts (1978), *Policing the Crisis: Mugging, the State, and Law and Order* (Macmillan: London).

Harris, T. (1986), "The Bawdy House Riots of 1688" 29 *Historical Journal* 536–56.

Harrison, Brian (1966), "Philanthropy and the Victorians" 9(4) *Victorian Studies* 353–74.

—— (1973), "For Church, Queen and Family: The Girls' Friendly Society 1874–1920" 61 *Past & Present* 107–38.

—— (1974), "State Intervention and Moral Reform in Nineteenth Century England" in Patricia Hollis, ed., *Pressure From Without in Early Victorian England* (Edward Arnold: London) 289–322.

Hart, H. L. A. (1963), *Law, Liberty, and Morality* (Oxford University Press: Oxford).

Hay, Colin (1995), "Mobilization Through Interpellation: James Bulger, Juvenile Crime and the Construction of a Moral Panic" 4 *Social and Legal Studies* 197–223.

Hay, Douglas (1977), "Property, Authority and the Criminal Law" in Douglas Hay, Peter Linebaugh, John Rule, Edward Thompson & Cal Winslow, *Albion's Fatal Tree: Crime and Society in Eighteenth Century England* (Allen Lane: London).

Hayek, F. A. (1973), *Law, Legislation and Liberty* (Routledge & Kegan Paul: London) Vol. I: *Rules and Orders*.

Hayley, William (1699), *Sermon Preach'd Before the Societies for Reformation of Manners at St. Mary's-le-Bow on 3rd October, 1698* (Jacob Jonson: London).

Hayton, David (1990), "Moral Reform and Country Politics in the Late Seventeenth-Century House of Commons" 128 *Past & Present* 48–91.

Heylyn, John (1729), *Sermon Preach'd Before the Societies for Reformation of Manners at . . . St. Mary-le-bow, January 8, 1728* (Joseph Downing: London).

Hill, Christopher (1969), "The Bawdy Courts" in *Society and Puritanism in Pre-Revolutionary England* (Panther: London) 288–332.

Hill, Marilynn W. (1993), *Their Sisters' Keeper: Prostitution in New York City, 1830–1870* (University of California Press: Berkeley).

Hofstadter, Richard (1955), *The Age of Reform: From Bryan to FDR* (Alfred A. Knopf: New York).

Hole, Matthew (1699), *The True Reformation of Manners* (Oxford).

Hollowell, James H. (1887), *Brotherly Honour versus Selfish Passion: An Address to Young Men and to Citizens* (Moral Reform Union: London).

Holmes, Geoffrey (1976), "The Sacheverell Riots: The Crowd and the Church in Early Eighteenth Century London" 72 *Past & Present* 55–85.

Holtzman, Ellen (1982), "The Pursuit of Married Love: Women's Attitudes Towards Sexuality and Marriage in Great Britain, 1918–1939" 16(2) *Journal of Social History* 39–51.

Honneth, Axel (1995), *The Struggle for Recognition: The Moral Grammar of Social Conflicts* (MIT Press: Cambridge, Mass.).

Hopkins, J. Ellice [1869], *Home Thoughts for Mothers and Mothers' Meetings* (2nd edn; Nisbet & Co.: London).

—— (1882a), *Grave Moral Questions: Address to the Men and Women of England* (Hatchards: London).

—— (1882b), *Early Training of Boys and Girls: An Appeal to Women* (Hatchards: London).

—— [1883] *The White Cross Army: A Statement of the Bishop of Durham's Movement* (Hatchards: London).

—— (1883), "Ellice Hopkins' 'Social Wreckage' " 4 *Chautauquan* 40–2.

—— (1899), *The Powers of Womanhood; or, Mothers and Sons, a Book for Parents and Those in Loco Parentis* (Wells, Gardner & Darnton: London).

Houghton, Walter E. (1957), *The Victorian Frame of Mind, 1830–1970* (Yale University Press: New Haven).

Howe, John (1698), *Sermon Preach'd Before the Societies for Reformation of Manners at Salter's Hall, February 14, 1698* (Thomas Parkhurst: London).

Hunt, Alan (1993), *Explorations in Law and Society: Toward a Constitutive Theory of Law* (Routledge: New York).

—— (1995), "Moralizing Luxury: The Discourses of the Governance of Consumption" 8(4) *Journal of Historical Sociology* 352–74.

—— (1996), *Governance of the Consuming Passions: A History of Sumptuary Regulation* (Macmillan: London).

—— (1998), "The Great Masturbation Panic and the Discourses of Moral Regulation in Nineteenth-Century Britain" 8(4) *Journal of the History of Sexuality* 575–615.

—— (1999a), "The Purity Wars: Making Sense of Moral Militancy" *Theoretical Criminology* (in press).

—— (1999b), "Anxiety and Social Explanation: Some Anxieties About Anxiety" *Journal of Social History* (in press).

Hunt, Alan, & Gary Wickham (1994), *Foucault and Law: Towards a New Sociology of Law as Governance* (Pluto Press: London).

Hunter, James Davison (1991), *Culture Wars: The Struggle to Define America* (Basic Books: New York).

Hyam, Ronald (1990), *Empire and Sexuality: The British Experience* (Manchester University Press: Manchester).

Hyland, Paul, & Neil Sammells, eds (1992), *Writing and Censorship in Britain* (Routledge: London).

Hynes, Samuel (1968), *The Edwardian Turn of Mind* (Princeton University Press: Princeton).

Ingram, Arthur [1909], *Social Purity: A Sermon* (Wells & Gardner: London).

Ingram, Martin (1984a), "Ridings, Rough Music and the 'Reform of Popular Culture' in Early Modern England" 105 *Past & Present* 79–113.

—— (1984b), "Religion, Communities and Moral Discipline in Late Sixteenth and Early Seventeenth Century England: Case Studies" in Kaspar von Greyerz, ed., *Religion and Society in Early Modern Europe 1500–1800* (George Allen & Unwin: London) 177–93.

—— (1996), "Reformation of Manners in Early Modern England" in Paul Griffiths, Adam Fox and Steve Hindle, eds, *The Experience of Authority in Early Modern England* (Macmillan: London) 47–88.

Innes, Joanna (1990), "Politics and Morals: The Reformation of Manners Movements in the Later 18th-Century England" in Eckhart Hellmuth, ed., *The Transformation of Political Culture: England and Germany in the Late Eighteenth Century* (Oxford University Press: Oxford) 57–118.

Irvine, Janice M. (1995), "Regulated Passions: The Invention of Inhibited Sexual Desire and Sexual Addiction" in Jennifer Terry & Jacqueline Urla, eds, *Deviant Bodies: Critical Perspectives on Difference in Science and Popular Culture* (Indiana University Press: Bloomington) 314–37.

Isaacs, Tina Beth (1979), "Moral Crime, Moral Reform and the State in Early Eighteenth Century England: A Study of Piety and Politics" (PhD dissertation, University of Rochester: Rochester, NY).

Jackson, Margaret (1994), *The 'Real' Facts of Life: Feminism and the Politics of Sexuality,* c. *1850–1949* (Taylor & Francis: London).

Jaeger, Muriel (1956), *Before Victoria: Changing Standards and Behaviour 1787–1837* (Chatto & Windus: London).

Jefferis, Benjamin Grant, & J. L. Nichols (1967), *Light on Dark Corners: A Complete Sexual Science and Guide to Purity* [1894] (Grove Press: New York).

Jeffreys, Sheila (1982), "'Free From All Uninvited Touch of Man': Women's Campaigns Around Sexuality, 1880–1914" 5(6) *Women's Studies International Forum* 629–45.

—— (1985), *The Spinster and Her Enemies: Feminism and Sexuality 1880–1930* (Pandora: London).

Jenkins, Philip (1992), *Intimate Enemies: Moral Panics in Contemporary Great Britain* (Aldine de Gruyter: New York).

Jordanova, Ludmilla (1989), *Sexual Visions: Images of Gender and Medicine Between the Eighteenth and Twentieth Centuries* (Harvester-Wheatsheaf: New York).

Kay-Shuttleworth, James (1970), *The Moral and Physical Condition of the Working Classes Employed in the Cotton Manufacture in Manchester* [1832] (Frank Cass: London).

Kellogg, John Harvey (1896), "Chastity and Health" in Aaron M. Powell, ed., *National Purity Congress* (American Purity Alliance: New York) 250–68.

—— (1974), *Plain Facts for Old and Young, Embracing the Natural History and Hygiene of Organic Life* [1877] (Heritage Press: Buffalo).

Kent, Susan K. (1987), *Sex and Suffrage in Britain, 1860–1914* (Princeton University Press: Princeton).

Kepel, Gilles (1994), *The Revenge of God: The Resurgence of Islam, Christianity, and Judaism* (Pennsylvania State University Press: University Park).

King, Peter (1989), "Prosecution Associations and their Impact in Eighteenth-Century Essex" in Douglas Hay & Francis Snyder, eds, *Policing and Prosecution in Britain 1750–1850* (Oxford University Press: Oxford) 171–207.

Kirk, Edward B. (1905), *Talk With Girls About Themselves* (Simpkin, Marshall, Hamilton, Kent & Co.: London).
Kneeland, George J. (1913), *Commercialized Prostitution in New York City* (Bureau of Social Hygiene, The Century Co.: New York).
Langum, David J. (1994), *Crossing Over the Line: Legislative Morality and the Mann Act* (University of Chicago Press: Chicago).
Laqueur, Thomas W. (1976), *Religion and Respectability: Sunday Schools and Working-Class Culture 1750–1850* (Yale University Press: New Haven).
—— (1990), *Making Sex: Body and Gender From the Greeks to Freud* (Harvard University Press: Cambridge, Mass.).
Laraña, Enrique, Hank Johnston & Joseph R. Gusfield, eds (1994), *New Social Movements: From Ideology to Identity* (Temple University Press: Philadelphia).
Lasch, Christopher (1965), *The New Radicalism in America, 1889–1963* (Alfred A. Knopf: New York).
—— (1975), *Haven in a Heartless World: The Family Besieged* (Basic Books: New York).
Latour, Bruno (1988), "Mixing Humans and Nonhumans Together: The Sociology of a Door-Closer" 35(3) *Social Problems* 298–310.
Leidhold, Dorchen, & Janice Raymond, eds (1990), *The Sexual Liberals and the Attack on Feminism* (Pergamon Press: Oxford).
Letwin, Shirley R. (1992), *The Anatomy of Thatcherism* (Fontana: London).
Levine, Philippa (1990), *Feminist Lives in Victorian England: Private Roles and Public Commitments* (Basil Blackwell: Oxford).
Lightner, Candace (1996), "Foreword" to Anita Spencer, *A Crisis of Spirit: Our Desperate Search for Integrity* (Plenum Press: New York).
Lofland, Lyn H. (1973), *The World of Strangers: Order and Action in Urban Public Space* (Basic Books: New York).
London Society for the Protection of Young Females (1839), *Fourth Annual Report* (LSPYF: London).
Lyttelton, The Revd Edward (1900), *The Training of the Young in the Laws of Sex* (Longmans, Green & Co.: London).
McHugh, Paul G. (1980), *Prostitution and Victorian Social Reform* (Croom Helm: London).
McIntosh, Mary (1988), "Family Secrets as Public Drama" 28 *Feminist Review* 6–15.
Mackey, Thomas C. (1987), *Red Light Out: A Legal History of Prostitution, Disorderly Houses, and Vice Districts, 1870–1917* (Garland: New York).
MacKinnon, Catharine (1982), "Feminism, Marxism, Method and the State: An Agenda for Theory" 7 *Signs* 515–44.
—— (1984), "Not a Moral Issue" 2 *Yale Law & Social Policy Review* 321–45.
Mackirdy, Olive, & William N. Willis (1912), *The White Slave Market* (Stanley Paul: London).
Macleod, David I. (1983), *Building Character in the American Boy* (University of Wisconsin Press: Madison).
McRobbie, Angela (1994), "The Moral Panic in the Age of the Postmodern Mass Media" in *Postmodernism and Popular Culture* (Routledge: London) 198–219.

Manchester, Colin (1988), "Lord Campbell's Act: England's First Obscenity Statute" 9(2) *Journal of Legal History* 223–41.
Mandeville, Bernard de (1957), *The Fable of the Bees, or Private Vices, Publick Benefits* [1705], ed. F. B. Kaye (Clarendon Press: Oxford).
[——] (1730), *A Modest Defence of Publick Stews* (London).
Mangan, James A., & James Walvin, eds (1987), *Manliness and Morality: Middle-Class Masculinity in Britain and America, 1800–1940* (Manchester University Press: Manchester).
Mann, Michael (1993), *The Sources of Social Power* (Cambridge University Press: Cambridge) Vol. II: *The Rise of Classes and Nation-States, 1760–1914.*
Marchant, James [1904], *National Purity Crusade, Its Origin and Results*, intro. Ellice Hopkins (Morgan & Scott: London).
—— [1909], *Aids to Purity: Seven Personal Letters* (Health & Strength: London).
—— (1909), *Social Hygienics: A New Crusade*, foreword H. J. Gladstone (Swann Sonnenschein: London).
—— (1917), *Birth Rate and Empire* (Williams & Norgate: London).
Marcus, Steven (1964), *The Other Victorians: A Study of Sexuality and Pornography in Mid-Nineteenth Century England* (Meridian Books: New York).
Marilley, Suzanne M. (1993), "Frances Willard and the Feminism of Fear" 19(1) *Feminist Studies* 123–46.
Martindale, Louisa [1908], *Underneath the Surface* (Southern Publishing: Brighton).
Marty, Martin E., & R. Scott Appelby, eds (1991–94), *The Fundamentalism Project*, 4 vols. (University of Chicago Press: Chicago).
Marx, Karl, & Frederick Engels (1976), "Manifesto of the Communist Party" [1848] in *Marx–Engels Collected Works* (Lawrence & Wishart: London) Vol. VI.
Mason, Michael (1994), *The Making of Victorian Sexuality* (Oxford University Press: Oxford).
Mather, Cotton (1703), *Methods and Motives for Societies to Suppress Disorders* (Boston).
Matthews, Nancy A. (1994), *Confronting Rape: The Feminist Anti-Rape Movement and the State* (Routledge: London).
Maudsley, Henry (1884), *Body and Will* (Appleton: New York).
Mayhew, Henry (1967), *London Labour and the London Poor: A Cyclopaedia of the Condition and Earnings of those that will work, those that cannot work, and those who will not work*, 4 vols. [1851–1862] (Frank Cass: London).
Mayo, Daniel (1717), *Sermon Preach'd Before . . . at Salter's Hall, July 1, 1717* (2nd edn; Emmanuel Matthews: London).
Mearns, Andrew (1883), *The Bitter Cry of Outcast London: An Inquiry into the Condition of the Abject Poor* (James Clarke: London).
Meese Commission (1986), *Attorney General's Commission on Pornography: Final Report*, 2 vols. (Department of Justice: Washington, DC).
Merton, Robert K. (1976), "The Sociology of Social Problems" in Robert K. Merton & Robert Nisbet, eds, *Contemporary Social Problems* (4th edn; Harcourt, Brace, Jovanovich: New York) 3–43.

Mill, John Stuart (1964), "Nature" [1854] in *Three Essays on Religion: The Nature and Utility of Religion* [1874] (Holt & Reinhart: New York).
Minson, Jeffrey (1993), *Questions of Conduct: Sexual Harassment, Citizenship, Government* (Macmillan: London).
Moore, Barrington (1978), *Injustice: The Social Basis of Obedience & Revolt* (Sharpe: White Plains, NY).
Moral Reform Union (1883), *Pamphlets and Leaflets* (British Library).
More, Hannah (1830), *The Works of Hannah More*, 11 vols. (T. Cadwell: London).
Morgan, Robin (1980), "Theory and Practice: Pornography and Rape" in Laura Lederer, ed., *Take Back the Night: Women on Pornography* (William Morrow: New York).
Morris, The Revd John (1885), *Our Sin and Our Shame* (J. S. Amoore: London).
Morrow, Prince A. (1904), *Social Diseases and Marriage: Social Prophylaxis* (Lea Brothers: New York).
Mort, Frank (1985), "Purity, Feminism and the State: Sexuality and Moral Politics" in Mary Langan & Bill Schwartz, eds, *Crises in the British State 1880–1930* (Hutchinson: London) 209–25.
—— (1987), *Dangerous Sexualities: Medico-Moral Politics in England Since 1830* (Routledge & Kegan Paul: London).
Mosher, Clelia D. (1980), *The Mosher Survey: Sexual Attitudes of Forty-Five Victorian Women*, ed. James Mahood & Kristine Wenburg (Arno Press: New York).
National Association for the Promotion of Social Purity (1870), *Principles and Objects* (NAPSP: London).
National Council of Public Morals (1921), *To Save the British Race* (NCPM: London).
National Vigilance Association (1887), *Report of the Executive Committee* (NVA: London).
Nead, Lynda (1988), *Myths of Sexuality: Representations of Women in Victorian Britain* (Blackwell: Oxford).
Nelson, Barbara J. (1984), *Making an Issue of Child Abuse: Political Agenda Setting for Social Problems* (University of Chicago Press: Chicago).
Neuberg, Victor E. (1977), *Popular Literature, a History and Guide: From the Beginning of Printing to the Year 1897* (Penguin Books: Harmondsworth.).
Newburn, Tim (1992), *Permission and Regulation: Law and Morals in Post-War Britain* (Routledge: London).
Nissenbaum, Stephen (1980), *Sex, Diet and Debility in Jacksonian America: Sylvester Graham and Health Reform* (Greenwood Press: Westport).
Nordau, Max (1895), *Degeneration* (William Heinemann: London).
Oestreich, Gerhard (1982), *Neostoicism and the Early Modern State* (Cambridge University Press: Cambridge).
Offe, Claus (1984), *Contradictions of the Welfare State*, ed. John Keane (Hutchinson: London).
Ollyffe, George (1709), *The Hindrance of Reformation: A Sermon Preach'd Before the Society for Reformation of Manners in the Parish Church of Wendover, May 5, 1709* (Joseph Downing: London).

Osborne, Thomas (1994), "Bureaucracy as a Vocation: Governmentality and Administration in Nineteenth-Century Britain" 7(3) *Journal of Historical Sociology* 289–313.

Overton, J. H. (1885), *Life of the English Church, 1660–1714* (Longmans, Green & Co.: London).

Pally, Marcia (1994), *Sex and Sensibility: Reflections on Forbidden Mirrors and the Will to Censor* (Ecco Press: Hopewell).

Palmer, Samuel (1706), *Sermon Preach'd Before the Societies for Reformation of Manners on 7th October, 1706* (London).

Pankhurst, Christabel (1913), *The Great Scourge and How to End It* (E. Pankhurst: London).

Parker, Alison M. (1997), *Purifying America: Women, Cultural Reform, and Pro-Censorship Activism, 1873–1933* (University of Illinois Press: Urbana).

Pearson, Michael (1972), *The Age of Consent: Victorian Prostitution and Its Enemies* (David & Charles: London).

Peiss, Kathy (1983), "'Charity Girls' and City Pleasures: Historical Notes on Working-Class Sexuality, 1880–1920" in Ann, Christine Stansell & Sharon Thompson, eds, *Powers of Desire: The Politics of Sexuality* (Monthly Review Press: New York) 51–73.

Perkin, Harold J. (1969), *The Origin of Modern English Society, 1780–1880* (Routledge & Kegan Paul: London).

—— (1989), *The Rise of Professional Society: England Since 1880* (Routledge: London).

Petrie, Glen (1971), *A Singular Iniquity: The Campaigns of Josephine Butler* (Macmillan: London).

Philips, David (1989), "Good Men to Associate and Bad Men to Conspire: Associations for the Prosecution of Felons in England, 1760–1860" in Douglas Hay & Francis Snyder, eds, *Policing and Prosecution in Britain 1750–1850* (Oxford University Press: Oxford) 133–70.

Pivar, David J. (1973), *Purity Crusade: Sexual Morality and Social Control 1868–1900* (Greenwood Press: Westport).

Pivar, David J. (1980), "Cleansing the Nation: The War on Prostitution, 1917–1921" 12 *Prologue: Journal of the National Archives* 29–40.

Platt, Anthony (1969), *The Child Savers: The Invention of Delinquency* (University of Chicago Press: Chicago).

Playfair, Giles (1969), *Six Studies in Hypocrisy* (Secker & Warburg: London).

Polanyi, Karl (1957), *The Great Transformation* (Beacon Press: Boston).

Pomfret, Samuel (1701), *A Sermon Preach'd to the Societies for Reformation of Manners on 6th October, 1701* (London).

Pornography and Sexual Violence: Evidence of the Links. The Complete Transcript of public hearings on ordinances to add pornography as discrimination against women, Minneapolis City Council, Dec. 12–13, 1983 (1988), (Everywoman: London).

Porter, Roy (1985), "Making Faces: Physiognomy and Fashion in Eighteenth Century England" 38 *Etudes Anglaises* 385–96.

—— (1991), "Is Foucault Useful for Understanding Eighteenth and Nineteenth Century Sexuality?" 1 *Contention* 61–81.

Porter, Roy, & Lesley Hall (1995), *The Facts of Life: The Creation of Sexual Knowledge in Britain, 1650–1950* (Yale University Press: New Haven).
Porter, Roy, & Mikula Teich, eds (1994), *Sexual Knowledge, Sexual Science: The History of Attitudes to Sexuality* (Cambridge University Press: Cambridge).
Portus, Garnet (1912), *Caritas Anglicana; or, an Historical Inquiry into those Religious and Philanthropic Societies that Flourished in England Between the Years 1678 and 1740*, intro. W. H. Hutton (A. R. Mowbray: London).
Powell, Aaron M. (1878), *State Regulation of Vice: Regulation Efforts in America: The Geneva Congress* (Wook & Holbrook: New York).
—— ed. (1896), *National Purity Congress* (American Purity Alliance: New York).
Price, Samuel (1725), *Sermon Preach'd Before the Societies for Reformation of Manners at Salter's Hall, June 28th, 1725* (Emmanuel Matthews: London).
Prochaska, Frank K. (1980), *Women and Philanthropy in Nineteenth-Century England* (Clarendon Press: Oxford).
Proclamation Society (1790), *Resolutions of the Magistrates deputed from the Several Counties of England and Wales, assembled at the St Alban's Tavern* (Hatchards: London).
—— [1800] *Report of the Committee of the Society for Carrying into Effect His Majesty's Proclamation Against Vice and Immorality, for the Year 1799* (Hatchards: London).
Proudhon, Pierre-Joseph (1923), *General Ideas of the Revolution in the Nineteenth Century* [1851], trans. John B. Robinson (Freedom Press: London).
Quinlan, Maurice J. (1941), *Victorian Prelude: A History of English Manners, 1700–1830* (Columbia University Press: New York).
Rajchman, John (1991), *Truth and Eros: Foucault, Lacan and the Question of Ethics* (Routledge: New York).
Reckless, Walter C. (1933), *Vice in Chicago* (University of Chicago Press: Chicago).
Reinarman, Craig (1995), "The 12-Step Movement and Advanced Capitalist Culture: Notes on the Politics of Self-Control in Postmodernity" in Marcy Darnovsky, Barbara Epstein & Richard Flacks, eds, *Cultural Politics and Contemporary Social Movements* (Temple University Press: Philadelphia) 90–109.
Riis, Jacob (1890), *How the Other Half Lives* (Charles Scribner's Sons: New York).
Roberts, M. J. D. (1983), "The Society for the Suppression of Vice and Its Early Critics 1802–12" 26 *Historical Journal* 159–76.
Robins, Elizabeth (1913), *Where Are You Going To?* (Heinemann: London).
Roe, Clifford G. (1910), *Panders and Their White Slaves* (Revell: New York).
—— (1911a), *Horrors of the White Slave Trade: The Mighty Crusade to Protect the Purity of Our Homes* (Chicago).
—— (1911b), *The Prodigal Daughter: The White Slavery Evil and the Remedy* (L. W. Walter Co.: Chicago).
—— (1911c), *The Great War on White Slavery; or, Fighting for the Protection of Our Girls* (G. G. Clows: Pennsylvania).
—— (1914), *The Girl Who Disappeared* (American Bureau of Moral Education: Chicago).
Rolph, C. H. (1961), *The Trial of Lady Chatterley: Regina v. Penguin Books Limited* (Penguin Books: Harmondsworth).

Room, Robin (1993), "Alcoholics Anonymous as a Social Movement" in Barbara S. McCrady & William R. Miller, eds, *Research on Alcoholics Anonymous: Opportunities and Alternatives* (Rutgers Centre of Alcohol Studies: New Brunswick, NJ).

Roper, Lyndal (1989), *The Holy Household: Women and Morals in Reformation Augsburg* (Clarendon Press: Oxford).

Rosanvallon, Pierre (1988), "The Decline of Social Visibility" in John Keane, ed., *Civil Society and the State* (Verso: London) 199–220.

Rose, Nikolas (1989), *Governing the Soul: The Shaping of the Private Self* (Routledge: London).

—— (1993), "Government, Authority and Expertise in Advanced Liberalism" 22(3) *Economy and Society* 283–99.

—— (1994), "Expertise and the Government of Conduct" in Austin Sarat & Susan Silbey, eds, *Studies in Law, Politics and Society* (JAI Press: Greenwich) Vol. 14: 359–97.

—— (1996), "Authority and the Genealogy of Subjectivity" in Paul Heelas, Scott Lash & Paul Morris, eds, *Detraditionalization: Critical Reflections on Authority and Identity* (Blackwell: Oxford) 294–327.

Rose, Nikolas, & Peter Miller (1992), "Political Power Beyond the State: Problematics of Government" 43(2) *British Journal of Sociology* 173–205.

Rosenthal, Michael (1986), *The Character Factory: Baden-Powell and the Origins of the Boy Scout Movement* (Pantheon: New York).

Ross, Dorothy (1991), *The Social Origins of American Social Science* (Cambridge University Press: New York).

Rothman, David (1978), "The State as Parent: Social Policy in the Progressive Era" in Willard Gaylin, ed., *Doing Good: The Limits of Benevolence* (Pantheon: New York).

Russell, Diana (1993), "Pornography and Rape: A Causal Model" in Diana Russell, ed., *Making Violence Sexy: Feminist Views on Pornography* (Open University Press: Milton Keynes) 120–50.

Russett, Cynthia Eagle (1989), *Sexual Science: The Victorian Construction of Womanhood* (Harvard University Press: Cambridge, Mass.).

Ryan, Mary P. (1979), "The Power of Women's Networks: A Case Study of Female Moral Reform in Antebellum America" 5(1) *Feminist Studies* 66–85.

Ryan, Michael (1837), *Prostitution in London, with a Comparative View of that of Paris and New York* (H. Bailliere: London).

Ryther, John (1699), *Sermon Preach'd Before the Societies for Reformation of Manners on 16th February 1698/9* (Thomas Parkhurst: London).

Sabine, William T. (1896), "Social Vice and National Decay" in Aaron M. Powell, ed., *National Purity Congress* (American Purity Alliance: New York) 42–56.

Sacheverell, Henry (1702), *The Character of a Low-Churchman* (3rd edn; London).

—— (1709a), *The Communication of Sin: A Sermon Preached at the Assizes at Derby, 15 August 1709* (London).

—— (1709b), *The Perils of False Bretheren: A Sermon Preach'd at Saint Paul's London.*

Scharlieb, Mary [1920], *Self-Control and Birth Control* (London Council for the Promotion of Public Morality: London).

Schivelbusch, Wolfgang (1979), *The Railway Journey: Trains and Travel in the Nineteenth Century* (Urizen Books: New York).

Schults, Raymond L. (1972), *Crusader in Babylon: W. T. Stead and the Pall Mall Gazette* (University of Nebraska Press: Lincoln).

Schwartz, Hillel (1986), *Never Satisfied: A Cultural History of Diets, Fantasies, and Fat* (Free Press: New York).

Scott, John (1807), *The Importance of the Sabbath: with Appendix on the Societies for the Suppression of Vice* (Browne & Radford: Kingston-upon-Hull).

—— [1807], *An Account of the Societies for Reformation of Manners and the Suppression of Vice* (Browne & Radford: Kingston-upon-Hull).

Sears, Hal D. (1977), *The Sex Radicals: Free Love in High Victorian America* (Regents Press of Kansas: Lawrence).

Segal, Lynn (1997), "Feminist Sexual Politics and the Heterosexual Predicament" in Lynne Segal, ed., *New Sexual Agendas* (Macmillan: London) 77–89.

Seidler, Victor J. (1987), "Reason, Desire and Male Sexuality" in Pat Caplan, ed., *The Cultural Construction of Sexuality* (Tavistock: London) 82–112.

Seidman, Steven (1992), *Embattled Eros: Sexual Politics and Ethics in Contemporary America* (Routledge: New York).

Sennett, Richard (1974), *The Fall of Public Man: On the Social Psychology of Capitalism* (Cambridge University Press: Cambridge).

Shoemaker, Robert B. (1991), *Prosecution and Punishment: Petty Crime and the Law in London and Rural Middlesex,* c. *1660–1725* (Cambridge University Press: Cambridge).

Showalter, Elaine (1990), *Sexual Anarchy: Gender and Culture at the Fin de Siècle* (Viking Press: New York).

Shubert, Adrian (1981), "Private Initiative in Law Enforcement: Associations for the Prosecution of Felons, 1744–1856" in Victor Bailey, ed., *Policing and Punishment in Nineteenth-Century Britain* (Croom Helm: London) 25–41.

—— (1950), "The Secret Society" in Kurt H. Wolff, ed., *The Sociology of Georg Simmel* (The Free Press: Glencoe) 345–76.

—— (1971), "Prostitution" in *On Individuality and Social Forms,* ed. Donald N. Levine (University of Chicago Press: Chicago).

Sims, George S. (1908), "Foreign Bullies" in National Social Purity Crusade, *The Cleansing of a City,* ed. James Marchant (Greening & Co.: London).

Sims, Edwin W. (1909), "The White Slave Trade of Today" in Ernest Bell, ed., *War on the White Slave Trade* (Charles C. Thompson: Chicago).

Smart, Carol (1992), "Unquestionably a Moral Issue: Rhetorical Devices and Regulatory Imperatives" in Lynne Segal & Mary McIntosh, eds, *Sex Exposed: Sexuality and the Pornography Debate* (Virago Press: London) 184–99.

Smiles, Samuel (1958), *Self-Help: With Illustrations of Conduct and Perseverence* [1859] (John Murray: London).

Smith, F. Barry (1971), "Ethics and Disease in the Late-Nineteenth Century: The Contagious Diseases Acts" 15 *Historical Studies* 118–35.

—— (1976), "Labouchère's Amendment to the Criminal Law Amendment Bill" 17 *Historical Studies* [Melbourne] 165–73.
—— (1990), "The Contagious Diseases Acts Reconsidered" 3 *Social History of Medicine* 197–215.
[Smith, Sydney] (1809), "On the Statement of the Proceedings of the Society for the Suppression of Vice" 13(26) *Edinburgh Review* 333–43.
Smith-Rosenberg, Carroll (1971), *Religion and the Rise of the American City: The New York City Mission Movement, 1812–1870* (Cornell University Press: Ithaca).
—— (1985), *Disorderly Conduct: Visions of Gender in Victorian America* (Oxford University Press: New York).
Snitow, Ann (1986), "Retrenchment vs. Transformation: The Politics of the Anti-Pornography Movement" in Kate Ellis et al., eds, *Caught Looking: Feminism, Pornography and Censorship* (Real Comet Press: Seattle).
Social Purity Alliance (1880), *Laws and Operations and Address* (Inchbold & Beck: Leeds).
—— (1884a), *Morality of the Masses: Who Is Responsible?* (Hatchards: London).
—— (1884b), *Schoolboy Morality: An Address to Mothers* (Social Purity Alliance: London).
Societies for Reformation of Manners (1694), *Proposal for National Reformation of Manners* (John Dunton: London).
—— (1699a), *An Account of the Rise and Progress of the Reformation of Manners in London, and Westminster, and other parts of the Kingdom; with a persuasive to persons of all ranks to be zealous and diligent in promoting the Execution of the Laws against Profaneness and Debauchery, for the effecting of a National Reformation* (London).
—— [1699b] *The Sodomite's Shame and Doom* (London).
—— (1700a), *An Abstract of the Penal Laws Against Profaneness and Vice* (B. Aylmer: London).
—— (1700b), *A Help to a National Reformation* (D. Brown: London).
—— (1703), *An Account of the Rise and Progress of the Reformation of Manners in England, Scotland and Ireland* (5th edn; Joseph Downing: London).
—— (1704), *An Account of the Societies for Reformation of Manners in England, Scotland and Ireland* (20th edn; Joseph Downing: London).
—— (1706), *An Account of the Rise and Progress of the Reformation of Manners in England, Scotland and Ireland* (14th edn; Joseph Downing: London).
—— (1708), *A New Catalogue of Books and Small Tracts Against Vice and Immorality* (2nd edn; London).
—— (1710), *A Letter to a Minister of the Church of England Concerning the Societies for Reformation of Manners* (Joseph Downing: London).
—— (1715), *A Representation of the State of the Societies for a Reformation of Manners Humbly offered to His Majesty* (London).
—— (1737), *A Declaration from the Present Society: Appendix to 42nd Account of the Progress of the Work of the Societies for Reformation of Manners* (London).
—— (1786), *An Account of the Societies for the [sic] Reformation of Manners in the Last Century; with some Remarks adapted to the Present Period* (London).
—— (nd1), *A Dissuasive from the Sin of Uncleaness* (London).

—— (nd2), *A Dissuasive against the Horrid and Beastly Sin of Drunkenness* (London).
—— (nd3), *Letter from Several Members of the Societies for Reformation of Manners to Thomas Jewison* (London).
Society for the Suppression of Vice (1803), *An Address to the Public from the Society for the Suppression of Vice* (London).
—— (1825), *Objects of the Society for the Suppression of Vice* (London).
Springhall, John (1977), *Youth, Empire and Society: British Youth Movements 1883–1940* (Croom Helm: London).
Spurr, John (1990), "'Virtue, Religion and Government': The Anglican Uses of Providence" in Tim Harris, Paul Seaward and Mard Goldie, eds, *The Politics of Religion in Restoration England* (Blackwell: Oxford): 29–47.
Stafford, Ann (1964), *The Age of Consent* (Hodder & Stoughton: London).
Stanhope, George, Dean of Canterbury (1702), *The Duty of Rebuking: Sermon Preach'd Before . . . December 28, 1702, to which is added a Postscript to the religious Societies* (T. Leigh & D. Widminster: London).
Stansell, Christine (1986), *City of Women: Sex and Class in New York, 1789–1860* (Alfred A. Knopf: New York).
Stanton, Elizabeth Cady (1898), *Eighty Years and More: Reminiscences, 1815–1897* (New York.).
Stead, William Thomas (1885), "A Maiden Tribute to Modern Babylon" *Pall Mall Gazette* (6–10 July).
—— (1886), *Speech Delivered at the Central Criminal Court, November 4, 1885* (Moral Reform Union: London).
Steinmetz, George (1993), *Regulating the Social: The Welfare State and Local Politics in Imperial Germany* (Princeton University Press: Princeton).
[Stephens, Edward] (1691), *The Beginning and Progress of a Needful and Hopeful Reformation in England with the First Encounter of the Enemey Against it, His Wiles Detected and his Design ('t may be hop'd) Defeated* (London).
[——] (1697), *A Seasonable and Necessary Admonition to the Gentlemen of the First Society for Reformation of Manners, Concerning the Reformation of Themselves, of the Bishops and of the House of Commons* (London).
Stone, Lawrence (1977), *The Family, Sex and Marriage in England 1500–1800* (Weidenfeld & Nicolson: London).
Storch, Robert D. (1977), "The Problem of Working Class Leisure: Some Roots of Middle-Class Moral Reform in the Industrial North, 1825–1850" in A. P. Donajgrodzki, ed., *Social Control in Nineteenth Century Britain* (Croom Helm: London) 138–62.
Susman, Warren I. (1984), *Culture as History: The Transformation of American Society in the Twentieth Century* (Pantheon: New York).
Swift, Jonathan (1709), "Project for the Advancement of Religion and the Reformation of Manners" in *Legacy to the Wicked Authors of the Present Age* (H. F.: Dublin) 33–74.
Swiney, Frances (1907), *The Bar of Isis; or, the Law of the Mother* (Open Road Publishing Co.: London).
Terrot, Charles (1959), *The Maiden Tribute: A Study of the White Slave Traffic of the Nineteenth Century* (Frederick Muller: London).

—— (1960), *Traffic in Innocents: The Shocking Story of White Slavery in England* (E. P. Dutton: New York).

Thatcher, Margaret (1993), *The Downing Street Years* (Harper Collins: London).

Thomas, Donald (1969), *A Long Time Burning: The History of Literary Censorship in England* (Routledge & Kegan Paul: London).

Thomas, Keith (1959), "The Double Standard" 20 *Journal of the History of Ideas* 195–216.

Thompson, Bill (1994), *Soft Core: Moral Crusades Against Pornography in Britain and America* (Cassell: London).

Thompson, E. P. (1968), *The Making of the English Working Class* (Penguin: Harmondsworth).

—— (1971), "The Moral Economy of the English Crowd in the Eighteenth Century" 50 *Past & Present* 76–136.

—— (1991), "Rough Music" in *Customs in Common* (Merlin Press: London) 467–531.

Thompson, F. M. L. (1988), *The Rise of Respectable Society: A Social History of Victorian Britain, 1830–1900* (Fontana: London).

Tönnies, Ferdinand (1955), *Community and Association*, trans. Charles P. Loomis (Routledge & Kegan Paul: London).

Trudgill, Eric (1976), *Madonnas and Magdalens: The Origins and Development of Victorian Sexual Attitudes* (Heinemann: London).

Tuckniss, The Revd W. T. (1967), "The Agencies at Present in Operation within the Metropolis for the Suppression of Vice and Crime" [1862] in Henry Mayhew, *London Labour and the London Poor: A Cyclopaedia of the Condition and Earnings of those that will work, those that cannot work, and those who will not work*, 4 vols. (Frank Cass: London) Vol. IV: xi–xl.

Turner, E. S. (1950), *Roads to Ruin: The Shocking History of Social Reform* (Michael Joseph: London).

Turner, George Kibbe (1907), "The City of Chicago: A Study of Great Immoralities" 28 *McClure's Magazine* 575–92.

—— (1909), "The Daughters of the Poor: New York City and the White Slave Trade of the World, Under Tammany Hall" 34 *McClure's Magazine* 45–61.

Valverde, Mariana (1989), "The Love of Finery: Fashion and the Fallen Woman in Nineteenth Century Social Discourse" 32(2) *Victorian Studies* 168–88.

—— (1991), *The Age of Light, Soap and Water: Social Purity and Philanthropy in Canada, 1885–1925* (McClelland & Stewart: Toronto).

—— (1994), "Moral Capital" 9(1) *Canadian Journal of Law and Society* 213–32.

Van de Velde, Theodore H. (1928), *Ideal Marriage: Its Physiology and Technique*, trans. Stella Browne (Heinemann Medical Books: London).

Van Krieken, Robert (1991), "The Poverty of Social Control" 39(1) *Sociological Review* 1–25.

Varley, Henry [1884], *Private Lecture to Youths and Young Men, January 18, 1883* (Christian Commonwealth: London).

Veblen, Thorstein (1967), *The Theory of the Leisure Class: An Economic Study of Institutions* [1899] (Viking Press: New York).

Vincent, John M. (1935), *Costume and Conduct in the Laws of Basel, Bern and Zurich 1370–1800* (Johns Hopkins Press: Baltimore).

Wagner, David (1997), *The New Temperance: The American Obsession with Sin and Vice* (Westview Press: Boulder).

Walkowitz, Judith R. (1980), *Prostitution and Victorian Society: Women, Class and the State* (Cambridge University Press: Cambridge).

—— (1982), "Jack the Ripper and the Myth of Male Violence" 8(3) *Feminist Studies* 543–74.

—— (1983), "Male Vice and Female Virtue: Feminism and the Politics of Prostitution in Nineteenth-Century Britain" in Ann Snitow, Christine Stansell & Sharon Thompson, eds, *Powers of Desire: The Politics of Sexuality* (Monthly Review Press: New York) 419–38.

—— (1992), *City of Dreadful Delight: Narratives of Sexual Danger in Late-Nineteenth Century London* (University of Chicago Press: Chicago).

Wallis, Roy (1979), *Salvation and Protest: Studies of Social and Religious Movements* (Frances Pinter: London).

'Walter' (1966), *My Secret Life* [*c.* 1880] (G. Legman: New York).

Ward, Edith (1892), *The Vital Question: An Address on Social Purity* (Lund: London).

Ward, Edward (1709), *The London Spy* (4th edn; London).

Ward, William (1700), *Sermon Preach'd Before the Societies for Reformation of Manners, 24th November, 1699* (London).

Ware, Vron (1992), *Beyond the Pale: White Women, Racism and History* (Verso: London).

Webb, Beatrice (1926), *My Apprenticeship* (Longman: London).

Weber, Max (1930), *The Protestant Ethic and the Spirit of Capitalism*, trans. Talcott Parsons (George Allen & Unwin: London).

Welter, Barbara (1966), "The Cult of True Womanhood: 1820–1860" 18 *American Quarterly* 151–74.

Wesley, John [1763], *A Sermon Preached Before the Society for Reformation of Manners, January 30, 1763* (John Flexney: London).

White, Arnold (1908), "Foreign Bullies" in National Social Purity Crusade, *The Cleansing of a City*, ed. James Marchant (Greening & Co.: London).

White, Melanie, & Alan Hunt (2000), "Citizenship: Care of the Self, Character and Personality" 4(1) *Citizenship Studies* (in press).

Whiteaker, Larry H. (1997), *Seduction, Prostitution and Moral Reform in New York City, 1830–1860* (Garland Press: New York).

Wiebe, Robert H. (1967), *The Search for Order, 1877–1920* (Hill & Wang: New York).

Wilberforce, Robert I., & Samuel Wilberforce (1838), *The Life of William Wilberforce*, 5 vols. (John Murray: London).

Wilberforce, William (1797), *A Practical View of the Prevailing Religious System of Professed Christians in the Higher and Middle Classes in this Country, Contrasted with Real Christianity* (Cadell & Davies: London).

Willard, Frances E. (1896), "Address to the National Purity Congress, Baltimore, 1895" in Aaron M. Powell, ed., *National Purity Congress* (American Purity Alliance: New York) 124–7.

Willis, Richard (1704), *Sermon Preach'd Before the Societies for Reformation of Manners . . . January 3, 1703/4* (Matthew Water: London).

Willis, William (1910), *White Slave Traffic* (M.A.P.: London).
Willis, William N. (1912), *The White Slaves of London* (Stanley Paul & Co.: London).
Wilson, Elizabeth (1987), "Thatcherism and Women: After Seven Years" in Ralph Miliband, Leo Panitch and John Saville, eds, *Socialist Register, 1987* (Merlin Press: London) 199–235.
Wohl, Anthony (1978), "Sex and the Single Room: Incest Among the Victorian Working Classes" in Anthony Wohl, ed., *The Victorian Family: Structure and Stress* (Croom Helm: London) 197–216.
Wollstonecraft, Mary (1967), *A Vindication of the Rights of Woman* [1792] (Cambridge University Press: Cambridge).
Wood, Nancy (1982), "Prostitution and Feminism in Nineteenth-Century Britain" 7 *m/f* 61–78.
Wood-Allen, Mary (1896), "Moral Education of the Young" in Aaron M. Powell, ed., *National Purity Congress* (American Purity Alliance: New York) 224–38.
—— (1901), *Marriage: Its Duties and Privileges* (Chicago).
Woodward, Josiah (1698), *The Duty of Compassion to the Souls of Others: Sermon Preach'd Before . . . December 28, 1696* (2nd edn; Simpson: London).
—— (1701), *Account of the Progress of the Reformation of Manners in England and Ireland* (J. Nutt: London).
—— (1702), *Sermon Preach'd at the Parish Church of St. James Westminster on the May 21, 1702 at the Funeral of Mr. John Cooper, a Constable who was barbarously murther'd at May-Fair in the Execution of his office, in Suppressing the Publick Disorders There* (Joseph Downing: London).
—— (1704), *Some Thoughts Concerning the Stage in a Letter to a Lady* (London).
—— (1711), *The Judgement of Rev. Dr. Henry Sacheverell Concerning the Societies for Reformation of Manners* (J. Downing: London).
Wrightson, Keith, & David Levine (1979), *Poverty and Piety in an English Village: Terling, 1525–1700* (Academic Press: New York).
Wynne, John (1725), *Sermon Preach'd Before the Societies for Reformation of Manners at St. Mary-le-Bow, 3rd January, 1725* (London).
Yeazell, Ruth B. (1989), "Nature's Courtship Plot in Darwin and Ellis" 2(2) *Yale Journal of Criticism* 33–53.
Young, Arthur (1784–1815), *Annals of Agriculture*, 46 vols. (Strahan: London).
—— (1797), *National Danger, and the Means to Safety* (W. Richardson: London).
Zouch, Henry (1786), *Hints Respecting the Public Police* (John Stockdale: London).

INDEX